Please return/renew this item by the last date shown
Thank you for using your library

Wolverhampton Libraries

The Past in the Present

Editor in Chief

Francis Robinson, Royal Holloway, University of London

Amit Chaudhuri

Clearing a Space

Reflections on India, Literature
and Culture

Peter Lang Oxford

Cover illustration: Portobello Road Market, London, 1959
© Sergio Larrain/Magnum Photos
Cover design: Dan Mogford

First published in 2008 by Peter Lang Ltd
International Academic Publishers, Evenlode Court, Main Road,
Long Hanborough, Witney, Oxfordshire OX29 8SZ, England
© Peter Lang Ltd 2008
www.thepastinthepresent.com, www.peterlang.com

The right of Amit Chaudhuri to be identified as the Author of this work has been asserted
in accordance with the Copyrights, Designs and Patents Act 1988.

British Library and Library of Congress Cataloguing-in Publication Data: A catalogue
record for this book is available from the British Library, UK, and the Library of
Congress, USA.

ISBN 978-1-906165-01-7 (Paperback)
ISBN 978-1-906165-06-2 (Hardback)

Printed in Hong Kong

For Peter D. McDonald

Contents

Acknowledgements   9
Introduction: On Clearing a Space   11

Part One
Towards a Poetics of the Indian Modern

Poles of Recovery   39
In the Waiting-Room of History: On *Provincializing Europe*   57
The Flute of Modernity: Tagore and the Middle Class   69
The East as a Career: On 'Strangeness' in Indian Writing   85
Argufying: On Amartya Sen and the Deferral of an Indian
    Modernity   100
This is Not Music: The Emergence of the Domain of 'Culture'   109
'Huge Baggy Monster': Mimetic Theories of the Indian Novel
    after Rushdie   113
Two Giant Brothers: Tagore's Revisionist 'Orient'   122
Travels in the Subculture of Modernity   140
Thoughts in a Temple: Hinduism in the Free Market   160
On the Nature of Indian Gothic: The Imagination
    of Ashis Nandy   165
'Hollywood *aur* Bollywood'   170
The View from Malabar Hill   182
Stories of Domicile   189
Notes on the Novel after Globalization   195
Anti-Fusion   214

Part Two
Alternative Traditions, Alternative Readings

Arun Kolatkar and the Tradition of Loitering   221
Learning to Write: V. S. Naipaul, Vernacular Artist   235

A Bottle of Ink, a Pen and a Blotter: On R.K. Narayan   243
'A Feather! A Very Feather upon the Face!': On Kipling   251
Returning to Earth: The Poetry of Jibanananda Das   265
Women in Love as Post-Human Essay   279
Champion of Hide and Seek: Raj Kamal Jha's Surrealism   295
Midnight at Marble Arch: On *The Reluctant Fundamentalist*
    by Mohsin Hamid   301
Beyond 'Confidence': Rushdie and the Creation Myth
    of Indian English Writing   308

Notes   312
Index   317

Acknowledgements

I am grateful to the editors of various journals in which these essays first appeared. Firstly, to Karl Miller and Mary-Kay Wilmers, for inviting me in 1988 to write for the *London Review of Books*, in which the greatest number of these essays have appeared. To the many editors there I have worked with, in the past and present – John Lanchester, Andrew O' Hagan, Paul Laity, Daniel Soar – I'm grateful. To the *Times Literary Supplement* and Lindsay Duguid I'm beholden for giving me room for long essays. I'd also like to thank editors and literary editors of the following publications in which some of these pieces have appeared: *Interventions, New Republic, New Left Review, Meanjin, New Statesman, The Observer*, the *Telegraph*, and the *Hindu*. I should also mention Edwin Frank of *NYRB Classics* for the very valuable suggestions he made to me for the introduction to *Jejuri*. And I should thank Penguin India for allowing me to reprint the introduction to the anthology of writings on Calcutta.

I am grateful to the following institutions for inviting me to present some of these pieces as papers: the Wissenschaftskolleg, Berlin, the Nehru Memorial Library, Delhi, the Royal Society of Literature, London, the Seagull Bookshop, Calcutta, the University of California at Santa Cruz, the Department of South Asian Languages and Civilizations at the University of Chicago, the Southern Asian Studies Institute, Columbia University, the Centre for South Asian Studies, Cambridge, the School of Oriental and African Studies, London, and the New Writing Worlds Partnership, Norwich. To my students at Columbia and Freie Universities, and at the University of East Anglia, I'm grateful for helping me to clarify and shape many of the ideas contained in these pages.

My special thanks to my editor, Alexis Kirschbaum, for her mixture of conviction, openness, and thoughtfulness, and for her unwavering support of this book, and her management of its fortunes, from the very start. To the general editor, Francis Robinson, for the personal warmth and generosity with which he received this project. And to Rukun Advani and

Anuradha Roy, my publishers in India, for asking me to put together this collection several years ago, and for their patience, kindness, and belief.

These essays are the result of conversations. I can't mention all my interlocutors by name, but should acknowledge, once again, Peter D. McDonald, to whom this book is dedicated. To various other friends, I am grateful. Dan Jacobson, for first kindling and guiding my interest in the essay. Finally, my wife Rosinka, from whose support and insight, as well as her knowledge of nineteenth-century Bengal, I have benefited in ways I can't begin to enumerate. No page of this sort in a book by myself can forget to thank my parents, for instilling in me, and making me constantly think about, their old-fashioned (in their time, new-fangled) belief in the importance of literary culture.

Introduction
On Clearing a Space

I have been writing these essays for about fourteen years now, mainly for the *London Review of Books* and the *Times Literary Supplement*, but for other journals and periodicals as well. From the beginning, I have been concerned with clearing a space for a particular kind of discussion; and, as I've become more and more aware of my own intentions, I've turned my gaze on the intentions themselves, and made thinking about them part of my inquiry.

I should say that, as an Indian writer of fiction in English, I have felt myself at an angle, from the start, from the project of the Indian English novel in the last twenty-five years. This angularity itself, and its minor enigma, provides a common thread or node that runs through the essays, whether they are about modernity, humanism, or individual authors; that they are the work of a writer to whom the experience of marginality, and the significance of the minority vantage-point, has been important – but who finds it difficult to adhere to, or accept, the post-colonial intellectual's or writer's exclusive right in the present moment to define what the minority or marginal experience might be. Could there be marginal experiences, to do with the imagination, that are crucial to the life of the writer that post-coloniality often finds itself unable to open up to; and does post-colonial theory become, paradoxically, an instructive and pedagogic discourse on marginality, providing an absolute definition of what it constitutes? Does the pressure of the marginal, in its turn, lead us towards affinities that may have little do with identity and language? These are a few of the questions these essays hopefully raise; implicitly, in the very necessity for their being written, and explicitly, as theme.

Part of the book's narrative involves, then, the expression and exploration of a temperament – of an Indian writer who doesn't trace, as he probably should, his creative lineage to Salman Rushdie and the mandatory 'hybrid' post-colonial usages of English, but to a variety of (often conflicting) sources and forebears, including European and vernacular Indian (specifically, the Bengali) traditions, where the modes of recuperation, or the processes through which those traditions are made available to the writer, are as important as the traditions themselves. For, besides the assumption of material formations and politics on the one hand, and something like spontaneous affinity on the other, the events that seem to us like 'chance' and 'accident' are also crucial to the creation of the writer's temperament, his or her *oeuvre*, and to the plotting of any intellectual history. These essays seek neither to deny nor ignore post-colonial theory, nor to speak for some previous orthodoxy that it has replaced, but, since that theory has itself become a significant orthodoxy, to often define themselves both against it and through it, to extend the field that it has opened up, and also to reconsider some of its underpinnings. I have tried, in some of these pieces, to clear a space for not only myself, but also those writers and traditions (principally the writers and traditions in the Indian vernaculars, but also the Indian English tradition that predates Rushdie and, in certain invisible tributaries, is contemporary with his work) that the critical language of post-colonial theory engages with very sparingly. And yet I don't think that the present-day marginality of the vernaculars, or of a certain kind of Anglophone writer preceding the 'boom' (such as R.K. Narayan, the novelist of the fictional pastoral, 'Malgudi', or the poet-scholar A.K. Ramanujan), is simply the consequence of their not having the international readership they would if they had been writing in English, or had been picked up and marketed by international publishing houses, or won the Booker Prize; the entire groundwork and the premises of internationalism, which informed the works of many of these writers (no matter who was reading or publishing them), have themselves been dismantled with globalization. 'Internationalism' is a way of reading, and not a demography of a readership; and what we're witnessing is not the rise of internationalism, but its interruption and eclipse, and its replacement by a new mythology of travel, displacement, movement, and settlement, with, paradoxically, its new anxious awarenesses of the 'other', the foreign, and the native. It's into the latter that, by subtle default, the debates about marginality, the vernaculars, commercialism, exoticization, and identity automatically fall. It's time, now, to begin to look at the debate from the outside, as it were; to be open to its anxieties, which one might share, but to use its terms at one remove. And when I speak of 'clearing a space', I should at least make an attempt to delineate what I mean by that 'space'; because I wouldn't like either its polemics or its largesse, its aim to open up and accommodate, to fall within and disappear among the oppositionalities I've hinted at. The essays were written over quite a length of time, and I can't guarantee that they were always successful in being immune to the terms of the debate; but an introduction is also an afterthought, a summation, and I can say that what I have been resisting is not just this or that orthodoxy, but the terms of the argument as they're given to us today, with the so-called '*bhasha*' or Indian-language writers on one side, and Rushdie and his putative progeny on the other; and that 'modernity', rather than identity, authenticity, or language (in that modernity itself produced a constitutive consciousness of these things), might be one way of shifting the focus, of remapping a history – modernity as a creator of myths, fictions, and artistic practice, as a phase in our history, as a site under threat, as a mutating sign.

My own sensibility was formed, to a large extent, by a Bengali humanism which has its provenance in Calcutta in the nineteenth century. There is no point in either making a secret of this fact or advertising it, but understanding what it means in this instance; because one presumes that no two cases of cultural formation can be exactly alike. Even categories such as European and Indian culture have made themselves available to me, I now realize, at least partly through the prism and filter of this humanism. And yet, as I didn't grow up in Calcutta, it didn't come to me via a pedagogic route, or from a source of authority; it wasn't, in other words, a conscious and privileged context. It has been, rather, indivisible from constant acts of interpretation, reconstruction, and imagining on my part, qualified firmly, too, by the ethos of elite pop culture (I use the oxymoron deliberately) in which I grew up in 1960s and 1970s Bombay. To say I am 'a product of', then, is already to mislead; it's to simplify what's essentially a somewhat idiosyncratic imaginative and critical project – a continual and shifting self-positioning – into a story about contexts and origins. Distance, and not an unequivocal sense of inheritance, necessitates the project; a Bengali immersed in this context from birth would almost certainly undertake it very differently. The itinerary, in my case, has been in some ways a circuitous one. Drawn to first reconsider that humanism through my own once-youthful absorption in European modernism, a taste for which might have actually been prepared in me by an intellectual formation of which I wasn't fully aware, it and its figures are now not so much a matter of cultural pride as a point of entry into a discussion through which I might define a place for myself as a writer. For instance, if I write about Tagore, it's not because I am primarily interested in him as an exemplary savant in our nationalist iconography (a subject that's been dealt with copiously in Anglophone India), but as a – in the words of an Indian writer – 'mere poet', and what the practice of a 'mere poet' might tell us about ourselves (something that Anglophone Indian writing, especially in the case of Tagore, has spent a relatively small amount of attention or time upon, and which serves as a reminder of the largely public nature of its self-awareness). Part of my speculations involve, of course, the compulsions, the necessity, of occupying and creating that space; because no space that's not commonly recognized is comfortable to inhabit.

The project, which is really an outsider's project, begs its own questions. It entails the manipulation, re-examination, and use of certain predilections and prejudices which have at once enriched and compromised one's view and experience of the world; among them, an apparent privileging of the 'real' and the 'ordinary'. My own explorations in tracing a trajectory, an arc, of the Indian 'real', the Indian 'everyday', and recuperating a genealogy of Indian 'reality' and the mundane – especially in the face of the epic and fantastic narratives that Indian literature has been made synonymous with – attest, hopefully, to the fact that the humanism I speak of is a critical resource, partly because its own true location is now peripheral and ambiguous. And so, even as I speak about 'humanism', I need to reiterate, and to remind myself and others, that what I'm attempting is not an expression of an allegiance, or to describe what it already recognizable, but that I am primarily involved in an act of distancing. In dwelling on 'Indian' or 'Bengali' humanism, I'm not trying to add to the knowledge of variants of humanism in the world, or issuing a corrective; nor am I interested in *returning* to a lost, utopian paradigm of 'high' modernity. What I *am* interested in are the elisions that direct the binaries (East, West; high, low; native, foreign; fantasy, reality; elite, democratic) within which, by some subtle but inescapable default mechanism, we generally position ourselves in relation to our cultural formation, binaries that, however, do not quite corroborate our experience of the world. Crucially, I am rethinking, too, my, and others', relationship with creative and critical language, and inquiring after what continues to validate, or neuter, that relationship.

A 'space' is also an absence; and I'll briefly try and account for how reflecting on space might be a consciousness of absences.

A couple of years ago at a student conference, a group of eminent academics, largely in the social sciences, gathered to explore a theme: the future of cultural studies. The opening statement was made by the political scientist and founding member of the 'subaltern studies' group, Partha Chatterjee; it was, in effect, a characteristically lucid and fair-minded summation and exposition on the relatively brief history of cultural studies as a discipline, and an acknowledgement that it was now at a crossroads:

where was it going to go from here? But what struck me most was a small, perhaps inadvertent glossing-over in Chatterjee's statement that was as revealing to me as anything else he said. Cultural studies, after the ground-work prepared by Stuart Hall in the 1970s, properly registered itself as a discipline and as a critical shift in England in the 1980s; and it represented, as Chatterjee pointed out (this much is beyond dispute), a now-famous 'turn'. The 'turn' was repeated in Indian academia in the early 1990s; in 2005, it was time to ask where it was going, and whether a renewal of vocabulary was necessary. But where – and I mean intellectual, not geographical, location – did that 'turn' occur? In the case of Stuart Hall, Cambridge, and the subsequent proliferation of cultural studies in Anglo-American academia, the answer is clear, and even crucial to the mythology; it took place in, and challenged, the old centres and discourses of the liberal arts and the humanities. It represented, as we know, a decisive reclamation and privileging of 'popular culture', both as a source of value and an area of study, over the mainly 'high' cultural preoccupations of the humanities till that time.

But where did the Indian 'turn' take place? The answer is far more problematic. It would seem, implicitly from Chatterjee's statement,[1] as well from his silence – but also from the way the practitioners in the field appear to conceive of this issue – that it too largely occurred in the West-ern academy. Indian 'cultural studies', it would appear, became a rewriting and extension of British and American cultural studies by defining its re-lationship to Western humanities through a specific lens and angle – that Indianness, post-coloniality, and popular culture were, under its rubric, conflated into a single entity or engine recuperated against the humanist assumptions of the Western liberal arts. What's ignored in this formula-tion, rather than, crucially, critiqued or quarrelled with, is the palpable space of literature, thought, and practice that comprises Indian 'high' culture. British cultural studies seemed clear that its quarrel lay with its own 'high' cultural academic and intellectual parameters; in a sense, it was a continuation and reworking of the very tension and the two-way traf-fic that have informed much of European modernism: between 'popular cultural' forms parodying, vulgarising, and travestying 'high' forms on the one hand, and 'high' forms appropriating, domesticating, and recycling 'low' forms on the other. But Indian cultural studies' emphasis on conflat-ing post-coloniality with popular culture means that it, effectively, refuses to recognize, engage with, and, most importantly, explore the formative history of tension with its own 'high' cultural space. Since there's a grow-ing, and indeed indispensable, informing presence for the post-colonial in the worldwide field of cultural studies, where the post-colonial is almost automatically associated with the cause of popular forms, it means that there's a huge, under-theorized, and even sentimental gap in the discourse; the gap involves not only an elision of the post-colonial 'high' cultural, but the elision of a tension between the 'high' and the 'low' that is not, at once, a narrative of the tension between the post-colonial and the imperial, or, for that matter, between the Indian and the Western.

There's a further problem; for, by the early 1990s, when Chatterjee says the 'turn' that Indian cultural studies represents took place, the principal practitioners (after the near extinction of art-house cinema) of 'high' culture in India were the writers in the vernacular literatures. These writers, faced with the market-intimate onslaught of Indian writing in English, had recourse to, in defence of their own practice, an incongruous variety of romantic-nationalist and post-colonial arguments, to do with identity, marginality, and linguistic authenticity; a recourse to everything, that is, except 'high' culture and the significance of the modernist aesthetic that, ironically, so powerfully informed their own experimentation and development. This is a telling and significant contradiction in their position that hasn't been taken up, probably because people on both sides of the argument, for very different reasons, are intent on avoiding formulations on the 'modern', while they're ready to leap towards competing (essentially pre- and post-globalization) articulations of 'Indianness'. It is another reason that the debate remains thin, emotional, and implausible. Moreover, in what way does the critique represented by the 'popular' relate to, and qualify, this eminent but evidently endangered group of writers, and the ambiguous domain they inhabit: that of vernacular 'high' culture, modernism, and experiment? Anyway, the marks by which we designate one kind of cultural output as 'elite' and another as not are complicated permanently, not to say productively, when we think of the century-and-a-half-old locations of cosmopolitanism and artistic experimentation in small towns and cities in India (for example, Baroda, Allahabad, Cuttack, Kishorganj), and the gradual eclipse of these intellectual centres by the relocation of the post-Independence Indian elite, especially in the last twenty-five years. This, including various other elements in the story, including what globalization has done not only to agriculture, employment, but also to the 'high' modernities in the Indian languages, leads us to a different consideration of what constitutes the 'elite' from the one we're accustomed to having.

I was reminded of the compelling gap, or space, I have mentioned, when I was in Lille in France in 2006, and happened to visit an excellent exhibition of Indian popular art – oleographs, lithographs, devotional posters, calendar images, studio backdrops – curated by the art historian

Jyotindra Jain. A wonderful array, and an indication, again, of the terrific work that Jain is now synonymous with; and yet marked by that same elision and conflation. The narrative logic of the exhibition, as one moved from left to right, from picture to picture, was to subtly make Indian popular art one with Indian art itself, and, by suggestion, location, and argument, to place it in the context of, and differentiate it from, the European museum, and the conventions of European art. Generally free of the language of cultural studies, Prof Jain's commentary was still marked by Indian cultural studies' silence on the location of Indian 'high' modernist culture, and the mutual situatedness of the popular and the 'high' in one another, their secret pacts and public warfare without which no history of the image is complete or comprehensible. An exhibition, say, of American popular art from the 1950s must say something about its revisions of artistic practice in the 'high' cultural domain, and, in doing so, will be reassessing not only the former, but the latter, and perhaps even questioning their accepted demarcations. For, just as there is no 'high' artistic practice that doesn't define itself against, while also being secretly in commerce with, 'low' forms, there is no 'popular' culture whose irradiation can be felt without a knowledge of the 'high' contexts that are shaping the same material in a different, contestatory way. The tension and give-and-take between the demotic and the refined directs the provenance and history of any tradition, and modernity reworks the quarrel in its own terms; further, arguing about what is 'high', or acceptable, and 'low', or inadmissible, is indispensable to the construction of nationality; in some of the essays below, I've hinted at some of its more extreme variants as being instances of (borrowing from English literature a term that brings together the political and the aesthetic) the 'gothic'. In other words, we can't neglect the inner tumult and debate that characterize a culture simply because the fact of colonialism tempts us to externalize the conflict; to shift the focus from the 'high' and the 'low' to the 'indigenous' and the 'foreign', the 'authentic' and the 'derived'; or, at least, we can't speak of the latter without possessing some sense of how, in modernity, they too are internalized and made versions of the 'high' and the 'low'. Can we, then, in India, while theorizing the 'popular', afford to take the realm of 'high' culture as a readymade, as an already invented and dismantled entity, as a meaning that has lapsed; for the polemic to have any power, surely it's a meaning that needs to be revisited constantly?

The narrative of modernity in India is a narrative of tension and conflict, of imprisonment and liberation. But the realm that this tension and striving for freedom inhabit can't entirely be contained by, though it is deeply

related to, the one we have been habituated to render it into: that of empire and nationalism. Some time in the late eighteenth or early nineteenth
century, the bourgeois self in India becomes aware of itself without having
properly named itself; for instance, we find Tagore (as we shall see below)
speaking rather distantly in the late nineteenth century of a 'substance
called the mind', as if he were still getting used to the idea of, or trying
to arrive at a vocabulary to describe, self-consciousness in modernity.
It's no longer the superstructure of religion or communal hierarchy that
orders life or assigns value; it's the light thrown on what is a new domain,
'reality', by the human consciousness, which also has other, provisional
appellations. By the second half of the nineteenth century, the importance
of light and space as both metaphors of, and habitations for, the human
self, or 'the substance called the mind', is absolute, especially with Tagore,
who, in a letter in 1894 to his niece, would demand, not political freedom
(though he came from a family whose experiments in nationalism are well
known), but 'more light, more space'. With the waning of religion and the
old self, light becomes logos; this is comically but appositely played out,
for instance, in the names of the some of the chief protagonists in the story
of how Bengali humanism defines itself. The first and obvious example of
this is Tagore, whose first name, by which he's usually invoked in Bengal,
means 'lord of the sun'; the late nineteenth-century rise of Tagore is literally the rising of the sun upon the Bengali consciousness, openly acknowledging, finally, the advent and reign of logos.

The other, later, equally recognizable figure from this narrative whose
name and profession have associations of reason, the human, and the lumi-
nous is the film-maker Satyajit Ray. There is, of course, the surname, which,
in the famous Westernized version in which it's familiar, lent itself to all
sorts of cheap, but unintentionally loaded, puns in newspaper headlines,
such as 'Ray of Hope for Indian cinema'. The notion of light as the primary
ingredient, indeed, the fundamental aesthetic, of cinema was crucial to Ray;
the shooting of his second film *Aparajito* involved the search, recorded in
'Extracts from a Banaras Diary', for the 'right' sort of light, allied as it was
both to the veracity of the medium and to a deeply moral sense of the real,
noted in the telegraphically terse diary entry: 'Morning scenes in the ghat
must be shot in the morning and afternoon scenes in the afternoon.' Then
there's the sense of light being Ray's vocation, provenance, and destiny,
especially in his memory that, at the age of twenty-two, well before it had
occurred to him that he would in any way work with film, an astrologer had
predicted to his mother that he would (the pun, again, is inevitable) make
his name 'through the use of light'. Light, for Ray, is the basic raw material
and foundation of film; as the newspaper headline mawkishly suggests, it's

also the foundation of 'seeing' ('He has only to keep his eyes open ...' the young Ray was advising the Indian film-maker in 1948), which, in turn, is intimately connected with reason and logos.

Both Rabindranath and Ray, custodians of illumination, separated though they are by about three generations, are products of the Brahmo Samaj; Tagore's father Debendranath being a founder, but Ray's father Sukumar, the brilliant writer of nonsense verse, also an active member and lampooner of this reform sect. The aura of light that surrounds these names and world-views needs to be situated, then, in the Samaj's disman- tling of the old religion, its intention of replacing the inherited sources of validation with, in effect, logos, and the new moral weight it places on 'seeing'. The embrace of light brings with it a privileging of the eye: thus, '*Alo amar alo ogo*', the simple but ubiquitous Tagore song, almost the first proper song any Bengali child growing up in Calcutta learns (as I grew up in Bombay, I was excluded from this education), runs: 'Light oh my light, the light fills the earth,/ My eye's washed by light, my heart's vanquished by light.' This light has an almost Shelleyan force, but it's conjoined with the ideas of daybreak, awakening, and looking, which is why it's sung by children in the morning at play-school in the way a religious hymn might be; as a rehearsal of the nineteenth-century arrival of the human and of logos. Ray's first film, *Pather Panchali*, has, early on, the apotheosis of the boy Apu's eye, shut as he pretends to sleep, opening onto the world (a moment cherished by Kurosawa) in the next frame.

Thereafter, this open, staring, meaning-proferring eye will recur in a number of guises in Ray's oeuvre: as the tear in the curtain in the young Apu's tiny rented rooftop room in Calcutta in *Apur Sansar*; as the slats in the Venetian windows and the binoculars in the heroine's hand in *Charulata*. This is not just a metaphorical allusion to the camera, but a brimming over from Ray's intellectual, artistic, and emotional formation, the nineteenth- century gaze of the self looking out at and ascribing value to the world. (A great deal has been said about the 'gaze' of the colonizer; very little, in comparison, about the moral and aesthetic significance of 'seeing' for the Indian modern – a reminder of post-coloniality's own blind spots, and its refusal to seriously engage with the role of the senses in the construction of bourgeois modernity.) As Ray's art-house practice becomes exhausted, he shifts the act of 'looking', with its associations of reason and logos, as well as its poetic engendering of meaning, to his children's films, with their figure of the amateur detective, the spy, the observer, culminating in a scene in *Joy baba Felunath* when the eponymous hero, Feluda, is hidden behind a string cot and is spying, through a rent, upon the possible suspect. The detective embodies, even more than the romantic drifter, rationality;

this intriguing and apparent dichotomy pertains to a significant part of Bengali children's literature as well – that often, especially in the proliferation of adventure, spy, and mystery genres in Bengali in the first half of the twentieth century, children's literature is not so much an escape from the humanist logos of 'high' literary practice, but a coming to its irreducible possibilities from a different direction.

What does the self look out on; what does light illumine? Space, of course. Space is figured in Tagore by a number of synonyms: among them, '*shunya*' or 'the empty', '*ashim*' or 'the infinite', '*akash*' or 'sky' – '*Amar mukti aloy aloy, ei akashe*'; 'My liberation's among the light, within this sky. ' These are variations and developments upon the spatially amorphous divinity 'without outline' (the Upanishadic *niraakar*) with which the Brahmo Samaj banished the erstwhile Hindu chaos of faiths and sacred apparitions. In Ray, space is the cinematic frame; which, by arresting the story and detail (a common accusation against Ray had to do with the slowness of his pacing), brings the frame as close as possible to space itself. It's as if, after the passing of the old world, this eye is intent upon dwelling on, and delineating the borders of, the reality that has replaced it, before hurrying to catalogue its features. It is an intensity of looking that's, today, for many, quite difficult to understand.

By the 1870s, nationalism – of both the cultural and political varieties – had begun to formulate itself pretty clearly. There was the creation of the 'Hindu mela', for one, in 1867 by the Tagore family and Nabagopal Mitra (man of many parts; educationist; editor; friend of the Tagore family), to restore, dignify, and celebrate indigenous crafts, music, and vocations; the setting up of the Indian National Association – a significant step towards bringing into existence a viable nationalist political organization – by Surendranath Banerjea in 1876; and the fact of the inauguration of the Congress in 1885 is, of course, well known. A different sort of upheaval, though, was registering itself at around this time in Tagore's work, one that would have recognizable and far-reaching echoes in the space of culture and creative practice in Indian modernity. The Bengali poets who precede Tagore (with the exception of Michael Madhusudan Dutt[2]) are either attempting to fashion narrative histories of the nation, or to make aesthetic objects out of the possibilities raised by the intersection of English and Bengali literary conventions. The self, at this moment, exteriorizes its relationships, especially via the entities it calls, after the vocabulary given to it by Orientalist scholarship, history and tradition; claiming each as a powerful and authentic constituent of identity, and distancing itself from each because of subjecthood and the story of India's 'decline': these moves will be indispensable, later, to both creativity and the possibility of a national-ist politics. And yet, at this time – the 1870s – the new literatures in English and Bengali are, by extension, an ancillary of the Orientalist and quasi-nationalist projects, an offshoot of social science preoccupations, lacking, as yet, their own arena; in some ways their position is not dissimilar to, and might even be an obverse mirror-image of, the role Anglophone literature in India has been playing in the last twenty-five years. It's only with Mad-husudan Dutt, with his strategic reworking of the *Ramayana*, that a 'turn' takes place *within* the self, and, by implication, a stake is made for culture and creativity being a primary and competing domain for self-expression (I explore this in the essay 'Poles of Recovery'). (There's also, of course, the novelist Bankimchandra Chatterjee, arguing belligerently but elegantly for a 'modern' Bengali literature in both his criticism and his practice.)

For Tagore, by the late nineteenth century – as nationalism finally falls into place around him in the public sphere – culture and literature are no longer just significant enterprises in the nationalist project, as history is, and will continue to be; they are competing and alternative sources of value. As far as Tagore is concerned, the principal master, the originator of meaning and language, and, therefore, of constriction and oppression, is not the colonizer, but the self, or logos; Tagore's main quarrel embod-ies a self-division, a suspicion of logos (which, as light or illumination, is contained in his own name), rather than a simple, overriding distrust of the colonizer. As a political being, Tagore is of course fiercely against English ideas of supremacy; like members of his family as well as many of his contemporaries, he's also a cultural nationalist, and, as a public figure, in the way he uses attire, as much of a political strategist as Gandhi. As an artist, though, he's profoundly wary of the logos on which nationalism depends, and accepts as a foundation; this alienates Tagore from himself, and causes him to search constantly, and relentlessly try to give expression to, a different kind of liberation; secular, but equally at odds with the old religious and the new political resonance of the word '*mukti*', or 'freedom'. This self-division, then, is most palpably present from the late nineteenth century onwards, into the great age of nationalist activity in the twentieth century. From then on, it becomes the characteristic mark of, and the most fecund context of production in, the realm of 'high' culture in modern India; its pressure is formative and evident in various languages – this is something I explore, again, in 'Poles of Recovery'. The fallout of the self-division explains, to some extent, the often unspoken but always crucial ambivalence this domain has had in relationship to nationalism, clarifying its subtle but persistent resistance, as a competing domain of value and freedom, to being incorporated into the narrative of the nation.

For roughly the last 125 years, then, our modernity has been a story of self-division; and, almost immediately, a pressing and occasionally vulgarized version of that story has made itself available, as a narrative of nationalism, of the native and the foreigner. All these elements, these contradictions, are enacted in language; as they are, for instance, in Tagore's essay on Bengali nursery rhymes.

'Children's Rhymes' ('*Chhelebhulano Chhara*'; literally, but only approximately, 'Rhymes to Entrance Children') is important because of its embodiment of the tensions I've been speaking about, as well for its repeated skirting round the valid but potentially slippery rhetoric of nationalism. It's striking, too, for proposing a modernist argument at a time (1894) that predates modernism and is roughly contemporaneous with the early Freudian absorption in childhood and word-association; it's an argument that, for all Tagore's later public bewilderment with modernism, reminds us that neglected, 'light' genres – here, the nursery rhyme – can be an occasion for making affiliations in a way that's more difficult in an artist's more orthodox practice.

The essay begins with a confession and a caveat that rehearses one of the frictions that will inform and shape it: 'For some time now, I have been collecting the rhymes current in Bengali by which women divert children. These rhymes may have a special value in determining the history of our language and our society; but to me, their simple natural poetic strain seems more worthy of regard' (Sukanta Chaudhuri's translation). Tagore, in the first sentence, seems to be relating himself to the important nationalist projects being undertaken in Bengal at the time, the attempts to create, for the want of a better word, a 'low' or oral history of the region that resulted most famously in 1883 in the Rev. Lal Behari Day's canonical collection in English, *Folk Tales of Bengal*. Our sense of that sort of undertaking must also include the archival activities – really labours of love – in the Bengali language by the poet Iswar Gupta and the critic and editor Akshay Chandra Sarkar in the 1850s. The investment in the local and its history would continue in a different way – informed, though, by the same romantic nationalism – at the end of the nineteenth century in the literary historian Dinesh Chandra Sen's work, in his ecstatic excursions from village to village in Bengal collecting manuscripts. In the second, *faux naïf* statement, Tagore immediately distances himself from romantic nationalism, using something he calls 'simple' and 'natural', '*sahaj sabhabhik*' (though it is anything but simple), to initiate a different sort of discussion. Tagore is concerned with the nature of thought here: on the one hand, analytical thought, which he identifies with critics and experts, who must have clear reasons for saying a poem is 'good' or 'bad';

on the other, the sort of thought, perception, or judgement that has no – or exceeds – justification. Very quickly, we begin to realize that Tagore is not speaking up for Bengali nursery rhymes as an Indian nationalist but as a modern; that it isn't national identity and its prestige, but the realm that lies beyond justification that exercises him; it is self-division and the tension with logos that he's dwelling on, as enacted by a general figure called the 'expert' on one side, and another utopian figure called the 'poet' on the other. He confesses:

> It is impossible for me to dissociate my delight in savouring children's rhyme from my memories of childhood. The present author does not have the acumen to judge how much of the sweetness of these rhymes is owing to those memories and how much to the perennial principles of literature. I should admit this at the outset.
>
> 'The rain falls pitter-patter [*tapur tupur* in the original], the river is in flood' – in my childhood, this rhyme was like a magic chant for me, and I have yet to overcome that magic ... Nor can I otherwise explain why so many epics and lyrics, theories and precepts, so much human labour and sweating toil should be spent in vain and forgotten every day, while these inconsistent, meaningless, wilfully composed verses should flow for ever through popular memory.

'Inconsistent, meaningless', '*asangata arthahin*': these are important terms in late nineteenth-century colonial rhetoric against 'subject races' and their literatures, as they would be, in a different way, for native progressives and reformers of the time, for whom much of tradition, defaced by superstition and custom, is *arthahin*. Tagore, in the context of the colonial rhetoric, will counter and reverse it in his own tit-for-tat, as I shall show in my essay on his idiosyncratic and powerful interpretation of the Orientalist legacy. And, as a direct progeny of the Brahmo Samaj, some of the progressive language and world-view would have rubbed off onto him, and would resurface in his response to Gandhi. But here, he's enacting a modernist self-division by actually using the notion of the 'inconsistent' and 'meaningless' in opposition to 'judgement', 'acumen', 'theories and precepts', and rationality; the target is not the colonizer, nor the English language, nor the dead weight of tradition, but the self as a source of illumination. 'Memory' and 'magic' become a counterpoint to history and nationalism, and the 'inconsistent' act of remembering – in that what is recalled is trivial rather than canonical – reorders the integrity of the self and what it values. In the following paragraph, Tagore is speaking in aphorisms and paradoxes, but is all the time developing upon the covertly modernist argument:

If we consider the matter rightly, nothing is so old as a child. Adult human beings have changed in so many ways by accidents of place, time, upbringing, and custom; but the child remains as he was a hundred thousand years ago ... The reason for that youthful permanence is that the child is nature's own creation. The adult, on the contrary, is largely a human creation. In the same way, these rhymes are children's literature: they have been born of themselves in the human mind.

At first glance, this reads like a revision of Wordsworth – 'The Child is the father of the Man' – but Tagore is not after 'natural piety' in his polemic; and, while Wordsworth might have been convinced about the necessity of habitually returning to the wellspring of childhood, there's no evidence that he believed that the adult human being was a construct, as Tagore appears to suggest. Indeed, for all his talk of 'permanence', Tagore is not so much speaking of the invention of the adult as he is of the invention of the child.

The immense role assigned to the moral and imaginative space of childhood, and its invention, in the modern Bengali consciousness has not only to do with a nationalist programme to produce a home-grown children's literature ('There was a time when even our fairy tales seemed to be manufactured in the factories of Manchester', Tagore would say seven years later), but, in some regards, to do with the opposite: the creation of a domain of play and anarchy that critiques the *bhadralok* self, which is invested in several serious enterprises, including rationality, progress, modernization, and the nation. Modernism sustains itself, in many ways, by challenging and berating the 'modern': it's a characteristic and powerful form of self-dividedness. That the suspicion of modernity and the rational is not automatically a resistance to the West, but a classic modernist turn within, and against, the self is what I'm trying to explore in the context of Tagore's essay on nursery rhymes. The paragraph that follows is intriguing:

> The phrase 'born of themselves' is significant. In the normal way, echoes and reflections of the universe revolve in our minds in a scattered, disjointed manner ... As in the atmosphere, roadside dust, flower-pollen, assorted sounds, fallen leaves, water droplets, the vapours of the earth – all the ejected, whirling fragments of this turning, agitated universe – float and roam meaninglessly, so it is in our minds. There too, in the ceaseless stream of our consciousness, so many colours, scents, and sounds; so many vapours of the imagination, traces of thoughts, broken fragments of language – hundreds of fallen, forgotten discarded components of our practical life – float about, unobserved and purposeless.

This manifesto of the arbitrary and unfinished, with its advocacy of the 'whirling fragment', *'uddina khandangsha-sakala'*, is striking for a number of reasons. Firstly, it tells us something about Tagore's aesthetic that is implicit in the characteristic subject matter of the songs and poems, but which we've largely chosen to ignore: the subtle, strategic domestication of the image and the fragment in his work. Secondly, the year of the essay's publication, 1894, makes it not only an unusual utterance, but a precursor-polemic for many of modernism's chief preoccupations. Thirdly, the astonishingly serendipitous and propitious phrase, *'nityaprabahita chetanar madhye'*, which the translator renders teasingly, but without comment, as 'the ceaseless stream of our consciousness', and which could also be translated as 'the everyday flow of consciousness' or 'the daily current of consciousness', begs several questions. Had Tagore already, in 1894, read William James's *Principles of Psychology* (1890), where, in the chapter 'The Stream of Thought', he elaborates upon ideas that would be of fundamental interest to English literature a few decades later; or seen the essay in *Psychology* (1892), where James actually uses the now canonical and well-worn term 'stream of consciousness' in the title? If Tagore had read either or both (which is not at all unlikely), it's a testimony to the extraordinary cosmopolitanism of that family and the city in which it lived; and it is even more remarkable for being almost certainly the first transposition of James's influential formulation from the fields of psychology and philosophy into that of literary activity. On the other hand, if Tagore hadn't read James, the essay on nursery rhymes is singular for embodying a parallel project, one that would take such a seminal and irrevocable form in the West, and from which, once it had, Tagore would feel compelled to distance himself. Both these possibilities are equally rich and astonishing; but my intention is not so much to score a historicist point on behalf of Tagore's aesthetic (who came first, or how early?), but to pursue the intentions of Tagore's polemics: who is its target? For, in speaking up for the 'superfluous' in the paragraph just quoted – *'anaavashyak'*, which Sukanta Chaudhuri translates as the equally plausible 'purposeless' – Tagore is distinguishing himself from his Bengali progressive contemporaries, for whom the jettisoning of the superfluous and obscure in favour of the clarity and the perspective of rationality is essential to onward movement. The 'superfluous' entails the reclaiming and reassessment of the marginal; and yet Tagore's definition of marginality is not a nationalist or post-colonial one; the marginal is not located in, or shored up by, identity or race; allied to the *anaavasyak*, the 'superfluous', and the *arthhaheen*, the 'meaningless', it is, actually, a sort of space that Tagore is talking about, a reconfiguration of emptiness, or a crack, a gap in the everyday realm of valuation. What, or who, the target of the polemic is becomes clear in the next paragraph:

When one starts to think consciously with a specific objective in view, these shadowy mirages vanish in a moment: one's intellect and imagination take on an integrated purpose and begin to flow in a single direction. The substance one calls one's mind is so authoritarian that when it awakens and emerges into the light of day, the greater part of the world within and outside us is obscured under its influence: its own retinue of attendants fills all creation under its power, its law, and its bidding. Think about it: the call of birds in the sky, the sough of leaves, the babble of waters, the hubbub of human habitations – so many thousands of sounds, big and small, rising without end; so many waves and tremors, comings and goings … yet only a small fraction of all this impinges on one's consciousness. This is chiefly because one's mind, like a fisherman, casts a net of integration and accepts only what it can gather at a single haul: everything else eludes it. When it sees, it does not properly hear; when it hears, it does not properly see; and when it thinks, it neither sees nor hears properly. It has the power to move all irrelevancies far away from the path of its set purpose.

Tagore's contribution to, and his ambivalence towards, nationalism is well known; and yet look at how these contrary impulses play themselves out here. By 1894, it's already the self, the 'substance one calls one's mind', '*mana-namak padyarthati*', with its authoritarian – '*prabhutwashali*' – and teleological characteristics, that Tagore feels is the primary source of constriction and discomfort. Progressive Bengalis of the two previous generations, in arguing with the *prabhutwashali*, the 'authoritarian', might almost certainly have been quarrelling with religion and tradition – especially as the word, deriving from *prabhu*, has resonances of 'lordliness' and religious power. (Even James, in fact, in his crucial notion of a sort of higher self, the 'I', and a more worldly one, the 'you', in his *Psychology*, is refashioning a religious argument for secular, phenomenological ends, and is probably influenced by his readings in Oriental philosophy.) But Tagore is not critiquing tradition, religion, or the 'higher' self in the Upanishadic vein; he carefully avoids loaded theological terms like *atma*, and settles for the common-or-garden *mana* ('heart' or 'mind'), and the secular-modern *chetana* ('consciousness'). Indeed, the 'high' and the 'low' are always on slippery ground in a piece that's difficult to fit, for all its advocacy of a popular genre, into a recognizable and reassuring 'cultural studies' paradigm; for a popular, academically neglected form is being championed in the interests of what is potentially a 'high' cultural notion, the 'stream of consciousness'. The target of the attack, then, is something – for want of more precise terms – more immediate and foundational than either tradition or foreignness, those familiar polarities in modern India; and what is posited against it is, curiously, not identity, history, or even the future, but the 'superfluous', the *anaavasyak*, which, on its second appearance in the

essay, Chaudhuri translates as 'irrelevancies'. Tagore's relationship to colonialism doesn't shape the argument either; in fact, his critiques of both
colonialism and nationalism are offshoots of this difficult and productive
self-division. For Tagore, the nation-state, both before and after Empire, is
a circumscribing, imprisoning space; according to him, as we know, one
can't become free by simply shaking off the colonizer. Tagore is not being
a utopian romantic here, as songs like 'Where the mind is without fear'
would lead us to believe; in arguing for the *anaavasyak* as a fundamental
constituent of freedom, he's taking on the self and its relentless allocation
of meaningfulness – while always qualifying it and making it contingent
('the substance one calls the mind'). It's in that crack, that gap or space –
the 'superfluous' – that much of our cultural activity has taken place, and
been challenged, in the last century and a half.

The history of logos in Indian modernity, as we know, is concomitant with,
and inextricable from, the emergence of the human and the secular. But
just as 'high' culture and nationalism have had a symbiotic but necessarily
competitive relationship in India – an inevitable mark of the self-division
that characterizes our modernity – there are, I think, powerfully competing
but symbiotically linked senses, or even spaces, in which the 'secular' exists
in our recent history. One sense, to put it simply, even crudely, is related to
what's called, pejoratively, 'high' cultural history, and to an interior, or (to
give this dichotomy a more complex dimension) a metaphorical, potential
space, a space not unrelated to the 'superfluous' that Tagore's arguing for.
The other sense of the 'secular' derives from a humanistic nationalism, and
exteriorizes and orders space, turning it into a civic and political domain.
In the story of our self-division, I'd say that, when it comes to the word and
notion, 'secular', the second meaning, which Tagore would have associated with the logos of nationalism, has vanquished the former; that the
history of the 'secular' as a cultural, humane, interstitial space in the midst
of logos, rather than logos itself, has lost out to the idea of the 'secular' as a
fundamental manifestation of the rationality of the nation-state, just as the
histories of modernity and cosmopolitanism in India have been subsumed,
in our time, and for a variety of reasons, by a history of the nation.
      In the last two decades, especially, the Indian understanding of the
'secular' has become primarily a constitutional one. When Indians speak
of the special Indian version of, or innovation upon, the 'secular' – especially in its metamorphosis into a noun, 'secularism', that sounds like an
ideology – they're speaking of a constitutional innovation and product
whereby a liberal guarantee is made for pluralistic and multicultural
practices in the nation-state. The signs of the 'secular' are at once exterior

and symbolic, simultaneously visible and statistical. So, in the space of the nation-state, about 80 per cent of the population comprise Hindus, who will coexist, ideally, in a peaceful way with the 12 per cent of Muslims and the 8 per cent of the remaining minorities. The peculiar Indian usage of the term 'cosmopolitan' is a corollary of this symbolic and statistical way of understanding space, what it is for, and those who inhabit it; the term is used, most frequently, or almost exclusively, as an adjective for the city of Bombay, and describes, typically, its multicultural demography – that, for instance, so many Gujaratis, Maharashtrians, Bengalis, Parsees, and Bohri Muslims live together in the neighbourhood of Teen Batti.

Informing this view of the 'cosmopolitan' and the 'secular' is the constitutional view of India, Indianness, and the nation-state as a symbolic but visible space, where numerical quantities of legitimate world-views and religions associated with the land will, when added up, amount to 'India' or 'Indianness'. This is fine; it is also important; and, unsurprisingly, the writers in India who speak of the 'secular' and the 'cosmopolitan' do so principally with a constitutional definition in mind. Among the most robust and like-able proponents of this constitutional understanding is Ramachandra Guha; among the most stylish and intelligent Sunil Khilnani. In fact, the feline stylishness of Khilnani's prose points to a history of the 'secular' and the 'cosmopolitan' in India different from the one he's most often writing about; his style emerges from a 'cosmopolitanism' that is a form of inner ex-ile, of a 'high' cultural eclecticism that has been the mark of outsiders, usu-ally Jewish writers, who have domesticated themselves as Europeans and have revised Europeanness from the inside; and from an idea of the 'secular' as a hidden space for the self, for daydreaming and literary ambition, and for identifying and ascribing value to a domain which, with the passing of religion and mythology, is called 'reality' (the writer works within 'reality' as he or she reorders it; writing is not, for one such as Khilnani, a caste or inherited vocation, but a constant gesture towards inhabiting a private but real world). The constitutional interpretation of the 'secular' – while it's indispensable for obvious reasons – gives us an attenuated grasp of how the imagination, the act of daydreaming, and the valuation of the 'real' have been the everyday business of the 'secular' in the past one hundred and fifty years in India; it gives us no access to the multiple, non-symbolic, invisible, onto-logical locations of the 'secular' in this country. This is so partly because, of course, we've always been, due to the unique mixture of nationalism, Marx-ism, and now post-coloniality in our intellectual discourse, uneasy with the idea of an ontology or phenomenology of what 'being Indian' means: what it means to see, smell, or touch as an Indian, or to live inside a dwelling, or to encounter a horizon, and how these experiences are not givens, but coterminous with the emergence with the 'secular' in our history; and this uneasiness means that we feel far more comfortable defining ourselves, in the context of the 'secular', through the external marks and symbols that a powerful constitutional notion gives to us.

'Liberation through renunciation – that path's not for me' ('*bairagyasadhane mukti, se amar noy*'); thus Tagore, in the poem '*Mukti*' or 'Liberation', from the 1901 collection, *Naivedya*. Wonderfully parodied in Parashuram's short story, 'Sri Sri Siddheshwari Limited', these words are spoken in it in a thick North Indian accent, by a canny Marwari businessman who's attending a meeting of Bengalis of dubious business acumen trying to set up an enterprise. Parashuram (or Rajshekhar Basu) is glancingly touching upon forms of worldliness: the sort expressed in Tagore's line, and another sort, ventriloquized through Tagore by the businessman. Tagore himself is drawing attention to the fact, as he has often (one thinks of the famous opening lines of the song 'I have been invited/ to the world's festival of joy'), that the poet's vocation (and the 'I' and 'me' in these works is principally the poet) involves not a religious rejection of the material and visible universe (that which is called '*moha*' or '*maya*' or 'illusion' in religion) but an embrace of it, a dwelling in it. Poetry is a form of dwelling in the world. And so, in the same poem: 'Whatever delight there is in a scene, in a smell, in a melody/ – your delight will reside at its core.' The 'you', addressed and praised here, is not named, as it never is by Tagore; it's the most affirmative product of his self-division, a self that makes dwelling in the world possible, and is available, evidently, only through poetry; a self that's a progeny, in fact, of the poetic act of making. Tagore, in other words, makes a case again and again in his work (notwithstanding his frequent longings for 'elsewhere') of the poem as a space for being in the world, for habitation, as Heidegger would state it in 1946 in his meditation on Hölderlin. The importance of fashioning this space, this world, is attested to by the loaded way in which Tagore generally uses the words '*rachita*', 'that which is composed', and '*rachana*', 'composition', in his poetry, as, at once, a deliberately self-referential and metaphysical paradox: an allusion to the poem, as well as to the metaphysics of occupying, and fashioning, the space of the literary. A moment on Tagore's peculiar use of the word '*maya*' would be appropriate here. There are, fundamentally, two recognized registers of the term; the first is the familiar religious-metaphysical register, to do with the unreality of the visible world. The second register, common in Bengal, is a homely one, and refers to the almost irrational attachment that human beings feel for another human being or place, as in, 'She felt a deep sense of *maya* for that awful boy, because he reminded her of her son.' To these two registers Tagore adds a third, a subtly, but decisively, modernist one: that of 'enchantment' – a celebration of, rather than a turning away from, the visible world, as appearance is remade through perception, poetry, and language. It's this sense, for instance, that informs '*ki maya dey bulaye, dilo sab kaaj bhulaye*' ('what's this enchantment stroking me, making me forgetful of my work'), in the song about the incursion of a bee into a room.

Despite Heidegger's residual but extreme cultural nationalism, it's clear that, in the essay on Hölderlin's line about 'dwelling poetically in the universe', he's formulating a view already in existence: of culture and the literary being a habitation for the human, in a way that incorporates the everyday and the local, but somehow transcends the national or the racial. To be part of this making is to be part of an attempt to create a dwelling for man, rather than to be only fashioning a national literature. The everyday, the specific, and the local become, in this notion of culture, aspects of that making; Western European literature, English literature, and even the literatures of an erstwhile colony like America, and certain literatures in the time of colonization, like Ireland's, have become essential to this Heideggerean, really 'high' cultural notion of poetry as dwelling. It's for this reason that we enter, say, the everyday or the neighbourhood of Joyce's *Ulysses*, or the landscape of Heaney's poems, or the terrain of Eudora Welty's stories, in order to visit the realm of the literary as habitation, rather than to, for instance, partake of the 'sights, sounds, and smells' of Ireland or the American South. All those literatures and cultures that have, for one reason or another, been excluded from that Heidegerrean dwelling become, in some senses, varieties of national or popular literature; the everyday and the particular become signs of, at once, nationality and the exotic; it is no accident that, when thinking of the physical world in Indian writing, it's characteristic to speak of the 'sights, smells, and sounds of India', rather than, say, the polemical and spiritual significance of the immediate, the earthly, for the modern. Part of this project – to produce, as it were, the marks of a national landscape rather than make the work of art and the habitation of the world in some profound sense coterminous with one another – part of the project began, unsurprisingly, with relatively early Anglophone writing in India, almost as a pact between members of colonial bourgeois society on different sides of the divide. So, in 1912, the critic Edmund Gosse, introducing Sarojini Naidu's[3] poems, could recount the heartfelt, yet shrewd, advice he'd given her:

> I implored her to consider that from a young Indian of extreme sensibility, who had mastered not merely the language but the prosody of the West, what we wished to receive was, not a *réchauffé* of Anglo-Saxon sentiment

in an Anglo-Saxon setting, but some revelation of the heart of India, some sincere penetrating analysis of native passion, of the principles of antique religion and of such mysterious intimations as stirred the soul of the East long before the West had begun to dream that it had a soul. Moreover, I entreated Sarojini to write no more about robins and skylarks, in a landscape of our Midland counties ... but to describe the flowers, the fruits, the trees, to set her poems firmly among the mountains, the gardens, the temples, to introduce to us the vivid populations of her own voluptuous and unfamiliar province; in other words, to be a genuine Indian poet of the Deccan, not a clever machine-made imitator of the English classics.

Of course, Tagore too is intent upon describing, with great specificity (and, significantly, through the Sanskrit poet Kalidasa), 'the flowers, the fruits, the trees'; often with polemical purpose, as I try to show in the essay 'Two Giant Brothers'. But his invocation of the particular, the 'real', doesn't just involve, as a solution to his self-division, the turning away from one culture and the embracing of another, but a resolve to occupy both the world and the work of art in a new way. The reason readers continually revisit Tagore and several writers after him in India – writers who all deal in the sensuous, the local, in every language spoken here, including English – is not for the sake of those sights and sounds, but for a renewing sense of how writing remakes language and culture as a habitation, a dwelling, which the reader, too, has occupied in India in the last century, in a manner that's very different from living in the nation-state. The poem, or literary work, as a space in our history: this, too, has to be adequately comprehended and described.

Not all 'Oriental' traditions in the time of modernity have been identified with being forms of religion, nationalism, or, in effect, popular literature or culture; or made exempt, for that matter, from the Heideggerean metaphysical-secular notion of the literary as habitation. Japan is an instructive case in point, an instance not without its own ambiguities and contradictions. Japanese literature and cinema in the twentieth century have generally been associated with the domain of 'culture', with forms of dwelling poetically, rather than, say, simply with the 'sights, smells, and sounds of Japan'. That's not to say that Japan hasn't been caricatured, even by its own artists. But the quality of the spatial that we used to, until not very long ago, ascribe to much that is Japanese, especially the juxtaposition of space (or an opening out) and order in its landscapes, paintings, flower arrangements, in the way a Japanese home is furnished, or in a film by Ozu, gives to its twentieth-century culture (in which I'd include its powerful reimagining of its past) an unformulated but distinct air of being a quasi-, or alternative, modernism, something related to, but at odds with (mirroring 'high' modernism's curious relationship to 'progress'), the Japan of modernity we all know about – with its black-suited office-goers, its tourists, its gift for manufacturing cameras and cars. The latter is connected, in our minds, and perhaps in Japanese self-awareness too, to a kind of 'Westernization' (and this has been the fate of the 'modern' in India, too; to be viewed as something that's essentially derived or imported). But the former, the domain of twentieth-century Japanese 'high' culture, is seen to be figuratively Japanese, but also allowed, in an odd, ahistorical, really New Critical way, to be part of the universal (implicitly European) space of 'high' culture in a manner in which probably Indian modernism (with the exception of Satyajit Ray) has not been. There's a tacit acknowledgement, in other words, that Japanese literature, for example, might arise from, and suggest, a context of modernism, rather than of religion or nationalism; although, admittedly, the Western (largely American) engagement has been mainly to do with individual writers or film-makers (Tanizaki, Mishima, Kurosawa, Ozu) rather than a movement or a discourse (which is what modernism is). Here, of course, I'm not speaking of the culture that's emerged from Japan in the last two decades, or of what it's contributed to, and absorbed from, globalization.

Junichiro Tanizaki, sensing the fundamentally European nature of the Western reading of Japanese 'high' culture, turns the table on the 'West' in his slim book on the Japanese style of dwelling, *In Praise of Shadows*. This is really a manifesto for modernism disguised, for strategic reasons, as a work of cultural nationalism; it's a strategy that 'high' cultural artists from the non-Western world have deliberately had recourse to; in 'Two Giant Brothers' below, for instance, I look at how Tagore, instead of arguing against the Enlightenment, argues for it having an older and truer history in India. In his short foreword to the book, the architect Charles Moore points out that 'in the West our most powerful ally is light.' "The sun never knew how wonderful it was," the architect Louis Kahn said, "until it fell on the wall of a building."' When Moore says 'our', he means American, possibly Western, architects; but he could be using the pronoun of the West itself, and its privileging of light and logos. But Western modernism, as he would know, also involves a profound critique of light and knowledge; with a precursor, especially in the visual arts, in Impressionism, it advocates a condition of imperfect visibility, holding up, against the total, the finished, and the perfect, the fragment, the incomplete, and, in the case of Benjamin's *flâneur*, an assortment of grimy urban knick-knacks. But, for Tanizaki, Western modernism's critique of logos, totality, and light is already intrinsically present in the Japanese aesthetic, and especially the way in which it informs the Japanese idea of habitation:

As a general matter we find it hard to be really at home with things that shine and glitter. The Westerner uses silver and steel and nickel tableware, and polishes it to a fine brilliance, but we object to the practice. While we do sometimes indeed use silver for teakettles, decanters, or sake cups, we prefer not to polish it. On the contrary, we begin to enjoy it only when the lustre has worn off, when it has begun to take on a dark, smoky patina.

In the next paragraph, broadening his argument from a Japanese nationalism to accommodate a wider Oriental nationalism, he offers what's really a Benjamin-like insight about the transformation of the ordinary objects of our modernity from usable things into junk, and, thereafter, into something that possesses a mysterious, magical, albeit secular, register (Tanizaki, who died in 1965, would not have read Benjamin; indeed, this essay, published in 1933, is contemporaneous with the German writer's work). Although what Tanizaki cites as an example is an object still in use, it is, for the conventional eye (which, in Tanizaki's clever inversion, is the 'Western' eye), something that is close to being unusable:

Chinese food is now most often served on tableware made of tin, a material the Chinese could only admire for the patina it acquires. When new it resembles aluminium and is not particularly attractive; only after long use brings some of the elegance of age is it at all acceptable. Then, as the surface darkens, the line of verse etched upon it gives a final touch of perfection. In the hands of the Chinese this flimsy, glittering metal takes on a profound and sombre dignity akin to that of their red unglazed pottery.

A couple of pages later, after brief reflections on jade, crystal, and wood – and the Japanese distaste for sparkle and polish – Tanizaki observes:

I suppose I shall sound terribly defensive if I say that Westerners attempt to expose every speck of grime and eradicate it. Yet for better or for worse we do love things that bear the marks of grime, soot, and weather, and we love the colours and the sheen that call to mind the past that made them. Living in these old houses among these old objects is in some mysterious way a source of peace and repose.

Tanizaki's essay is a tract, that, in effect, is a defence of 'dwelling poetically'; and it precedes by more than a decade Heidegger's meditation. Heidegger, as he thinks about Hölderlin's poem, brings together the notions of making and inhabiting with the idea of the special space that poetic language gives to the human being. Tanizaki is doing the same; at the centre of his thoughts is the self-effacing, unnamed, but subversive presence of the writer, his craft, and his vision of habitation; there's a constant reciprocity between the interiors that are being written about, the act

of writing, and, by implication, the space of culture that makes *this* view
of space real: here, too, there is a definite, suggestive reciprocity. But there
is the other, obvious conflation, through which Tanizaki is arguing that
Oriental aesthetics almost organically involves a 'high' cultural sensibility
in the modernist sense; in constructing this polemic, Tanizaki is bringing
to the surface the unspoken exclusivist, European component in the Western notion of the 'poetic' (Heidegger's essay is probably a good example),
and yet rejecting neither 'high' culture nor the ambition of 'dwelling poetically', but rewriting them with a mixture of nationalist aggression (always
qualified with apologies) and a sophisticated, leisurely modernist attentiveness to the changed value of the appurtenances of existence. Tanizaki's
also performing a kind of self-division that's a familiar fulcrum of Indian
modernity; it entails naming certain aspects of the self as 'Western', or
foreign, as outside of the zone of habitation. Unsurprisingly, what's felt to
be most oppressive is also what's most intimate, and foundational, to the
modern's, and the modernist's, sense of self and dwelling: light, or logos.
Thus, Tanizaki on lacquerware:

> An Indian friend once told me that in his country ceramic tableware is
> still looked down upon, and that lacquerware is in far wider use. We,
> however, use ceramics for practically everything but trays and soup
> bowls; lacquerware, except in the tea ceremony and on formal occasions,
> is considered vulgar and inelegant. This, I suspect, is in part the fault of
> the much-vaunted 'brilliance' of modern electric lighting. Darkness is an
> indispensable element of the beauty of lacquerware.

There are roughly three reasons why I have spoken about the notion
of 'space' in this introduction, and they all have something to do with the
position I've been trying to arrive at in the essays contained in this book.
The first, as I've already hinted at, has to do with the persistent sense of
deferral or absence one encounters in India with regard to 'high' culture
and modernity; it's a strange but perhaps logical absence, in that it makes
things easier for us; it engenders a space that's cocooning and enveloping,
where notions of the secular and of culture are, despite all our reservations about elite practices, reassuringly patrician and constitutional ones.
By simplifying our idea of the 'foreign', we escape the curious tensions and
contradictions – to take just one example, our resistance to the colonizer
on the one hand; our openness to the colonizer's culture on the other –
that have shaped our creative life in modernity; the simplification of the
'foreign' has also made our secular bourgeoisie, in the last twenty years,
enact its own contradiction, involving a voluble advocacy of marginality
(which, implicitly, becomes synonymous with identity) and an increasing

wariness, or eliding, of the outsider (who becomes a subterranean figure for the foreigner). The suspicion – or more accurately, the de-recognition, if there might be such a word – of the outsider cuts through to, and undermines, the core of our constitutionally backed democracy.

My second reason for an interest in 'space' has to do with the idea of it being the domain of the 'real' in the secular world. With the passing of religion as a principal source of value, and in anticipation of another complete cosmology (such as globalization) taking the place of the old world, the space of modernity seems more and more like not only an interstitial space, but a transitional one; modernism itself seems, in hindsight, not so much a settled and authoritative hegemony as one of the longest periods in the history of culture celebrating its own transitionality, its expectancy not to arrive at some final meaning, but to hold indefinitely to, and shape, the pause between one meaning, one period, and another. With globalization, the self-consciously transitional nature of the modern becomes clearer; as does the quality of the 'real' within that space, as a form of pregnancy of meaning, rather than a species of dead fact. The role of that space in India, from the vantage-point of the new world we inhabit now, and the charged pregnancy of its 'reality', is surely worth looking at, before we rush, in a characteristic move, to make the 'real' synonymous with the Western Enlightenment, and proceed to ignore it.

Finally, the narrative of the manner in which that 'high' cultural space was appropriated, reworked, and argued, for a number of reasons, by Indian, even non-Western (I'm thinking again of Tanizaki), artists, and in what way the rhetoric of the indigenous and of identity was, or wasn't, useful to those appropriations, is an important story, and one probably far more complex than the one about our recent, apparent annexation of the English language. But it might help us to understand that putative annexation better. In what way is the talk about English being 'an Indian language', situated as it is in the vocabulary of free-market globalization, superficially similar to, but also fundamentally different from as well as an overturning of, the simultaneously nationalist and 'high' cultural preoccupations of modernity?

It's not within my capabilities to tell that story, but to try to be true to my sense that it exists.

Amit Chaudhuri
2 September 2007
Calcutta

Part One

Towards a Poetics of the Indian Modern

Poles of Recovery

The Moor's Legacy

When I was an undergraduate at University College London in the early 1980s, cultivating a life of self-imposed loneliness, I would be pursued by a man of indeterminate nationality. He could have been from Latin America; when I asked him where he came from, he replied with a snort, 'Let us say ... from one of the industrialized nations.' His interest in me wasn't amorous; his intention was, curiously – once he'd found out I was from India – to humiliate me in the way I've just mentioned.

I think he was lonelier than I was; bearded, overcoated, his face raw with a skin disorder and his eyes framed by thick glasses, he had the air of a graduate student whose project had gone nowhere. He lighted upon me on the steps of Senate House or the Students Union Building, or on one of the roads outside. It was in front of Dillon's Bookshop that he asked me (he'd obviously discovered I was a student of English, and that I had ambitions as a writer, though I can't recall when I divulged this information to him) a question that caused me some discomfort: 'Why don't you write in your own language?' I mumbled something in reply; I hoped he'd go away. It's not that I didn't have a reason: I, a Bengali, had grown up in Bombay, and, not having been taught Bengali in school, didn't know it well enough to write poetry or fiction in it. My literary models and aspirations belonged to the English language; yet, secretly, I'd long been troubled by what my inquisitor implied: that you can't achieve anything worthwhile in literature unless you write in your 'own' language.

It becomes easier to understand my particular disquiet, the reasons for my being in England, standing outside Dillon's, and my ambition to be a writer in the English language, by looking back to Michael Madhusudan Dutt, with whom, in India, such journeys and disquiets largely begin. I, indeed, found myself reacquainting myself with his life and, in a small way, his work, for the purposes of an anthology I was editing. He was, of course, already familiar to me as a mythological figure in my childhood, the first figure to give literary history in India, in effect, a sense of theatre; like Shakespeare's Moor, to whom his contemporaries compared him, his life and practice form a parable of inner and actual exile, a negotiation between the 'civilized' and the 'barbaric'.

Dutt was born in 1824 into a well-to-do middle-class family, in a Bengal where a native bourgeoisie and intelligentsia had already come into being. Inscribed into his life is another narrative, to do with the secular, middle-class Indian self's struggle between disowning and recovering its – for the want of a better word – 'Indianness', a struggle that, as I was compiling material for the anthology, I found was a paradigm around which a substantial part of 'modern' Indian literature and culture was structured.

Dutt studied at the Bishop's College and the Hindu College in Calcutta, where, not long before, the Anglo-Portuguese poet, Henry Louis Vivian Derozio, had taught. By the time Dutt arrived there, the major articulations of modernity by Indians, in the spheres of religious and social reform, were already marked by conflicting currents of disowning and recovery. Raja Rammohun Roy had founded the reformist sect, the Brahmo Samaj, in 1828; it constituted, after Roy's contact with the culture and religion of the British colonizer (and owing not a little to the Islamic culture of the past), a rejection, or disowning, of the polytheistic, idolatrous aspects of Hinduism. But instead of completing this act of disowning, and converting to Christianity, Roy transformed it into an act of recovery by turning back to the *Upanishads*, and enlisting the nameless monotheistic deity in their passages as the foundation for a transcendental protestantism.

The figure of Michael Madhusudan Dutt belongs to this context – of Roy, of the intermittently comic, but nevertheless seminal, radicalism of Young Bengal, of the breaking of dietary and religious taboos, of social reform. In his personal and creative life, we see, again, the related impulses towards, on the one hand, the disowning of tradition, and its recovery as a creative constituent of the secular self on the other. Crucially, however, he translates the public acts of disowning and recovery that, so far, marked the spheres of religious debate and social reform, into the personal sphere of art. In a sense, almost, he suddenly, and unprecedentedly, gifts the Bengali a relationship between identity, rebellion, creativity, and the subconscious.

Dutt began his creative endeavour by writing poetry in the English language, and completed a substantial work, *The Captive Ladie*; his ambition was to be a canonical 'English' poet. When still a student, he converted to Christianity; this was his first great act of disowning. Whether he converted in reaction to the Hinduism he, like many of his generation, had come to feel impatient with, or in his desire to become more completely 'English' (and further his career as an 'English' poet), or in defiance of his father, is not known. At any rate, he hardly seems to have led a conventional 'Christian' life. If Dutt disowned his father and his religion, his father, in turn, disowned him, quite literally. The Oedipal conflict between father and son may not necessarily be the most productive way of looking at Indian culture, but it would certainly seem to play a part in shaping Dutt's life; it would appear modernity entered Bengali culture and poetry, via Dutt, not by a slaying of the colonizer, but of the father.

Around the late 1850s, after the long process of disowning, began the process of recovery, the reappropriation, by Dutt, of the Bengali language and culture, culminating in his epic poem, *Meghnadbadhakabya*. Now, rejecting the language in which he had invested his literary ambitions, he turned to his mother-tongue, not yet quite a respectable language for the middle class. Already, before embarking on the epic, he had written the long Bengali poem, 'Tilottama Sambhava'; in a long vivid letter written in English, on 15 May 1860, he had confessed to his friend Raj Narain: 'I am going on with Meghnad by fits and starts. Perhaps the poem will be finished by the end of the year.' Then, in some flippant sentences, he delineated the nature of the recovery he was undertaking: 'I am glad you like the opening lines. I must tell you, my dear fellow, that though, as a jolly Christian youth, I don't care a pin's head for Hinduism, I love the grand mythology of our ancestors. It is full of poetry.' This is followed by an exclamation both excited and desperate, an almost maritime, Raleigh-like view of literary possibility: 'What a vast field does our country now present for literary enterprise! I wish to God, I had time.' The word 'enterprise' is both striking and estranging; it reminds us, at once, of the material contexts, in a Bengal of middlemen, of Dutt's epic inversion; and of the fact that the literary pioneer is part visionary and part adventurer.

Dutt's comic but grandiose remarks about not caring 'a pin's head for Hinduism', but loving, all the same, 'the grand mythology of [his] ancestors' for its poetry contain a serious and, till then, unexpressed truth. For Dutt speaks not so much as a 'jolly Christian youth' as a very early vehicle for what we now rather vaguely call the 'secular' Indian sensibility, to which the rejection of indigenous culture and religion, relegating them to the realm of superstition and irrationality, would be an important act on the one hand; as would, on the other, its recovery of that very culture as a life-giving, if perennially problematic, part of itself. Roughly after Dutt's casual exhortations, the gods and goddesses would begin to appear not as deities, as they would to a devotee, but as actors upon the stage of the 'secular' consciousness, to which their meaning and power would no longer be orthodoxly religious, but nevertheless profound. It was a form of 'darshan'; but the passive and grateful devotion of the worshipper had been transformed into the slightly adversarial gaze of the romantic visionary.

Disowning and recovery are, indeed, written into the very composition of *Meghnadbadhakabya*: Dutt's rejection of English in favour of Bengali for the purposes of writing his epic was itself an immensely significant, almost an exhibitionistic, act of recovery. They are inscribed, too, into the subject matter, and Dutt's treatment of it; Dutt's epic reworks an episode from the Hindu epic, the *Ramayana* (which he'd heard from his mother as a child), except that, as we know, Dutt made the son of Ravana, the hero Rama's traditional adversary, the tragic protagonist of his poem. Dutt used the Miltonic inversion of *Paradise Lost* to make the transition from the certainties of a religious epic, and religion itself, to the ambivalences of a 'secular' work; 'I hate Rama and all his rabble,' said Dutt in another of his letters, speaking with the voice of an India that would find imaginative sustenance in its epics and religious texts while never literally engaging with their sacredness. Literature, with Dutt, and for the sort of modernism he ushers in, doesn't quite become a *substitute* for religion, as it was for Arnold; it becomes, in its relationship with religion, a process of self-division, of qualified wonder, of aesthetic joy and a not-quite-rational anger and fear, of immersion and distancing, of open-armed welcoming and angry refutation. All these registers are audible in Dutt's meditations, in his letters, upon his 'enterprise'.

The 'Turn'

In 1862, after his epic poem had been published, Madhusudan Dutt left for England, registering at Gray's Inn to study law – to be joined there, later, by wife and children. Dutt's arrival in the land where he'd once wished to be recognized as an 'English' poet went unremarked; he was miserable and soon short of funds. He moved to Versailles; here, he concentrated his efforts to introduce the sonnet (which had, itself, once travelled from Italy to England) to Bengali literature, calling it the 'chaturdashpadi', which one might loosely translate as 'the fourteen-line stanza'.

The sonnet, used to express the sentiments of courtly love at its inception, had lent itself to troubled meditations and to ambivalent sexual registers with Shakespeare; later, the seemingly pacific Wordsworth used it to propagate subliminally revolutionary messages. Yet the sonnet, even with Shakespeare, was a self-reflexive literary form; its subject, from the outset, had been itself. Dutt took the sonnet's self-reflexivity, and also its ability to address the political, and used them to play out, explicitly, the drama of disowning and recovery, of exile and homecoming, that had shaped both his life and his artistic choices.

One of his most celebrated sonnets is called 'Bangabhasha' ('The Bengali Language'); an earlier, equally well-known version of this poem, 'Kabi-Matribhasha' ('The Poet's Mother-Tongue'), is inserted into a letter written in English in late 1860 in Calcutta; it is probably his first attempt at the poem. Dutt says in the letter: 'I want to introduce the sonnet into our language and some mornings ago, made the following ...' The poet begins 'Bangabhasha' with a complaint to his 'mother', Bengal, of the miseries of exile:

> O Bengal, there are many treasures in your keeping; –
> Yet (fool that I am!), neglecting these,
> Senseless with lust for others' possessions, I've travelled
> To a foreign country ... (my translation)

The trope of exile (not unknown to Bengali devotional verse) is a prescient one: two years after the composition of the first version of this sonnet, Dutt would depart for England. In the ninth line, the addressee instructs her petitioner to return to the treasures hidden in his mother's, or motherland's, womb.

> Then, in a dream, the goddess of my lineage proclaimed.
> 'O child, your mother's womb is profuse with jewels,
> Why then are you in this state of destitution?
> Go back, ignorant one, go back to your home!'

The final couplet seals the issue; it records the poet's obedience to this directive, his withdrawal from the destitution of exile, and the discovery of those 'treasures', of which the principal one is his mother-tongue: 'Happily I obeyed; in time I found/ The riches of my mother-tongue, in the great web of treasures.'

The simultaneously questioning and self-reflexive dimensions of the Shakespearean sonnet (a form which Dutt didn't always use) serves him well here. To make a brief comparison: in 'Shall I compare thee to a summer's day?' Shakespeare, in the first eight lines, praises the beloved's beauty while noting, and querying, its transitoriness. The 'turn', the 'But' at the opening of the ninth line, or third quatrain, introduces us to the conviction that the poet's art, 'where in eternal lines to time thou growest', will preserve that mortal beauty from extinction. The final couplet encapsulates and summarizes this argument; here, the sonnet self-reflexively praises its own, and language's, power to preserve and renew.

This Shakespearean structure, and the psychological movement it embodies, is employed, by Dutt, to dramatize the colonial, and post-colonial, movement from spiritual and geographical exile to cultural recovery. The general questions regarding exile and identity are posed in the first eight lines. Exile, distancing, or cultural disowning are represented implicitly by the probable location of the sonnet's revision, Versailles (Dutt was to write most of his sonnets in France); they are represented, generically, by the sonnet itself, which too is an exile and wanderer across cultures, although its incursion into the vernacular of a colonial culture was, till then, unprecedented. At the ninth line, the 'turn', the Shakespearean 'But', occurs as an interjection from the goddess, and the process of cultural recovery begins in the midst of exile; the 'turn' of the sonnet becomes a cultural and almost physical turning towards the mother-tongue and one's indigenous antecedents. The concluding couplet, which completes the act of recovery by attesting to the poet's discovery of his language in the 'web of treasures', also confirms, in effect, that the sonnet is now an indigenous form; the self-reflexivity of the Shakespearean couplet is freighted, in Dutt, with an added colonial self-consciousness.

As if taking the goddess's imperative to heart, Dutt returned to India not long after. He did, though, take his exams at Gray's Inn, and came back to Calcutta a qualified barrister. Spiritual homecomings are all very well, especially when they lead to artistic voyages rather than actual ones; but real homecomings are a different matter. In Calcutta, Dutt practised, often controversially, at the High Court, lived extravagantly and beyond his means, and raced impatiently towards an untimely death. Both his and his wife's health worsened, although there were brief periods of convalescence. He died in 1874, at the age of 50, reportedly a few hours after his wife Henrietta did. He is buried at the Park Circus cemetery, one of his sonnets (addressed to a passer-by or itinerant), which he'd composed as his own epitaph, engraved on a plaque outside.

Editing the anthology of modern Indian writing, I discovered that the paradoxes played out in Dutt's relatively short life, and the trajectories and metaphors of exile and homecoming that define it, are patterns that repeat themselves in subsequent narratives of Indian modernity. Certainly, the lives of a substantial number of the major Indian writers of the twentieth century, and, significantly, the shape and arc of their work, appear to be structured around these patterns. Briefly consider, for instance, the life and works of the novelist, O.V. Vijayan, that hugely influential figure in Malayalam literature.

Vijayan was born in 1930 in Palghat, Kerala; his first novel, *Khasak-kinte Itihasam* (*The Legends of Khasak*), published in 1969, 107 years after Dutt's epic, is seen to represent a turning point in modern Malayalam literature. Based upon actual experience, it tells the story of an educated, rationalist young man who arrives as a schoolteacher in an obscure South Indian village in which time hasn't moved. An ambivalent but character-istic psychological movement is revealed to us; the young man, who had come from elsewhere to enlighten, finds himself unexpectedly touched and transformed by the existence of the village; not only is the protagonist transformed, but also the novel; what might have been a social realist fic-tion about conscience and duty becomes *something else*. Vijayan, who, like many young men in Kerala at the time, was a card-carrying member of the Communist Party, tells us, several years after the novel was originally written, how it not only fictionalizes an episode in his life, but, as it were, enacts the pattern of disowning and recovery.

He recalls, in an Afterword to the English translation, the provenance of his novel; how, as a young college graduate who'd lost his job, he'd taken a job as a schoolteacher in Thasarak through 'a State scheme to send bare-foot graduates to man single-teacher schools in backward villages'. He was, at the time, a member of the Communist Party, and had already published 'two long stories depicting imaginary peasant uprisings'. He now wanted to write a 'revolutionary' novel. Having grown up in the Palghat countryside himself, he was 'familiar with its landscape … and its hilarious dialects', and believed that the character of the 'city-bred schoolmaster coming to the village' could be developed as the perfect 'pilgrim-revolutionary'.

The novel, then, was planned as a radical act of disowning of, or as a riposte to, the feudal, the oral, the indigenous. 'Looking back,' he says, 'I thank Providence, because I missed writing the "revolutionary" novel by a hair's breadth.' Two things changed the direction the novel might have taken. The first was a historical event, the killing of Imre Nagy in Hungary, leading to Vijayan's disillusionment with communism. The other was Vi-jayan's arrival at the village itself, an arrival which was augmented into a sort of spiritual homecoming; just as, in Dutt's sonnet, the neglected mother-tongue becomes the goddess who instructs and commands, the obscure village, in Vijayan's fiction, becomes instructor to the schoolteacher: 'The Stalinist claustrophobia melted away as though it had never existed. Ravi, my protagonist, liberation's germ-carrier, now came to the village and re-entered his enchanted childhood. He was no longer the teacher, in atone-ment he would *learn*. He would learn from the stupor of Khasak.'

One might also find in this narrative, as in Dutt's career, an implicit mirroring of the movement from the English language to the mother-tongue; for Vijayan, before he wrote his first novel in Malayalam, was a student of English literature, and had a Master's degree in English. And this, as it happens, is a movement that recurs in the lives and works of many of the most influential writers in the regional literatures of what we call 'modern India'; Qurratulain Hyder (Urdu), U.R. Anantha Murthy (Kannada), Mahashweta Devi (Bengali), Ambai (Tamil), to name only a handful of living contemporaries, have all been students, even teachers, of English literature. The cleaving of the tongue is symptomatic, again, of how disowning and recovery permeate and shape the creation of the vernacular – which, in our literary history, is a synonym for, rather than a counter to, the 'modernist' – sensibility.

An Inversion in the Pattern

Disowning, recovery; the cleaving of the tongue: U.R. Anantha Murthy's story of how he embarked upon his first work, the short novel *Samskara*, is, again, as in Dutt and Vijayan, a narrative of homecoming in the middle of exile, recovery in the midst of physical, and inward, distancing:

> It was [sic] nearly a little more than twenty-five years ago that I wrote *Samskara* … I was in England as a student, and fatigued with speaking the English language most of the time. I needed to recover my mother-tongue, living in the midst of English … It all started when I went to see a Bergman film – *Seventh Seal* – with my teacher, the famous novelist and critic, Malcolm Bradbury. The film had no subtitles. My incomplete comprehension of it started a vague stirring in me. I remember having told Dr Bradbury that a European has no living memory of the middle ages and hence constructs it through knowledge acquired in books. But for an Indian like me, centuries coexist as a living memory transmitted through oral conditions. This set me off to rewrite a story which I had originally written for a journal.

Anantha Murthy returns to his room; behaves like one instructed; starts to rewrite the seminal fiction; the role of Dutt's 'goddess', the 'kula-lakshmi' who visited the poet in Versailles, is played here, in Birmingham, by, oddly, a 'familiar compound ghost' of Bergman and Malcolm Bradbury.

This little story echoes an account of A.K. Ramanujan's. (Ramanujan was, we know, an important Indian English poet; but it was also as a translator of ancient Tamil poetry that he made a profound impact on our idea of the relationship between English, the contemporary Indian self, and the 'little', non-classical traditions of Indian antiquity.)

Once more, in a foreign country – America, in this case – Ramanujan discovered the poems in ancient Tamil which he'd later translate:

Even one's own tradition is not one's birthright; it has to be earned, repossessed ... One comes face to face with it sometimes in faraway places, as I did ... One chooses and translates a part of one's past to make it present to oneself and maybe to others. In 1962, on one of my first Saturdays at the University of Chicago, I entered the basement stacks of the then Harper Library in search of an elementary grammar of Old Tamil, which I had never learned ... As I searched ... I came upon an early anthology of classical Tamil poems ... Here was a part of my language and culture, to which I had been an ignorant heir. Until then, I had only heard of the idiot in the Bible who had gone looking for a donkey and had happened upon a kingdom...

Here's an almost mystical discovery made within 'secular' parameters, like Dutt's discovery of the 'grand mythology of [his] ancestors'. The language moves from the vocabulary of individual choice – 'earned', 'repossessed', 'one chooses' – to that of chance and grace – 'I came upon', 'happened upon'. Self-knowledge is connected to ignorance – 'which I had never learned', 'ignorant heir' – as it is by mystics. Again, there's an air of exhortation, of instruction, on the one hand, and supplication and surrender on the other; the 'kulalakshmi' who, in the time of modernity, seems to have appeared before Indian writers-to-be in what Dutt called 'paradesh', 'foreign lands', is here as well, in the Chicago basement; she is invisible but palpable. Dutt, I'd said earlier, introduced an element of theatre into Indian literary history; that element of theatre recurs in both the small dramas mentioned above. Locations are worth noting in these stories of discovery and inauguration – the dark theatre with the foreign film without subtitles; the stacks in the basement; the sense of excavation, of artificial night; a narrative of the subconscious to which I'll return later.

We've been talking about 'turns' – a turning towards, a turning away from. They occur in these authors' texts, in the break in Dutt's sonnet, in Vijayan's protagonist's mutation from teacher to disciple in the obscure village, in the Brahmin hero's alienation from his caste and clan in *Samskara*; and they occur in the authors themselves, as protagonists in the literary history they're creating. Disowning and recovery give to our literary (and perhaps political and cultural) history a pattern as formal and passionate as that of a sonnet. Of this pattern, Nirad C. Chaudhuri's *The Autobiography of an Unknown Indian* presents a startling variation, even inversion, a turning away from the 'turn' itself, a conferring of new values to exile and to homecoming.

With Dutt originated the literary ambition of going outward, toward England and Europe; occasionally substituted, as in Vijayan, by a journey to a remote place. The journey seems to be followed by a crisis, a break, an epiphany, a spiritual homecoming to the mother-tongue. Chaudhuri muddied and complicated this sequence in all kinds of ways; and it's worth studying his career and his mental life for their remarkable continuities, and disjunctions, with Dutt's.

Although he didn't travel to England till he was fifty-seven years old, Chaudhuri's whole life, till then, had, in a sense, been a preparation for that journey. By the time he made it, he'd already memorized the features of England and Europe from his reading, as he tells us in *A Passage to England* – '... my mind was not a clean slate ... it was burdened with an enormous load of book-derived notions.' Entering England, he compared the authorized version of the England he already knew with the makeshift version that was presented to him: 'The famous chalk cliffs did not stand out glimmering and vast, as Matthew Arnold had described, but seemed like white creases between the blue-grey sheet of the Channel...' This predilection for attributing a veracity to text or word over 'actual' landscape or location is a habit of the colonial mind. It had been made famous by Wilde in 'The Decay of Lying': 'Where, if not from the Impressionists, do we get those wonderful brown fogs that come creeping down our streets, blurring the gas-lamps ...?'

By the time Chaudhuri made his journey, he was, of course, unlike Dutt, already famous in the language and country in which Dutt had aspired to make his name. The *Autobiography*, which was published in 1951, had received some very favourable reviews in the British press. The pattern I've been following takes on an intriguing shape with the writing of this book. Dutt had moved, about a hundred years previously, from the English language to the mother-tongue, thereby, in a sense, creating an avenue for Bengali literary culture, and Chaudhuri now reversed the direction. At the time of his writing the autobiography, and even long after, it was unusual, indeed exceptional, for a Bengali to embark upon a literary project, major or minor, in anything but his own tongue; at the time, the Bengali language was, for the Bengali writer, the legitimate vehicle for cosmopolitan, middle-class expression. But the cultural legacy of the putative but inescapable Bengal Renaissance, which was still coming into being when Dutt was writing, had obviously stratified sufficiently into a orthodoxy for Chaudhuri, born at its peak in 1897, and formed by it intellectually, to want to distance himself from it.

Chaudhuri had served a long apprenticeship as an 'unknown Indian' by the time he published his autobiography at the age of 54. Gravitating from a small town, Kishorganj, to Calcutta to read History at the Scottish Church College, he stood first in the BA exams in Calcutta University, probably then the colonial world's premier institution of higher studies.

As spectacularly, he proceeded to fail his MA. He then took up a series of jobs; and, for a time, was secretary to the nationalist Sarat Bose. Yet he continued to feel uneasy with Indian nationalism, and with the post-Independence Bengali, and Indian, middle class.

Besides, the Bengali 'bhadralok' worshipped a good degree, but never forgave or forgot a bad one; it extolled professional success and berated lack of ambition. Chaudhuri evidently knew what it meant to be judged by these standards; in his Preface, he said: '... after passing the age of fifty I am faced with the compulsion to write off all the years I have lived and begin life anew. My friends say I am a failure; and I daresay they will now think I am trying to excuse that failure; I will not concede the point.' Dutt turned from English to Bengali with a similar refusal to accept failure; to leave behind him the rejection from *Blackwood's Magazine*, the uncharitable reviews in Calcutta in the *Bengal Harkaru* and the *Hindu Intelligencer*, his difficult European odyssey; Chaudhuri turned from Bengali, and, in effect, Bengalis, in order to compose an epic, a panoramic picture, of the Bengali sensibility. Neither his literary practice, his choice of language, nor his anti-nationalism can be seen in isolation; I see them, in fact, as unexpected, sometimes estranging, elaborations upon a pattern.

Talking to Oneself

All his life, Chaudhuri strove both to express his Bengaliness and to escape it; if his first act of distancing was to write his autobiography in the English language, his second act of distancing himself from his intellectual antecedents was his lapidary dedication itself, placed at the beginning of the book, which made him infamous in his own land:

> TO THE MEMORY OF THE
> BRITISH EMPIRE IN INDIA
> WHICH CONFERRED SUBJECTHOOD ON US
> BUT WITHHELD CITIZENSHIP;
> TO WHICH YET
> EVERY ONE OF US THREW OUT THE CHALLENGE:
> 'CIVIS BRITANNICUS SUM'
> BECAUSE
> ALL THAT WAS GOOD AND LIVING
> WITHIN US
> WAS MADE, SHAPED AND QUICKENED
> BY THE SAME BRITISH RULE

This twelve-line signpost of Indian literary history, announcing its striking act of disowning while proclaiming its embarrassing allegiance, is absent, however, from the 1999 Picador reissue of the *Autobiography*; handling the book, I couldn't understand why it felt incomplete, why I felt something was missing. When I realized, at last, what it was, I phoned the publisher, Peter Straus; he confessed to being as surprised as I was, and promised he'd investigate. Later, he told me the dedication had been lost somewhere in the course of the book's publishing history, and that Picador had inherited the text the way it had appeared from its former publishers. Straus reassured me, of course, that the dedication would be restored. Why the dedication disappeared at all is mysterious; certainly, one has no reason to believe that Chaudhuri disowned, at some point, his own act, and proclamation, of disowning. Was it, then, censored, or excised, by a well-meaning Western publisher?

The dedication itself is a curious artifact, curiously arranged. The eighth line consists of one word only – 'because'; it serves as a sort of fulcrum around which the dedication turns; and as the 'turn' in Dutt's sonnet veers it towards the 'kulalakshmi', the goddess, and, finally, the mother-tongue, the 'because' here parodies the form and logic of the sonnet, and takes us in the opposite direction, 'All that was good and living/ Within us/ Was made, shaped and quickened/ By the same British rule.' The word 'us' occurs three times in the dedication; it's used with deliberate, and provocative, irony. Who is the 'us', after all, that the author of the dedication claims kinship with? For the dedication, in fact, represents a permanent break with that 'us', a relinquishing, by Chaudhuri, of his participation in the collectivities of post-Independence India. Seldom, I think, has the triumphalist collective pronoun been used in contemporary India with such lonely and perverse intent.

In choosing English, Chaudhuri was, of course, offering himself to a worldwide audience, if by 'world' we mean the Anglophone West. The 'unknown' in the title, thus, is also partly ironical, a slap in the face of a society he felt had largely ignored him. When Dutt published his epic, the Bengali readership was relatively amorphous, itself a kind of transitional text. Dutt could write to his friend: 'Many Hindu ladies, I understand, are reading the book and crying over it.'

He could also relate to the same friend, Raj Narain, in another letter, an account of an evolving readership charged with subterfuge and wonder; it is a moment of theatre, the sort of theatre that permeates Dutt's life, the poet himself acting out his two selves, the self that disowns and the self that recovers, posing first as Anglophone philistine, then proudly declaiming his own poem in Bengali:

Some days ago I had occasion to go to the Chinabazar. I saw a man seated in a shop and deeply poring over Meghanad. I stepped in and asked him what he was reading. He said in very good English; – 'I am reading a new poem, Sir!' 'A poem!' I said. 'I thought there was no poetry in your language.' He replied – 'Why, Sir, here is poetry that would make my nation proud.' I said, 'Well, read and let me know.' My literary shopkeeper looked hard at me and said, 'Sir, I am afraid you wouldn't understand this author.' I replied, 'Let me try my chance.' He read out of Book II that part wherein Kam returns to Rati … How beautifully the young fellow read … I took the poem from him and read out a few passages to the infinite astonishment of my new friend. How eagerly he asked where I live? I gave him an evasive reply, for I hate to be bothered with visitors.

The question of the 'audience', however, is a vexed one today for Indian writers in English, complicated by ideas of post-coloniality, appropriation, and authenticity: on a more banal level, it has become something of a nuisance. 'Which audience do you write for?' is a question asked indefatigably of Indian English writers published in the West, its underlying presumption being that the only morally defensible answer is, 'For an Indian audience'. Such choices are hardly ever simply made or have a simple history; Chaudhuri's autobiography, written, by strategic and deliberate self-admission, for a Western readership, gives to the issue the complexity it deserves.

If English, for Chaudhuri, is the language by which he disowns Bengaliness, it's also his sole means for expressing it; it's probably these contrary and subconscious usages that give his formal language its unexpected tactility; every sentence in the book – in the poetry of its descriptions of the East Bengali landscape, and its portrayal of Calcutta – is imbued with the Bengaliness it also implicitly rejects.

For Chaudhuri, recovery begins, indeed, in the midst of acting as interpreter to a non-Bengali, non-Indian audience. For instance, in his small prefatory note, Chaudhuri refers to Kishorganj as a 'little country town'; a page later, in the first sentence of the first chapter, he is already dismantling the canonical English and literary resonances of the phrase in order to convey a lived, but unacknowledged, reality. His description occurs, as we see, between two definitions, one disowned, the other recovered: 'Kishorganj, my birthplace, I have called a country town, but this description, I am afraid, will call up wholly wrong associations. The place had nothing of the English country town about it, if I am to judge by the illustrations I have seen and the descriptions I have read …' What, then, is the Kishorganj he posits against the English phrase? It is something in-between, a colonial construct, like 'Bengaliness' itself: 'one among a score of collections of tin-and-mat huts or sheds, comprising courts, offices, schools, shops and residential dwellings, which British administration had raised up in the green and brown spaces of East Bengal'.

To embark upon the *Autobiography* in English was a solitary project. It was like being in an echo chamber, your ear peeled for your own voice. Dutt had had the 'literary shopkeeper' to read his poem to; Chaudhuri had himself. In an essay called 'My Hundredth Year', Chaudhuri recalls how, when he began to write his book, the act of composing involved a play of echoes (audible as well as literary ones) and a talking to oneself: 'I read what I had written aloud and then also read a passage from some great work of English prose in the same way. If the two sounds agreed I passed my writing.'

The reason for this, as Chaudhuri puts it, was 'an acute anxiety', a sense of dispossession, for 'I did not learn English from Englishmen, nor hear it as spoken by native speakers of the language till late in life.' Chaudhuri, like many of his generation and his background – I think, here, of my wife's paternal grandfather and my own father, about twenty years younger than Chaudhuri, and, like him, a graduate of Scottish Church College – learnt English as a second language. English prose style, in the hands of writers like Chaudhuri and Naipaul, has been an instrument of ambivalence; besides, neither of these two writers, among the most individual stylists of English prose from the 'colonies', came from the upper reaches of their respective societies.

On the other hand, Rushdie's 'khichdi' idiolect, with its 'Bombay mix' of Hindi, English, and Indian English, is a hegemonic language; the increased use of a similar English in films and advertisements ('Britannia khao/ World Cup jao') signals the coming of age and the spending power of an upper-middle-class generation in post-Independence, post-liberalization India. This is not to either praise or condemn it, but to point out that, in order to appreciate its comedy and excitement, it's important to remember that this 'khichdi' language is very far from an African creole or pidgin, or being a language of the dispossessed.

On the other hand, English prose style, in Chaudhuri's hands, becomes the measure of one who doesn't quite belong. It's partly a language of suggestion, which is why sound and rhythm are such significant components of it. Chaudhuri, notoriously, believed in opinions and positions; but he believed (this is worth remembering) equally in the prosody of the English sentence: 'There is no such thing as one standard rhythm of English prose. English prose rhythms are bewilderingly diverse ...' There's a greater tension between sense and sound, between the different registers, audible and half-heard, of what Chaudhuri says, than either his readers or even he has given himself credit for. The auditoriness of English prose style becomes, for this astonishing and intractable writer, a mapping of an area between control and dispossession, between the authority of words and the suggestion of sound.

Postscript

My purpose in describing the pattern of disowning and recovery in the lives and works of certain writers – Madhusudan Dutt; Vijayan; Ramanujan; Anantha Murthy; Nirad Chaudhuri – is to propose an alternative story of modernity and modernism; to distinguish it from both European modernism and the narrative of post-coloniality.

The difference between the story of this modernism, and the more famous one that unfolds itself in Europe from the early twentieth century onwards, has to do, it seems, with the invention of the past and the artist's relationship to it. For the European and, especially, the American-born modernist, the past is threatened by the banality and the violence of the present: by popular culture; by the machine; by the venality of the marketplace, for which, often, Jewry is a figure; by the Great War. The European past returns, or is recuperated, in fragments, in the works of, say, Pound, or Eliot, or David Jones; it can no longer be inhabited, or made available, in its entirety. It's not surprising, as we now know, to find this powerful nostalgia for 'high' European civilization in Fascism, or that Western modernism had emotional ties and a certain sympathy with the latter. The *volkisch* philosophy of an Oswald Spengler, according to which cultures are essential, untranslatable, and rooted, plant-like, to a particular soil or habitat, finds its artistic counterpart in the great works of modernism, in which the European past is threatened, fragmented, but nevertheless organically and indispensably present.

The story of 'our' – if I can presume to use that pronoun – modernity is somewhat different. Firstly, as colonials, our idea of 'high' culture lay elsewhere. 'Our' past, in spite of its apotheosis by Orientalist scholars, was viewed with a degree of objectivity, ambivalence, even, occasionally, loathing. It was *this* past that, once neglected or rejected, presented itself to the artist – to Dutt, for example – with its renewing creative possibilities. A conspiracy of chance and circumstances brought about this renewal; and the source of the renewal appears to be often random and paradoxical. In Dutt's case, it was Milton and Versailles; for Vijayan, the death of Imre Nagy and the journey to a village; for Anantha Murthy, a Bergman film without subtitles; for Ramanujan, a basement in Chicago. Very few seem to have turned to a past that they didn't feel they'd once neglected; and very few seem to have encountered it in expected circumstances, or an expected place or shrine. Even Debendranath Tagore, whose epiphanic meeting with his spiritual heritage involves a more conventionally acceptable source, a page from the *Upanishads*, came upon the page accidentally, as it was being blown away by a breeze.

To take another example: Satyajit Ray. Here was a man born into a Brahmo family, whose enthusiasms, as he was growing up, were Western classical music and Hollywood movies, particularly John Ford's. A combination of roughly three events appears to have caused the 'turn' towards local landscape, the Bengali language, and the past that we find in Ray's first film – his discovery of Italian neo-realist cinema; Jean Renoir's visit to Calcutta; and a commission to illustrate an abridged version of *Pather Panchali*, which he hadn't read before. Indian modernism's (if I can call it that) relationship to the autochthonic past is comparable, in some ways, to European modernism's relationship to the industrialized present; in that its provenance is surreptitious, and the hint of illegality in the relationship makes it the more compelling.

The randomness of situations that lead to that 'turn' speaks less of an ideological move than of associations formed suddenly in the subconscious; indeed, this aleatory quality rearranges the purposes, the telos, of colonialism and nationalism. What else but the subconscious can make Milton, Imre Nagy, *The Seventh Seal*, Mozart, the *Ramayana*, Nischindipur, Basavanna, Kerala, Chicago, Calcutta, France, not seem like delirious babbling, but part of a single literary history? And it's the dimension of the subconscious that distinguishes this tale of modernity from the narrative of post-coloniality.

In the latter, a confrontation takes place between Empire and local culture; English and indigenous forms of knowledge; colonizer and colonized. But in the story I've told, the battle, the struggle, takes place *within* the self, and not just between the self and an enemy outside it; the story of modernity is as much a story of self-division as the post-colonial narrative is one of Empire, domination, and resistance. In the narrative of post-coloniality, the mother-tongue, 'Indianness', or 'Bengaliness' are natural properties of the colonized, threatened by the processes of Empire. In the story of modernity, the mother-tongue and the English language are part of a transaction that, through disowning and recovery, define the 'modern' self; the transaction is modulated from artist to artist, from moment to moment, and takes a radically new, but provisional, form in the work of the Anglophone writer – but it's precisely this inward tension that both enables and disfigures creativity in the life and career of the Indian 'modern'.

For me, this extraordinary tale takes about 120 years to unfold, and, in literature at least, it comes to an end circa 1981, with the publication of *Midnight's Children*. Here is the classic postmodern Indian text, and I name it thus not only because it possesses all the recognizable window-dressing of postmodernity: polyphony; the conflation and confusion of fantasy with history. In Rushdie's novel, the tension between rejection and recuperation which gave the modernist Indian literary text its inexhaustible light and shade is replaced by something new: a promiscuity of meaning. Nothing is either disowned or recovered; all is embraced. The inward struggle that, from Dutt to Ramanujan, gave Indian modernism its particular meaning, is replaced, in *Midnight's Children*, by infinite play.

And yet I don't think the modernist paradigm I've described is altogether dead. Its residues perhaps survive even now; and, although I'm fifteen years younger than Rushdie, I think that my artistic practice has been informed and shaped by that older, residual pattern. This is probably true of other writers among my contemporaries, but I'll restrict myself to a personal retelling. The 'turn' in my life occurred around 1978; and though it didn't have anything to do, directly, with my apprenticeship as a writer, it had everything to do with my creative life. The 'turn' took place in my relationship to an art that was, for me, extremely important but still secondary at the time: music. One fine day, almost, I became a lifelong student, and then exponent, of Hindustani classical music.

Nothing had prepared either my family, or myself, or my friends for that 'turn'. My father belonged to the upper reaches of the Bombay corporate world; that was the desert island I grew up on. My mother was, and is, primarily a singer of Tagore-songs; and the genteel, hybrid, Tagorean world of the bhadralok has always kept classical music, with its zamindars, ustads, and tawaifs, at arm's length. (The associations of Western classical music were, for the European bourgeoisie, unambiguously 'high' cultural; the hostility it provokes is a hostility towards elitism. For the Indian, especially the Bengali, middle class, on the other hand, Hindustani classical music always had the air, at once, of profundity, intricacy, and disrepute.)

When the 'turn' came, however, it was complete and seemingly final. Prior to it, I dallied, unsurprisingly for one who'd grown up in Bombay, with American folk, blues, and rock music; played the acoustic and electric guitars; even composed songs. Almost overnight, I set aside my guitars; calluses gradually grew on the fingertips that, six months before, had borne the deep, embedded lines of frets and strings. I stopped listening to my huge record collection; it was only recently, after about twenty-two years, that I once more began to play, with extraordinary shyness, my Joni Mitchells and James Taylors. In 1980, what I had was a sort of theological conversion;

I decided that the music I'd listened to and sung so far was out of joint with the world around me, with 'India', its seasons, its times of day; only the *raags* of the tradition I now embarked upon were appropriate and apposite to that reality. In fact, Western popular music fitted in with Bombay, and the scene I saw from my balcony – the Marine Drive, the Queen's Necklace, Chowpatty Beach, the nocturnal lights and incandescent messages of the city – rather comfortably; but it was as if, in pursuing Hindustani classical music, I was assigning new values to reality – to light, to air, to evening, to morning.

When I look back to Dutt and the 150 years of our cultural history, what happened in my life, and the suddenness with which it happened, the radical break it constituted, seem no longer surprising; indeed, they fit in quite well with the pattern of disowning and recovery through which the nation, the self, experience, and creativity have made themselves available to us in modernity. You turn to a language that seems the only language adequate to your altered vision of reality, and of yourself; heretofore neglected, this becomes the authentic language of nationhood, experience, self-consciousness. In the poets and writers I've mentioned, the mother-tongue was thus constructed; in my case, that 'Indian' language was Hindustani classical music. I've begun, once more, as I said, to listen to my old records; but the calluses on my fingers healed so completely that I don't think I will touch the guitar again.[1]

In the Waiting-Room of History
On *Provincializing Europe*

I went to a Protestant school in Bombay, but the creation myth we were taught in the classroom didn't have to do with Adam and Eve. I remember a poster on the wall when I was in the Fifth Standard, a pictorial narrative of evolution. On the extreme left, crouching low, its arms hanging near its feet, was an ape; it looked intent, like an athlete waiting for the gun to go off. The next figure rose slightly, and the one after it was more upright: it was like a slow-motion sequence of a runner in the first few seconds of a race. The pistol had been fired; the race had begun. Millisecond after millisecond, that runner – now ape, now Neanderthal – rose a little higher, and its back straightened. By the time it had reached the apogee of its height and straight-backedness, and taken a stride forward, its appearance had improved noticeably; it had become a Homo sapiens, and also, coincidentally, European. The race had been won before it had properly started.

This poster captured and compressed the gradations of Darwin's parable of evolution, both arresting time and focusing on the key moments of a concatenation, in a similar way to what Walter Benjamin thought photographs did in changing our perception of human movement:

> Whereas it is a commonplace that, for example, we have some idea what is involved in the act of walking (if only in general terms), we have no idea at all what happens during the fraction of a second when a person actually takes a step. Photography, with its devices of slow motion and enlargement, reveals the secret. It is through photography that we first discover the existence of this optical unconscious; just as we discover the instinctual subconscious through psychoanalysis.

The poster in my classroom, too, revealed a movement impossible for the naked eye to perceive: from lower primate to higher, from Neanderthal to human, and – this last transition was so compressed as to be absent altogether – from the human to the European. These still figures gave us an 'optical unconscious' of a political context, the context of progress and European science and humanism. Here, too, Benjamin has something to say. In a late essay, 'Theses on the Philosophy of History', he stated: 'The concept of the historical progress of mankind cannot be sundered from the concept of its progression through a homogeneous, empty time.'

'Homogeneous' and 'empty' are curious adjectives for 'time': they are more readily associated with space and spatial configuration. Certain landscapes glimpsed from a motorway, or the look of a motorway itself, might be described as dull and 'homogeneous'; streets and rooms might be 'empty'. My mentioning motorways isn't fortuitous. When Benjamin was formulating his thoughts on progress and history, and writing this essay in 1940, the year he killed himself, Hitler, besides carrying out his elaborate plans for the Jews in Germany, was implementing another huge and devastating project: the Autobahn. The project, intended both to connect one part of Germany to another and to colonize the landscape, was begun in the early 1930s; it's clear that Hitler's vision of the Autobahn is based on an idea of progress – 'progress' not only in the sense of movement between one place and another, but in the sense of science and civilization. In India, in other parts of the so-called 'developing' world, even in present-day New York, London or Paris, it's impossible properly to experience 'homogeneous, empty time' because of the random, often maddeningly diverse allocation of space, human habitation and community. It is, however, possible to experience it on Western motorways and highways. Hitler was a literalist of this philosophy of space and movement: he wanted space to be 'homogeneous', or blond and European. Benjamin knew this first-hand; he was writing his 'Theses on the Philosophy of History' as a Jewish witness to Nazism and one of its potential victims. Hitler's anxiety and consternation at Jesse Owens's victory in the 100 metres at the Berlin Olympics in 1936 came from his literalism of space, his investment in progress and linearity. That idea of space was at once reified and shattered when Owens reached the finishing line before the others.

Benjamin had been thinking of history in terms of space for a while; and, not too long before he wrote about 'homogeneous, empty time', he'd posited an alternative version of modernity and space in his descriptions of the *flâneur*, the Parisian arcades and nineteenth-century street life. The Parisian street constitutes Benjamin's critique of the Autobahn: just as the crowd, according to Benjamin, is 'present everywhere' in Baudelaire's work, and present so intrinsically that it's never directly described, the Autobahn is implicitly present, and refuted, in Benjamin's meditations on Paris. The *flâneur*, indeed, retards and parodies the idea of 'progress'.

'Around 1840 it was briefly fashionable to take turtles for a walk in the arcades,' Benjamin writes in a footnote to his 1939 essay on Baudelaire. 'The flâneurs liked to have the turtles set the pace for them. If they had had their way, progress would have been obliged to accommodate itself to this space. But this attitude did not prevail; Taylor, who popularized the watchword "Down with dawdling!", carried the day.' The *flâneur* views history subversively; he – and it is usually he – deliberately relocates its meanings, its hierarchies. As far back as 1929, Benjamin had explained why the *flâneur had* to be situated in Paris:

> The flâneur is the creation of Paris. The wonder is that it was not Rome. But perhaps in Rome even dreaming is forced to move along streets that are too well-paved. And isn't the city too full of temples, enclosed squares and national shrines to be able to enter undivided into the dreams of the passer-by, along with every shop sign, every flight of steps and every gateway? The great reminiscences, the historical frissons – these are all so much junk to the flâneur, who is happy to leave them to the tourist. And he would be happy to trade all his knowledge of artists' quarters, birthplaces and princely palaces for the scent of a single weathered threshold or the touch of a single tile – that which any old dog carries away.

There's an implicit critique of the imperial city, and the imperialist aesthetic, in this description of Rome, with its 'great reminiscences' and 'historical frissons', and in the contrast of 'national shrines' and 'temples' with the 'touch of a single tile'. Benjamin is not alone in using these metaphors; both Ruskin and Lawrence (who probably took it from Ruskin) use Rome as a metaphor for the imperial, the finished, the perfected, as against the multifariousness of, say, the Gothic, the 'barbaric', the non-Western. Benjamin doesn't quite romanticize the primitive as Lawrence at least appears to: instead, he comes up with a particularly modern form of aleatoriness and decay in the 'weathered threshold' of a Parisian street.

Of course, the *flâneur* was not to be found in Paris alone. There was much wayward loitering in at least two colonial cities, Dublin and Calcutta. This – especially the emergence of the *flâneur*, or *flâneur*-like activities, in modern, turn-of-the-century Calcutta – would have probably been difficult for Benjamin to imagine. Benjamin's figure for the *flâneur* was Baudelaire, and for Baudelaire – and, by extension, for the *flâneur* – the East was, as it was for Henri Rousseau, part dreamscape, part botanical garden, part menagerie, part paradise. Could the *flâneur* exist in that dreamscape? Dipesh Chakrabarty, the author of *Provincializing Europe*, whose meditations on the limits of Western notions of modernity and history are impelled by Benjamin but who also has the word 'postcolonial' in his subtitle, was born in Calcutta. His inquiry is partly directed by the contingencies of being a South Asian historian in America, and also by being a founder member of the subaltern studies project, which attempted to write a South Asian or, specifically, Indian history 'from below', by bringing the 'subaltern' (Gramsci's word for the peasant or the economically dispossessed) into the territory largely occupied by nationalist history. But the inquiry is also shaped by the Calcutta Chakrabarty was born in, much as Benjamin's work is shaped by the Paris he reimagined and, to a certain extent, invented. From the early nineteenth century, the growing Bengali intelligentsia in Calcutta was increasingly exercised by what 'modernity' might mean and what the experience of modernity might represent, specifically, to a subject nation, and, universally, to a human being. Chakrabarty's book is not only an unusually sustained and nuanced argument against European ideas of modernity, but also an elegy for, and subtle critique of, his own intellectual formation and inheritance as a Bengali. The kind of Bengali who was synonymous with modernity and who believed that modernity might be a universal condition – irrespective of whether you're English, Indian, Arab or African – has now passed into extinction. Chakrabarty's book is in part a discreet inquiry into why that potent Bengali dream didn't quite work – why 'modernity' remains so resolutely European.

Chakrabarty's writing is not without irony or humour; the cheeky oxymoron of the title is one example. At least a quarter of Chakrabarty's work was done, and his challenge given an idiom, when he reinvented this terrific phrase, which was probably first used with slightly more literal intent by Gadamer. According to Ranajit Guha, who is or used to be to subalternist historians roughly what Jesus was to the apostles, the 'idea of provincializing Europe' had 'been around for some time, but mostly as an insight waiting for elaboration' before Chakrabarty articulated and substantiated it so thoroughly. The 'idea' itself is set out and argued for in the introductory chapter. Chakrabarty begins with a disclaimer: '*Provincializing Europe* is not a book about the region of the world we call "Europe". That Europe, one could say, has already been provincialized by history itself.' The essay has two epigraphs: the first, from Gadamer, seems to speak of Europe as a 'region of the world'; the second, more tellingly, from Naoki Sakai, describes the 'West' as 'a name for a subject which gathers itself in discourse but is also an object constituted discursively'. What Chakrabarty wants to do with 'Europe', then, is in some ways similar to what Edward Said did with the 'Orient': to fashion a subversive genealogy. But instead of Said's relentless polemic, Chakrabarty's book features critique and self-criticism in equal measure. For me, Chakrabarty has the edge here, because for Said the Orient is a Western construct, an instrument of domination: he doesn't – and never went on to – explore the profound ways in which modern Orientals (Tagore, say) both were and were not Orientalists. Chakrabarty's work suggests, I think, that the word 'Eurocentric' is more problematic than we thought; that, if Europe is a universal paradigm for modernity, we are all, European and non-European, to a degree inescapably Eurocentric. Europe is at once a means of intellectual dominance, an obfuscatory trope and a constituent of self-knowledge, in different ways for different peoples and histories.

Said's great study takes its cue from the many-sided and endlessly absorbing Foucault, in its inexhaustible conviction and its curiosity about how a body of knowledge – in this case, Orientalism – can involve the exercise of power. Much post-colonial theory, in turn, has taken its cue from Said and this strain of Foucault. Chakrabarty's book comes along at a time when this line of inquiry, which has had its own considerable rewards and pitfalls, seems one-dimensional and exhausted. In spite of the 'postcolonial' in the subtitle, it owes little to the fecund but somewhat simplified Foucauldian paradigm. Instead, its inspiration seems post-structuralist and Derridean, and it rehearses a key moment in Derrida: the idea that it is necessary to dismantle or take on the language of 'Western metaphysics' (which for Derrida is almost everything that precedes post-structuralism and, in effect, himself), but that there is no alternative language available with which to dismantle it – so that the language must be turned on itself. For Derrida's 'Western metaphysics' Chakrabarty substitutes 'European thought' and 'social science thought':

> European thought . . . is both indispensable and inadequate in helping us to think through the various life practices that constitute the political and the historical in India. Exploring – on both theoretical and factual registers – this simultaneous indispensability and inadequacy of social science thought is the task this book has set itself.

This is not very far from Derrida, who writes at an important juncture in *Writing and Difference* of

> conserving all these old concepts within the domain of empirical discovery while here and there denouncing their limits, treating them as tools that can still be used. No longer is any truth value attributed to them: there is a readiness to abandon them, if necessary, should other instruments appear more useful. In the meantime, their relative efficacy is exploited, and they are employed to destroy the old machinery to which they belong and of which they themselves are pieces. This is how the language of the social sciences criticizes *itself*.

Derrida is reflecting here on Lévi-Strauss, who when confronted with South American myths finds the tools of his trade obsolete but still indispensable. The idea of Chakrabarty registering a similarly self-reflexive moment about thirty years later, in relation to Europe, modernity and 'life practices . . . in India', is poignant and ironic: he belongs to the other side of the racial and historical divide; to a part of the world that should have been, at least in Lévi-Strauss's time, and by ordinary European estimation, the object rather than the instigator of the social scientist's discipline. It would have been next to impossible for Lévi-Strauss to foretell that something resembling his anxiety about the social sciences would one day be rehearsed in the work of a man with a name like Dipesh Chakrabarty.

And this, of course, is the crux of Chakrabarty's book. 'Historicism – and even the modern, European idea of history – one might say, came to non-European peoples in the nineteenth century as somebody's way of saying "not yet" to somebody else.' To illustrate what he means, he turns to John Stuart Mill's *On Liberty* and *On Representative Government* – 'both of which', Chakrabarty says, 'proclaimed self-rule as the highest form of government and yet argued against giving Indians or Africans self-rule.'

> According to Mill, Indians or Africans were *not yet* civilised enough to rule themselves. Some historical time of development and civilisation (colonial rule and education, to be precise) had to elapse before they could be considered prepared for such a task. Mill's historicist argument thus consigned Indians, Africans and other 'rude' nations to an imaginary waiting-room of history.

The 'imaginary waiting-room of history' is another of Chakrabarty's compressed, telling images. I don't know if he picked it up from the German playwright Heiner Müller, who uses it of the 'Third World' in a 1989 interview; but he employs it to great effect. The phrase has purgatorial resonances: you feel that those who are in the waiting-room are going to be there for some time. For modernity has already had its authentic incarnation in Europe: how then can it happen again, elsewhere? The non-West – the waiting-room – is therefore doomed either never to be quite modern, to be, in Naipaul's phrase, 'half-made'; or to possess only a semblance of modernity. This is a view of history and modernity that has, according to Chakrabarty, at once liberated, defined, and shackled us in its discriminatory universalism; it is a view powerfully theological in its determinism, except that the angels, the blessed and the excluded are real people, real communities.

Chakrabarty's thesis might seem obvious once stated; but the 'insight waiting for elaboration', to use Ranajit Guha's words, must find the best and, in the positive sense of the word, most opportunistic expositor. In Chakrabarty, I think it has. (The urge to provincialize Europe has, of course, a very long unofficial history. It's embodied in jokes and throwaway remarks such as the one Gandhi made when asked what he thought of Western civilization: 'I think it would be a good idea.' Shashi Tharoor is having a dig at historicism when he says, in *The Great Indian Novel*, 'India is not an underdeveloped country. It is a highly developed country in an advanced state of decay.') Chakrabarty has given us a vocabulary with which to speak of matters somewhat outside the realm of the social sciences, and to move discussions on literature, cultural politics and canon formation away from the exclusively Saidian concerns of power-brokering, without entirely ignoring these concerns.

In the light of Chakrabarty's study, Naipaul's work begins to fall into place. Here is a writer who seems to have subscribed quite deeply to the sort of historicism that Chakrabarty describes. From the middle period onwards, in books such as *The Mimic Men, A Bend in the River* and *In a Free State*, Naipaul gives us a vision – unforgettable, eloquent – of the Caribbean and especially Africa as history's waiting-room. Modernity here is ramshackle, self-dismantling: it exists somewhere between the corrugated iron roof and the distant military coup, the newly deposed general. The 'not yet' with which Forster's narrator indefinitely deferred, in *A Passage to India*, the possibility of a lasting friendship between Fielding and Aziz are also the words that describe Naipaul's modern Africa. The opening sentence of *A Bend in the River* (which so exasperated Chinua Achebe) – 'The world is what it is; men who are nothing, who allow themselves to become nothing, have no place in it' – owes its tone less to religious pronouncements than to a belief in what Benjamin called 'the march of progress' in the 'homogeneous, empty time of history'. Naipaul's theology stems not so much from Hinduism, or the brahminical background he's renowned for, as from Mill. It was Mill, as Chakrabarty points out, who consigned certain nations to a purgatory, in which, in different concentric circles, they've been waiting or 'developing' ever since. In fiction, the greatest explorers of this Millian terrain have been Naipaul and Naipaul's master, Conrad.

Chakrabarty's study also helps to clarify the ways in which we discuss and think of the 'high' cultures of the so-called developing countries: not only the ancient traditions, but the modern and modernist ones as well. This is an area of self-consciousness, and a field of inquiry, that is potentially vast, important and problematic; it also happens to be one that 'cultural studies' has largely missed out on, being more concerned with popular culture and narratives of resistance to empire. Yet for almost 200 years, in countries like India, there has been a self-consciousness (and it still exists today) which asks to be judged and understood by 'universal' standards. It isn't possible to begin to discuss that self-consciousness, or sense of identity, without discussing in what way that universalism both formed and circumscribed it.

In some regards, then, cultural studies is hostage to the kind of historicism that Chakrabarty talks about: it can't deal with the emergence of high modernism in post-colonial countries except with a degree of suspicion and embarrassment, partly because of the elite contexts of that modernism, but partly, surely, for covertly historicist reasons, such as a belief that no modernism outside Europe can be absolutely genuine. Take the Bengal, or Indian, Renaissance: the emergence of humanism and modernity in nineteenth-century Calcutta. The term 'Renaissance' was probably first applied to this development by the eminent Brahmo Shibnath Shastri; it was later employed by Marxist historians such as Susobhan Sarkar. But other Marxist and, later, subalternist historians have with some justification raised their eyebrows at the term. They have tried to dismiss it as intellectually meaningless, mainly because they see it as an elite construct, an upper-middle-class invention that raises too many questions, and which, while identifying too closely with British ideas of 'progress', was also an instrument of vague but voluble nationalist blarney. All this is true. But it ignores the fact that a construct can be a crucial constituent of an intellectual tradition. The European Renaissance is a case in point: we now know that it is largely a nineteenth-century invention, but that doesn't reduce the role it has played in the drama of European intellectual and cultural history – it only problematizes it.

The opening of Susobhan Sarkar's *Notes on the Bengal Renaissance*, which first came out as a booklet in 1946, makes clear the unease that historians felt on first using the term:

> The impact of British rule, bourgeois economy and modern Western culture was felt first in Bengal and produced an awakening known usually as the Bengal Renaissance. For about a century, Bengal's conscious awareness of the changing modern world was more developed than and ahead of that of the rest of India. The role played by Bengal in the modern awakening of India is thus comparable to the position occupied by Italy in the story of the European Renaissance.

Whether these claims are true or not is open to debate; but they're disabled by their uncritical investment in the idea of Europe as the source, paradigm and catalyst of progress and history, both in an earlier and in the colonial age. The habit, in the context of Indian culture, of not only invoking Europe but making it the starting point of all discussion, was inculcated by nineteenth-century Orientalists: the translator and scholar

William Jones called Kalidasa, the greatest Indian poet and dramatist of antiquity, the 'Shakespeare of the East'. To do this, Jones had to reverse history – Kalidasa preceded Shakespeare by more than a thousand years. Jones is not so much making a useful (and supremely approbatory) comparison as telling us inadvertently that it's impossible to escape 'homogeneous, empty time': that as far as Kalidasa is concerned Shakespeare has already happened. This language persisted in the subsequent naming of periods in culture, and of cultural figures; and educated Bengalis followed the example of the Orientalist scholars. Thus Bankimchandra Chatterjee, India's first major novelist, became the 'Walter Scott of Bengal'. Both Scott and Chatterjee wrote historical novels, but when the comparison was first made, on the publication of Chatterjee's first novel, Chatterjee claimed he'd never read Scott. Even if he had, to call him the 'Walter Scott of Bengal' is subtly different from, say, Barthes remarking, 'Gide was another Montaigne,' where a continuity is being established, a lineage being traced. In the phrase that describes Chatterjee, however, an inescapable historicism refuses a literary continuity, and turns Chatterjee into an echo. Walter Scott in Bengal is Walter Scott in the waiting-room.

The 'first in Europe, then elsewhere' paradigm that Chakrabarty speaks of – what is now the developmental paradigm – is what made the process of modernization in non-Western countries seem to many, European and non-European, like mimicry. 'We pretended to be real, to be learning, to be preparing ourselves for life, we mimic men of the New World,' Naipaul's narrator, Ralph Singh, says in *The Mimic Men*; Chakrabarty's friend, the exuberantly impenetrable Homi Bhabha, has an essay on mimicry and colonialism, 'Of Mimicry and Man: The Ambivalence of Colonial Discourse', that has long been part of every post-colonial primer. In it he tries, using Lacan and referring in passing to Naipaul's great, intractable novel, to complicate and even rescue the idea of mimicry, to make it subversive: mimicry undermines the colonizer's gaze by presenting him with a distorted reflection, rather than a confirmation, of himself. Some of the essay's formulations about mimicry – 'almost the same but not quite'; 'almost the same but not white' – are close enough to the kinds of problem Chakrabarty addresses. Once again, though, as with Said, I think Chakrabarty's work gives us a richer, more penetrating language to deal with modernity and the colonial encounter. There's a barely concealed utopian rage in Bhabha against the compulsion towards mimicry, and also an unspoken nostalgia for a world in which mimicry isn't necessary. For Chakrabarty, 'Europe' is a notion that has many guises, and these guises have both liberated us and limited us, whichever race we belong to. There is, therefore, a valuable element of self-criticism in his study: to *provincialize* Europe is not to vanquish or conquer it – that is, provincializing Europe isn't a utopian gesture – but a means of locating and subjecting to interrogation some of the fundamental notions by which we define ourselves.

Despite its title, it might be more productive to read *The Mimic Men* with Chakrabarty's book rather than Bhabha's essay in mind. Ralph Singh, a failed politician from the Caribbean island of Isabella, now retired at the age of forty to a boarding-house in London, and writing something like a memoir, is not so much disfigured by 'mimicry' as haunted, even entrapped, by the language called 'Europe'. It's not a life story he wishes to compose. 'My first instinct was towards the writing of history,' Singh says, and he returns again and again to an analysis of a way of thinking and seeing. 'I have read that it was a saying of an ancient Greek that the first requisite for happiness was to be born in a famous city,' he writes. 'To be born on an island like Isabella, an obscure New World transplantation, second-hand and barbarous, was to be born to disorder.' 'Second-hand', like 'half-made', is a word weighted with the historicism that gives Singh his sense of being a failure from the start, and Singh's creator much of his pessimism. Even memory, the site of renewal for the Romantics and modernists, is deceptive: 'My first memory of school is of taking an apple to the teacher. This puzzles me. We had no apples on Isabella. It must have been an orange; yet my memory insists on the apple. The editing is clearly at fault, but the edited version is all I have.' The orange exists in the waiting-room. Its historical and physical reality counts for little; Ralph Singh's memory is 'discursively constituted', and has its own truth; and, at the time of the narrative's composition, it is all he has of Isabella.

Connecting the two halves of Chakrabarty's study – the first largely a self-reflexive appraisal of social science writing, the second a critical engagement with modern Bengali culture – are not only the themes of historicism and modernity, but the figure of Benjamin. Chakrabarty picks up the key insight about the 'homogeneous, empty time of history'. The phrase was made current in the social sciences by Benedict Anderson in his classic discussion of the rise of the nation-state, *Imagined Communities*; but Chakrabarty's usage of it, concerned primarily with the European notion of modernity, is Benjaminesque in spirit. Yet the references to Benjamin after the introduction are relatively few. This is an interesting and intriguing elision: perhaps Chakrabarty needs him to be an invisible presence. In the second half of the book I sensed him most powerfully in the chapter '*Adda*: A History of Sociality'; and it might have been enriching to have the connection made explicit, or to know whether Chakrabarty himself was fully conscious of it. 'The word *adda* (pronounced "uddah") is translated by the Bengali linguist Sunitikumar Chattopadhyaya as "a place" for "careless talk with boon companions" or "the chats of intimate friends" ... Roughly speaking, it is the practice of friends getting together for long, informal and unrigorous conversations.' Never was *adda* so theorized and romanticized as it was in Calcutta, as both a significant component and symptom of Bengali bourgeois culture in the first three-quarters of the twentieth century. Even the usage of the word is different in Bengali from Hindi, say, where it means a meeting-place not a practice. Chakrabarty goes on:

> By many standards of judgment in modernity, *adda* is a flawed social practice: it is predominantly male in its modern form in public life; it is oblivious of the materiality of labour in capitalism; and middle-class *addas* are usually forgetful of the working classes. Some Bengalis even see it as a practice that promotes sheer laziness in the population. Yet its perceived gradual disappearance from the urban life of Calcutta over the last three or four decades – related no doubt to changes in the political economy of the city – has now produced an impressive amount of mourning and nostalgia. It is as if with the slow death of *adda* will die the identity of being a Bengali.

The figure who comes to mind when I read this is Benjamin's *flâneur*; and, though Chakrabarty doesn't explore the correspondence between *flânerie* and *adda*, the resemblances are striking. Both *adda* and *flânerie* are activities whose worth is ambivalent in a capitalist society: they rupture the 'march of progress'. *Flânerie* is 'dawdling', and *adda* a waste of time which, at least according to one writer, Nirad C. Chaudhuri, 'virtually killed family life'. Neither *flânerie* nor *adda* is a purely physical or mental activity; both are reconfigurings of urban space. The *flâneur*, as Benjamin saw him, walked about the Parisian arcades of the nineteenth century, but as Hannah Arendt pointed out, he did so as if they were an extension of his living-room: he deliberately blurred the line dividing inside from out- side. Something similar happened with *adda* in Calcutta in the twentieth century; it either took place in drawing-rooms, in such a way as to disrupt domesticity and turn the interior into a sort of public space; or on the *rawak* or porches of houses in cramped lanes, neither inside the home nor in the street. For historical and social reasons, both activities are largely the preserve of the male; there are few female *flâneurs* and, as Chakrabarty points out, female participation in an *adda* is exceptional.

Benjamin's relationship to the *flâneur* and his subterranean affirma- tion of daydreaming in his meditations on *flânerie* lend his work an odd poignancy and ambivalence; given that Benjamin was a Marxist, the *flâneur* could never be wholly legitimate either outside or inside his work. Some of Chakrabarty's concerns in this book – modernity, *adda* and the shadow of Benjamin's *flâneur* – occupy a similarly ambivalent position in relationship to his provenance as a subalternist historian. The subaltern is certainly an interloper in this book (especially in a terrific essay, 'Subaltern Pasts, Minority Histories'), but the modern is an equally problematic one: they both challenge the historian, in this case the subalternist historian, with the limits and responsibilities of his discipline. It is the ambiguity of Chakrabarty's own position as both critic and archivist of modernity that gives his study its poetic undertow and its intelligent irresponsibility.

The Flute of Modernity
Tagore and the Middle Class

Rabindranath Tagore was born on 7 May 1861, or the twenty-fifth day of Baishakh in the Bengali calendar. The twenty-fifth of Baishakh is still celebrated in Bengal, especially in Calcutta, with performances of Tagore's songs and dance dramas, and the heat of midsummer is associated in the minds of Bengalis with Tagore's birthday. His name itself conjures up light and heat, for Rabindranath means 'lord of the sun'. For quite a few years, however, the celebrations have had the slightly exhausted air of ritual, a ritual by which Bengalis not only commemorate an anniversary but also observe the passing away of something more than Tagore, the passing of something that defined themselves and their own Bengaliness; though this is never articulated in so many words.

In 1778, roughly a century before Tagore's birth, an English scholar-administrator named Nathaniel Halhead wrote the first Bengali grammar, probably with the collaboration of Brahmin *pandits*. Calcutta was then the East India Company's main port of trade, and Bengal, of which Calcutta is the capital, was the province upon which the commercial and cultural exchange of the colonial world would leave a profound impress. Halhead wrote the grammar for the instruction of English officials and administrators. Though the machinery of colonialism had already begun to whir after Mughal rule was deposed in Bengal in 1757, officials of the Company still behaved like traders in a foreign land, taking the trouble, for their own purposes, to comprehend the local language and customs.

William Jones arrived at Calcutta from Oxford in 1783. He had been an Arabist before, but now in Calcutta he unofficially inaugurated Orientalist scholarship *within* India, translating Sanskrit texts into English, most famously the works of Kalidasa, whom he touchingly and misleadingly called the 'Shakespeare of the East'. Kalidasa was the court poet in King Vikramaditya's court in the fourth or fifth century AD, and he became famous in nineteenth-century Europe, especially for his play *Sakuntala*, which Jones translated and Goethe admired. Kalidasa was also to become Tagore's favourite poet, and this, too, must surely owe something to the renewed attention directed to the long-dead poet by the Welshman in one of the earliest in a series of cultural collaborations that characterized the formation of modern Indian culture.

An overarching, to all outward purposes secular, narrative about the historical past, in the crude sense in which we understand it now, was arguably absent from the consciousness of Indians at the time; and the spiritual and political history of India reconstructed by Orientalist scholars in the late eighteenth and early nineteenth centuries supplied, substantially, that narrative. By the 1830s, the young Anglo-Portuguese poet and teacher Henry Louis Vivian Derozio, who was born in Calcutta and identified himself as 'Indian', had taken the presence of that golden past sufficiently as a given to mourn its passing in sonnets such as 'To India – My Native Land', which is studied and recited in schools even today. That sonnet was one of the first utterances of an incipient nationalism, a collective identity that had crossed over into the domain of the aesthetic; and Derozio's students at the Hindu College, Calcutta, members of newly formed middle class, who would read Tom Paine and have their heads full of radical notions, were among the first to articulate nationalist ideas. But they – especially Derozio – were also quick to bring nationalism into the domain of aesthetics, and create a crucial reciprocity between the two; to not only involve the beginnings of secular 'culture' in a nationalist project, but make the nation, once and for all, a cultural one. It's a reciprocity that's given our democratic and daily lives in India their recognizable texture, and probably led to the obfuscations, both right-wing and secularist, with which we're now so familiar.

Tagore's approach to this reciprocity is angular, and significant for being so. He seems to be reminding us that the recovery of history, for the Indian, was fraught with ambiguity; this becomes clearer with the passage of time in the nineteenth century. History was like the subconscious; it had been buried, and now, in an act of translation, it was being recovered. It was as if Indians, in invoking history, were recalling a past that they did not quite remember having forgotten. Thus while Derozio, in the early nineteenth century, is proprietory about the past, declaiming about 'our days of glory past', Tagore, eighty years later, is ambivalent and full of doubt: like the subconscious, history, for the Indian modern, is both one's own and the Other. The awareness of tradition and heritage is accompanied not only by the vantage-point of modernity and identity, but also by a sense of loss and imprisonment very different from the elegiac Orientalist and Derozian narrative of national decline from the Golden Age to the present.

These paradoxes are played out in Tagore's poem 'Meghaduta', or 'The Cloud Messenger', which is about Kalidasa's long Sanskrit poem of the same name, set in the rainy season, a season beloved of Tagore; Kalidasa's poem is an ode to nature and a record of romantic, metaphysical separa-tion (*biraha*). The speaker in the poem asks the rain-carrying clouds to carry a message from him to his beloved in the faraway city of Alaka. And Tagore's poem about this poem is not only a characteristic celebration of the rains, but a gesture towards the intellectual ambience of early colonial India; a striking refashioning, then, of what was already an artistic legacy.

Kalidasa had become world-famous in the early nineteenth century, well before Tagore's birth, with Jones's translation; and the scholar H.H. Wilson had translated the *Meghaduta* in 1813, a translation that was well known in educated middle-class Bengali circles. By the time of Tagore's birth, Calcutta was not only a site of scholarship, it had printing presses proliferating in Bengali and English, and was producing more books than almost anywhere else in the world except London. William Dune, the editor of a journal published from Calcutta called *The World* (a telling and ambitious name for a colonial journal, but indicative of the city's interna-tionalist temperament and of the construction of a certain self-image), had observed in 1791 that 'in splendour London now eclipses Rome … and in similar respects, Calcutta rivals the head of the empire. But in no respect can she appear so eminently so, as in her publications… we may place Calcutta in rank above Vienna, Copenhagen, Petersburg, Madrid, Venice, Turin, Naples or even Rome.' It was almost inevitable that Kalidasa would be present in the library of a cosmopolitan family such as the Tagores – benefiting in all kinds of ways from the articulations of 'world literature' – which was itself instrumental in reshaping that cosmopolitanism.

Tagore's poem is an implicit tribute to that intellectual ambience and the possibilities it created; and it is also a tribute to the secular, silent act of reading, which, in that culture, had become a significant activity whereby old texts, and the printed page, were being placed in new contexts, and reassessed and reimagined. Tagore's poem is pervaded both by the sound of thunder (it is raining outside as he reads) and the inward silence of perusal:

Today is a dark day, the rain is incessant …

In a gloomy closed room I sit alone
And read the *Meghaduta*. My mind leaves the room,
Travels on a free-moving cloud, flies far and wide.
There is the Amrakuta Mountain,
There is the clear and slender Reva river,
Tumbling over stones in the Vindhya foothills …

(translated by William Radice)

Yet recalling the past meant, in this Tagorean configuration, confronting the question: why, and at what point, had the Indian modern ceased to have recourse to it, as an entity clearly available to rational apprehension? As Tagore wrote, in an essay on Kalidasa: 'Not merely a temporal but an eternal gulf seems to separate us from the great slice of ancient India – stretching from the Ramgiri to the Himalayas – through which life's stream flowed in the form of the *mandakranta* meter of the *Meghaduta*.' In his poem, Tagore brilliantly reworks Kalidasa's tale of separation from the loved one into a narrative of the separation of the self from history; the beloved pining in the city of Alaka becomes a figure of the past, intimate but distant, beautiful, but not quite recoverable. From the English Romantics Tagore had learned of the Imagination, and here he uses Kalidasa's cloud in a Wordsworthian way, making it a symbol for the modern Indian's desire to be one, through the Imagination, with his identity and history:

My heart travels thus, like a cloud, from
        land to land
Until it floats at last into Alaka – Heavenly,
        longed for city
Where pines that most loved of loves,
        That paragon of beauty. Who but you,
        O poet,
Revealer of eternal worlds fit for Lakshmi
        to dally in,
Could take me there? To the woods of
        undying spring flowers
Forever moonlit, to the golden-lotus-lake …
Through the open window she can be seen –
Wasted in body, lying on her bed like a
        sliver of moon
Sunk low in the eastern sky.

> Poet, your spell has released
> Tight bonds of pain in this heart of mine.
> I too have entered that heaven of yearning
> Where, amidst limitless beauties,
> Alone and awake, that adored one spends
>   her unending night.
> The vision goes ... I watch the rain again
> Pouring steadily all around.
>
> (translated by William Radice)

While Tagore wrote charming, implicitly patriotic verses, often for children, about the heroes and heroines of pre-colonial India (there was a renewed focus on these figures among the Bengali intelligentsia, owing to influential Orientalist histories such as James Tod's *Annals and Antiquities of Rajasthan*), he was also the first poet to articulate, to, in effect, fashion an iconography for, the educated Indian's anxiety about the recovery of the past. In another poem, 'Dream', Tagore invokes his sense of his historical past not in the aestheticized language of the new nationalism (as, say, Derozio might have invoked it), but in terms of fantasy, loss, and incommunicability:

> A long, long way away
>
> in a dream-world, in the
>   city of Ujjain,
> by River Shipra I once went to find
> my first love
> from a previous life of mine.
>
> (translated by Ketaki Kushari Dyson)

And ten stanzas later:

> I looked at her face,
> tried to speak,
> but found no words.
> That language was lost to me ...

'That language': the nineteenth century in India, and especially in Bengal, was a time of radical crossings-over in language, when languages were in the process of being both lost and regained. Derozio and his circle of contemporaries and students at the Hindu College wrote in English, the language that was present at the inception of the Indian middle class and that would always, in one way or another, define its existence. Michael Madhushdan Dutt, one of those who studied there after Derozio died, began his career as a poet who wrote in English, and whose ambition it was to be a canonical 'English' poet. (He even converted to Christianity, possibly to expedite this process.) But later in 1861, faced with failure, he wrote the first modern poem in Bengali, which was also, in a sense, a translation and a revision: *Meghnadabadhakabya*, an epic poem based on an episode and a character from the ancient Indian epic the *Ramayana*, written in blank verse as a gesture towards Milton, and using Milton's sympathy 'for the Devil's party' to invert the epic.

A few years later, Bankimchandra Chatterjee, a Bengali magistrate who worked for the British, wrote the first Indian novel in English, *Rajmohan's Wife*, an economical exploration of the Bengali family and domesticity. Partly from a feeling of nationalism, Chatterjee crossed over to Bengali, and embarked on the project of creating the first modern corpus of Bengali, indeed Indian, fiction. Once, Sanskrit and Persian had been the official and 'high' languages, Brajbhasha a northern and eastern Indian literary language; more recently, English, among the Bengali bourgeoisie, had briefly played its part in this constellation.

With the adoption of English and the formation of the middle class, there came, in the shape of a well-known paradox, the idea of writing in the mother-tongue. Bengali, whose grammar had been written approximately 100 years ago by Halhead, became a respectable language of self-expression for the Bengali bourgeoisie and its intellectuals. So began what's been often, and for a long time debatably, called the Bengal Renaissance, one of the greatest (despite anxieties to do with categorizing it) cultural efflorescences of the modern age, its critical demands all the more intriguing because of its disputable nature. Tagore was at once its product, its spokesman, its inquisitor.

Krishna Dutta and Andrew Robinson have produced a very readable and generally sympathetic biography of Tagore[1]. Dutta and Robinson wish to give us Tagore in his time, his public persona, and so they tend to put him in the company of other world figures of his day, such as Gandhi and Einstein; though it must be said that they do a good job of rendering also the inward complexity, the self-contradictoriness, and the insecurity of the man. What is most missing from this life of the poet is the poetry. This is partly because the authors have set out to avoid the gauzy, reverential literary effusions of earlier biographers. And yet a biography that takes the poetry into account with knowledge and sensitivity is absolutely essential.

(Almost the only thing of this sort in English is the Buddhadeva Bose's elegant monograph on the poet, now available only on a few dusty library shelves.[2])

Dutta and Robinson do provide an interesting, and sometimes penetrating, account on Tagore's ancestry and his family. The Tagores were Brahmins; they apparently moved to Bengal around AD 1000. Yet they came to exist at one remove from their caste, for members of a section of the family converted to Islam in the seventeenth century, and they were ostracized for it. Ostracism probably pushed the Tagores away from a more conventional Brahminical lifestyle towards entrepreneurship. They became successful middlemen, and were among the first to benefit substantially from trade with the British.

In the eighteenth century there was a rift within the family, and this led to the departure of Nilmoni Tagore, Tagore's great-great-grandfather, from the family home at Pathuriaghat and to his arrival at Calcutta, where he would build, in Jorasanko, the mansion in which Tagore would be born three-quarters of a century later. 'From then on,' Dutta and Robinson write, 'especially during the high noon of Empire in India after 1857, the two branches of the Tagores at Pathuriaghat and Jorasanko would have little to do with each other.' This small history of migration, ostracism and fracture is important, for it allegorizes the split, gradual but irrevocable, between the old Bengal, and the old India, and the new; and it helps us to comprehend the independent-mindedness of Tagore's immediate family, and in what way it had been prepared, by the time of Tagore's birth, to contribute to an emergent India.

The contrast between Tagore's father and his grandfather is obvious. Tagore's grandfather, 'Prince' Dwarkanath Tagore, was one of the first great Bengali entrepreneurs (a gradually disappearing breed, since business acumen came to be looked down upon in bourgeois Bengal). He was famous for his dinner parties in London; Dickens wrote about him in terms at once disparaging, scandalized, and envious. When he died he left his son Debendranath his lands and his debts. Debendranath was a Platonic figure, and could have been one of the philosopher-aristocrats of the *Republic*: a man both this- and other-worldly. Probably sometime in 1838, he experienced an epiphany after reading, by chance, a page of the *Upanishads*. He became a founding member of the Brahmo Samaj in 1843, a Hindu reform movement that owed something to Protestant Christianity; for it turned away from what it perceived to be the polytheism of middle and late Hinduism to the philosophical monotheism of the early Hindu texts, the *Vedas* and the *Upanishads*. The gods and the goddesses were replaced by a *nirakaar* force, a spiritual meaning without form or name.

The Brahmo Samaj went on to become one of the most powerful intellectual movements to shape modern, secular India. Indeed, one might argue that the aesthetic parameters of secular India (by 'aesthetic', here, I mean the transposition of historical and political entities into forms of self-imaging and self-consciousness) were prefigured by its basic tenets. In place of a varied, polyphonic, amorphous heterogeneity, there was now a unifying, all-encompassing meaning that was capable of accommodating and subsuming what it had replaced; and if this was the Brahmo Samaj's reworking of the Hindu religion, it was also Nehru's concept of what India as a nation-state should be. It's no wonder that, with hindsight, the bases of the Brahmo Samaj seem to lead so logically to those of secular, Nehruvian India.

Debenranath's Brahmoism was a great influence on his son, though Tagore was never altogether comfortable with it. Tagore's poetry, especially his songs, are among the first and the most profound utterances of a secular Indian sensibility, and they speak of an old world that is lost but is being transformed into something new. Here are the first two lines of a familiar and well-loved song:

> I haven't seen him with my eyes as yet,
> I have only heard a flute playing.

A couple of clarifications need to be made about the translation of those lines, which is my own. First, my line has the pronoun "him" in place of intermediate Bengali *taare*; the Bengali pronoun never specifies gender, but derives it through context. Second, I have deliberately translated the second line literally. The Bengali reader or listener would automatically interpret Tagore to be saying 'his flute'; yet the exact literal meaning suggests only 'a flute' or 'the flute'. And both these points, small as they are, are pertinent to our understanding of the Brahmo-influenced, secular spirituality of Tagore's poetry, the leap he is making, very subtly, from the old world to the new.

In a traditional devotional song, the flute would be played by Krishna, the Hindu cowherd-god. In Tagore's song, the player is not named, and the indeterminate Bengali pronoun is apposite to the nameless, secular meanings of modern India that have replaced the hallowed, familiar names and significances. The old world has become invisible and cannot be seen 'with my eyes'; what remains is the auditory signal that the flute sends forth. And by not using a possessive pronoun, by saying 'flute' instead of 'his flute', Tagore causes another fracture, a small disjunction, to occur. The sound of the flute represents the seductive appeal of Hindu divinity; it represents the known and the yearned for. But the flute cut off from its original context becomes a more ambiguous sign; it represents what is unknown, new, transformed. The listeners of the song traverse a distance as they hear these two lines, and it is the distance between the old feudal faith and the psychological terrain of modern India.

Growing up in the great house in Jorasanko, Tagore would have experienced the stirrings of the new urban cosmopolitanism around him, and sensed them, indeed, in the presence of his own family. Here Dutta and Robinson's biography is useful and involving. There was Tagore's father, of course; but there was also his older brother Dwijendranath, who, according to the biographers, 'was the most intellectual and the least worldly of the siblings. Deeply immersed in the study of Indian philosophy, mathematics and geometry, he also revelled in folding complex paper boxes and was responsible for inventing the first Bengali shorthand and musical notations.' Another brother, Satyendranath, was the first Indian to enter the Indian Civil Service. And the most remarkable of Tagore's elder brothers was probably Jyotirindranath, who, among other things, composed his own songs on the piano.

Tagore was the youngest of thirteen children, and he grew up in that house with something of the solitariness and the freedom of an only child. There are whole pages in his memoirs, *Jiban Smriti*, or *My Reminiscences*, which appeared in 1911, devoted to meticulous descriptions of the hours that he spent daydreaming as a boy. He was a recalcitrant pupil, he hated school, and much of his education took place at home. The English language was especially hated, but it was compulsory; Tagore's account of himself as a boy hoping, on a rainy day, that his English tutor would fail to turn up, and his deep unhappiness, a few minutes later, upon seeing the tutor's black umbrella approaching stubbornly through the rain, is a classic of Bengali children's literature.

Meanwhile, Tagore's father would be away for long spells, either overseeing his lands, or doing the opposite, withdrawing from his worldly duties to some Himalayan resort in the North for a period of sustained meditation. His often unannounced returns home created consternation, joy, and a tumult in the household; and these seemingly far-off tremors were also felt by the family's youngest member. Indeed, Tagore's relations with his parents are more mysterious than they at first might appear to be.

His mother is a figure largely in the background; she enters his poetry as a generalized maternal presence. The father's incarnation in his son's imaginative writings is more intriguing. Debendranath's mixture of aristocratic power and renunciatory spirituality and his relative inaccessibility seem to have made him, in Tagore's poems, a natural emblem for a certain kind of divinity that was spiritual and non-materialistic, masculine and powerful. Both the power of the old aristocracy and the reformist spiritualism of the Brahmo Samaj – contraries that were brought together in Debendranath – are integral to Tagore's idea of divinity in many of his poems. It is no accident that the divine being is called 'Raja', or 'king' in the poetry. A poem called 'Arrival', for instance, seems to recall those sudden returns home by Debendranath:

> Our work was over for the day, and now
>   the light was fading;
> We did not think that anyone would come
>   before the morning.
> All the houses round about
> Dark and shuttered for the night.
> One or two amongst us said, 'The King of
>   Night is coming.'
> We just laughed at them and said, 'No one
>   will come till morning.'

(translated by William Radice)

But later:

> O where are the lights, the garlands,
>   where are the signs of celebrations?
> Where is the throne? The King has come,
>   we made no preparation!
> Alas what shame, what destiny?
> No court, no robes, no finery
> Somebody cried in our ears, 'O vain,
>   O vain this lamentation':
> With empty hands, in barren rooms,
>   offer your celebration.

These stanzas, in, Bengali, not only convey the physical upheaval Debendranath's return caused in the household of Jorasanko; they imply, too, the complex, dazzling paradox that the appearance of a figure such as Debendranath – aristocratic but unworldly, a 'King' but of 'Night' – signified on the horizon of Bengali culture. His appearance caused not only a tumult, but also a reordering of values and an anxiety, in the household.

Tagore's first memorable literary endeavour was accomplished when he was probably sixteen, in shape of a literary fraud. Pessoa-like, the young Tagore created a 'heteronym', Bhanusingha, a medieval poet who wrote in Brajabuli, one of the older literary languages; and Bhanusingha's oeuvre of songs are sung today as part of the Tagore repertoire. Years later, in his memoirs, Tagore was still gleeful that these songs had deceived an authority on Bengali literature, who would later mention Bhanusingha in a thesis on medieval Bengali poetry.

The literary models and inspirations behind Tagore's imaginative leap are interesting in themselves, and they remind us of the hybrid context of Tagore's work and, indeed, of that Bengal Renaissance. This is worth pointing out, because cultural commentators today often lazily identify post-colonial uses of English with hybridity and the indigenous languages of once-colonized countries with some sort of authenticity. Yet more than one language is written into Tagore's poetry.

Around the time that Tagore composed the *Bhanusingher Padabali*, Bengal was in the midst of unprecedented intellectual activity. Bengali scholars had recently collated the works of the great medieval Bengali poets, Chandidas and Bidyapati, and compiled the *Vaishnav Padavali*. It was the music of these poets with which the young Tagore fell in love, and he was moved to produce a comparable music through the persona of Bhanusingha. Yet the idea for the pastiche (if that is what it was) came from Chatterton, whose work Tagore also loved. Tagore's heteronym leads us to a moment of transition in the development of an artist and a culture. It is evidence of the pressure exerted upon him by what one might tentatively call a polyphonic, multilingual reality, but in a way seemingly different from the way we understand such transactions today; the notion of 'pressure' itself, and secrecy, and the idea that polyphony is not necessarily extroverted display, but might involve a long history of ellipses, concealment, and self-effacement, are, by now, somewhat alien to us. Here, again, Pessoa reminds us it might be otherwise.

Tagore began his career in print as a lyric poet in the strictest sense: he was a writer of songs. His first book of poems, *Prabhat Sangeet*, or *Morning Songs*, was published in 1878, when he was still sixteen. The core of his achievement may lie in his songs; and for these he was both admired and, at first, reviled by his contemporaries. It was for his own inexact prose version of another book of songs, the *Gitanjali* (a compilation, in the English version, of songs from the original collection and two others), that Tagore was awarded the Nobel Prize many years later.

The story of his rise to international celebrity and the Nobel Prize is well known: Tagore completing his English "translations" (they were really reworkings) on board a ship to England in 1912; the painter Rothenstein reading the handwritten 'translations' and, stunned, passing them on to Yeats; the excitement thereafter; Yeats introducing Tagore to an elite circle of friends in London, including Pound, who would confess to feeling like a 'painted pict with a stone war-club' when he met the poet; publication of some of the prose poems in Harriet Monroe's *Poetry* on Pound's recommendation; the Nobel Prize in 1913; Pound's and Yeats's swift and shocking disenchantment with Tagore; Tagore's ascension as a world figure from the 'East' coinciding with his banishment from the serious Western literary establishment. A part of this story is given in Dutta and Robinson's anthology[3] of Tagore's writings, in intermittent epistolary form, beginning with Tagore's letter to Yeats in 1912: 'It has been such a great joy to me to think that things that I wrote in a tongue not known to you should at last fall in your hands and that you should accept them with so much enjoyment and love.'

Few poets have led, in the modern age, so public a life, have lectured and spoken on so many subjects, occasionally badly and verbosely. And few poets in the modern age have mastered and left their mark on so many other genres: on musical composition, on the novella, and on the short story (the writer Buddhadeva Bose pointed out that Tagore brought the modern short story to Bengal at a time when it had hardly any practitioners – Kipling is the obvious exception – in England), not to speak of the novel, the theatre, and even painting.

In their anthology, Dutta and Robinson have attempted to give the reader a sense of this range, though it doesn't seem that the quality of the translations of much of the poetry (I have in mind especially Tagore's own problematic "reworkings") will do much to alter Tagore's reputation outside Bengal, or to extend his readership beyond what has long been his constituency in the West: Indophiles, amateur religious enthusiasts, and admirers of Kahlil Gibran. I say this despite the fact that Dutta and Robinson have bravely tried to make Tagore real, and historical, by including some of his letters, his lesser-known essays, and some of the marvellous early letters written in Shelidah, when Tagore was looking after his father's estates and was still young and obscure. In those letters he recorded, in casual but heightened prose, the life of the estates, the local people who worked on or around them, the weather, and the faint traces of the colonial world: from these experiences would come the first short stories, full of air and light, bringing the ordinary Indian citizen of the colonial world – a postmaster, a servant girl – into Indian fiction for the first time. For all this, one still feels that it is time that Tagore's most recent translators settle their differences, and bring out a volume of their own best translations of Tagore's poems and stories; for there have good translations by each of them, a fact that tends to get lost with each new attempt, as well as with each translator's implicit assumption that his or her Tagore is the 'true' one.

Few poets, then, have been so prolific and in so many ways, and, also, in their lifetime, have been so written and spoken about. Yet it is crucial to note that few poets in their work – in the output on which both their popular and critical reputations rest – have devoted so much of their gift to describing what is half understood, partially grasped, unclear, or ambiguous – but that is the temperament of Tagore's songs and his lyricism. This is ironic, of course. In the West, and sometimes in India, Tagore has traditionally been seen as a purveyor of Eastern wisdom, a man who tended to make recondite, timeless utterances. He himself, when not composing poetry, made repeated assertions about 'creative unity' and 'universalism' in ways that, by now, beg not to be taken at face value. Yet his Bengali lyrics have everything to do with uncertainty, with hesitation, with the fleeting and the momentary, and the beauty that resides in the moment of incomplete perception.

How did a lyric, rather than an epic, poet come to be Bengal's national poet? And a poet of uncertainties and absences, which make him an unusual national poet, to say the least. The reason for this is probably that Bengal was the site of India's first modern middle-class culture, a culture neither feudal nor entrepreneurial. Unlike the Indian cultures with ancient feudal and religious traditions, Bengal – though it possessed its own rich stream of pre-colonial culture – found its most characteristic voice in the late nineteenth century, in its bourgeoisie. Modern Bengal began, no doubt, with an entrepreneurial flourish, with the lives of those like Tagore's grandfather Dwarkanath Tagore; but in Tagore's family itself, the gradual distancing, over the next two generations, of the world of business activity from the world of 'cultured' or *bhadra* society becomes apparent. More and more, ambitions related to commerce would come to be disdained.

Both old feudal societies, with their internalized religious and mythic landscapes, and new entrepreneurial societies, with their external upheavals, need epic poets. Thus the ancient poetry of the *Mahabharata* and the *Ramayana* sustained the feudal Indian consciousness until the nineteenth century, and does so even now. Yet the genteel Bengali middle class – the *bhadralok*, literally, the 'civil person' or 'civilized person' – chose for its national poet one who sang of the small incommunicabilities of human language. Occupying a perpetual in-between space in history, that middle class, which no longer possessed the language to speak of the past that had vanished or of the world that had opened up before it, found in this poet's metaphors a vocabulary of self-definition. Thus, both *diganta*, or 'horizon', which suggests that opening-up, and *katha*, or 'word', 'language', or 'story', suggesting self-expression and history, recur in Tagore's songs.

The Bengali middle class consisted of barristers, advocates, school-teachers, lecturers, doctors, civil servants, people who were both partaking of colonial power and revising its meaning. They constituted the first indigenous governing class in India who experienced power while being cut off from its source. Theirs was a jealously protected world, composed of known and concrete social and secular values: the family; the child; education; respectability; marriage; entry (for males and, gradually and less commonly, for women) into one of the professions. The unknown, for them, was the glimmer of the past, all that their small but all-encompassing world had replaced; the past, and their own buried selves.

Tagore's poetry, especially in his songs, captures this psychological dichotomy with precision. The Bengali bourgeois world of the social, the worldly, the known, becomes in his songs the concrete and physical world of sensation and appearance, of detail; the buried self becomes a passer-by or traveller – a *pathik*, seldom met or seen – or a guest – *atithi* – awaited by someone who stands at a window. These are Tagore's recurring motifs.

One can see this duality inform the opening lines of a song chosen at random, though it is a famous song (the translation is mine):

> O moment's guest,
> Whom did you come searching for at dawn
> Climbing a path strewn with shefali blossoms?

The acts of noticing and compression are enshrined in the third line. A Bengali would know that the white, star-shaped *shefali* flowers, redolent with perfume in the evening, fall from their branches in the course of the night, so that the feet of a person trampling them at dawn would be the first things to disturb them from their repose, the first human influence of the day to agitate nature; and the unseen traveller, ghost-like, would leave no sign of his passing except the disturbance of the dead shefali flowers. The line is as abbreviated a statement as a line in a haiku; the detail is as oblique as the one in Edward Thomas's 'In Memoriam (Easter 1915)', where the presence of the war is suggested in terms of the bushes heavy with flowers, because the men who would pick those flowers for their sweethearts are all away.

The physical world, then, is evoked concretely; but the traveller, the stranger, is blurred and indefinite. And he, being a guest, reminds us of what is both ours and not ours. It is as if the poem's speaker at once longs to be hospitable to, and is distanced from, his innermost self. This – the tensions between the physical, the familiar, the minute, and the unclear and potentially distant – perfectly captures and dramatizes the psychological dichotomy of the Bengali bourgeoisie: the dichotomy, in the middle-class psyche, between the social-secular-rational-colonial world and the world of the subconscious and the pre-colonial.

Again and again in Tagore's songs, the secular world perceives the glimmer of the known or the partially known – the complex religious and feudal world that has vanished, with the self that belonged there – either through a window or while confronting the horizon (which transforms the landscape into a great window). The word *kichhu*, which as an adjective means 'a little', and as a noun 'something' or 'anything', is a common enough word in the language. Tagore makes it a key word in his songs, using it repeatedly to define the half-understood 'something' that exists on the edge of the secular world. It is a euphemism for history and the subconscious. Tagore also uses it to mean 'something unsaid'; and here, too, a complex emotional register is created, for it evokes the poignancy of the trajectory of Bengali middle-class life, with its *bhadralok* propriety, gentility, rationality, and its ironic lack of fulfilment. Here are the first lines of another song; I have italicized the words that are translations of *kichhu*:

> You may as well sit by me for a *little* while more;
> If you have *anything* more to say, say it, whatever it is,
> See the autumn sky pales.
> The vaporous air makes the horizon shine.

The imperfectly perceived, partially known, unnamed presence – whether it represents the spiritual source of the pre-colonial world now made semi-visible and nameless, or the regeneration of the new one – is always associated, in Tagore's songs, with conflicting emotions of resignation and joy: resignation, because that spirituality is inaccessible now except through these spots of time; and joy, because these spots of time open up new possibilities, new ways of deriving sustenance from the old. Thus, songs such as 'From time to time I catch glimpses of you' and 'Because I wish to find you anew/ I lose you moment to moment' are accompanied by conflicting impulses of acceptance and excitement in the interpreter of the song and its listener; they capture the sense of incomplete but revivifying spiritual possibility in the interstitial world of the Bengali, and the Indian, middle class.

Indirectness, in these songs, is both Tagore's literary mode and his subject matter. This indirectness, this articulate evasiveness, was also reflected in the life of the Bengali middle class before, and to a certain degree after, independence. This middle class has been the source of much that is modern about modern India; but it has also been traditionally cut off, and sometimes it has cut itself off, from central political power. It is at least partly for this reason – Bengal's distance from direct political control in the colonial and even the post-colonial age – that epic sweep and candour, in the poetry of Bengal's national poet, have been replaced by lyric sugges-tion and reticence. At crucial junctures of nationhood, poets narrate and re-create their nation's history in the form of epic; but Bengal was both a nation and not a nation, a region with its own community and history but also a part of the larger nation-state that had been conceptualized, early on, in no small measure by some of its own intellectuals. Thus Tagore's most enduring creative legacy to the Bengali bourgeoisie was both epic-like and yet not an epic, a gift of songs in which the consciousness of Bengali mo-dernity first found utterance and in which the impress of its creation and its history was subliminally contained, while relinquishing the overarching narrative of the epic for lyric moments of implication and inquiry

The problem with reading and judging Tagore is not only a problem of translation, or of understanding a seemingly untranslatable and exotic culture. Tagore needs to placed in the context of modern Indian history, and more specifically in the context of an almost permanently interstitial Bengali middle-class culture, before the texture of his work can be under-stood, and the same holds true the other way round. But, alas, India is commonly perceived as either possessing no history at all, as being an en-chanted place of ancient myths and verities (the jacket of Dutta and Rob-inson's anthology of Tagore's writings promises that it an 'essential guide for readers seeking … wisdom'); or else its history is seen as a parable of postcoloniality, of the confrontation of the colonized with the colonizer. But Tagore does not fit into either formulation, and neither does most of modern India. Tagore is one of the figures who stand at the forefront of India's extraordinary and often traumatic reinterpretation of itself in this century. And his most profound engagement with history – his principal enactment of his role within it – lay not in his asides to Gandhi or his opinions on Mussolini, but in the reticent, self-repeating, half-lit world of his poems and his songs.

The East as a Career
On 'Strangeness' in Indian Writing

Legacies of Orientalism

At readings by Indian writers in English, two related questions, or some version of them, will invariably be asked by a member of the audience, whatever the setting – bookshop, university seminar or literary festival. The first question is, 'Which audience do you write for?'; and the second, 'Are you exoticizing India for a Western audience?' I'm not entirely sure why people don't tire of asking these questions; but I notice that all kinds are interested in asking them – among others, the type whose reading consists almost entirely of recent fiction, an odd mixture of *The Da Vinci Code*, Pico Iyer, and Vikram Seth; people who read almost nothing but magazines, and whose views on, and affective response to, writers derive not so much from books, but almost entirely from what's circulating about those books and their authors in print; and people in academic disciplines like cultural studies or literature, to whom, especially since the rise of the former, and the latter's surrender to the former's protocols, such questions are bread and butter.

The questions seem to arise from some residue of an idea of a moral custodianship of literature, at a time when no one – neither the reader, nor the person who attends readings because of the free drinks, nor the academic – seems to have a clear or reliable notion of what 'literature' is. What is it we're trying to protect when we ask these questions? What is literature, or, for that matter, 'Indian writing in English', entities largely created by writers, and apparently so susceptible to being sold and peddled like wares by them?

'Literature', as a category, has, for some time now, lost its integrity and recognizability; and there is no persuasive and intelligent debate, let alone a consensus, on the nature of Indian writing in English. Ever since

the politics of representation, rather than the definition of literary practice, became a principal preoccupation of literary departments, many of
us have been left with one or two tired moral gestures in lieu of a robust
and ongoing discussion of, and inquiry into, what it is we're making those
gestures on behalf of. And the politics of representation – for questions
about a writer's audience, and his or her use of the 'exotic', are political
questions – has passed into the common parlance, in the way that more
complex ideas from, say, Rousseau or Freud or Marx have in the past been
translated into the public sphere, where they're free to be used sometimes
as a knee-jerk response to the problematic.

As to the questions above, I think it's safe to say that most people
who ask them – whether they're nameless literary buffs, or pillars of society, or teachers or students of literature – think the questions arose within
themselves spontaneously as an immediate response to a situation or context; there's an assumption that these questions have no history or source.
But surely these questions tell us more about the intellectual formations
and compulsions of our time, and about this moment in Indian literary
history, than their supposed answers would illuminate us about the impulses that go into the act of writing? The questioner, anyway, is hardly
as interested in those impulses – that is, in the answers to the questions
(for it's perfectly possible, even plausible, that there are Indian writers who
conceive of their projects with something like a 'Western readership' in
mind; Nirad C. Chaudhuri, embarking on his great autobiography, is an
example, and one that at once complicates the issue) – as in stating certain
moral parameters for writing and thinking. Where did those particular
parameters come from? The questions aren't timeless, but the questioner
invests them with the authority of timelessness. And yet, to my knowledge,
no one asked Bibhutibhushan Banerjee or Manik Bandyopadhyay whom
they wrote for, or if they were 'exocitizing' rural Bengal for a metropolitan
readership.

English, then, is part of the problem; the act of writing in English
was, in India, potentially an act of bad faith, and some version of the old
suspicion regarding the motives of those who write in English remains
and is still at work among us. But the focus in those earlier attacks on
Indian writers in English, such as the famous one led by the Bengali critic
Buddhadeva Bose, was artistic practice, even if that practice entered the
discussion negatively, with a metaphysical fatalism; it was apparently impossible for writers to fully and deeply address their subject except in a
language that was their 'own'. By bringing the audience into the picture,
the emphasis and the debate shift from writerly practice to cultural, social,
and economic transactions – from the mystery and riddle of the creative

act to the dissemination of texts and meanings, by publishers and newspapers, in the academy and in bookshops, from meaning to the production of meaning.

This is where Edward Said comes in; Said who, in a devastatingly effective substitution, replaced 'meaning', in the post-structuralist inquiry (still fresh at the time) into its production, with 'the Orient'. The notion is brought in, almost casually, as an interjection, when Said says that his concern in his study, *Orientalism*, is to examine the 'enormously systematic discipline by which European culture was able to manage – and even produce – the Orient'. That 'and even' shouldn't distract us from the fundamental importance Said and others after him have attached to this notion. In the last few decades, there's been a palpable but often unspoken feeling that the production of the Orient has moved beyond Europe, and Europeans, into the realm of the so-called diaspora, and of Indian writing in English. And the spread of globalization and the free market coinciding roughly with the advent of the post-Rushdie Indian novel in English returns us to the epigraph from Disraeli in Said's book: 'The East is a career'. For the production of the Orient involves, implicitly, its consumption; the circle is incomplete without the 'audience'.

But the concern with this form of 'production' has given us not so much a critical eye or sensibility, but a sense of vigilance, and, at a cruder level, a kind of vigilantism; this is where the astringency and aggression of those questions come from. More than a year after Said's death, we can reflect on the legacies of *Orientalism* – the book, not the phenomenon described within it – and say that this particular brand of vigilantism too is one of them. It's the Saidian inheritance that gives those questions their urgency; but since they seem to have no provenance, and little critical content, I'd say they are vulgarized legacies of *Orientalism*, among the many by-products of that great polemic that are both ubiquitous and don't bear close scrutiny. This doesn't prevent those questions from being reiterated, as a constant, irrefutable challenge, and their standpoint from remaining unexamined; vulgarizations permeate language, and become a habit of thinking.

The Storyteller

Maybe we could inquire about what sorts of presuppositions these questions – 'Which audience do you write for?' and 'Are you exoticizing your subject for a Western audience?' – are based on. Take the first question first, which accuses, by implication, the Indian writer in English of being removed from his or her 'natural' readership: an Indian one. The question relies on utopian ideas which are present everywhere and all the time in the way we think of these matters.

For instance, the 'Indian audience' is itself a utopian idea; and, like all utopian fictions, it makes us flushed with emotion, and fills us, according to the situation, with a sense of pride or injustice or protectiveness. Yet it's difficult to construct an ideal readership, waiting to receive or judge new works by writers, in a country in which even the Anglophone urban middle class – a minority – is divided and differentiated by disharmonies of interest: political, social, intellectual, not to speak of pettier reasons for disagreement. Possibly the question arises from an Arcadian vision of Indian history – India as a womb of storytelling and myth, where audience and storyteller or performer are umbilically united. And possibly it comes from a particular view of other cultures, including modern ones, where writers are perceived to write for a bourgeois constituency that also provides them with a 'natural' habitat – so that the problem of the audience is seen to be a problem special to the deracinated, dislocated Anglophone Indian (a belief shared by many Anglophone Indians themselves), who has, as it were, stepped out of, or turned against, nature.

Yet the dissonance between audience and writer goes into the heart of modernism, and the modern, itself: not only as a form of elitism, a high-handed, inhumane rejection, by the modernists, of the ordinary person. I mean that the dissonance is written into the text; that it's a profound and complex resource for the writer. For instance, the rift between reader and writer not only surrounds the novel, *Ulysses*, and its reputation; it's a powerful component in the work. We know that the Ulysses-figure in the novel, Leopold Bloom, the *petit-bourgeois* copywriter, is not the kind of man who'd read *Ulysses*, or is exactly the sort who wouldn't. Bloom's reading comprises the trashy magazine, *Titbits*, which he peruses in the lavatory, 'seated calm above his own rising smell'. Later, as if it were a modernist 'readymade' that had unsuspected uses, he turns it to toilet paper: 'He tore away half the prize story sharply and wiped himself with it.' A great gap, in terms of writer and audience, divides Joyce from Bloom. Stylistically, artistically, Joyce, in writing his novel, had no intention of closing that gap, but only of widening it; but imaginatively, he needed to make the journey toward Bloom so that his novel might move outward into the world from the circumference of Stephen's persona, and onward from the *Portrait*. In writing it, Joyce defines no clear-cut, consoling relationship to his audience; the novel is built upon a paradox, upon both the necessary embracing and the necessary rejection of Bloom by his creator.

Let me cite another instance of this dissonance, this time in a story from a vernacular Indian literature, where (so the person who asks the

Indian English writer the question about the audience implies) author and reader are at one in prelapsarian harmony. The story is '*Suryana Kudure*', or, in A.K. Ramanujan and Manu Shetty's translation, 'A Horse for the Sun', by the Kannada writer, U.R. Anantha Murthy, whom I very much admire, but whose public pronouncements have got him into a sort of critical rut. These pronouncements largely consist of repeated airings of the belief that the vernacular or '*bhasha*' writer has an immediate and organic access to his readership and community that the Anglophone Indian writer doesn't and, really, can't. Yet his own finest work tells us something quite different about the location of the modern Kannada writer, and the tensions latent in the latter's relationship to his or her readership. In 'A Horse for the Sun', the narrator, a person very like the author, even down to his name, 'Anantha', a city-dwelling intellectual, a disillusioned Marxist, returns briefly to his village, and, accidentally, runs into a childhood friend, Venkata – a bit of a clown, a buffoon, a person who hasn't moved on or achieved anything; by Anantha's social and moral standards, a failure.

Anantha is disappointed in, even repelled by, his old friend; but, oddly, he's also attracted to his air of sensuousness and freedom, his apparent unburdenedness. Venkata's domestic life is a mess; but he embodies an elemental, physical joy. Later in the day, in his house, he tells a reluctant and tired Anantha that he'll administer him a head-massage; while doing so, he launches into a near-meaningless, extraordinary soliloquy. Newsprint and faeces mingle with one another in Bloom's toilet; in Venkata's bath, Anantha's various tortured cerebral speculations dissolve into Venkata's rapturous pre-verbal utterance and the body's sensations. Venkata is the story's subject, but, as Anantha knows, he will not be its reader; and it's precisely the physical closeness and intellectual disconnectedness that Anantha feels toward Venkata that impels and shapes the story, that gives its sense of thwarted desire and its calamitous ending. Anantha Murthy, the spokesman and propagandist for Kannada literature, and flagellant of Indian English writing, believes the 'bhasha' writer belongs to an organic community; the vision of Anantha Murthy, the artist, arises compellingly from the conviction that no organic community is possible.

No writer has a given and recognizable audience, except, perhaps, in our fabular reconstructions of antiquity or medieval history. A writer, sooner or later, has to come to terms with this, in a much more painful and thoroughgoing way than the questioner in the audience will understand. The reader too needs to come terms with it, if he is to have more than a passing interest in what literature does; for the writer not only speaks to the reader, but interrogates the unbridgeable gap between the two. Any theory of reading that doesn't take this into account will leave itself open to question. Benedict Anderson's narrative of nations coming into being through 'imagined communities' of readers is, for instance, yet another utopian conflation of nationality with readership, which never incorporates, into its study, the notion that discontinuities are as important to the formation of the modern imagination as collectivities. It's not only the reader who takes the decision of rejecting or accepting a writer; the writer, too, depending on what his objective is at that moment, and how he means to achieve it, gives himself to, or withholds himself from, the reader.

Life Itself

What does the 'exotic' in 'Are you exoticizing your subject for a Western audience?' – a question asked indefatigably of Indians who write in English – what does the word mean, or in which sense is it meant? Dictionaries will give you a range of meanings, such as 'foreign' – where 'foreign' is usually 'tropical' – and 'strange' and even 'bizarre'. But the dictionaries' interpretations are almost entirely positive; the exotic has to do with a certain kind of allure, the allure of the strange and faraway. They still haven't taken into account the post-Saidian registers of the word, by which it has become a habitual term with which to count the spiritual costs of colonialism: 'inauthentic' and 'falsified' are still not options among their list of meanings. The word's stock had never been very high, but its reputation has declined in the way the reputation of 'picturesque' had earlier; although the latter never transcended its status of being a minor aesthetic term into becoming the populist catchphrase that the former has become.

   Said, of course, feels compelled to use the word in the first page of *Orientalism*, where he notes that a French journalist, on 'a visit to Beirut during the terrible civil war of 1975–1976 … wrote regretfully of the gutted downtown area that "it had once seemed to belong to the Orient of Chauteaubriand and Nerval."' For the European, for the French journalist, to mourn the demise of this Orient was almost natural, for, as Said goes on to say, this Orient 'was almost a European invention, and had been since antiquity a place of romance, exotic beings, haunting memories and landscapes … Now is was disappearing' – in the Middle East, especially, as the French journalist saw it, into the tragic mess of contemporary history. In a salutary reminder, characteristic of Said both in his study and his political work, the reader is told of the simple but, till then, often ignored, irony of the fact that the Orient was also a real place, even in the time Chauteaubriand and Nerval; that, even then, 'Orientals had lived there, and that now it was they who were suffering'; however, 'the main thing for the European visitor was a European representation of the Orient and its contemporary fate ...'

Characteristic, too, of Said in much of his literary critical work (his political writings and activism are almost a compensation for this), is, as he fleetingly admits himself, his own study's turning away from the Oriental, except in his or her itinerary in European texts, and from the Oriental representation of the Orient. This – the Orient's representation of itself – is presumably what the 'almost' in 'the Orient was almost a European invention' refers to, and also suppresses: that the Orient, in modernity, is not only a European invention, but also an Oriental one, an invention that has presumably created and occupied an intellectual, cultural, and political space far larger and more important than its European counterpart. The book about the Oriental invention – and I mean that word in both senses, as 'creative' and 'spurious' production – of the Orient is still to be written; for now, we have to be content with that 'almost'. Dipesh Chakrabarty, in his *Provincializing Europe*, wryly observes that a literary commentator, while describing the provenances of *Midnight's Children*, its mixture of 'Western' and 'Eastern' elements, makes specific references to what she considers the Western resources of Rushdie's novel (*The Tin Drum, Tristam Shandy* etc.), but refers to the Eastern ones only in blurred and general categories: 'Indian legends, films and literature'. Chakrabarty gives this sort of critical viewpoint a hilarious definition: 'asymmetric ignorance'. While one should hesitate before ascribing to Said an ignorance of modern Oriental cultural traditions, that 'almost' in his sentence certainly constitutes an asymmetry – an asymmetry whose logic he pursues implicitly but quite relentlessly in his study.

What does this asymmetry mean to our understanding – our specifically Said-inflected understanding – of the 'exotic'? In the sense that we use the term today, the 'exotic' doesn't just mean 'foreign', but a commodification of the foreign: an intrinsic part of the 'production' of the East that Orientalism entails, and which is, crucially, made possible by the spread of capitalism and of markets. When the person in the audience asks the Indian writer in English about exoticization, he means to say that the writer is a sort of deracinated Oriental who, in an act of betrayal, has become involved in the production of the Orient. We've inherited the Saidian asymmetry along with the Saidian critique; it leads us to believe that Oriental and, for our purposes, Indian history was a bucolic zone untouched by the market until, probably, the Indian novelist in English came along; that the Orient has been in a state of nature in the last 200 years, translated into the realm of production and consumption only by Western writers and entrepreneurs. And in this way, we exoticize exoticization itself, making it impossibly foreign to, and distant from, ourselves.

A glance at the cultural history of our modernity, however, tells us that we've been 'producing' the Orient, and exoticizing it, for a very long time; that the exotic has been a necessary, perhaps indispensable, constituent of our self-expression and political identity, as given voice to in popular culture, in calendar prints, oleographs, the 'mythologicals' of early Hindi cinema, as well as the lavish visions of Indian history in the latter – these are the signatures of the cultural and political world of the anonymous; a 'production' of the East more challenging or significant than anything the word 'Orientalism' can hope to encapsulate, and part of whose inheritance, as seen in the core of kitsch in the BJP's version of *Hindutva*, is ambiguous. So persuasive is this production and its peculiar language that outsiders, and even Indians, often see it – say, in its incarnation as the genre today called, inexactly, 'Bollywood' cinema – as essentially or even immemorially Indian, not realizing that these forms emerge at a crux and juncture in the nineteenth and early twentieth centuries when religion and tradition begin to respond to the incursion of capital; that the forms are quite different from the highly impersonal, stylized variations of folk art prior to capitalism; and that they make, for the first time, the notion of 'bad taste' a powerful contender in Indian cultural life.

A certain sort of middle-class flirtation with the exotic goes back to the formation of our modernity: in some of the paintings of, say, Abanindranath Tagore, or especially those of Ravi Varma. This particular strain of exoticism, which appears in the late nineteenth century, is marked, really, by an appropriation of realism, of photographic and naturalistic detail. In the case of Ravi Varma, it involves a commodification of the native in the terms of Western, sometimes pre-Raphaelite utopias, each mythic scene depicting the outcome of both mental and actual journeys made between India and Europe, in particular, Germany (Varma set up his printing press outside Bombay in collaboration with German print technicians). This new utopian naturalism distinguishes Varma's (and others') vivid exotica from the Kalighat *pats* and oils of the early decades of the nineteenth century, which, with their combination of stylized figures in the folk style and their greedy assimilation of elements of the colonial world (hairstyles, attires), represent a vital, mischievous, and self-critical pupal phase in modern popular culture, and especially in the local artist's early response to capital; a genuine deflection of the exotic through the sensuousness of the line itself. But, of course, the Indian production of the exotic also later becomes important – far more so than its Western counterpart – to canonical artists like the film-maker Satyajit Ray as something they define their art, even their very sense of the 'real', against: what's stifling to the young apprentice director in 1948, in an essay called 'What is Wrong with Indian Films', is not his burden as a post-colonial, but his burden as a modern – the presence, on all sides, of a powerful home-grown 'exotic' in cinema, a descendant, in the moving image, of Varma's utopian realism;[1] what Ray calls elsewhere the 'mythologicals and devotionals' that 'provide the staple fare for the majority of Bengal's film public'.

This 'production' of the East in cinema has already quite a long history in India, he notes dourly in 1948: 'Meanwhile, "studios sprang up," to quote an American writer in *Screenwriter*, "even in such unlikely lands as India and China." One may note in passing that this springing up has been happening in India for nearly forty years.' The call to turn away from this home-grown production is quasi-religious, Vivekananda-like: 'The raw material of the cinema is life itself. It is incredible that a country which has inspired so much painting and music and poetry should fail to move the film maker. He has only to keep his eyes open, and his ears.'

'Life itself': this brings us to the second part of what's so problematic about the recent history of the term 'exotic' in our country. When Ray speaks of 'life' and the 'raw material' of life, he's speaking of a refutation of the spectacular that comprises the exotic, in favour of the mundane, the everyday, and the transfiguration of the mundane. 'Life', 'the everyday', 'reality' or 'vastav', rather than 'reality' as 'satya', with its connotation of spiritual 'truth': all these were invented by the modernist bourgeois Indian imagination in the nineteenth century as categories inextricable from 'Indianness'; and then the 'real' is transfigured by the artist in the new, secular domain of culture emerging at the time. The crucial role of the transfiguration leads, in the 1940s, to Ray's directive to the film-maker to 'keep his eyes open, and his ears': the words not only echo Vivekananda, but Tagore, who, in a song invoking the givens of nature – light, air, grass – says, 'kaan petechhi,/ chokh melechhi'; 'I have kept my ear peeled,/ I have gazed upon.' The act of 'seeing', or 'recognizing' the 'real', once it has emerged, becomes a secular act full of spiritual urgency, sacred and yet displaced from and mostly unconnected to religious topoi, antithetical in its own eyes, importantly, to the equally vital project of commodifying and 'producing' the local.

That transfiguration involves a making foreign or strange the 'raw material' of the commonplace; a process that is, indeed, for artists like Ray, a critique of the 'strangeness' of the 'mythologicals', of popular culture, of the exotic. Tagore defines it at the conclusion of the same song: 'janaar majhe ajaanare korechhi sandhaan'; 'I've searched for the unknown/ in the midst of the known'. The 'raw material' of estrangement, for the modern artist, is *not* the extraordinary, but as much light, grass, air, as it is the dross that surrounds us: verandahs, advertisement hoardings, waiting rooms, pincushions, paperweights.

All these, in a process both elusive and fundamental to art, are made new and distant – but, in India, critical language, especially in English, has for some time lacked a vocabulary with which to engage with this transformation and its contexts and questions. Even much of the bafflement that attended Ray's early and middle work in India, and the complaint that he lacked political content, has probably something to do with the inability to understand the defamiliarized in art.

On Strangeness

It's the matter of strangeness in art – what Viktor Shklovsky called, almost a century ago, 'defamiliarization' – that brings me to the late Arun Kolatkar, and to a short and unique book, called *Jejuri: Commentary and Critical Perspectives*, edited and, in part, written by Shubhangi Raykar. *Jejuri* is Kolatkar's famous sequence of poems which was published in 1976, and won the Commonwealth Poetry Prize the following year. It mainly comprises a series of short lyric utterances and observations through which a narrative unfolds – about a man, clearly not religious, but clearly, despite himself, interested in his surroundings, who arrives on a bus at the eponymous pilgrimage town in Maharashtra where the deity Khandoba is worshipped, wanders about its ruined temples and parallel economy of priests and touts, and then leaves on a train. In some ways, the sequence resembles Philip Larkin's 'Church Going'; except that, where Larkin's distant, sceptical, bicycle-clipped visitor 'surprises' in himself a 'hunger to be more serious' inside the church, the hunger to be more curious is characteristic of Kolatkar's peripatetic narrator.

Kolatkar was a bilingual poet who wrote in both Marathi and English; in Marathi, his oeuvre is shaped by a combination of epic, devotional, and weird science-fiction and dystopian impulses. In English, Kolatkar's impetus and ambition are somewhat different: it's to create a vernacular with which to express, with a febrile amusement, a sort of urbane wonder at the unfinished, the provisional, the random, the shabby, the not-always-respectable but arresting ruptures in our moments of recreation, work, and, as in *Jejuri*, even pilgrimage. Kolatkar was, in the fledgling tradition of Indian writing in English, the first writer to devote himself utterly to the transformation and defamiliarization of the commonplace; given that Indian writing in English has, in the last twenty years or so, largely taken its inspiration from the social sciences and post-colonial history, that avenue opened up by Kolatkar has hardly been noticed, let alone explored, by very many contemporary writers. By 'defamiliarization' I mean more than the device it was for Shklovsky; I mean the peculiar relationship art and language have to what we call 'life', or 'reality'. 'Realism' is too inexact, loaded, and general a term to suggest the gradations of this process, this relationship, and its perpetual capacity to surprise and disorient the reader. In India, where, ever since Said's *Orientalism*, the 'exotic' has been at the centre of almost every discussion, serious or frivolous, on Indian writing in English, the aesthetics of estrangement, of foreignness, in art have been reduced to, and confused with, the politics of cultural representation. And so, the notion of the exotic is used by lay reader and critic alike to demolish, in one blow, both the perceived act of bad faith and the workings of the unfamiliar.

Kolatkar died in 2004, and his death means he's safely passed into the minor canonical status that India reserves for a handful of dead poets who wrote in English. But the present consensus about him shouldn't obscure the fact that his estranging eye in his English work has been problematic to Indian readers. Shubhangi Raykar's commentary was published in 1995 with, she says, 'the modest aim of helping the undergraduate and graduate students in our universities'. Her book is, of course, indispensable to any reader not wholly familiar with the references to various myths and legends, especially those to do with the deity Khandoba, that recur in the poem. But there's another difficulty, one to do with reading, that Raykar draws our attention to:

> Yet another aspect of *Jejuri* is that it is a poem that can be fully understood and enjoyed only when the reader is able to 'see' it. *Jejuri* is, thus, a peculiarly visual poem. Repeated references to colour, shapes, sizes, textures of objects and many other details … are outstanding aspects of *Jejuri*. And yet these very aspects bewilder the students.

Among the 'critical perspectives' included in Raykar's book is the Marathi critic Bhalchandra Nemade's essay, 'Excerpts from Against Writing in English – An Indian Point of View', originally published in 1985 in *New Quest*, a journal of ideas published from Pune descended from the influential *Quest*, which itself was modelled on *Encounter*. Nemade's opening paragraphs are fortified by a range of allusions to linguistic theory; but the nationalistic tenor of the essay doesn't demand too much sophistication or imagination from the reader: 'A foreign language thus suppresses the natural originality of Indian writers in English, enforcing upon the whole tribe the fine art of parrotry.' The typo-ridden text has 'ant' for 'art', and the juxtaposition of 'tribe', 'ant', and 'parrot' gives both the sentence and its subject matter an odd anthropological texture. Unlike the Bengali writer and critic Buddhadeva Bose, who worried that the Indian writer in English would have nothing either worthwhile or authentic to say, Nemade is as interested in the realm of consumption, in the possibility of the East being a career (to adapt Disraeli's epigraph to Edward Said's great polemic), as he is in the validity of the creative act itself: 'An Indo-Anglian writer looks upon his society only for supply of raw material to English i.e. foreign readership.' He mentions three instances of what, for him, are acts of 'aesthetic and ethical' betrayal: Nirad C. Chaudhuri's *The Autobiography of an Unknown Indian*, Narayan's *The Guide*, and Kolatkar's *Jejuri*. And the now-familiar question, still relatively fresh in 1985, is asked and sardonically answered: 'What kind of audience do these writers keep in mind while writing? Certainly not the millions of Indians who are "unknown" who visit Jejuri every year as a traditional ritual ...'

Here is the mirage of the organic community that so haunts our vernacular writers – the idea that those who write in their mother-tongue are joined to their readers in Edenic harmony; anyhow, Nemade doesn't ask himself if the readership of *New Quest* is an extension of, or an interruption in, that community. Kolatkar's poem he classifies as a form of 'cynical agnosticism' and 'philistinism'. Quoting one of the most beautiful lines in the sequence, 'Scratch a rock and a legend springs', where the narrator is noting, with evident detachment, the incorrigible way in which the apparently barren landscape generates mythology, Nemade says, 'he writes with little sympathy for the poor pilgrims, beggars, priests and their quite happy children at Jejuri'; instead, 'Kolatkar comes and goes like a weekend tourist from Bombay.' Nemade is a distinguished critic and writer, but this isn't a particularly distinguished offering. Yet it's interesting because of its rhetoric, in the way, for instance, it uses the word 'tourist', to create a characteristic confusion between estrangement as a literary effect, and the threat of the 'foreign', with its resonances of colonial history. The aesthetics of wonder is inserted into, and enmeshed with, a politics that is partly nationalistic, partly xenophobic.

That interpreting the operations of the random or the unfamiliar in the work of the Indian writer in English is a problem beyond malice or wrong-headedness becomes clear when we look at Raykar's notes, which give us both sensitive close readings of the poems and a great deal of enlightening information about the local references and terrain. Yet Raykar, who is obviously an admirer of Kolatkar's, seems oddly closed to the experience of estrangement. In fact, estrangement becomes, once more, a form of cultural distance, and the notes a narrative about alienation; a narrative, indeed, of semi-articulate but deep undecidedness and uncertainty about what constitutes, in language, poetic wonder, citizenship, nationhood, and in what ways these categories are in tension with one another. Examples abound, but I'll give only two. The first concerns her note to 'The Doorstep', a poem short enough to quote in its entirety:

> That's no doorstep.
> It's a pillar on its side.
>
> Yes.
> That's what it is.

For Raykar, these lines betray a 'gap between the world of the protagonist and the world of the devotees'. For 'a traditional devotee,' she says,
'every object in the temple exists at two levels. One is the material level
which the protagonist can see and share with the devotees. The other level
transforms a mundane object into a religious, spiritually informed object.'
Raykar points out that this 'level is not at all accessible to the protagonist.' But surely there's a third level in the poem, in which a significance is
ascribed to the mundane, the superfluous, that can't be pinned down to
religious belief; and it's this level that Raykar herself finds inaccessible, or
refuses, for the moment, to participate in.

My second example is her note on 'Heart of Ruin', the poem that precedes 'The Doorstep' in Kolatkar's sequence. As Raykar tells us – and this
is the sort of information that makes her book so useful, and, since it's one
of a kind, indispensable – the poem is 'a detailed description of the then
dilapidated temple of Maruti at Karhe Pathar.' From the first lines onward,
Kolatkar gives us a portrait of a casual but passionate state of disrepair:
'The roof comes down on Maruti's head./ Nobody seems to mind./ ...
least of all Maruti himself.' This is how Kolatkar catalogues the dishevelled
energy of the scene, as well as his bemused discovery of it:

> A mongrel bitch has found a place
> for herself and her puppies
>
> in the heart of the ruin.
> May be she likes a temple better this way.
>
> The bitch looks at you guardedly
> past a doorway cluttered with broken tiles.
>
> The pariah puppies tumble over her.
> May be they like a temple better this way.
>
> The black-eared puppy has gone a little too far.
> A tile clicks under its foot.
>
> It's enough to strike terror in the heart
> of a dung beetle

and send him running for cover
to the safety of the broken collection box

that never did get a chance to get out
from under the crushing weight of the roof beam.

Morosely, the narrator concludes – and Kolatkar's abstemiousness
with commas serves him well in a sentence in which the second half is
neither a logical extension nor a contradiction of the first – 'No more a
place of worship this place/ is nothing less than the house of god.'

Raykar's gloss, again, translates Kolatkar's laconic, estranging sensibility into the neo-colonial, or at least the deracinated, gaze: 'To a visitor
with an urbanised, westernised sensibility it is always an irritating paradox
that the almighty god's house ... should be in such a sorry state of disrepair ... Hence the ironic, sardonic tone.' I think Raykar's and Nemade's
response to the superfluous and random particular in *Jejuri* (comparable,
in some ways, to the impatience Satyajit Ray's contemporaries felt with the
everyday in his films) is symptomatic, rather than atypical, of a certain kind
of post-Independence critical position, which obdurately conflates the
defamiliarization of the ordinary with the commodification of the native.
With the enlargement of the discourse of post-coloniality in the last two
decades, the critical language with which to deal with defamiliarization has
grown increasingly attenuated, while the language describing the trajectory of the East as a career has become so ubiquitous that, confronted with
a seemingly mundane but irreducible particular in a text, the reader or the
member of the audience will almost automatically ask: 'Are you exoticizing
your subject for Western readers?'

The two poems by Kolatkar I've quoted from, as well as Nemade's
criticisms, remind me of a short but intriguing essay by the social scientist
Partha Chatterjee, called 'The Sacred Circulation of National Images', and
I'd like to end by dwelling on it briefly. Chatterjee is puzzled and engrossed
by what has happened to these 'national images' – for instance, the Taj Mahal; Shah Jahan's Red Fort – as they've been represented in our textbooks
in the last forty or fifty years: that is, in our relatively brief, but palpably
long, history as a republic. He discovers that early photographs and en-
gravings found in textbooks dating back, say, to the 1920s, are gradually
replaced in textbooks after 1947 by a certain kind of line drawing. He finds
no economic *raison d'être* for this change: 'Are they cheaper to print? Not
really; both are printed from zinc blocks made by the same photographic
process.' But the more telling change occurs in the nature of the representations themselves, as the pictures of certain monuments are transformed
into 'national icons'. The earlier pictures and photos, Chatterjee finds, have

an element of the random in their composition – an engraving of the Taj Mahal has a nameless itinerant before it; an early photograph shows a scattering of 'native' visitors before the same building; early pictures of the Red Fort or the *ghats* in Benaras have the same sort of 'redundant' detail – a group of men, a dog – in the foreground.

As these monuments are turned into 'national icons' in post-Independence history textbooks, the pictures are emptied of signs of randomness, emptied, indeed, of all but the monument itself, and a new credo and economy of representation comes into existence: 'There must be no hint of the picturesque or the painterly, no tricks of the camera angle, no staging of the unexpected or the exotic. The image must also be shorn of all redundancy ...' We all know what Chatterjee is talking about from our own memories of the textbooks we studied as children, from the functional but implicitly absolute representation of monuments they contained. Although the impetus behind the 'emptying' of the textbook image seems partly Platonic – a nostalgia for the ideal likeness, unvitiated by reality's unpredictability – Chatterjee places it in the context of the Indian nation-state, identifying it as the process by which national monuments are turned to 'sacred' images.

It seems to me that both Nemade's and Raykar's literary responses to *Jejuri* are, with different degrees of intensity (and, in Nemade's case, belligerence), really part of a larger discussion of what constitutes nationality and the nation-state; that the sacredness they invest in and are anxious to protect in Jejuri is less the sacredness of Khandoba and of religion, and more that of an absolute idea, or ideal, of the nation. Kolatkar's doorstep, his broken pillars, roofs, and beams, his mongrel puppy and dung beetle, violate that idea and its space, as I think they're meant to, just as much as the itinerant or animal the anonymous engraver introduced into his representation was at once accidental and intentional. Defamiliarization not only renovates our perception of familiar territory; it dislocates and reframes our relationship of possessiveness to that territory in ways that the discussion on nationality, on what is authentic and what foreign, what's exotic and what native, not only cannot, but actually suppresses. For Kolatkar, the break that the superfluous brings about in the telos of Nemade's and Raykar's unstated but undeniable national narrative is a small ecstasy; for Raykar, and Nemade especially, a source of puzzlement and unease.

Argufying
On Amartya Sen and the Deferral of an Indian Modernity

Amartya Sen's *The Argumentative Indian* is a civilized polemic about India. Many of the facts and citations that Sen marshals towards his polemic would be familiar to people acquainted with studies of Indian culture and history; but the moment and manner of the polemic make it unusual. It's directed, mainly, against two views of India, views that might seem remotely connected to one another, or even adversarial. Both emphasize – even invent – an India synonymous with religion, magic, antiquity, 'spirituality', the irrational, the non-modern. The first of these views has a powerful and venerable history; it's the principal Western perception of India, and that perception, even when it's an empathetic one, begins and ends with India's spiritual significance. With imperialism, the perception becomes a justification – to differentiate the conquered from the conqueror as being less rational, less capable of individual and independent action, less intrinsically free.

The second view that Sen's concerned with has made a relatively recent appearance, although its hidden history in India is a long and troubled one. Sen points out that this second view, which has to do with the invention of a particular India by right-wing Hindus (represented by the BJP and ancillary political organizations like the RSS), bears a striking resemblance to the Western invention, notwithstanding the BJP's strident and melodramatic nationalism. The BJP's interpretation or vision of Hinduism – *Hindutva* – is political and emotional, but owes hardly anything to traditions of rationality.

Sen's purpose is to remind us that the democracy and the secular inheritance we value in India today are not an accident, and neither are they merely a gift from the West; nor are they, on the other hand, something that an idealized Hindu identity needs protection from. Towards the middle of the book, Sen addresses both the Western misrepresentation and the Hindu mystification, and the point at which these antithetical streams unexpectedly flow into each other:

> The special characteristics of Western approaches to India have encouraged a disposition to focus particularly on the religious and spiritual elements in Indian culture. There has also been a tendency to emphasise the contrast between what is taken to be 'Western rationality' and the cultivation of what 'Westerners' would see as 'irrational' in Indian intellectual traditions. While Western critics may find 'anti-rationalism' defective and crude, and Indian cultural separatists may find it cogent and penetrating (and perhaps even 'rational' in some deeper sense), they nevertheless agree on the existence of a simple and sharp contrast between the two heritages. The issue that has to be scrutinised is whether such a bipolar contrast is at all present in that form.

For Sen, the 'bipolar contrast' is a construct that's circulated widely in the academic, political, and popular imagination, but which doesn't bear close examination. India, says Sen, has a long, even pioneering, tradition of argumentation, scientific achievement, secular debate, free thinking, scepticism. It's a tradition in which, for example, its democracy, its freedom struggle, its intellectual and cultural developments in the last 200 years, and, by implication, Sen's own trajectory from economist to public intellectual – an archetype of the rational, argumentative Indian modern – need to be placed.

Sen, of course, is not alone among Indians in espousing the secular, the rational, the 'high' cultural: indeed, Enlightenment values and a humanist vision of the world in general, and of India in particular, have accompanied and indelibly shaped the growth and formation of the Indian middle class from the early nineteenth century onward. The humanist discourse (for the want of a better word) has been, by common consensus, the elite discourse in India; and it's against it that, on the one hand, raw, emotive, right-wing critiques like *Hindutva* have been raised, and, on the other, as Sen notes, critiques such as subaltern studies – which trace the itinerary of the Indian peasant – whose provenances are Gramscian, and belong to the left. The political expression of this modernist, enlightened humanism is usually referred to by the catch-all term 'Nehruvian', although it doesn't by any means emanate from Nehru alone; it would be as much a mistake to identify that political temper with a single figure, despite Nehru's personal vision of his country, as it would to reduce the Elizabethan age to Elizabeth I. For the philosophical underpinnings and the first explorations of the basis of that humanism we need to go back further to the late eighteenth century, to the polyglot scholar Raja Rammohun Roy, who, in taking issue both with Brahmin orthodoxy and Christian missionaries, 'made in two decades', as the historian C.A. Bayly has said, 'an astonishing leap from the status of a late-Moghul intellectual to that of the first Indian liberal', and who 'independently broached themes that were being simultaneously developed in Europe by Garibaldi and Saint-Simon'.

But if the discourse of modernity and of the human has been the elite discourse in India for almost two centuries, this elitism and hegemony is rather an unusual one in that it appears to have no official intellectual or existential expression, no central text. It's been translated into policy, state-craft, and institutional practice, into democracy, free speech, and ideas of social equality, and its most eloquent author and guarantor is the Constitution; it's observable as the context in which not only political activity, but the growth and development of literatures, the writing of histories, the creation and contestation of meanings, have taken place since the early to mid-nineteenth century. Yet, if one were to turn to look toward a body of work, or a single significant statement, for a full-blown genealogy and definition of the human in India, and, especially, its cognitive basis, we wouldn't find a great deal. It's fine to deconstruct or historicize that cognitive basis – what it means to *be*, to think and feel as, a modern and an Indian – by placing it in its social and institutional contexts, but only when we have a thorough idea of what it is, or at least more than the dim and generalized sense we have of it now. Indeed, it's likely that we'd get a more vivid idea of the Indian modern in critiques of Indian modernity, in the works of, say, Ashis Nandy or the subaltern studies historians, than in its own putatively formative domain. Or we might agree that such a thing as Indian modernity, with its notions of rationality, science, and 'high' culture, existed by arriving at it by a process of elimination: very large areas of Indian history in the last two centuries will simply not fit comfortably into a category such as, for instance, 'post-colonial'. The film-maker Satyajit Ray, watching Kurosawa's *Rashomon* for the first time in Calcutta, noted in startlement that a work or sensibility of such sophistication couldn't be a one-off or a freak occurrence; that it must emerge from a culture 'fully formed'. We might say the same of any Indian modern, including Ray. And yet our canonical sense of the 'fully formed' cultural history – compared to, say, that of European or American modernity – in which we must locate the modern Indian self and its impulses is relatively poor, notwithstanding salutary overviews undertaken recently by the likes of C.A. Bayly, and Sugata Bose, Ayesha Jalal and various others. A somewhat odd hegemony, then – what makes Indian modernity, especially its subjective space, so elusive?

Sen has attempted – successfully, I think – to write an erudite but accessible handbook on, and defence of, what is in effect secular Indian modernity (although, tellingly, like other Indians, Sen too isn't wholly comfortable with the term 'modern'), on its roots in antiquity, and its possible journey in the future. Sen's idea of situating the modern 'argumentative' Indian in the lineage of traditions of science, scepticism, and rationality that go back in history – to figures like the Moghul emperor Akbar, a peerless liberal, in Sen's eyes, and then further into antiquity, to mathematicians like Aryabhatta – bears some resemblance to the notion of the 'early modern' advanced by certain South Asian historians fairly recently. These historians don't go back quite as far as Sen does, to texts like the *Upanishads*, but restrict themselves, on the whole, to the period between the fifteenth and eighteenth centuries. In the hands of a historian like Sanjay Subrahmanyam, it's a fecund and challenging notion; it qualifies, as Sen too tries to, our assumption that modernity in India was the inadvertent gift of colonialism. For Subrahmanyam, this period in India isn't just a medieval age defined by feudal and religious interrelationships, but a time when certain 'early modern' structures come into place, in institutional practice, modes of dissemination of knowledge, social mobility, the role of the individual, or subtler cultural registers like, as Subrahmanyam notes, the 'shift in the portrayal of the empirical individual' in the painting of the 'Mughal school'. The usefulness of the notion of the 'early modern' is indubitable, although it's never entirely clear what the Indian 'late modern', or, simply, 'modern' is through whose filter we're looking back, presumably, at its early foundations. The methodology seems to be a bit like Borges's in his essay, 'Kafka and his Precursors', where the narrator notes wryly that it became possible, after Kafka's appearance on the horizon, to trace a line of precursors, both notable and obscure, stretching back from him – an ironical reversal of the orthodox teleology of traditions developing and leading up to a 'great writer'.

But there's little doubt that the 'early modern' helps us to look back at history and uncover new formations in it. For me, there are, in addition to what our historians have written about, two key 'early modern' moments. The first has to do with the significance of domiciled natives, or, to borrow from Heaney, 'inner émigrés', to the Indian sense of nationality. There are two crucial figures in this regard: the first is the great thirteenth-century scholar, poet, and innovator in music in the Delhi Sultanate, Amir Khusrau; the second, the early nineteenth-century Anglo-Portuguese poet, Henry Louis Vivian Derozio, who lived and died at the age of twenty-three in Calcutta, and whose sonnets in English to his 'native land', India, are still studied in schoolbooks. Khusrau's father, who was Turkish, migrated to

India from Central Asia; Khusrau patriotically called himself, by all accounts, 'Turk-e-Hindavi', or an 'Indian' Turk. Derozio, approximately six centuries later, chose to give voice to the first rumblings of Indian identity as we know it now in his sonnets and poems. Both these men are definitive instances of the journey the 'early modern' makes towards the 'modern', especially in that they prefigure what we now suspect to be true of Indian nationality: that it not only transcends race, but complicates and perhaps includes within itself the notion of 'otherness' and foreignness. This is why, in the last elections in India, secular Indians who might not have been admirers of Sonia Gandhi nevertheless found themselves deeply uncomfortable with the attempts to marginalize her from the political process because she'd been born an Italian.

The other key 'early modern' moment, for me, involves a transgression – a quasi-Oedipal one – that is, everywhere, constitutive of modernity. This is the son's breach, in the nineteenth and twentieth centuries, of the father's mercantile, bourgeois status, towards a daydreaming, irresponsible, and possibly artistic life, realigning and reassigning, in the process, the values of the bourgeois order. This transgression is the subject of Mann's novels, it lies, silently, at the core of Kafka's life, and is charted in a progression in the history of the Tagores in Bengal, from the life of the entrepreneur 'Prince' Dwarkanath, to that of his otherworldly but landowning son Debendranath, to, finally, that of his grandson (at first, a disappointment in the family), the poet Rabindranath. Might the well-known turning of certain landlords from their feudal responsibilities, before and at the cusp of colonialism, towards the classical arts, especially music (Tarashankar Banerjee's tragic story, 'Jalsaghar', about this turn in the life of one landowning family was later made into a film, *The Music Room* by Ray), be an 'early modern' prefiguring of that bourgeois and profoundly modern transgression? Certainly, one of the most important junctures in the story of colonialism in India, the annexation of Oudh by the British, involves a king, Wajid Ali Shah, who was seen to have abnegated his monarchical responsibilities for music and dance, and is credited with facilitating one of the most popular of semi-classical musical forms, the *thumri*. From the point of view of the history of colonial, nationalist, and Marxist histories, these abnegations of duty signify decadence, the waning of the Mughal order, the failure of an old social class which left itself vulnerable to either the new, parvenu bourgeoisie or the colonizer. From the point of view of the history of modernity, is not the lapse of the artistic landlord or king an 'early modern' rehearsal of a definitive moment, when the old is transgressed and transformed unrecognisably into the new?

Probably one of the principal reasons that the word 'modern' is problematic for Indians, that modernity remains, in South Asia, an unofficial and potentially embarrassing reality in spite of being a hegemonic and foundational one, is its filial involvement with the 'colonial'. For some influential South Asian historians today, 'colonial modernity' is the rubric under which everything that was produced or occurred from roughly the mid-nineteenth century onwards falls – from the great novels of Bankim-chandra Chatterjee, Hindu oleographs, educational policy, the scientific temper, the railways, the creation of popular culture, to nationalism. But while theorists of the 'early modern' and the 'colonial modern' have tried, often with a high degree of excellence, to describe what actually happened in South Asia in the last 500 years, one feels that the very terms, 'early modern' and 'colonial modern', are inflected with a nostalgia for what never did happen, or what might have – an indigenous, home-grown modernity, in whose narrative the problematic moment of colonialism never occurred. Is it because of this (and not just to pursue a Borgesian irony) that the historians of the 'early modern' never clearly specify what its late phase is – because it was interrupted and compromised by colonialism? And is this why the status of the 'colonial modern' is never less than ambiguous, and it's never accorded more than a provisional and slightly controversial acceptance: because Indians believe modernity is both theirs and not theirs, because they feel that it was authored, at least in part, elsewhere? Perhaps this is why the modern in India has been both a hegemony and an inheritance that Indians have been consistently equivocal about; why its features are obvious and also partly concealed. This is a pity, because we've never known any other modernity but the one we've had: in spite of its privileging of, and investment in, human agency, it's true we can probably no more choose our history of modernity than we can our relations. The secret, utopian longing, in India, for another, 'purer' modernity possibly explains why we fail to engage completely with the implications and radical achievements of this one.

For, while it's true that Indian modernity as we know it is concomitant and congruent with colonialism, it's also true that the construction of 'Indianness', or 'being Indian', in that period transcends, complicates, and makes fluid the fixed identity of the colonial subject. In what way, and how, did 'being Indian' become a point of departure from all sorts of more specific marks and occlusions towards a seemingly transparent, absolute, spontaneous human identity? The question hasn't been adequately answered. At what point in the nineteenth century, for instance, did a person in India reading either Tagore, or Shakespeare, or the *Bhagavad Gita*, or Tom Paine, or an editorial in a newspaper, become someone who was reading not only as a colonial subject, or an upper-caste or upper-class Hindu, or as an aristocratic Muslim, but as an 'Indian'; how was it that being 'Indian' was to possess a national identity but also to be 'human', and, in an unexpected sense, to be at one with the colonizer? This category – 'Indianness' – was an extraordinary invention; in its double location in the national and political on the one hand, and in the universal and human on the other, it was at once oppositional and closed and receptive and open-ended; it provided the basis for resistance to the colonizer and, on another level, an intriguing empathy with him. This empathy came not just from submission and acquiescence (submission, anyway, leads to mimicry, not empathy), but the translation, through the cognitive basis of 'being Indian', of the self from colonial subject to 'universal' human being. This – and not just class elitism – is what gives Indian modernity, in the nineteenth and early twentieth centuries, its dislocating, distinctive note of confidence and its magpie-like instinct toward intellectual entitlement; the note is audible, and that instinct manifest, in this statement that Tagore made in a letter to C.F. Andrews, which Sen quotes in his book: 'Whatever we understand and enjoy in human products instantly becomes ours, wherever they might have had their origin.' In 1816, the conservative Indian founders of the Hindu College, asking the Chief Justice Edward Hyde East to set up an institution in Calcutta that would provide Indians a European education, and being asked, in turn, by Hyde East if this wouldn't upset traditional sensitivities, said – the sentiment and note of confidence look forward to Tagore's – that they wished to take from Europe 'that which they found good and liked best'. By 1816, then, presumably, the 'universal human being' had emerged in India, side by side with, and subsuming, the early colonial subject; for these gentlemen, otherwise conservative by nature – they had marginalized Rammohun Roy from this very initiative for being too radical – spoke not only as native opportunists, but as human beings exercising judgement in a context where such judgement had come into play. This note of confidence is seldom heard in Western modernism, despite its cosmopolitanism and its reputation for radical experiment; although the Western modern has done, in relation to non-European culture, exactly what the Indian wanted to do in regard in relation to the European, that is, taken what it 'thought good and liked best' (one thinks of Van Gogh's Japanese prints and Picasso's African mask). The non-European is silently domesticated and naturalized in the space of European modernity; the latter is shaped by a secret sense of the 'other' in a way that Indian modernity isn't. The note of confidence and celebratory entitlement we hear in Tagore and the founders of the Hindu College is, perhaps for this reason, absent from Western modernism; but it's possibly present in other modernities. Certainly, its most powerful expression comes from Borges in 'The Argentine Writer and Tradition': 'I believe our tradition is all of Western culture, and I also believe we have a right to this tradition, greater than that which the inhabitants of one or another Western nation might have.'

Sen himself, by this Indian definition, is a 'late modern'; although deeply anti-colonial (as, indeed, many of the Indian artistic and intellectual elite were, including Tagore), he's marked by a particular kind of confidence in relationship to European and other cultures that places him in the line of the founders of the Hindu College; and, in spite of his concern with placing Indian rationality and science within their own cultural traditions, seems unaffected by the nostalgia for an uncontaminated, indigenous modernity that secretly impels some of the most acute of postcolonial thinkers. What he has to say may not be as groundbreaking as the work of these writers has occasionally been; but his book rumbles, despite its civility, with a private and timely discontent that reminds us that the problem of Indian modernity and humanism needs to examined afresh; that, if Indian modernity is a way of viewing the world, we haven't scrutinized, enough, the gaze in the mirror.

In one regard, I'd modulate Sen's thesis. Sen draws our attention to the two world-views that have invented a 'spiritual' India: that of Europe and, closer to home, of *Hindutva*. But there is a third, more imaginatively significant invention of Indian spirituality; it comes from the rational, humanist, secular middle class whose archetypal representative Sen calls the 'argumentative Indian'. The romantic creation of a spiritual India has been crucial to secular Indian moderns, to their paradoxical, poetic sense of rootedness in, and exile from, the country they belong to. Sen quotes with approval the social scientist Partha Chatterjee's discussion of the emergence of a 'domain of the spiritual' in India:

> … anticolonial nationalism creates its own domain of sovereignty within colonial society well before its battle with the imperial power. It does this by dividing the world of social institutions and practices into two domains – the material and the spiritual. The material is the domain of the 'outside', of the economy … of science and technology… where the West has proved its superiority. The spiritual, on the other hand, is an 'inner' domain bearing the 'essential' marks of cultural identity. The greater one's success in imitating Western skills in the material domain, the greater the need to preserve the distinctiveness of one's spiritual culture.

This is very persuasive. But there is another powerful reason for the creation of a 'domain of the spiritual' in India, as there is in the West: the disappearance or passing of its old locations in religion. The new domain of the spiritual that emerges, then, is something called 'culture', and it is integral, not antithetical, to the emergence of secular modernity. This explains why key national figures who have transgressed orthodox religious denominations like Gandhi and Tagore are marked by residues of the old domain of religion while actually inhabiting the domain of culture, why they have a saint-like air while being political strategists or secular artists. The narrative of 'spiritual India' will have to do without its most productive incarnation if we only look for it in Western representation, or in *Hindutva* revisionism, and neglect the space it occupies in the secular subconscious and dreamscape.

This is Not Music
The Emergence of the Domain of 'Culture'

At a recent paper-reading by, and discussion with, Perry Anderson at the Seagull Resource Centre, the subjects attended to were multiculturalism; its relationship with religion; the role of the left; and multiculturalism in three relatively 'new' nations – India, Israel, and Ireland – all three having been carved out on the basis of religion. There was an involved debate, for quite some time, on religion, and secularism in India. Anderson wanted to know, for instance, why Marxism had taken root in Bengal and Kerala, and not elsewhere; was it because the thrust of the mainstream religion, Hinduism, was tempered here by Islam and Christianity? An interesting question, not fully answered; the other reason for the tempering of Hinduism in Bengal – the Brahmo Samaj, the so-called Bengal Renaissance – was touched upon by a well-known historian, but not dwelt on; it was a point of view popular in the 1960s, he said, but never pursued with 'proper sociological rigour'. The same historian, reflecting on religion, said its public and even bellicose aspects, which Anderson had referred to in his talk, should be distinguished from religion as a more private, 'spiritual' practice.

To me, what was missing from a lively debate on the nature of the 'secular', with politics and religion occupying the two poles of reference, was a notion of the role of culture. It took me back to the fact that, in our country, the debate around the secular is largely constructed around the discourses of politics and religion; that, if culture is introduced into the debate, it's done so in its guise as political and religious culture, and rarely as 'culture' in the secular and modern sense. 'Sociological rigour' or not, this leaves a very large gap, or silence.

The history of the secularization of the West can't be written without taking into account the separation, at a certain point in history, of religion and culture, so that they came to occupy two distinct, umbilically related, but oppositional spaces; and the emergence of the secular is concomitant with the rise of the notion of culture as a space separate from religion. Something similar happened in India, and in Bengal, in the nineteenth century, but let me stay with Europe for a moment.

The discussants had distinguished between religion in the sphere of politics and community, and religion as a 'spiritual' practice; but, in the West, a second site of the 'spiritual', *outside* religion, came into existence with secularization: that site was culture. The forms of culture in secular Western society that embodied and interrogated the 'spiritual' were, of course, the arts: music, painting, literature. These were activities that existed in the secular domain, that were sceptical of orthodox religiosity, but had a deep investment in the sense of the sacred, the transformative. I'm using the word 'culture' here, of course, not as anthropologist might, to denote the sum total of the life-practices of a community, but in the problematic but influential Arnoldian sense; and the Arnoldian sense of culture, as a non-religious but nobly creative domain, permeated the construction of the secular not only in post-industrial England, but also, surely, in Bengal in the time of colonialism, more deeply perhaps than we can acknowledge and understand. It was Matthew Arnold who became chief propagandist for the idea of culture, specifically literature, as a space both transcendental and secular; who argued for poetry as a 'substitute' for religion in an age in which faith had become a 'melancholy, long, withdrawing roar'; who argued for the Bible to be read not as 'dogma', but as 'literature'. Some of these extraordinary inversions of values and meanings will be familiar to us from the unfolding of the narrative of the secular and the modern in India and in Bengal.

The most influential poet-critic in English after Arnold, T.S. Eliot, was particularly impatient with the grand claims Arnold made on the behalf of poetry. At first reading, Eliot's wry but outraged objection to Arnold's substitution of religion with poetry seems to suggest that he's arguing for a view of poetry at once more complex and pragmatic than the one Arnold had. But one must remember that Eliot was an orthodox believer who finally 'came out'; that perhaps he's pleading not so much on behalf of poetry as of religion; nothing, for Eliot, is a substitute for religion. For all that, it's worth recalling that we don't read the poems Eliot wrote long after it was public knowledge he'd become Anglo-Catholic – for instance, *Four Quartets* – as if they were expressions of religious faith; we read them, and they ask to be read, according to the conventions of a secular 'work of art': *Four Quartets* belongs, that is, not to the domain of religion, but to the domain of culture. This paradox itself redirects us to the ways in which, in the West, we inhabit the secular space of culture, and that space inhabits us.

Much of the secular 'imaginary' of Western art and literature derives from, as we well know, an aspect of religion that Anderson didn't mention in his talk: mythology. To many of the great Romantics and modernists in the post-industrial West, and to those on the cusp of Romanticism and modernism, like Rilke, mythology became a great secular cultural inheritance. Protestant Christianity had no mythology to speak of; the icons of antique religions – from Greece, Rome, even India – became part of the creative hoard of the Western secular imagination.

I've revisited all this because something comparable happens in India, in Bengal, in the nineteenth century; at a certain point of time, religion and culture come to occupy related but oppositional spaces; the composition of the *Meghnadbadhakabya* might be said to constitute an important moment, a moment when a poem with an overtly religious subject was transplanted from the domain of religion into the domain of culture; in looking back at the space in which that poem was written and read, we become witness to the outline of a secular, modern space that is also 'spiritual' and mythopoeic. But there's a difference between this and what had happened earlier, and would continue to happen, in Europe; Hindu mythology, unlike the Greek, was a living continuum; in what way, then, was it 'recovered'? I think the moment of Orientalist scholarship is significant here; it was William Jones, among others, who transferred Indian mythology and religion to the domain of 'culture' in the modern, secular, Arnoldian sense. Others, more gifted than he, brought to that domain, in various Indian languages, a spiritual, existential, and artistic richness and complexity.

The legacy of those transactions, the complex experience of that richness, are fundamental to the Indian secular: they return to us, for instance, when we listen to a *puja* song by Tagore, and the act of listening becomes not a religious but a cultural act. Similarly, the Tagore *kirtan*, which belongs not to the temple but to the drawing room: the latter, then, becomes the secular, Anoldian space in which art accommodates spirituality, but not religious belief. The traditional classical and devotional arts were also reconstituted in the time of modernity; that's why I can listen to a Meera *bhajan* sung by Paluskar and admire its artistry, and also be moved by its spiritual immediacy, without necessarily believing in the existence of Krishna; the Paluskar *bhajan*, for me, exists in the domain of Arnoldian 'culture' rather than religion.

The secular, in India, is identified as a national space in which multiple religions are tolerated; in this political sense, as Sanjay Subrahmanyam and many others have pointed out, 'secularism' is an Indian word that has no exact Western equivalent; it is a post-Independence, constitutional construct. But the 'secular', in modern India, has also surely, especially in its incarnation as culture, been an alternative site, as it is in the West, for the spiritual, the existential, the experiential; in its aspect of 'culture', the 'secular' in India shares with Europe the complex spiritual inheritance of modernity. This inheritance has been exhaustively investigated in the West, but very little in comparison in India, where the discussion of the 'secular' (to the cost of our understanding, I think) remains an exclusively political one. The trajectory of culture I've been speaking of is certainly not equally valid for everyone, and in every place, in the modern world. On Brooklyn Bridge, I recall a Sudanese taxi driver playing a haunting tape of a muezzin with a particularly lovely and melodious voice. 'This music is beautiful,' I said. He corrected me angrily: 'This is not music. This is the Koran!' 'But it is beautiful,' I insisted.

The iconography of secular culture in India is predominantly, even hegemonically, Hindu; but we should pause before we rush to conflate it with *Hindutva*, as many commentators do these days. Firstly, we shouldn't confuse a cultural hegemony with a religious one; the predominance of Hindu imagery in the construction of the secular Indian imagination also delinked those images from their original parameters to all moderns, both Hindus and non-Hindus, just as the cultural hegemony of secular Europe made itself available even to those on its margins, like Joyce in Dublin and Dutt in Calcutta; Christianity itself, for the colonized middle class, could never achieve the unexpected multiplicity of register, and the reach, of European modernity.

The construction of secular universals is a double-edged sword; it both injures and empowers. Thus, the universal 'human' in Europe was covertly European, but it didn't remain the property of Europe alone; similarly, the secular 'Indian' is secretly Hindu, but is every Indian's property: so, Hussain can paint Saraswati and Qurratulain Hyder write about Sita – the domain of culture, unlike the domain of religion, belongs to the modern in a way that doesn't presume or demand allegiance or belief. Surely the principal project of *Hindutva* is to destroy this domain of culture that was created in modernity, to subsume it under an all-encompassing interpretation of religion; to command Hussain to abjure the modern painter's, rather than a believer's, adoration of Saraswati.

'Huge Baggy Monster'
Mimetic Theories of the Indian Novel after Rushdie

In the past eighteen years, after the publication of *Midnight's Children* and the rise of the Indian novel in English, Indian fiction in English has not only come to seem central to the idea of Indian literature in the minds of both the popular media and the academic intelligentsia, but has also edged out from everyday consciousness those indigenous languages and their modern traditions that seemed so important a few decades ago, and were so crucial to the evolution of modern Indian identity or identities. Neglected, too, now, is the narrative of how the poets and writers in English who preceded Rushdie (*Midnight's Children* having been erected as a sort of gigantic edifice that all but obstructs the view of what lies behind it) practised their craft when conditions at home and abroad were, in several senses, inimical to the enterprise they were involved in. The two words, 'Indian' and 'English', which sat next to each other so uneasily, their juxtaposition looked upon with as much suspicion from every side as if they were the progeny of warring families (which, in a sense, they were), are now wedded in a marriage that not only seems inevitable but health-giving; what might have been a tragedy has been turned, apparently, into a happy ending with numberless possibilities. In fact, the word 'Indian' is almost only ever used, as a taxonomic term in contemporary literature, in connection with the word 'English'; no one speaks of the Indian novel in Bengali, or Urdu, or Kannada. There is an implication here that only in the English language do Indian writers have the vantage-point, or at least feel the obligation, to articulate that post-colonial totality called 'India' (on the other hand, it sometimes seems that the post-colonial totality called 'India' only exists in the works of Indian English novelists, or in the commentaries they engender). The construction of the post-colonial

Indian English novel, after Rushdie, has, in critical and popular discourse, become inextricably entangled with the idea and construction of 'Indian-ness' and post-coloniality; it is an idea that has taken on new and, in some ways, more prescriptive meanings since the days of the poet A.K. Ram-anujan, the novelist R.K. Narayan, and the memoirist Nirad C. Chaudhuri (to name, at random, three important Indian practitioners of the English language).

The publication in 1981 of *Midnight's Children*, a Nehruvian epic, coincided, oddly, with the beginning of the end of Nehruvian India. Since then, Indian writers in English have become increasingly visible, especially in the English-language media in India, and have become less like God's spies and more like members of the English royal family, involved in trivial curiosity and national prestige, and receiving inordinate amounts of at-tention. In the way Rushdie's work, or an idea of that work, is interpreted and represented perhaps lies a key to the way Indian writing is supposed to be read and produced – Rushdie both being the godhead from which Indian writing in English has reportedly sprung, revivified, and, almost more importantly, a convenient shorthand for that writing. It is probably possible to look individually at some of the assumptions which inform the expectations of publishers, writers and critics, even when they haven't been consciously articulated by them.

The first is the tautological idea that since India is a huge baggy mon-ster, the novels that accommodate it have to be baggy monsters as well. Indeed, different Indian writers in English have taken different routes to the goal of hugeness. Rushie and others have created 'magical', bustling, post-colonial narratives, while Vikram Seth and Rohinton Mistry have an-nexed the nineteenth-century European novel. It is their privilege to do so. But while the large novel might have come to seem typical of the Indian literary enterprise, it is actually not. It contrasts with forms that writers of fiction have chosen in, say, Bengali, where the short story and novella have predominated at least as much as the novel, often in the hands of the major novelists of the first half of the century, such as Bibhutibhushan and Tarashankar Banerjee. The writer and critic Buddhadeva Bose reminds us that Tagore brought the modern short story into Bengal in the late nine-teenth century, some time before it was introduced to England (Kipling is an exception, of course). In a South Indian language such as Kannada, the novella became a seminal form in the hands of a major contemporary, U.R. Anantha Murthy; in their choice of form, these writers hoped to suggest India by ellipsis rather than by all-inclusiveness. Paradoxically, the large, postmodernist Indian English novel, while apparently eschewing realism, pursues a mimesis of form, where the largeness of the book allegorizes the largeness of the country it represents. It is worth remembering that those who write in the languages of India, whether that happens to be English or one of the modern 'vernaculars', do not necessarily write about 'India' or a national narrative (that narrative, anyway, wasn't present in any clear way before Independence), but about cultures and localities that are both situated in, and disperse the idea of, the nation. They write, to take examples from only twentieth-century vernacular traditions, about villages (such as the Bengali village, Nishchindipur, of Bibhutibhushan Banerjee's great modernist novel *Pather Panchali,* published in 1929; later to become Satyajit Ray's first film), or particular cities and places, like, say, the Lucknow or London or Sylhet in Qurratulain Hyder's Urdu stories, or even the Czechoslovakia of Nirmal Verma's Hindi short fiction, or the Africa that Bibhutibhushan wrote about in *Chaander Pahaad (The Moon Mountain),* an Africa he had never been to. None of these fictional landscapes is, thus, necessarily India; yet none of them is situated outside the consciousness of what it means to be Indian; they extend our idea of what 'Indianness' is, while opening that idea to question.

Post-Rushdie, the Indian novel in English has been constructed, in both popular and critical terms, as something distinct from – indeed, as an alternative to – the conventional English novel. Rushdie's writing is not my subject here; the nature of its achievement and legitimacy is a separate issue altogether; it is the construction, after *Midnight's Children,* of a particular idea of both the post-colonial novel and Indian writing in English, where the heterogeneity of the genre is glossed over and where these terms are used as a substitute for a more demanding form of engagement, that is intriguing. Rushdie's style, robustly extroverted, rejecting nuance, delicacy and inwardness for multiplicity and polyphony, and, moreover, the propensity of his imagination towards magic, fairy tales and fantasy, and the apparent non-linearity of his narratives – all these are seen to be emblematic of a non-Western mode of discourse, of apprehension, that is at once contemporaneously post-colonial and anciently, inescapably Indian. Again, although the emphasis on the plural and the multivocal, in this reading, is postmodern, the interpretative aesthetic is surprisingly old-fashioned and mimetic: Indian life is plural, garrulous, rambling, lacking a fixed centre, and the Indian novel must be the same. Delicacy, nuance and irony apparently belong properly to the domain of the English novel and to the rational traditions of the European Enlightenment; and inasmuch as these traditions have been involved with the history of colonialism, nuance and irony must be looked on with suspicion. A cursory glance at the ancient and modern literary traditions of India – one thinks even of translations such as Ramanujan's English renderings of ancient Tamil poetry or

Arvind Krishna Mehrotra's versions of Prakrit love poetry – will confirm
that delicacy and nuance are not the prerogative of the rational, bourgeois
West alone, but are central to, and manifested with great skill and beauty
in, all significant examples of Indian writing. To celebrate Indian writing
simply as overblown, fantastic, lush and non-linear is to risk making it a
figure for the subconscious, and to imply that what is ordinarily called
thinking is alien to Indian tradition – surely an old colonialist prejudice.

A related way of assigning a fundamental Indianness, even non-
Westernness, to the post-colonial Indian novel in English is to place its
'magical' subject matter and its expansive, non-realist narrative mode
in the lineage of epics such as the *Ramayana* and the *Mahabharata*, and
texts like the *Thousand and One Nights*. While there are many differences
between the traditional Indian epic and the post-colonial Indian English
novel, one seems to be of particular importance; the mythic imagination
from which those epics sprang was disturbingly amoral and estranging (I
recall some of the British critics of Peter Brook's *Mahabharata* noting in
wounded tones the Machiavellian, unfathomable nature of the Hindu god
Krishna), and it is through this amorality that the epics reveal to us the
mystery of human nature and the universe. The post-colonial novel, on the
other hand, is frequently rooted in the liberal middle-class conscience and
founded on humanist verities: multiculturalism is good; colonialism and
fundamentalism are bad, etcetera. Further, it often rehearses a national
narrative that every middle-class Indian child has learnt in school and
which every member of the Indian ruling class is defined by: the narrative
about colonialism and independence, and the idea of India as a recognizable totality. William Carlos Williams said of *The Waste Land* that it had
returned poetry to the classroom; and there are those who, when reading
some post-colonial narratives, will feel that they have gone back to their
Indian Certificate of Secondary Education history textbook.

There is yet another way in which the post-colonial Indian novel is
interpreted mimetically: in the proposition that, because the post-colonial,
often diasporic, Indian is a hybrid entity, the language of the post-colonial
too must be hybrid, with a scattering of untranslated Indian words and
phrases and odd sentence constructions. What is perceived to be, or even
constructed as, standard English is seen to be linked to an alien sensibility and to the verbal traditions of colonialism, and perhaps less adequate
to the hybrid, multilingual nature of post-colonial, Indian consciousness.
Hybridity, however, can frequently enter texts in subtly disruptive, rather
than obvious, ways; it need not be worn like national costume. In his
famous story, 'Pierre Menard, Author of the *Quixote*', Jorge Luis Borges,
himself a multilingual, Anglophile Argentinian writer who was preoccu-

pied with the idea of what constituted difference, and with a multiplicity of voices, invents Pierre Menard, a modern French writer who 'did not want to compose another *Quixote* – which is easy – but the *Quixote* itself'. Borges, who was shaped both by English and Spanish literatures, meditates, mischievously, on the nature of translation and artistic creation, and the subtle ways in which a hybrid, multilingual sensibility relates itself to language. Menard is French; but he does not attempt to appropriate Cervantes's language, nor Gallicize it; instead, he creates the *Quixote* by producing it verbatim. Let me quote two passages by other writers. The first is from a biography:

> It was a curious town with one long main street running through it, called Cavalierstrasse. The street was very long and had pavements on both sides. But so little traffic passed over it that it had to be weeded from time to time to get rid of the grass which came up through the chinks of the stones. The houses generally had only one storey, and some of them were mere cottages. Almost every house had a mirror fastened outside the main window, like the driving mirrors of today, so that the inmates could get notice of an approaching visitor.

The second is from an autobiographical novel:

> Rabbits came out to play on the snow, or to feed. A mother rabbit, hunched, with three or four of her young. They were a different dirty colour on the snow. And this picture of rabbits, or more particularly their new colour, calls up or creates the other details of the winter's day: the late-afternoon snow-light; the strange, empty houses around the lawn becoming white and distinct and important.

The first passage offers a description of a nineteenth-century German town, and is from Nirad C. Chaudhuri's life of Max Mueller, *Scholar Extraordinary*, the second is a description of Wiltshire from V.S. Naipaul's novel *The Enigma of Arrival*. Both passages could have been written by an English writer, in which case they would have been elegant and unremarkable; their peculiar meaning, however, operates in the fact that they are nevertheless the products of hybrid sensibilities and histories, sensibilities belonging in one case to an Indian writer, and in the other to a writer of Indian origin; and these sensibilities and histories are not present in the writing in any obvious way, but are immanent in it. These writers, like Menard, create a new language by seemingly reproducing the old (apparently Chaudhuri does this, in effect, literally, and, in a Menard-like move, takes the details of his description almost verbatim from Mueller), a language of altered meanings in which hybridity and post-coloniality reside like the colour of snow and the rabbits in Naipaul's passage, on the border of absence and recognition.[1]

One of the subtlest ways, indeed, in which the multilingual imagination enters an Indian text has to do with the use of English words – not transmuted or 'appropriated and subverted for the post-colonial's own ends', as the current dogma has it, but, estrangingly, in their ordinary and standard forms; yet this is a practice whose import has been insufficiently acknowledged or studied. The peculiar excitement of the poetry that Ramanujan, Arvind Mehrotra or Dom Moraes (to take only three examples) wrote in the 1960s and 1970s derived not so much from their, to use Rushdie's word, 'chutnification' of the language, but, in part, from the way they used ordinary English words like 'door', 'window', 'bus', 'doctor' 'dentist', 'station', to suggest a way of life. This was, and continues to be, more challenging than it may first appear; as a young reader, I remember being slightly repelled by the India of post offices and railway compartments I found in these poems; for I didn't think the India I lived in a fit subject for poetry. The poets I have mentioned appeared to make no overt attempts to 'appropriate' or 'subvert' the language, because the English language was already theirs, linked not so much to the colonizer as to their sense of self and history; these poets' use of language had less to do with the colonizer than with modern Indians' exploration, and rewriting, of themselves.

English words had entered Indian languages, their original shapes and meaning intact; and when Satyajit Ray, in his film *Kanchenjunga*, had his characters switch constantly between Bengali and English, he was neither, as his first American viewers concluded, depicting a set of deracinated Indians, nor celebrating as a curiosity Indian 'hybridity', but speaking directly to a middle-class Bengali audience in a language they already understood, a language of different linguistic, cultural and emotional registers. Buddhadeva Bose notes the excitement he felt in the 1940s on encountering the English word 'ball' in a poem by the great Bengali poet Jibanananda Das; not because it illustrated some notion of hybridity still decades from coming into fashion, but because Das's use of the word revealed some ordinary, inevitable, but resonant constituent in the intellectual and emotional texture of modern Bengali life that was then in the process of being articulated. Bose's recording of his excitement is not unlike Larkin's contentious and characteristically self-confident comment on Auden in an essay that appeared in 1960: 'He was, of course, the first "modern" poet, in that he could employ modern properties unselfconsciously ("A solitary truck, the last/ Of shunting in the Autumn") ...' The 'modern' was not only an era, but an argument for a language, and poets everywhere had set about defining it, and discovering the ways in which they were defined by it.

Fredric Jameson has called the 'national allegory' the most characteristic form of the post-colonial novel, and has deemed pastiche the most
characteristic literary form of postmodernism. This leads us to the way in
which the construction of the post-colonial Indian novel in English – with
its features of hybridity, national narrative, parody and pastiche – is connected to the movements and changes in the history of the West itself,
especially in the late twentieth century, and to the possible notion that,
in the Indian English novel, the West had found a large trope for its own
historical preoccupations at least as much as it has discovered in itself a
genuine curiosity for, and engagement with, Indian history and writing.
From the 1970s onwards, and, in Britain, from the early 1980s – which was
also, as it happens, the time of the publication of *Midnight's Children* and
the rise of the new Indian English novel – the West has seen a decisive and
sometimes invigorating assault on what Derrida has called 'the metaphysics
of presence in the history of Western thought', in the form of Continental
philosophy and American and European cultural movements; specifically,
post-structuralism, postmodernism, and post-coloniality, the latter a discourse created mainly by migrant intellectuals. The impulse behind these
schools and movements, if they can be called such, has been a sometimes
necessary overturning of old certainties and hierarchies; the blurring of
the line dividing 'high' from 'popular' culture; the rejection of authenticity in favour of 'difference' and hybridity; the preference, after Bakhtin, of
the parodic over the original; in cultural studies, after Foucault and Said,
the shift towards historical discourse and away from the literary; and the
deconstruction of the idea of the author. Some of the reasons for this are
clear and are related to Western history. Colonialism, for instance, has
been based on a misrepresentation of the culturally different, as Said has
shown, and the politics of exclusion and misrepresentation are involved
in the creation of canons, which are formed by leaving out the 'different'.
Any kind of 'authenticity', whether canonical, cultural, or textual, is thus in
question. And this has to do not so much with the history of countries like
India, where, during the nineteenth and twentieth centuries, a sense of the
authentic was indispensable to the sense of self and the past, and where it
has also been imbricated with a sense of hybridity and evolving plurality
that has characterized its cultures for centuries, but with Western history,
where 'authenticity', or 'purity', and 'hybridity' have not only existed, since
the nineteenth century (if not since the Enlightenment), in mutually exclusive intellectual and cultural compartments, but where, more recently,
after Auschwitz, 'authenticity' is associated with extreme right-wing politics and the destructive propensities of masculine fantasy. At this point in
Western history, hybridity is morally preferable to the authentic, quota-

tion or discourse to 'presence', and post-colonial culture, in particular, the post-colonial novel, becomes a trope for an ideal hybridity by which the West celebrates not so much Indianness, whatever that infinitely complex thing is, but its own historical quest, its reinterpretation of itself.

When Derrida and the post-structuralists, taking as their forebears those philosopher-subversives, Nietzsche, Marx and Freud, began their attack on the relationship of the word to the world, of the text to 'presence', they were perceived as raising a critique of Western logocentric thought and creating a space for marginalized, even non-Western, cultures and voices. Ironically, in one respect this critique belongs to mainstream Western tradition, and goes back to its source: Plato. In a chapter in the *Republic*, Socrates reveals two orders of reality to his disciples; one, the reality of the phenomenal world, in which exist concrete objects like, say, a table, and the other the world of ideal form, in which the idea of the table exists immutably and timelessly. The idea of the table, Socrates suggests, is truer than the actual table. But, Socrates goes on to say sardonically, there is another, third table distinct from either of these; and when his befuddled disciple inquires what this is, Socrates furnishes a rather beautiful Protean description of the poet, and says that the third table exists in the work of the poet, and that the poet, incredibly, claims it is as real as the other two. Plato, here, is Derridean; any claim that the creative text or language makes to magically represent the world or capture reality is looked on with suspicion. Derrida's and Plato's quarrel concerns the ideal form, which Plato considers the only truth, while Derrida would see it as a logocentric construct or a 'transcendental signified'; however, they are both in agreement about the duplicity of the poet's claim that he can somehow represent, and in doing so convey, reality, or 'presence'. This is worth remembering whenever we think that realist art is a profound constituent of the Western tradition, and that fantasy is somehow non-Western. Realism – the relationship that modes of representation have to the seasons, human life and the universe – has been a fundamental and unquestioned component of Indian art, from classical dance to the epics of Valmiki and Vyasa, the court poetry of Kalidasa, and the modern lyrics of Tagore; on the other hand, in Western culture, realist art, with its special claim to renovate our perception of the world, has always resided somewhat uneasily at the centre, repeatedly called on, like an immigrant, to justify the legitimacy of its existence.

The post-structuralist philosophers and postmodernist writers taught us to be playful and at the same time to disbelieve in the real with the ferocity and scepticism with which the atheists and materialists of old disbelieved in God. In the global, postmodern world, we live in the materialism of the sign. The old command economies pretended to cater to the wants of the needy; in the free-market economy the needy remain, an intractable and unaddressed signified, while money generates itself around the signifier, the idea of wealth and desire; wealth does not feed the poor, but itself. In a world of representations, what happens to the practices of reading and publishing? One hears, in relation to the novel, especially the Indian novel in English, that commerce and art have come together, that literary works of quality are becoming commercial successes. Can this be true? It doesn't really mater. In a culture of signification, the issue of what a 'real' masterpiece is, or whether such a thing can even exist, is an irrelevance; what matters is the marketing and consumption, after each successful publicity campaign and the awarding of each prize, of the signifier, the idea of the masterpiece, the idea of the Indian novel in English. What Indian fiction is, what the traditions and histories and languages are from which this real and heterogeneous entity emerged, is a signified that, paradoxically, almost has no presence.

Two Giant Brothers
Tagore's Revisionist 'Orient'

Edward Said's *Orientalism*, published in 1978, gave intellectuals and writers (themselves, like Said, often migrants) from once-colonized nations a language that liberated and shackled in almost equal measure. The liberations that Said's critical perspective provided, which gave both Europeans and non-Europeans a shrewder and more unillusioned sense of the subterranean ways in which power operated through the cultures of Empire, are now so familiar that we might make the mistake of taking them for granted: which would be foolish, as Eurocentrism is alive and well, and takes new and unexpected forms with every political epoch. Besides, as Said himself knew, the force of his critique has diminished and ossified over the years into professional interests and job profiles; this was something he was clearly troubled by.

The limitations of Said's seminal study have to do with the idea it's given us about how the post-colonial might engage with the colonizer's (that is, European, or Western) culture, and with history; and, explicitly, how the European engages with non-European antiquity. And so we're left with a somewhat monochromatic type where both the post-colonial and the European are concerned: a type whose relationship to European or Oriental culture, as may be the case, is defined almost exclusively by questions of power and appropriation, and whose own culture and past are at once static and strangely blurred. *Orientalism*, at least at first glance, doesn't seem to tell us or explain where its author, in all his many-sidedness, comes from – Western metropolitan intellectual; radical political activist; post-colonial critic; champion of canonical European literature; classical pianist. What is it about the long histories of colonization and modernity that produced these intriguingly separate, even contrary, selves in Said? *Orientalism*, at least the way we read it now, doesn't seem to give us an explanation; and for Marxist critics like Aijaz Ahmed, the contradictions are a sign of bad faith.

Yet it's this book that contains a celebration of the author of *La Ren-aissance Orientale*, Raymond Schwab, and gives us, in Schwab, an outline of another idea of, and way of responding to, the Orient, and, by exten-sion, to any culture other than one's own. Schwab, Said notes, himself looks back to another figure while describing the startling penetration of European culture by the Orient, or their interpenetration by one another: the figure is Abraham-Hyacinthe Anquetil-Duperron (1731–1805), 'an ec-centric theoretician of egalitarianism, a man who managed in his head to reconcile Jansenism with orthodox Catholicism and Brahmanism', and who, journeying to Asia, 'travelled as far east as Surat' in India, 'there to find a cache of Avestan texts, there also to complete his translation of the *Avesta*'. Here, Said quotes Schwab on what the latter saw to be Anquetil-Duperron's legacy; it is one of the most affirmative and exuberant passages on cultural contact ever written, though its rhetoric needs to be distin-guished somewhat from declamations on hybridity that are common to-day:

> In 1759, Anquetil finished his translation of the *Avesta* at Surat; in 1786 that of the *Upanishads* in Paris – he had dug a channel between the hemispheres of human genius, correcting and expanding the old humanism of the Mediterranean basin … Before him, one looked for information about the remote past of our planet exclusively among the great Latin, Greek, Jewish, and Arabic writers … A universe in writing was unavailable, but scarcely anyone seemed to suspect the immensity of those unknown lands. The realisation began with his translation of the *Avesta*, and reached dizzying heights owing to the exploration in Central Asia of the languages that multiplied after Babel. Into our schools … he interjected a vision of innumerable civilisations from ages past, of an infinity of literatures …

According to Said, the fact that certain Europeans opened them-selves, in the late eighteenth and the nineteenth centuries, to the cultural store of the Orient resulted, in those individuals, in a 'new, triumphant eclecticism'. Among the figures he mentions are, of course, Anquetil-Dup-erron, and Sir William Jones, the founder of Indology, whose researches on the Orient, Hinduism, and the Sanskrit language include translations from – and, in effect, a recovery of – the great fourth-century Sanskrit poet Kalidasa. Yet Said is hard on the latter – 'Whereas Anquetil opened large vistas, Jones closed them down, codifying, tabulating, comparing' – as if Jones somehow embodied more of the colonial project and less of the 'tri-umphant eclecticism' than Anquetuil-Duperron did. This is borne out, for Said, by Jones's personal itinerary, and, for us, by the way Said describes it: 'In due course he was appointed to "an honourable and profitable place in the Indies", and immediately upon his arrival there to take up a post with the East India Company began his course of personal study that was to gather in, to rope off, to domesticate the Orient and thereby to turn it into a province of European learning.'

This reservation about Jones or what he represents – Jones as a symbol of nineteenth-century European scholarship's 'domestication' of the Orient – has been echoed by others. The historian, Dipesh Chakrabarty, says something similar while enquiring into why he finds it possible to engage in a form of serious intellectual commerce with European philosophers, but not with the many Indian ones going back to antiquity: 'Sad though it is, one result of European colonial rule in South Asia is that the intellectual traditions once unbroken and alive in Sanskrit or Persian or Arabic are now only matters of historical research for most – perhaps all – modern social scientists in the region.' But were intellectual traditions in South Asia 'once unbroken and alive' – 'once' referring to the hazy and golden period before colonization? This speculation is all the more surprising because it comes only a few sentences after Chakrabarty admits, pertinently, that the idea of an 'unbroken' European intellectual tradition going back to the Greeks is a relatively recent construct. The idea of an unbroken Indian tradition is itself probably an Orientalist invention, and Jones one of its early architects.

The 'Orient' itself comes into being in the early period of colonialism, and with Orientalist scholarship, as it never had before; and one of the earliest writers to perceive its great cultural, emotional, philosophical, and political potential is Tagore. Certainly, a hundred years prior to Tagore (and to Jones and his researches), no poet in Bengal beheld the Orient and its unbroken past as a foundation, a point of origin, and a parameter for the self and for creativity; there is no 'Orient', or 'East', for the medieval poets Chandidas, Vidyapati, or Jayadeva, as there is, so profoundly, for Tagore. Nor would it have occurred to Chandidas to locate himself in history, and to claim and create pan-Indian lineages with certain Indian poets and texts, with Kalidasa or the *Upanishads*, as Tagore does. And, for Chandidas, naturally, there is no Europe; for Europe was born, for the Indian, at about the time the Orient was – twins, though not identical ones, that had, in the Indian's mind, a momentous and painfully coeval birth. The researches of the likes of Anquetil-Duperron and even Jones brought to certain Europeans a 'new, triumphant eclecticism', says Said; but that eclecticism had a relatively brief legacy in the West: by the early twentieth century, it had narrowed itself to an almost exclusively European definition, so that words like 'cosmopolitan' were more or less interchangeable with 'European'. Said doesn't mention – maybe it doesn't occur to him – that the true and most significant inheritors of Anquetil-Duperron's 'triumphant eclecticism' weren't Europeans, but Orientals; that it was they who took fullest intellectual and artistic advantage not only of the advent of Europe in their consciousness, as they did, but of the fact of the 'Orient', the 'correction' and 'expansion' of 'the old humanism of the Mediterranean basin'. It's in this context that we must situate the importance of Tagore, born roughly eighty years after Anquetil-Duperron's translation of the *Upanishads*, in 1861; and, indeed, that of Said, as one of the latest in that line of Orientals appropriating and complicating Anquetil-Duperron's inheritance.

'A nineteenth-century Orientalist was therefore either a scholar... or a gifted enthusiast ... or both,' says Said, after pointing out that 'there was a virtual epidemic of Orientalia affecting every major poet, essayist, and philosopher of the period... this is a later transposition eastwards of a similar enthusiasm in Europe for Greek and Latin antiquity during the High Renaissance.' But the resemblance with the Renaissance ends there. The Orient, in Europe, continued to remain the province of arcane scholars and gifted enthusiasts; in the realm of culture, it retained, and still does, the ethos of 'Orientalia'. Unlike Greek and Latin antiquity, which becomes an indispensable resource and even a romantic myth for modernism, the Orient, with a handful of exceptions, such as the final lines of *The Waste Land*, is never inserted into modernist self-consciousness. Its domain becomes, in Europe, largely the domain of popular culture, of kitsch and the exotic. Even in nineteenth-century Indian art, the Orient occupies the soft, hazy space of 'Orientalia' in popular artists like Ravi Varma; indeed, the Oriental paintings – the faux Mughal miniatures – of Tagore's nephew Abanindranath, often seen to be the father of modern Indian painting, have their life-blood, partly, in the kitschy, the popular. This is not to make a value judgement about one sort of artist, or art, and another, but to try to map the moment and to be as true as possible to its impetus. It would have been easy enough for Tagore to turn, as a poet and writer, to the Orient as a magical and occult resource, as Yeats did, in some of his writings, with Ireland. Instead, radically, he inscribed it, in his vast oeuvre, into the trajectory of humanism and the 'high' modern; Easternness, in his work, is no longer incompatible with individualism, with the self-consciousness about the powers and limits of language, or the awareness of the transformative role of the secular artist. In fashioning these paradigms, modes of consciousness, and roles for himself, Tagore seems to be addressing, instructing, and even rebutting not a Brahmin, but a bourgeois, orthodoxy in Calcutta; and, unprecedentedly, conflating his identity as an Oriental and his vocation as a secular artist in doing so.

By the time Tagore was born in 1861, the first wave of Orientalist enthusiasm and the most significant phase of Orientalist scholarship were over. In 1813, Byron had advised Thomas Moore, 'Stick to the East ... it [is] the only poetical policy.' The 'policy' had impelled him, Southey, and Moore to write about the *gul-e-bulbul* (the stock Persian metaphor for the nightingale in the garden), and probably also stimulated Edward Fitzgerald's 'translation' of the *Rubaiyyat* of Omar Khayam. By the second half of the nineteenth century, the excitement, despite the appearance of Max Mueller, had largely passed. (T.S. Eliot's misgivings about Fitzgerald's poem, despite his not being immune to its appeal, is representative of modernism's distrust of 'Orientalia'. How Tagore escaped, albeit briefly, this distrust, with the help of Pound, of all people, isn't easy to understand, and I'll return to it later.)

In 1879, 'Oriental' poetry received a final fillip with the publication of *Light of Asia*, Edwin Arnold's life of the Buddha in narrative verse. As early as 1817, Thomas Moore had received the unheard-of sum of 3000 guineas as an advance for his poem *Lalla Rookh*; now, once more, *Light of Asia* became an immense success on both sides of the Atlantic, and was reprinted eighty times. When Matthew Arnold visited America, he found he was confused by many with Edwin. Of course, the notion of 'high seriousness' that Matthew Arnold had himself formulated would prevail upon the culture of the time, guaranteeing that his reputation would outlast the frenetic but essentially light efflorescence of the 'Oriental' poem; here, too, in the contrast between the two Arnolds, we're reminded that 'seriousness' in literature remained a European or Anglo-Saxon province, and the 'Oriental' was marked by lightness, colour, and momentary success. The matter of success in the marketplace (one of the first things we associate with a certain kind of Indian writing today) and its relationship to the Orient has a lineage, then, stretching back to the early nineteenth century.

The example of the Tagore family shows us that, in Calcutta itself, the creation of a space for culture had everything to do with a humanistic embracing of 'high seriousness', and a turning away from commerce and material reward: the same turn that marks the emergence of modernism in the bourgeois cultures of Europe. Tagore's grandfather, 'Prince' Dwarkanath, was a man who made his fortune out of the opportunity the colonial moment presented him with, as a middleman for the Company in Calcutta. He travelled to London and threw lavish parties; he died with his financial affairs in disarray. The disarray – not to speak of the vast estates – was inherited by his son Debendranath, who paid off his father's debts and made his family financially secure again. But the turn away from commerce and entrepreneurship (if not from inherited land) that would come to characterize middle-class or *bhadralok* Bengali culture already marks Debendranath, who, besides being a man of property, became a philosopher-mystic – 'maharshi' or 'maha rishi', the 'great sage'. What facilitated Debendranath's increasing philosophical leanings was his discovery of the *Upanishads* – a text that his father's friend, the scholar, reformer, and thinker Rammohun Roy had translated into English in the early nineteenth century, and which Anquetil-Duperron, too, had brought to the world's attention in the eighteenth century in his French translation. The *Upanishads*, then, became, for both Roy and Debendranath Tagore, a prism through which they recovered not only their own spiritual inheritance, but the lineage of a humanism to be found outside the Mediterranean basin.

The break with commerce that Debendranath represented was deepened emphatically and with finality in the next generation, especially by two of his fourteen children: Jyotirindranath, his fifth son, and Rabindranath, the youngest. (Tagore's biographers, Krishna Dutta and Andrew Robinson, have noted perceptively that, although the poet speaks constantly of his father in his memoirs and elsewhere, he elides the subject of his grandfather Dwarkanath.) Jyotirindranath, with his experimentations in theatre, literature, and especially musical composition (in the 1870s and 1880s he was composing Bengali songs on the piano), was a great influence on Rabindranath, as was Jyotirindranath's young wife, with whom he had an ambiguous relationship: part fraternal, part romantic, the sort of semi-articulate bond that animates many of his fictions and especially his songs, a bond that almost thrives on the permanent impossibility of consummation –

> I could speak to her on a day like this,
> on a day when it rains as heavily.
> You can open your heart on a day like this –
> when you hear the clouds as the rain pours down
> in gloom unbroken by light.
>
> Those words won't be heard by anyone else;
> there's not a soul around.
> Just us, face to face, in each other's sorrow
> sorrowing, as water streams without interruption;
> it's as if there's no one else in the world.
> (my translation)

These, the first two verses of a song, echo, with their promise of secrecy and revelation, what Tagore wrote to Kadambari in the concluding piece in a collection of jottings and musings published not long before her death:

I offer something more with these thoughts, which only you will notice. Do you remember that moment by the banks of the Ganga? That silent dark? Those wanderings in imagined worlds? Those deep discussions in low, serious voices? The two of us sitting silently, saying nothing? That breeze at sunrise, that evening shadow! And, once, those rain-bearing clouds, Sravan's downpour, the songs of Vidyapati? ... I have concealed a handful of contentment and grief in these thoughts; open these pages once in a while and look upon them with affection, no one but you will be able to see what's in them! The message inscribed into these words is – there's one writing that you and I shall read. And there's another writing for everyone else.

These three – Jyotirindranath, Kadambari, and Rabindranath – formed, along with certain gifted members of a subsequent generation, the core of what was probably India's first 'artistic' family: 'artistic' in the sense of self-consciously pursuing the arts as a vocation, with a quasi-religious Victorian fervour, while moving away from, as self-consciously, the pre-ordained responsibilities defined by caste, class, property, and even gender. This salon – at once embarrassing, silly, and deeply creative and original – and Tagore's part in it were permanently shadowed by Kadambari's suicide in 1884. The reasons for it are unclear; though speculations range from her attachment to Rabindranath, who was married a few months before she took her life by consuming opium, to her husband Jyotirindranath's flirtation, possibly liaison, with an actress he came into contact with during his forays into theatre, and whose letters Kadambari discovered in his pocket; again, a scene retold in the novel *Chokher Bali*.

Part of the immediate legacy bestowed on Tagore by his father Debendranath was that of the Brahmo Samaj, the reformist sect within Hinduism founded by Rammohun Roy. The sect developed a curious but compelling mixture of protestant high-mindedness and Hindu metaphysics; its prayers and meetings were conducted in a 'church'; its central text was the *Upanishads*. In rejecting the idolatrous practices and the deities of ordinary Hinduism and replacing them with the *niraakar* (formless) One of the *Upanishads*, Brahmoism supplied Tagore not so much with a religion – he was never entirely convinced by, or interested in, its claims to being one – as an aesthetic. It was an aesthetic that corresponds closely with the Flaubertian dictum that would define a substantial part of the modernist enterprise: 'The author, like God in the universe, is everywhere present but nowhere visible in his works.' This is a notion of God, and his relationship to creation, that goes to the heart of Brahmoism's vision of the world. Indeed, you have to wonder if Flaubert had been reading Anquetil-Duperron, and had aestheticized an Upanishadic idea. Certainly, Tagore *did* perform that aestheticization in his own work, introducing to Bengali literature a new sort of self-reflexivity as he did so; seldom referring to God in his writings, but speaking of the 'kabi' or 'poet' while referring to both author and divinity, and punning on the word 'rachana', or 'composition', to mean both text and creation.

Tagore's education was an unusual one. Admitted to the Normal School at a 'tender age', he was deeply unhappy there, and was mainly educated at home by tutors. His least favourite lesson was English, and he pokes fun at the language in *Jiban Smriti*, his memoirs: 'Providence, out of pity of mankind, has instilled a soporific charm into all tedious things. No sooner did our English lessons begin than our heads began to nod.' Later, in 1878, when his first book of songs appeared, he would go to England to study law, attend lectures for a few months at University College London, travel through the country and observe English culture (his remarks on Western music are particularly interesting) with a mixture of empathy and resistance, and finally return to Calcutta in 1880, without a degree. Tagore, like Kipling, his younger contemporary, was secretly traumatized by what Foucault called the 'disciplinarian' society: the cluster of institutions comprising schools, universities, hospitals, prisons. The trauma, strangely, ended up making Kipling an official spokesman for the disciplinarian society; but Tagore always remained ill-at-ease in it. Not just his opposition to imperial England, but his suspicion of nationalism and the nation-state seem to derive from it; as does his fanciful experiment in a more open and relaxed form of learning in a place he wistfully chose to name 'Shantiniketan'. From childhood onward, Tagore had been looking out of windows and partitions; the word '*khancha*', or 'cage', recurs in the songs and poems, as do the possibilities and avenues of egress that victims of a disciplinarian society fantasize about – '*batayan*' or window; '*kholo dwar*', the exhortation to open doors; the famous speculation at the end of a poem about the flight of wild geese, '*hethha noi, hethha noi, onno kothhay*', 'not here, not here, but elsewhere'.

When Tagore published his first book of songs at the age of 16, he was praised by the foremost writer of the time, Bankimchandra Chatterjee. But his relationship with Bengali literary culture was no means easy. Although he was probably Bengal's foremost poet by the end of the nineteenth century, he had several vociferous detractors (among them contemporaries like the poet D.L. Roy), whose comments on his work ranged from the snidely witty to the piously outraged. Even after the Nobel Prize, which he got in 1913, the passages in which Tagore had begun to write a new colloquial Bengali prose were included by Calcutta University in the MA paper in Bengali as specimens to be rendered by examinees into 'chaste Bengali'. The Nobel itself was the climax of a series of meetings and accidents. On board a ship to England in 1912, Tagore had completed his translations of the metrically strict but delicately agile Bengali songs of his *Gitanjali* into loose English prose-poems with a hint of Biblical sonority: 'The pages of a small exercise-book came gradually to be filled, and with it in my pocket I boarded the ship.' Once in London, Tagore lost the attaché case in which he was carrying the manuscripts on the Underground, but rediscovered it in the Lost Property Office: a tribute to British civic sense, and possibly a reminder that the case contained nothing that would be of use to anyone. He gave the translations to the painter William Rothenstein, a friend of his nephew Abanindranath's, who had met Tagore in the winter of 1910–11 in the house in Jorasanko, Calcutta. Rothenstein had then been intrigued by both Tagore's presence and his silence during conversations; not knowing of his reputation as a writer, his curiosity grew when he happened to read a story by Tagore in Calcutta's *Modern Review*. Rothenstein was astonished and immensely moved by the translations in the *Gitanjali* (the English *Gitanjali* doesn't quite correspond to its Bengali counterpart, but also contains a selection from two other books of songs); he showed them to Yeats. The Irish poet seems to have responded to them as business executives are reported to respond to Paul Coelho: 'I have carried the manuscript of these translations about with me for days, reading it in railway trains, or on the top of omnibuses and in restaurants, and I have often had to close it lest some stranger would see how much it moved me.'

Why Tagore translated the songs into a language he'd once found so tedious, and which he used with a degree of insecurity ('That I cannot write English is such a patent fact that I never had even the vanity to feel ashamed of it,' he confessed to his niece Indira), is mysterious. Also mysterious is how they excited and even instructed, albeit for a relatively short while, the most exacting figures of literary London, Ezra Pound included. The English *Gitanjali* is a shadowy approximation of the marvellous original; if it continues to be of interest, it's for cultural and even psychological, not literary, reasons – and the same is true, as it happens, of the 'Orient'. The writers who'd once promoted Tagore went off him not long after he got the Nobel in 1913; in 1917, Pound wrote in a letter: 'Tagore got the Nobel Prize because, after the cleverest boom of our times, after the fiat of the omnipotent literati of distinction, he lapsed into religion and was boomed by the pious non-conformists.' The word 'boom' is striking; the economist Amartya Sen, in his recent book *The Argumentative Indian*, seems to pick up that word and both recall and refute Pound when, speaking of Tagore's reputation, he places it within the logic of capital and the free market by saying it was a victim of the 'boom and bust' cycle that most Oriental enthusiasms constitute in the West. Tagore's star waned irrevocably in the

Occident; or at least the Oriental Tagore's did – the humanist Tagore's star had never appeared in that firmament.

The Oxford Tagore Translations, whose general editor is Sukanta Chaudhuri, gives us pause, and a renewed opportunity to take stock of the achievement and its historical moment. The series gives us not only an overview of the vast range of the work – there are separate volumes of poetry, critical essays, writings for children, short stories, and one novel (that leaves the paintings and plays) – but is a fresh attempt to assuage the anxiety that Tagore has seldom been well translated, least of all by himself, and to allay the fear that he cannot be. But the nature of the 'bad' Tagore translation has not only to do with insufficient fidelity to the original, or inadequate mastery of the target language; it's do with a naïve and specious spirituality or Easternness in the English version that's present in the original in complex and oblique ways. The 'bad' translations, including Tagore's own, insert Tagore into 'Orientalia'. The Oxford Tagore Translations, then, is itself a late instance of the sort of humanist project that Tagore, in large measure, began in Bengal in the late nineteenth century; his emphatic rejection of Orientalia in Bengali, despite his slipping dangerously close to it in English; his situating of the Oriental in the human and universal, and vice versa. The Oxford Tagore series is an attempt to capture and be true to this process; of the way in which Easternness, in Tagore's oeuvre (and, implicitly, in those of us – his editors, translators, readers – for whom Tagore is a formative inheritance), becomes so integrally a part of the narrative of the human: till then largely the domain of the West. That the editors and translators don't always seem fully conscious of the process they embody reminds us how quickly and deeply that conflation of the Oriental with the universal was internalized amongst Indian moderns, while its features remain only sketchily delineated in critical language.

How, in creating his oeuvre and opening up the possibilities of a new tradition – a modern literature in India – did Tagore position himself as a modern? His view of himself, expressed in and across his essays, is that he is an Oriental, bringing to bear upon the modern world the special insight of the Oriental; that he is a Bengali, having recourse to the emotional terrain of Bengal; and that, as a poet, he is a 'universal' human being, with access to a humanity that is deeper than civilizational borders, or conflicts, or even the fact of colonization. Each one of these personae (for the want of a better word) is assumed by Tagore at different points of time, and developed and pursued according to the appropriateness of the moment or the argument, without any sense of self-contradiction or confusion or embarrassment. By European modernism itself, represented to him mainly by the early T.S. Eliot and his urban despair in poems such as 'Preludes', he was deeply distressed, but nevertheless studied it dutifully, if balefully. Here he positioned himself as an Oriental who, implicitly, brought a far more profound response to life than Eliot's shallow (as Tagore saw it) urban angst. Tagore's rejection of Eliot and the decaying industrialized city of modernism led younger poets and admirers like Buddhadeva Bose (who had a long, eloquent debate with him on the subject not long before his death in 1941) to classify Tagore as probably something of a late romantic – as someone not quite modern. It's an impression that persists even today; as if a rejection of modernity as subject matter – tenement housing, electric lights, offices, scenes of urban dereliction – were itself an infallible sign of a distance from modernism; as if the fact that Tagore claimed Indian antiquity as a great part of his intellectual inheritance, and invoked nature repeatedly in songs and poems, marked him simply and uncomplicatedly as a Romantic.

In listening to these criticisms, Tagore was exceptionally patient; and yet, while officially stating his reservations about the modernists and about Eliot (with the exception of 'Journey of the Magi', which he was greatly moved by), and his disagreements with Bose, he was also studying and taking cues from them. Tagore was an astonishingly canny and gifted learner; and the topoi and characteristics of much of his work of his middle and late periods – the experiments in fragmentary and free verse; the appearance of the lower-middle-class city in a poems like 'Banshi' or 'Flute' (translated in this series by the novelist Sunetra Gupta, who also gives us some very striking renditions of some of the prose poems); the unfinished and provisional quality of much of the late poems and especially the paintings – are partly the irresolvable marks of what Edward Said called 'late style', and partly a working out of Tagore's problematic relationship with stimuli he felt compelled to reject, and yet couldn't ignore. Very few modern poets, except Yeats, have aged as intriguingly as Tagore; very few, in age, continued to be such gifted, if often recalcitrant students, while appearing to the world as a master.

Yet it would be a mistake to impose a dichotomy on Tagore's work, between the modern, the political, the 'critical', on the one hand, and the Romantic, the ahistorical, the organic on the other, as two of the most intelligent critics of Bengali culture, Buddhadeva Bose in the Forties, and, more recently, Dipesh Chakrabarty have done. It's a dichotomy that Tagore seems to invite and to confirm in his own pronouncements, but which his work dismantles profoundly. For Bose, and others after him, Tagore's turning away from the crises of modernity – urban squalor, man's alienation from the industrialized landscape – distinguishes him decisively from the modernists. Bose's idea of the modern, as of Bengali critics after him who've written about Tagore and modernity, seems to have its source in Eliot's essay on Baudelaire. Tagore's late poem 'Banshi', about a clerk (modernism's 'little man') who lives in a squalid tenement in Calcutta, is seen, then, to be an attempt by the poet to come to terms with the Baudelarian inheritance and milieu of modernism. But this is to identify modernism by theme alone, and ignore the radical revisions in forms of perception that it constitutes. Two of the fundamental preoccupations of the modernist imagination, the moment in time as a means of accessing the transformed present, and the image, which can't be entirely broken down or reduced, are both integral to Tagorean poetics and his view of the world – the moment, in his work, is 'kshan', and the image 'chhabi', or 'picture', and they recur in his poems, especially in his songs, in an infinity of contexts. 'Banshi', as it happens, is a Romantic poem about modernity; but the so-called romantic songs about the weather, the beloved, and nature, are replete with the modernist's fragmentary apprehension of the real, and of the irreducible image.

Chakrabarty, in an essay on Tagore, distinguishes the poet's 'critical eye', which he finds in his stories, and which, for Chakrabarty, negotiates history and society, from the sensibility, or gaze, found in the poetry, which he describes as the 'adoring eye': romantic, transcendent, bucolic. A 'division of labour' is at work here, and this is how Chakrabarty puts it:

> At the same time … as he employed his prosaic writings to document social problems, Tagore put his poetic compositions (not always in verse), and songs to a completely different use. These created and deployed images of the same category – the Bengali village – but this time as a land of arcadian and pastoral beauty overflowing with the sentiments that defined what Tagore would increasingly – from the 1880s on – call 'the Bengali heart'.

This is true; and yet, to get a fuller sense of the impact nature had on Tagore, and the one it has on us through his writing, we have to take into account the long and intriguing itinerary it had in his intellectual development. In fact, Tagore's natural world, in the songs and poems, has little of the finished repose of arcadia, but is beset by continual physical agitation, either subtle – tremors, tricks of light – or violent and Shelleyan, as in the famous poem about the flight of the wild geese in the collection *Balaka*. But the conception of nature Tagore theorized in his essays all his mature life *is* arcadian, and that arcadian conception is not incompatible with Tagore's politics, but is actually indispensable to it. That arcadia is India, or ancient India, and its source and mediator is Kalidasa. That notional arcadia has a deceptive tranquillity; for Tagore, nature is as much a political metaphor, an instrument for national contestation, as it is for

John Clare and Ted Hughes. Critics like Tom Paulin and Mina Gorji have drawn our attention to the ways in which nature becomes a metaphor for an embattled 'Englishness' in Clare and Hughes; the unfinished 'naturalness' of nature is conflated with the 'rude' qualities of Northern speech or English dialect, and set, implicitly, against the refined and false graces of Southern England, and of the court and the city. So, as Paulin points out, the thistles in Hughes's poem of the same name become 'a grasped fistful/ Of splintered weapons and Icelandic frost thrust up/ From the underground stain of a decayed Viking.' The thistles, in the poem, enact the contestation over what Englishness, and English speech, constitute: 'They are like … the gutturals of dialect'; mown down, their 'sons appear, / Stiff with weapons, fighting back over the same ground'.

Tagore's deployment of nature in his politics and aesthetics is as ideological as Hughes's, and has equally to do with nationality; but it moves in the opposite direction, critiquing imperialism while overturning the verities that we've now come to associate with post-colonial writing and identity. If Tagore were to fit in with our stock idea of the post-colonial writer, he would have enlisted the wildness of nature, of the indigenous landscape, as a trope of resistance against European civilization and the Enlightenment. Instead, for Tagore, nature is *the* site of civilization, refinement, and of certain ideals of the secular Enlightenment, such as the ideal of living in harmony with the world: and it's a specifically Indian location for these things. Tagore, audaciously, not so much critiques the Western Enlightenment and humanism, and the idea of 'civilization' itself, but snatches them away from their expected location and gives to them another source and lineage in India and its antiquity; cheekily, he implies this lineage might be the more authentic one. Here, both nature and Kalidasa – for him, the ur-poet of the physical world – are crucial to his purposes. Tagore's engagement with Kalidasa is all the more astonishing when we think of Chakrabarty's honest, if remorseful, admission that modern Indian intellectuals are unable to enter into a fruitful dialogue with their forebears; for the dialogue Tagore has with Kalidasa is not just instinctive and emotional, but pressing and contemporary. We begin to understand, as we read him theorising about nature and the Sanskrit poet, the radically revisionist nature of his project – not only to insert the Orient into Western humanism, but to subsume the more true, the more humane, tradition of humanism under the Orient. Towards the end of an essay, 'The Religion of the Forest' (not included in the Oxford translations), Tagore reflects on two broad, and conflicting, civilizational impulses:

When, in my recent voyage to Europe, our ship left Aden and sailed along the sea which lay between the two continents, we passed by the red and barren rocks of Arabia on our right side and the gleaming sands of Egypt on our left. They seemed to me like two giant brothers exchanging with each other burning glances of hatred, kept apart by the tearful entreaty of the sea from whose womb they had their birth.

For Tagore, 'the two shores spoke to me of two different historical dramas enacted.' In Egypt, he sees a civilization that grew around a 'noble river, which spread the festivities of life on its banks across the heart of the land. There man never raised the barrier of alienation between himself and the rest of the world.' On the other hand, on 'the opposite shore of the Red Sea the civilization which grew up in the inhospitable soil of Arabia had a contrary character to that of Egypt. There man felt himself isolated in hostile and bare surroundings.' And so, his mind 'naturally dwelt upon the principle of separateness. It roused in him the spirit of fight, and this spirit was a force that drove him far and wide.' For Tagore, these 'two civilizations represented two fundamental divisions of human nature. The one contained in it the spirit of conquest and the other the spirit of harmony.' Tagore concludes that 'both of these have their truth and purpose in human nature.'

It's clear, however, which side Tagore is on, and what the purpose of this elaborate meditation is. 'Egypt' is a trope for the Orient, 'Arabia' for the colonizer, and, therefore, by extension, for the West. (Tagore is not the first Indian poet to view the Arab as a 'conqueror'; Henry Louis Vivian Derozio, an important but comparatively minor figure of the early nineteenth century, does the same. It's something they inherited from the work of the early British Orientalists; but since both Derozio and, here, Tagore turned the Arab into a covert trope for the English colonizer, it's something they also turn against the people they inherited it from.) That Tagore means the English colonizer is left in no doubt if one looks at the textual analysis that he undertakes in most of this essay, a comparison between literary responses to nature in English and in Sanskrit. The English works mainly comprise Shakespeare, who is found wanting: 'In the *Tempest*, through Prospero's treatment of Ariel and Caliban we realize man's struggle with Nature and his longing to sever connection with her.' In *Macbeth*, all we evidently get of the non-human world is a 'barren heath where the three witches appear as personifications of Nature's malignant forces'; in *King Lear*, 'the storm on the heath' is a symbol of the human tumult enacted in the play. Moreover, the 'tragic intensity of *Hamlet* and *Othello* is unrelieved by any touch of Nature's eternity'. Tagore glances at play after play, before judiciously washing his hands of both the English poet and the culture he belongs to: 'I hope it is needless for me to say that these observations are not intended to minimise Shakespeare's great power as a dramatic poet but to show in his works the gulf between Nature and human nature owing to the tradition of his race and time.' Not even Milton is exempt; although the 'very subject' of *Paradise Lost* ' – Man dwelling in the garden of Paradise – seems to afford a special opportunity for bringing out the true greatness of man's relationship with Nature', Tagore detects a disturbing element of mastery in Milton's account of that relationship: 'Bird, beast, insect or worm / Durst enter none, such was their awe of man.'

As Tagore reads these poets, he seems to argue that Western humanism – and its idea of 'civilization' – is complicated, and compromised, by its compulsion to dominate and colonize nature. It's a conclusion remarkably similar to D.H. Lawrence's *Etruscan Places*; Lawrence's metaphors for colonizer and colonized are the Romans and the Etruscans respectively, where the former's civilization is marked by territorial conquest and the domination of nature, the latter's by its investment in agricultural and spiritual regeneration. Extraordinarily, in his essay, Tagore notes a particular break in the English imagination after the Renaissance with the advent of Romanticism; the break is characterized by a new relationship to nature, a new definition of the human, and its source, Tagore claims, is the Orient: 'We observe a completely different attitude of mind in the later English poets like Wordsworth and Shelley, which can be attributed in the main to the great mental change in Europe, at that particular period through the influence of the newly discovered philosophy of India which stirred the soul of Germany and aroused the attention of other Western countries.'

Tagore, in spite of his use of the word 'philosophy', is not so much thinking of Max Mueller, Schiller, Schelling, and German Indology here, but of nature and poetry, of Kalidasa, and of Goethe's enthusiasm for the *Shakuntala*. This is more than Tagore's version of what Schwab called the 'correction and expansion of the old humanism of the Mediterranean basin'; it's a wresting of the humanist and civilizational initiative from the West. Tagore, then, is not as interested in critiquing the Western Enlightenment in the now-familiar post-colonial manner, as he is in relocating its original impetus in the Orient and in India. This relocation, of course, was an obsession with a branch of Orientalist scholarship, and with figures like William Jones; but, while the Orientalists were content to discern certain features of the Enlightenment in Indian antiquity, Tagore wants to trace a lineage from antiquity to modernity, from Kalidasa to, specifically, himself, and to use that lineage to rebuff the colonizer. For these purposes, Kalidasa and Shakespeare and their imaginative relationships with nature continue to be contrasted strategically by Tagore; his own advocacy of Kalidasa is also shrewd and strategic, besides being passionate.

At the time Tagore was writing, traditional Indian literature was seen (as it still is sometimes) to be almost indistinguishable from mythology and religion; Tagore himself, although his own poetry and imagination were radically secular, was translated as a public figure into the realm of mythology and mysticism, partly because of this reason, and partly through his own connivance. Yet the nature of his engagement with Kalidasa tells us of a very different concern, a different agenda, which also brings him much closer to the modernist preoccupation (prevalent in Europe at the time) with exactness, concreteness, and sensory perception than one would ordinarily think. The reasons for Tagore more or less ignoring, as a practising poet, the influence of his immediate as well as not-too-distant precursors in Bengal, such as the devotional poets Chandidas and Vidyapati (except in a youthful pastiche he did of the latter's work), and turning to a North Indian Sanskrit poet of antiquity are manifold. In claiming Kalidasa as a precursor, Tagore is seeing him as a proto-modern, as someone whose primary subject was the physical universe, unmediated by religion, and whose primary concern was language itself, and its ability to convey and enrich ways of seeing. The devotional poets of India referred to the physical world – to the landscape and to the weather – in stock images that circulated in their work; one would expect, then, that Tagore learnt to 'look' at the real world from the English Romantics he admired. Tagore is aware of this, and is at pains to tell us that he learnt it from Kalidasa, from whom, too, according to Tagore, the Romantics inherited, consciously or indirectly, the habit of looking at the world. It's no accident, surely, that the lines Tagore quotes from Kalidasa in his essay, 'The *Meghadutam*', about Kalidasa's great poem-sequence, not so much invoke tradition as much as contemporariness: they're lines in which perception, memory, and immediate physical sensation have come together in a single moment and image, and are quite unlike anything in Chandidas or Vidyapati: 'The breezes from the snowy peaks have just burst open the leaf-buds of deodar trees and, redolent of their oozing resin, blow southward. I embrace those breezes, fondly imagining they have lately touched your form, O perfect one!'

Kalidasa is crucial to Tagore's revisionist notion that a fundamental strain of Enlightenment humanism – the idea that the individual fashions and reorders his relationship to the physical universe through language – is more authentically Indian, or Oriental, than European. As a colonial subject, Tagore would have known that, ever since James Stuart Mill wrote his contemptuous diatribe on the Indian epics, the *Ramayana* and the *Mahabharata* , the common English view of Indian writing was that it was overblown, grotesquely overwritten, and excessively romantic. In Mill's words:

These fictions are not only extravagant, and unnatural, less correspondent with the physical and moral laws of the universe, but are less ingenious, more monstrous and have less of any thing that can engage the affection, or excite admiration ... Of the style in which they are composed it is far from too much to say, that all the vices which characterise the style of rude nations ... they exhibit in perfection. Inflation; metaphors perpetual, and these the most violent and strained ... repetition; verbosity; confusion, incoherence; distinguished the Mahabharat and the Ramayan.

Through Kalidasa, Tagore wishes to show his readers that classicism – refinement and obliqueness in language; impersonality in perception – is not only native to India, but has older roots there than in Europe. In another, brilliant essay on Kalidasa, in which he compares *Shakuntala* to the *Tempest*, Tagore turns Mill's rhetoric upon Shakespeare, claiming, in effect, Hellenic classicism as an essentially Oriental literary characteristic, and Orientalizing, in Said's sense of the word, Shakespeare and the European poets:

Universal nature is outwardly serene, but a tremendous force works continually within it. In *Shakuntala* we can see an image of this state. No other drama exhibits such remarkable restraint. European poets seem to grow wild at the least chance of displaying the force of nature and impulse. They love to bring out, through hyperbolic utterance, how far our impulses can lead us. Examples aplenty can be found in plays like Shakespeare's *Romeo and Juliet*. Among all Shakespeare's dramatic works, there is no play as serenely profound, as restrainedly complete and perfect as *Shakuntala*. Such love dialogue as passes between Dushyanta and Shakuntala is very brief, and chiefly conveyed through hints and signs ... Precisely where another poet would have looked for a chance to let the pen race, [Kalidasa] quells it.

Reading the essays on Kalidasa in the Oxford Tagore Translations, one feels that Tagore is trying, in recuperating the Sanskrit court poet, to do in the realm of literature what Rammohun Roy and his own father Debendranath had done not very much earlier in the realm of religion and philosophy. Faced with the charge that the Hindu religion was incorrigibly polytheistic, these figures, instead of rejecting the European humanism from which that charge emanated, turned to ancient texts like the *Upanishads* to claim that, in a sense, the Enlightenment had an older lineage in India than it did in Europe. The story of that Indian rewriting of humanism wouldn't be complete without an acknowledgement of how Tagore enlarged it in the field of literature; for him, and for the narrative of Indian literature in the context of humanism, Kalidasa and his arcadia is as significant and loaded with meaning as the discovery of the *Upanishads* was to the Brahmo Samaj. 'Universal nature is outwardly serene, but a tremendous force works continually within it': it's as if, in speaking of nature, Tagore actually means literature, and the politics of literature, as it appears to a man living in a momentous and turbulent time.

Travels in the Subculture of Modernity

Last year[1], I was invited to teach a course on Indian literature at the Writing Division at Columbia University, to a group of graduate students working towards an MFA degree. My brief was to civilize the natives. The students at the Writing Division had never been offered a course on a non-European literature before; besides, they had relatively little exposure to non-American literatures. My presence was intended to mysteriously enrich their world.

My class comprised eleven charming and intelligent people of diverse backgrounds – Irish and Australian; a diversity of ethnic American identities; and two particularly helpful and courteous white Anglo-Saxon Protestants. I was relieved my assignment had not so much to do with reading and assessing students' stories, as with teaching them literature. My principal text was an anthology I'd edited, the *Picador Book of Modern Indian Literature*, whose appearance in America had been delayed by the ineptitude of the British publisher. This was the main text, though there were departures from it in the form of, among others, V.S. Naipaul and Junichiro Tanizaki.

The benign powers-that-be in the Division had taken pains to emphasize the non-academic nature of my assignment. I was to teach my students literature, but through the prism of their needs as aspiring writers. I kept this advice in mind and ended up ignoring it the moment the classes began – not intentionally, but because the nature of our discussions indicated that my students were not inimical to 'theory', if by that word we mean a process of abstract and analytical thought. Eliot's ironical formulation with regard to James, of a literary mind so fine that it was never marred by a single idea, appeared to be a deliberate ideal for the Writing Division. But my students' minds *were* marred – by speculations about the future, uncertainty about their own gifts, and, not least, by intellectual inquiry.

Something like a theological split had taken place in relation to literature in the last thirty years in American universities. The split was enacted

in Columbia by the uneasy relationship between the Writing Division
and the Department of English and Comparative Literature. Whether
the Writing Division or the English department represented, in this theological divide, mind or matter, spirit or body, or vice-versa, or from time to
time took on both dispensations, is difficult to say. I suppose the Writing
Division accused the English department of being too theory-ridden, and
in fundamental ways uninterested in and even hostile to literature. The
antipathy the creative writer has harboured toward the professorial – expressed, for example, by Virginia Woolf in *To The Lighthouse* and W.B. Yeats
in 'The Scholars' – this antipathy, health-giving in some ways to the writer,
had finally, in a sense, been industrialized, in that it was now responsible
for salaries and tenure applications. There are, of course, some grounds for
the Writing Division's unease; after post-structuralism, a new dimension
was added to the feud between professor and writer, in that critical theory
doesn't look with suspicion upon only this or that writer, as previous critical regimes did, but upon the claims the creative impulse makes for itself,
and upon the category of the 'literary' in general.

In turn, the English department, where I was an occasional interloper
and infrequent participant, believed the students at the Writing Division
were historically naïve and badly read. It was a version of the old, post-Ro-
mantic quarrel between art and politics, spontaneity and abstraction; the
quarrel, now anyway badly dated, had, at least for the English department,
been simplified and banished to Siberia with the creation of the creative
writing department. But here I was, nevertheless, to teach my students
literature, or *a* literature. Many of them, I noticed, had first degrees in History or English from Ivy League colleges; twenty years ago, a young man
in India or England who'd chosen English as a discipline because he was
interested in serving an apprenticeship to writing, would, after taking his
BA, possibly turn to graduate work for the cushion of institutional backing
while he continued to search for his voice as a writer and, quite probably,
a publisher. That is why I, for instance, had enrolled for a doctorate at Oxford after taking a first degree in English at University College London;
my motives were subterranean, not fully plausible even to myself, and
not so much academic-careerist as impelled by desire, a faith in the literary, a reliance on providence, and an eye on the main chance. It was also
important for me, as an Indian, to be at or near a Western metropolitan
centre. Many of my contemporaries shared, I'm sure, my motives, and the
number of dropouts from the MLitt/DPhil programme wasn't low. I went
on to complete my doctorate, despite my frequent temptation to abandon
it, partly because, as an Indian, it was a means to ensure my residency in
England, so important, I thought then, to the fruition of my writerly ambi-

tions. The plan worked almost too well; my second novel was published a
week before my viva.

I wonder whether, had I enrolled for an MFA rather than a DPhil,
I would have had a choice at the time. But it seemed to me that the MFA
students, too, lacked a choice in fundamental ways. The doctoral idiom
of much present-day criticism, the disappearance of the writer-critic from
English departments, the redefinition of those departments as purely
functional spaces, all these seem to be features of postmodernity.

If I'd been teaching the course at the English department, my experience might have been subtly different. Although I'd have been teaching
substantially from the same anthology, I might have – who knows – been
teaching it as a post-colonial literature, which is a somewhat different
value. There is a considerable gap to be bridged between 'Indian' and
'post-colonial', a gap that's almost, if not quite, as palpable between these
two categories and 'the West'; I mean all these denominations are, in their
different ways, related, sympathetic, and antithetical. To ask, for instance,
'Is there such a thing as post-colonial literature?' or 'Does a post-colonial
literature exist?' is problematic, but the questions, of course, have a triumphalist answer, to do with the 'writing back', the clearing of space, we've
all heard about. To ask, however, 'Is there an Indian literature?' or 'Does
an Indian literature exist?' is not necessarily to be insulting, but to invite
one to conceptualize the matter in a new way. I had attempted to ask this
question with my anthology; some readers, though not all, had taken the
anthology to be a statement rather than a question.

The anthology, like most anthologies, is an odd book. Its particular
oddity had been noticed and illuminated by reviewers like Alok Rai, who
had claimed it 'draws attention to the necessarily unfinished nature of such
a project'. The more disgruntled reviewers had loudly drawn attention to
its 'unfinished' nature themselves. Why was there so much Bengali and
English; and so little Tamil, and no Punjabi? For them, 'Indian literature'
was the sum of its significant parts; you would arrive at it if you added them
all up. This reminds me of Franco Moretti's article in the *New Left Review*,
where he wonders if one could *know* more 'world literature' by reading
more and more. Where would such a project end, and at what point does
it induce panic? I don't agree with all of Moretti's assumptions and conclu-
sions, but the following holds true for 'Indian literature' as well: 'That's the
point: world literature is not an object, it's a *problem*, and a problem that
asks for a new critical method: and no one has ever found a method by
just reading more texts.' But the fact is that you can't escape reading; the
decision concerns what sorts of readings are possible or viable. The huge
Sahitya Akademi anthologies of modern Indian writing, with a translated

extract from a different writer on almost every page, comprise a numb-ingly thorough and dull artefact, and an intriguing sociological/meta-physical document, a Borgesian attempt to map infinitude. Ironically, they partly mimic, in a way not entirely unknown to our post-Independence bureaucracy, the colonial explorer's striving toward control of alien terrain through classification and sampling.

At the Southern Asian Institute in Columbia in October, I gave a talk in which I asked, 'Is there an Indian literature?' and attempted to relate it to the anthology. In retrospect, the algebraic formula, $a + b + c = x$, where x is 'Indian literature' and a, b, and c writers in the various languages, and the quota solution, where 3 per cent of an anthology should be devoted to Meghalayan writing if Meghalaya forms 3 per cent of the total population, have failed. These are not so much solutions as symptoms of a bureaucratic cast of mind indispensable to the high moral tone of post-Independence India, and which can be found in all spheres of activity, including the criti-cal and the creative.

Are there other strategies? I can speak of them, again, with hindsight and self-analysis, because they were not entirely clear to me when I was putting the book together. I'll describe them briefly; they might appear far-fetched, and probably are, but perhaps no more so, in perspective, than the alternatives I've mentioned so far. I began by abandoning the assump-tion that 'modern Indian literature' was 'out there' in the world, available for judicious representation and transposing to within the covers of a book. A literature, like an anthology, is not a collection of extraordinary achievements but a field of interrelationships; and it is part of the antholo-gist's job – his or her critical function – to contribute to interpreting and even creating one possible version of that field.

The first anthology that had performed, for me, this critical function in 'Indian writing' was Arvind Krishna Mehrotra's *Twelve Modern Indian Poets*. Until I discovered this book, I'd read anthologies – mainly British and American ones – solely as collections of marvellous extracts: an ideal or improved microcosm of a literature. The British and American canons to which these extracts belonged one took for granted, as abstractions that had as much solidity as real objects. Given this model, the many-volume *Oxford Anthology of English Literature*, for instance, represented critical reassessments of great intelligence; a startling omission, like the absence of Virginia Woolf from the modern period, did not really disturb, and in some ways reinforced, the conviction that modern British literature was 'already' in existence when the anthology came into being, and would continue to exist with or without it. In contrast, Indian poetry in English, despite the several anthologies devoted to it, especially in the 1970s and

1980s, was a sort of rumour no one was entirely persuaded by. Just as you might have met a Canadian in 1970, and presumed he'd therefore come from a country called Canada, without yourself either having seen Canada or having any proof of the fact, you ran into Indian poems in English and presumed they must belong somewhere – and where else but to a body of work, a *raison d'être*, called 'Indian poetry in English'? But there was no pressing reason to come to this conclusion, at least until Mehrotra's anthology came along.

Mehrotra's book both mirrored and refuted an earlier influential selection, R. Parthasarathy's *Ten Twentieth-Century Indian Poets*. Both books were edited by poets; both editors wrote significant, manifesto-like introductions; both prefaced the selection from each poet with a prose piece that was something between a headnote and a small essay. Mehrotra's critique of the earlier book didn't take the form of a radical departure from Parthasarathy's selection; in fact, the two books had several poets in common. The difference seems to me that Parthasarathy believed in the *a priori* existence of something called 'Indian poetry in English'; his selection took place after the fact, and offered, purportedly, the 'best' this body of work might have to offer. Mehrotra's book, on the other hand, seemed less informed or guided by this *a priori* existence; instead, it tried to locate coordinates in clusters of poems, and clusters of poets, that might constitute a field. In many ways, Mehrotra's anthology was not so much a collection as a critical essay, and both the individual prefaces and the poems were part of its narrative.

This is one of the ways in which I think of the Picador anthology: as an extended essay with very large quotations. I have used the model of general introduction, individual prefaces, and deliberately subdivided my selections into clusters. The narrative has emerged with the growth of this essay and the juxtapositioning of these clusters. In connection to the idea of the quotation is a related idea that I find pertinent: the anthology as modernist text, an accumulation of fragments. A crucial component of the modernist aesthetic is failure, as James Wood has pointed out in relation to Virginia Woolf: the impossibility of representing totality, the acknowledgement of the incompleteness of perception, the subsequent privileging of the fragment, the unfinished, the moment. Can 'failure', as a principle of modernist creativity, be a model to the anthologist? And what is the anthologist trying to create out of failure? Well, it might even be 'modern Indian literature', or 'Indian poetry in English', or 'world literature', not so much as a myth that exists outside the text as a trope that operates inside it. In a sense, something like 'modern Indian literature', which cannot be identified with any one language, or 'Indian poetry in English', which we can't ally to any one history, must be a continual work, and product, of the imagination; we must believe in it whenever we encounter it, in the special way we believe in all fictions. But we can't encounter it as we might English or German or Bengali literature, as a universal, in the realm of abstractions, which transcends its particulars; 'Indian literature' is only present in its material configuration, in the clusters and constellations of texts; and there is no single or ideal configuration.[2]

Before I go on to say something about the nature of my explorations with my students, I'll try and describe my location during those months – comprising Manhattan's upper West side and the Writing Division – and how it appeared to me. I speak not as a scholar, or a writer, but as a traveller: a person who, during his travels in what might be the middle period of postmodernity, confronts competing, even substitute, forms of modernity.

In New York, I discovered versions of modernity in three distinct, but equally protected, environments: in the Writing Division, in the stretch of Broadway I often walked down, between 108th and 116th Streets, and in three papers I used to dip into intermittently – the *New York Review of Books*, the *New Yorker*, and the *New York Times*.

By modernity, I mean here a certain liberal bourgeois sensibility and ethos that held sway in culture, in rivalling interpretations and with local variations, from the late nineteenth century to roughly the 1970s: consisting of a privileging of 'high' over 'popular' culture, the idea of art as a self-enclosed space that might observe and comment on the world in which it exists, and the persistence, or haunting, of Enlightenment presuppositions of universality, rationality, and individual freedom. In literature and, specifically, literary style, the forebears, whose ghosts are still palpable, if in an entirely implicit and secret way, in these New York zones, would be Flaubert and Pound; not so much their fascination with suggestion and cadence, as their cherishing of the well-chosen word, and language's capacity for exactness and concreteness. However, one of the most important aspects of modernism in particular, in which it was both at odds and in tune with modernity as a whole, I found largely missing in the three broad locations I've mentioned: the tolerance, and even the encouragement, of the obscure and the difficult.

In the three papers I've named, it seemed there was a commonality of purpose as far as style is concerned. Their sentences were elegant, often short, clean, and uncluttered. Arguments were lucidly put forward; it was the sort of educated and cultivated voice one might have heard in the 1950s or the 1960s, holding out against the establishment. It had now *become* the establishment, in both the cultural and, despite civilized marks of distaste for aspects of contemporary American politics, political sense; the cultivated anti-establishment posture was now a rehearsal of a moment in modernity, an exercise in nostalgia. With the *New York Review*, style almost had to do with the assumption of the persona and voice of a defunct type, the erudite amateur; consequently, despite the many professorial contributions, there seemed to be, in the paper, a hostility to contemporary university-backed professionalism, and, therefore, a refined whiff of anti-intellectualism. In the *New Yorker*, the policy was to keep the prose, and the prose fiction in particular, largely free of sub-clauses and syntactical complexity, and the same could be said of the prose style of the *New York Times*. The allegiance to the civilized tone and subject matter of 'high' culture in the *New York Review* and the *New York Times* – shunning, equally, vulgarity, radical politics, and excessive theorizing – was notable. Someone said to me, approvingly, that you might see a report on the Spice Girls on page one in the *Guardian*, Britain's most intellectual daily, but you would never see it in the *New York Times*. This was a version of modernity; modernity as a protected space; and the enshrining of the liberal-educated mind one associated with that moment in history. The *auteur* that organized and produced this modernity was not an author-figure, that locus of origination that postmodernists spent so much time dismantling, but a team of editors, a collective *auteur* that forfeited the myth of spontaneous creation for the right to control and manage material, to take out and put in. The transaction between editor and author has been formative in all, and especially American, modernity; in postmodernity, the editor, dominating both writer and material, has taken over in certain parts of America in preserving, curating, and producing a lapsed, but still eagerly awaited, cultural tone.

The stretch between 108th and 116th Streets on Broadway resembled the *New York Times* and the *New York Review* in this regard: that it was defined by a notion of the liberal European sensibility – cosmopolitan and educated – that was once coterminous with a significant aspect of modernity. The charming second-hand bookshops on the pavement sold Nietzsche, Melville, Wallace Stevens, William James, and Alfred Kazin; the university bookshops had an air of seriousness and intellectual germination; and even the newsagents sold copies of the *Hudson Review*. There was hardly a chain store in sight, notwithstanding the Burger King on 110th, which was rendered invisible to me by the fact that no one I knew frequented it. All this made the stretch a bit like Europe, the sort of Europe that only upper-class East Coast America was capable of producing in the time of modernity; I noticed that Paris itself, when I last visited it, was overrun by MacDonald's outlets. (It's worth placing the enthusiastic discovery of the late W.G. Sebald and his European angst by certain sections of the American intelligentsia in this particular context and history. I heard the Irish poet Tom Paulin say of Sebald during a conversation in New York, 'Yes, very interesting – it's a kind of postmodern antiquarianism. I thought: this is very like the real thing, but actually a million miles away from it.') This, then, was a heritage modernity, and it constituted a whole physical and intellectual ethos, which essentially ignored, while in important ways being sponsored by, the engines of mass culture and global capitalism that drove the society it was situated in. Part of the everyday life of this heritage modernity was a consumption of the sort of cultural activity that might have existed three or four decades earlier, or before then; the intersection of café leisure with reading and writing, the confluence of bistros and bookshops. It brought with it a wide-eyed provincialism, a deep ignorance of cultural movements elsewhere in the world, while being convinced one was at the centre of it, and an odd self-congratulation that comes when you are not so much in the midst of a cultural efflorescence as consuming the idea of one. The arts were doing fine in America, I was told; American writing was in boom; and Philip Roth, whose resuscitation in old age and whose parables of impotent men undone by lust allegorized this efflorescence, was, like a miracle, everywhere.

This, then, was the spiritual and geographical location of the Writing Division. And here, too, the beacon for the apprentice writers, the exemplar who, whether or not they knew it, had set the parameters for their apprenticeship, was Joyce's mentor Flaubert. Their eye was being trained to spot the unnecessary word, their ear to hear the false note; and they were being taught to approach the art of prose writing with the attention and reverence due to a 'high' art form. Naturally, this little island of modernity – because that it is what it was, with the waning of these cultural assumptions elsewhere – couldn't be preserved except through substantial amounts of funding, and the funds came from the students themselves. For two magic years, they would pay to consume, partake of, and even suffer, some of the most powerful aesthetic principles of modernity. Into this, I arrived with my anthology. What would the authors in it have to say to them?

It gradually became apparent to us as we read these writers – most of them unknown to the students, who nevertheless read them with an unusual degree of sensitivity and intelligence – that they did not represent the sort of self-conscious 'difference' one has come to associate with and expect from Indian writing. None of the token narrative gestures towards demarcating 'difference' from Western literary traditions – polyphony; fantasy;

non-linearity – was necessarily present. Indeed, what we encountered was a powerful engagement, in craft and vision, with classical modernism; and modernism's characteristic quarrel with, and negotiation of, certain Enlightenment values – clarity of perception; rationality; the presupposed relationship between language and reality – in terms given to it by the Enlightenment itself. What is interesting is that, as we saw, this engagement wasn't played out as a negotiation between a 'native' idiom and a 'foreign' cultural paradigm, nor as an exclusive highbrow aesthetic project in a historical void, but as a relocation of the meanings of modernity, modernism, native idiom, history, aesthetics, and politics, in a way we might not have been familiar with if we'd only read the European or American modernists. It was this relocation of meaning that both I and my students had to deal with.

I will furnish an example of what I mean. The Hindi writer Nirmal Verma, who is credited with being one of the principal creators, in the 1960s, of the *'nai kahani'* or 'new story', with its obvious echo of and putative debt to the *nouveau roman*, spent some formative years in his writing life in what was then Czechoslovakia. My anthology includes one of his 'East European' stories, 'Terminal'; its style embodies a curious paradox that is characteristic of this subgenre in Verma's fiction: an exquisite attention to the nuances of perception, the gradations of everyday detail, and, on a broader level, a deliberate emptying of the story of specificity – for this story, strikingly, lacks all proper names, whether of its characters, country, or town. The only proper name in the story (or out of it) is, as I say in the anthology, 'Nirmal Verma'; it is this name in whose locus and history this story exists. Without it, it might just be a Czech story in Hindi translation; the name 'Nirmal Verma' catalyses the story into a state of 'being translated', into an evolution of significances. Names are important to abstract art in modernism, to Cubism and late forms of Impressionism: just as the daubs that compose Picasso's *Night Fishing at Antibes* congeal into a scene only once we know the name of the picture, so it seems to me that the painstakingly realized realism of 'Terminal' both breaks up and re-forms into an abstract pattern when we place the narrative in the name, 'Nirmal Verma'. This, then, is not a late modernist story about a symbolist terrain, although its physicality clearly has a symbolist glow; nor is it a diasporic post-colonial narrative of emigration – there is no mention of exile in the story. When I spoke of this work at the Southern Asian Institute, Gayatri Spivak, who was present, commented on Verma's 'double bind' as she saw it – his compulsive and meticulous emptying of his narrative of specificity indicated, strikingly, the very fact of his being haunted by what he wanted to escape: locale, nation. One might put this slightly differently. Invisibility, the transcendence of specificity, and the escape into universality have been the desire of most, if not all, modern writers. But it's precisely by embedding themselves or their work in some sort of convention, or the canon, or the particular, that they have attempted to transcend the contingent and efface their historical selves. By deleting certain fundamental specificities from his story, Verma is, paradoxically, denying it invisibility, and drawing attention to its midway state of being – its lack of location in any one canon or tradition – and thereby placing it anew in what would otherwise be less obvious: a historical and cultural moment. It is these odd dislocations of meaning, which we would perhaps not encounter if we had been exposed to nothing but the classic works of Western modernity – if we had read, for example, only Kafka, whose locale and temperament in some way 'Terminal' evokes, but not Verma himself – that I am speaking of.

My students were, of course, themselves practitioners. And though it became apparent that these various texts of 'modern Indian literature' didn't represent a 'difference' from their Western counterparts as theories of post-coloniality would have us construct that 'difference', it slowly became clear to us, as readers and also writers, that these fictions constituted a 'difference', an 'otherness', in terms of the possibilities of the *practice* of fiction in modernity. For, despite the verities we admired in these works, as we might admire them in any modern or modernist work, something was happening here that at once dislocated and instructed us, the sorts of registers the students, especially, hadn't thought modern fiction capable of accommodating, or even proper to its conception. It was these registers that marked a 'difference', but not the sort of 'difference' we have been taught to associate with Indian or post-colonial or subaltern fiction. It was a 'difference', to rewrite an old-fashioned literary critical word into the realm of cultural translation, of 'tone'.

I will give two examples of these, to us, unsettling but subtle registers of 'difference', or changes of 'tone'. For the first, let me return to Verma's 'Terminal'. This story, as I've said, is set in an unnamed East European town that is probably Prague. A man, obviously an outsider, and a woman meet each other by accident at a performance of Mozart's *The Magic Flute*, and fall in love. The woman develops an obsession: she wants to know what their future together will be like. One day, she forces the man to accompany her to a fortune-teller; they journey on a tram to the old town. The fortune teller sees something appalling in their future; when asked by the woman to describe what she's seen, she can't, but contrives to 'show' it to the woman rather than tell her what it is. The woman is badly shaken. She and the man return together on the tram; the woman gets off at her stop, and we know she won't see him again. The man continues his journey.

These are the bare bones of the story, whose psychological and physical details are rendered with great beauty; and despite, or perhaps because of, its air of mystery and the supernatural, we feel we're on sure ground as we read, in the hands of a master who's married together the symbolist and realist streams of narrative experience. There's a point in the story, however, in which an unobtrusive change in tonality occurs, before we are returned once more to the symbolist-modernist landscape. The man, on his way to the fortune teller with his lover, recalls, on the tram, the strange way in which the two had met: he'd turned up late for *The Magic Flute*, all the tickets had been sold, and this woman, whom he didn't know, had provided him with a ticket, which enabled them to sit together and their relationship to begin. The narrator tells us:

> One day, after they had got to know each other, he had asked her, 'That night when we met at the Mozart opera, who had you bought that other ticket for?'
> 'For you,' she had replied with a laugh.
> 'No, tell me truthfully, who were you waiting for?'
> She was silent for a while. She had neither laughed nor said anything. 'There is nothing to tell … I won't tell you because you won't believe me.'
> Suddenly anxious, he had said, 'Don't make excuses … You don't want to tell me who you were waiting for …'
> 'For you …' she had said.
> 'But we didn't even know each other.'
> 'That's why I didn't want to tell you. Such things happen to me often. I feel as if something is about to happen, like a signal from a distance. I see it only once, but I know it is asking me to be ready. That day I was the first in the queue to buy tickets. When a voice from the ticket-window asked, "How many?" I replied, "Two." After I had bought them, I wondered who the second ticket was for. It was then that I saw you.'
>
> (Alok Bhalla's translation)

This appears to fit in, at first glance, with the story's unspoken themes of fatedness, supernatural intervention, and private neuroses. It is so expertly done, so integrated into the whole, that we don't notice at once the alien register; that we are being introduced, in the midst of the metaphors of modernity and a vision that arises from it, to the sentimental, the absurd, something we should properly encounter outside this space, in the realm of the popular song or even the Hindi film. This register should be distinguished from modernist extremities of language and experience, which disrupt neither the high-cultural tone nor aspirations of the text, and indeed confirm them. Again, we aren't introduced to this shift in 'tone' as we would in a postmodern text, jubilantly, through parody and pastiche; instead, we're made to recover in ourselves, very briefly, the capacity to feel, within the incompatible context of the symbolist landscape, the tenderness and empathy for that absurd moment of possibility and the miraculous that the person in the cheap seat of the Hindi cinema hall is habituated to experience. This was unsettling to the class not only in our role as readers, but as practitioners. I questioned my class, 'Would you, if you'd been on your way to crystallizing a perfectly formed symbolist narrative, have taken a similar risk by introducing such a moment?' They acknowledged, now that they were conscious of the moment, they would not have; that they wouldn't have thought of steering the story in that direction, because it represented a risk and a gamble whose rewards, like the future – foreseen but undisclosed – in the story, were difficult for the writer to predict, discern, or describe.

Some of these 'changes in tone', these 'miracles' – not O. Henry's or Anatole France's quasi-Christian miracles, nor miracles entirely qualified by distance and irony, nor the self-conscious miracles of postmodernity, of the *echt*-Rushdie narrative, but something cheap and woven into, rather than transcendental of, lower-middle-class reality, a form of wish-fulfilment – confronted us repeatedly: those interested should look up Manto's stories, 'Peerun' and 'The Black Shalwar', in the anthology. My second example here comes from Vaikom Muhammad Basheer (1908–94), the great storyteller from Kerala. It concerns a character called 'Basheer' who is incarcerated in the Central Jail for mildly seditious activities (the writer Basheer was an admirer of Gandhi) during the time of the freedom struggle. The jail is evoked both as a place of abeyance and a pastoral, in which 'Basheer' comes into contact with freedom-fighters, petty criminals, murderers, warders, and a whole way of life. The walls of the jail separate it, as it happens, from the women's jail, from the direction of which there emanates an unmistakable feminine scent. 'Basheer', one day, finds himself conversing with a woman, whom he can hear but can't see; these conversations, as the days pass, become more passionate; their absences from one another more difficult. They signal their presence to one another by the means of a twig thrown up in the sky. They decide to find a way to meet; but just when the possibility of doing so offers itself, 'Basheer's' long-drawn-out prison term comes to an end, and the warder informs him he's free.

Here, too, as in 'Terminal', and the two Manto stories I've referred to in passing, the notions of the stranger, the invisible, and the unknown future facilitate the entry of the absurd; I don't use the word in the existential and artistic currency given it by Camus or Beckett, but to identify a moment of disruption and enrichment in modern Indian literature: a moment not antithetical, but essential, to Indian modernity. As in 'Terminal', the physical and incidental details in Basheer's story – the making of tea, the hoarding and smoking of tobacco – are marvellously drawn, and human relationships portrayed with a mixture of mockery and affection that Verma eschews. One of my students arrived for the class on Basheer with a worried look. She was full of admiration for the story, but was puzzled by her own response. 'I've just come from a class on Ondaatje, where we've been criticizing his bad poeticisms. But I've been wondering about how some of the things work in this story that you wouldn't expect to. I've been wondering why I accept them here but not in Ondaatje, whether I'm moving the goalposts and judging it by different standards because it's an Indian story.' She sounded gloomy.

I told her that I didn't think she was moving the goalposts, but that it was worth inquiring further into Basheer's story, and its style, and our own response to it. I asked them to consider a curious passage that occurs fairly early in the story, after the narrator's described the pervasive scent of woman he keeps inhaling or imagining, and not long after a terrific account of making a *chakki*, a prisoner's cigarette-lighter improvised out of a few bits of thread. The passage in question is an apostrophe to night; 'Basheer' is unable to sleep in his cell because of the electric light shining outside it. He suddenly realizes what a beautiful thing night is, and embarks on his apostrophe:

> One thing I came to understand then – I had never seen darkness. O primeval, deep, amazing darkness! O millions of stars that twinkle and flash in the endless vastness of the skies! O glorious, glorious, moon-drenched night! Why have I never seen you?
>
> (Nivedita Menon's translation)

This continues for several sentences. We are puzzled and delighted by this long passage; puzzled both by its existence in the space of the modern short story, and by our delight, the terms on which we find ourselves accepting its existence. It has a hint of absurdity; we ourselves wouldn't have put it in; but it makes us laugh in an affirmative way, and, at the same time, it conveys the desperation of a man who can't go to sleep. We aren't laughing *at* the voice, though. One might say the text, at this point, displays a lack of embarrassment as a source of aesthetic energy; its humour and poignancy derive neither from parody nor sentiment, but from a quality one might call corporeality, in that it invokes in us emotions similar to what we feel – laughter and pathos – when we see an ordinary person display his body without self-consciousness or embarrassment. Basheer, it could be said, modelled his attire on Gandhi, except that he wore a lungi and not a dhoti, and is 'half-naked' in many of his photographs. This nakedness, however, differs from the Romantic idea of nakedness, with its resonances of revelation, confession, innocence, and nature. Basheer's semi-nakedness is both self-revelatory and woven into a social fabric; similarly, the passage in question has, at once, the air of spontaneity and being theatrically well-rehearsed.[3]

One of my students, Mia Alvar, in her final paper, took a fresh look at these 'changes of tone' in Basheer, from the absurd to the comic to the poetic, in a brilliant analysis of Basheer's exclamation marks in the context of his use of humour. (Notice, too, the exclamation marks in the small extract I've quoted.) She calls it Basheer's 'indulgent use of exclamation points'. 'These marks', she notes, 'manage to convey an earnestness that is the opposite of sarcasm while preserving their status as sarcastic devices themselves. "Walls" is rife with exclamation points, but in the first two dialogues between the characters Basheer and Narayani, I counted *thirty nine* of them.' She continues:

> I believe that these, and all other exclamation points throughout the story, are supposed to conjure hysteria, epic poetry, high drama, comic books, religious worship, and the movies all at once, because Basheer's sarcasm allows his language to operate on several registers, even his punctuation manages to contain the shallowest and most serious of connotations.
>
> Because of this, the exclamation points in the last few pages of 'Walls' allow us to contain both the ridiculous melodrama and the genuine pathos of the story's ending. When Anian Jailor tells the narrator, 'You can go Mr Basheer. You are free!', we absorb both the glee and sorrow of his exclamation and what it means to the narrator, who will have to leave his unseen sweetheart behind in prison. Having played with the sheer amount of things an exclamation point can contain, the narrator earns this right merely to place it on the page and trust that we automatically absorb its bittersweet range of emotions. The exclamation that closes the story, 'God be with us!' similarly hits excessively melodramatic and painfully true notes all at once; the narrator is simultaneously exaggerating and earnestly meaning what he says. The effect is powerful.

In text after text, we were having to deal with, and pinpoint, this incursion of the alien register, and its movement in a story we could otherwise admire with the tools and language given us both by classical modernism and the tutors of the Writing Division. As the range of Mia's phrases reveals ('excessively melodramatic'; 'painfully true'), it was a 'change of tone' we occasionally resisted, but equally came to respect as that point of 'difference' in which the story began to do something that the Writing Division hadn't acknowledged it was necessarily expected to. But the 'difference' didn't come to us through the by now conventional routes of postmodernity and post-coloniality; it occurred in representative texts of Indian 'high' modernity, if one could make a claim to such an entity.

I have no clear explanation for this 'change of tone', this incursion, and the way in which it inhabits the work successfully and significantly, except in terms of a link to pluralism in modern India. I make this link tentatively. An epigraph to an essay on Cochin by Ashis Nandy, from Raimundo Panikkar, a priest and theologian of Spanish and Hindu parentage, kept returning to me as I taught and reread these stories:

> For over a quarter of a century the Indic world confirmed what since my birth was only a blurred feeling: the self-identity of Man is transcultural, and thus cannot have any single point of reference ... Pluralism is not synonymous with tolerance of a variety of opinions. Pluralism amounts to the recognition of the unthinkable, the absurd, and up to a limit, intolerable ... Reality in itself does not need to be transparent, intelligible.

I can't pretend to a deep understanding of either the Indic world or of Man; but I find the caveat about pluralism not being 'synonymous with tolerance of a variety of opinions', but a recognition of the 'unthinkable' and the 'absurd' instructive in the context of the peculiar modernist sensibility incarnated in these fictions, and the political processes of the modernity in which they arose. As we know, the Gandhian mass movement, the political aspirations of the subject country, and independent India itself involved the idea of universal adult suffrage. This was put into fruition after Independence, an experiment which, as subaltern historians have put it, introduced both the bourgeoisie and the peasantry, with their belief in the supernatural, the literate and the illiterate, into what were essentially Enlightenment concepts – individual choice and democracy. This, in Indian modernity, has created a pluralism that is not just a 'tolerance of a variety of opinions', as Western or even Nehruvian pluralism might be, but a teetering towards, and acceptance of, the 'absurd'. Is it far-fetched to suggest that something like this political process finds it mirror-image in, and leaves its impression on, the modernist or modern stories in the anthology, and the ways in which they ask to be read?[4] My students, as I've mentioned earlier, were being inculcated in the Writing Division in a more classical, even a heritage, version of modernity. The authors in the anthology were bringing, surreptitiously, into the students' field of vision registers and 'changes of tone' that they were being taught, in other classes and workshops, were anathema to fiction, and which they were being trained to detect and delete. For them, it must have been – as it was for me in that situation – a curious but hopefully challenging interface.[5]

In December, I returned to India. The travels out of which this piece has arisen were almost, but not quite, over. One evening in January, I heard my fourth novel, *A New World*, had won the Sahitya Akademi award in the English-language category – by chance, most probably, I thought, or by mistake. Nevertheless, I had to fly to Delhi a month later to receive the prize. For four or five days, I, sometimes with my family, skulked intermittently around the conferences, gatherings, and teas organized around the awards ceremony (a writer in every recognized Indian language would collect an award for the best book in that language; this, indeed, is the only official, government-sponsored Indian accolade that actually acknowledges the eligibility of English as one of those languages). I was brought into contact with a world that I knew relatively little of, or only fitfully; the mix of bureaucracy and culture, the proximity of government, the presence of creative idiosyncrasy and scholarly earnestness, of factionalism and large-heartedness, the absence of the substantial monetary incentives available to prose writers in the West. The annual Sahitya Akademi do is a major, if not universally popular, forum for those who were once called writers in the Indian vernaculars, and these days, as misleadingly, are called 'bhasha' writers: for 'bhasha' means language, and all writers, even those who write in English, have to have a 'bhasha'.

I'd got to know some of the more senior writers while compiling the anthology; and now I met my co-prizewinners, a few of whom were important national figures, but most of whom I'd never heard of, and some of whom wrote in languages that, to the uninformed outsider, didn't possess a proper literature at all. I was struck by the range of genres that the judges of the prize had given recognition to: poetry, memoir, criticism, the novel, the novella, the story; every known literary genre, in fact; and the observance of the relevance of some of these genres, such as poetry, the memoir-sketch, and the literary-critical exposition, was appropriate to a modernity in which those genres had gathered importance. This formed, say, an interesting contrast to the Booker Prize, which only recognizes fiction as literature, and the novel as fiction, and has long been subtly but aggressively trying to bridge the gap between the literary and the popular, at a real cost to the former, purportedly to enrich both our lives and the book trade. The Booker Prize's pious mission has ushered in an age of dubious democracy to the novel, presuming nothing existed in the place it redefines; one might recklessly say, but not entirely without seriousness, that this mission is a soft-focus, literary version of American foreign policy. The Sahitya Akademi, on the other hand, is a universe of bureaucracy, feuds, nepotism, its claustrophobic air inflected by an exclusive, unashamed, and occasionally incongruous devotion to the literary, the serious, the high-cultural; an unlikely, possibly an inimical, but an unmistakable greenhouse for a certain aspect, or ideal, of modernity. This was true even of the President, the Urdu literary critic, Gopi Chand Narang, who had been elected to his post in unusually controversial and rancorous circumstances, and to whom was attributed the importing of postmodern theories into Urdu literary discourse: here, too, was a man, it seemed to me, whose private and public roles were the creation of both Indian bureaucracy and a modernist conception of 'high' culture.

I listened to speeches; made a short one myself; I was struck by the amount of poetry quoted during these occasions. Of course, one knows that Indians use poetry – say, a couplet from a ghazal – in their speeches in the way the English use jokes and anecdotes in theirs; to make a direct connection with the audience. But I was struck by the persistence of the habit, and the seriousness with which verse was deployed; not by politicians, in these instances, but by writers, quoting modern poetry, some of it their own. The idea that poetry – modern, not performance poetry – might be used in this way, strategically, to supplement or reinforce a cultural observation, or a confession, is unusual in postmodernity. The persistence of poetry reminded me again of the plethora of literary forms I'd encountered here, which, elsewhere, in postmodernity, has been largely forfeited in favour of the novel's hegemony and definitiveness. The 'bhasha' writers, say, in Kannada, Urdu, or Hindi, continue to write stories and literary criticism and poetry and still enlarge their reputations as important writers. In a sense, the paradigm that rules them is the modernist one, in which these forms once flourished.

In this context, I have returned to the Irish writer Frank O'Connor's classic study of the short story, *The Lonely Voice*, a book now out of print and forgotten by all except a few. My memory told me that O'Connor's thesis was that the modern story, unlike the novel, depended upon the existence of an underground subculture. Having tracked down, at some expense, a second-hand copy of the book, I found that O'Connor's own words are 'submerged population group' – 'a bad phrase', said O'Connor, 'which I have had to use for want of a better'. At first, it seems that the 'submerged population group' supplies the short story with its characters: O'Connor, recalling Pushkin's claim that all Russian literature had emerged from Gogol's 'The Overcoat', turns to that story and finds in its protagonist a precursor to modernism's Little Man, a failed non-entity, a member of the nation's, or society's, 'submerged population group'. It gradually becomes clear that O'Connor's 'submerged population group' is also the site, in his view, of the creation and reception of the short story; that it provides the story not only with its characters and subjects, but with the cultural context for its production, and for the sort of reading it demands. Thus, he asks certain questions, and considers the 'peculiar geographical distribution of the novel and the short story' in the Anglophone world. 'For some reason,' he says, 'Czarist Russia and modern America seemed to be able to produce both great novels and great short stories, while England, which might be called without exaggeration the homeland of the novel, showed up badly when it came to the short story. On the other hand my own country, which had failed to produce a single novelist, had produced four or five storytellers who seemed to me to be first-rate.'

O'Connor's insight was, from the first, debatable and provocative; I wish, here, to tap it for its latent irony, and both qualify and extend it by placing it in a new configuration. O'Connor attributes the demographic phenomenon he mentions in the extract I've just quoted to the lack of cultural visibility of 'submerged population groups' in imperial England; their presence in nineteenth-century Russia and modern America; and their predominance in modern Ireland. He sums these distinctions up with: 'In America as in Czarist Russia one might describe the intellectual's attitude to society as "It may work," in England as "It must work," and in Ireland as "It can't work."' I think it's fair to say that by 'the novel', O'Connor means the nineteenth-century realist novel, which he situates, experientially and culturally, in mainstream bourgeois culture. The novel's mode of representation, and its aspiration, is totality; it presumes the existence of, and also the possibility of representing, a continuous fabric of human and social interrelationship. The short story, on the other hand, aspires towards the fragmentary and the partial; its very form imposes upon it an admission of the impossibility of totality. Long before the continuities between nation and narration were posited, O'Connor was implicitly proposing the novel as a nation-metaphor. He was not alone in speaking of the novel in this way. At least one other writer, W.H. Auden, in poems such as 'The Novelist' and 'Letter to Lord Byron', constructs the novelist, in contrast to the poet, as a bourgeois, respectable, citizen-type: dull, conscientious, hardworking, interested equally in every segment of society, making up in maturity and grown-upness what he lacks, especially vis-à-vis the poet, in imagination. Auden's novelist is, then, a pillar of society and nationhood; even reading and writing novels demands a degree of social responsibility and maturity very different from the perceived trance-like activity of reading and writing poetry. The poet, in his solitary vision, annihilates the national and social fabric in which the novel embeds itself.

All this is certainly true of the sort of novel Jane Austen – of whom Auden spoke with a mixture of distaste, respect, and mockery in 'Letter to Lord Byron' – and George Eliot and many others wrote; the novel as an exposition, analysis, and product of mainstream concerns. Dostoevsky and Dickens are obvious exceptions to O'Connor's thesis, and to Auden's. Although O'Connor did not believe so, the modernist novel is itself discontinuous with nation, and points (if we subscribe, for a moment, to this theory) towards the existence of subcultures. Both its protagonists and its narrative mode become disjunctive, idiosyncratic, private. Elsewhere, O'Connor said that *Ulysses* was not so much a novel as a very long story, for the novel records the effects of the passing of time on its characters, and Joyce's novel only covers a single day. In this comment lies a key to the poetic paradox of key modernist novels like *Ulysses* and *Mrs Dalloway*; at their heart lies the epiphanic moment, which, magnified and augmented into twelve or twenty-four hours, seems to contain everything in it, and is still fleeting, temporal, fragmentary, incomplete. The novel, then, becomes a poetic act of perception on a large scale; essentially, it abnegates its responsibility to represent and contain totality, and becomes a disjunction in the fabric of the nation with its assumption of a knowable and representable – both politically and imaginatively – reality. One might say, then, that modernity was a time when both new nations came into being, and subcultures that proclaimed imaginative allegiances distinct from those allied to nationhood were also powerfully operative. Certainly, the site of the flowering of modernity in India, between the mid-nineteenth and the mid-twentieth century, was, in the various languages, and in the context of colonial subjugation, the discourse of a huge subculture, a very large 'submerged population group'.

The idea of the continuities between the discourse we call 'the novel' and the discourse we call 'the nation' has been crucial, if not endemic, in the time of postmodernity and post-coloniality. This has led me to rephrase and rework some of O'Connor's demographic queries. Why did modern Bengali produce both great novelists and great short-story writers? Why is the pre-eminent writer of modern Urdu literature a short-story writer who was harangued in his lifetime, Saadat Hasan Manto, and why has it produced no major novelist except Qurratulain Hyder? Why is the emphatically predominant mode of contemporary Indian writing in English the novel; why does it not seem to give us stories and poems; and by what means has the Indian English novel become a synecdoche for all Indian writing? Why is it that 'all Indian writing' actually constitutes the short story, poetry, the novella, far more than it does the novel? My tentative answer would be – and some of this, of course, has been remarked on before – that the mainstream culture of postmodern India is to a considerable extent the product of the diasporic Anglophone Indian; it is he or she who largely constructs and repeatedly disseminates the idea of the nation;

it is he or she who both writes and consumes the novel, and especially the idea of the novel. This idea of the nation, and the novel, is a transcontinental way of 'being'. But I don't think modernity – as a location for, and a form of, self-consciousness – has altogether vanished; it has become a subculture. In contrast to many of the Anglophone Indian novelists, the 'bhasha' writers live in an immense subculture, the subculture of modernity, situated in that real, verifiable but waning location, the modern nation-state, and their ideas of the literary, of identity, of even the nation, are ideas that modernity gives to them, in occasionally distorted form. It is in this context that they write and discuss novels, stories, poetry, and literary theory; the nation, for them, is not a discourse that becomes, at a certain moment, indistinguishable from their practice, but a (sometimes corrosive) network of state patronage and political positions, and also, it has to be said, a place to live, work, and imagine in. I don't mean that they are 'behind the times'; the government of the country they live in has already taken measures to introduce it, economically, to globalization and postmodernity. I do not mean that modernity is 'flourishing' here; nor is it a heritage modernity, preserved by money, such as I encountered in New York. But it is a living and in some ways definitive, if also mauled and sometimes disfigured, force. We should not be surprised, therefore, if we encounter, for instance, the figure in painting in this location. It is not because the artists here haven't developed along contemporary Western lines, and are 'lagging behind'; it is because the figure is still a powerful visual tool in modernity. It, like the poem and the story, constitutes and expresses the experiences of a 'submerged population group', a subculture, and, travelling through that subculture, you once more feel briefly those forms' renewing imaginative and social function.

Thoughts in a Temple
Hinduism in the Free Market

Two weeks ago, I went for a walk with my daughter to the Birla temple. It is not far from where I live; and I have seen it coming up for years, from a time when I did not actually live in Calcutta, but when, during long or short periods of transit, I would look at it from the balcony of this flat. It was built – this plush Orientalist artefact – by the family after which it is named: the Birlas, whose forefather moved from Rajasthan to Calcutta and made his fortune here. I can't say I unreservedly enjoy going to this temple; there are, however, only so many places to walk about in Calcutta. My daughter, though, does enjoy going there, without reservation; and this was both her second visit and mine. The first time must have been almost exactly a year ago; I remember the warm marble floor under our bare feet from that excursion, the floor that must have absorbed the heat all day to give it out in the evening. I can also remember my daughter, a year younger, running across the space before the main shrine; on our second visit, the marble was warm again beneath our feet.

On this visit, the precincts of the temple were more crowded than the first time I went there; it was a site of recreation – men and women, and some children, sat in the large space before the steps that led to the sanctum in which the *arati* (evening prayers offered to the deity) was being performed. They looked content, like people at the seaside. My daughter, easily frightened, was alarmed at the sound of the bell, and did not want to investigate the *arati* – the familiar tune, which one can hear these days even when certain domestic water filters are used, was being played on a tape – and so we roamed around the premises. A thought came to me: would these people condone, or at least defend, what was happening in Gujarat?

The question was probably grossly unfair, but impossible to keep out of my head, or leave unasked. In the last ten years, gradually, the idea of the 'peace-loving Hindu' has been turned inside out. The most innocent-seeming of activities appear to be charged with unarticulated violence. To walk in the Birla temple was to sense – perhaps to imagine; but to imagine powerfully – that subterranean violence which Hinduism is now charged with in its totality: because you cannot isolate one kind of 'religious' activity from another.

Perhaps it was the location; perhaps I wouldn't have felt this discomfort if these people had gathered at a more ancient, less ostentatious place of worship. I have never really cared for the Birla temple, for its security guards who hover not very far from you once you enter, its marble floor and enormous chandelier, its expansive air of a lobby in a four-star hotel, its spotless, garish, unimpeachable idols.

This spectacle is part of the production of a version of Hinduism that has been a steadily developing enterprise in independent India: Hinduism as a rich man's, a trader's, religion. Although aggressive exhortations are made on behalf of Lord Ram, the principal deities of this religion are Ganesh and Lakshmi: not Ganesh, the wily and rapid transcriber of the *Mahabharata*, but the bringer of good fortune to the black marketeer; not Lakshmi, the agrarian goddess, but the goddess who presides over the urban dowry-system. As ever, our divinities bless their devotees indiscriminately. I have heard Hinduism celebrated for the resilience with which it, unlike other religions, has embraced capitalism; but perhaps it has embraced capitalism a little too well. It has left the Hindu with an importunate will to fit into the modern world, and without a social conscience.

Hindutva – the BJP's frequently used ontologically and culturally assertive term for 'Hinduness' – does not so much promote religion as it does material success for the followers of the Hindu religion. Success, in the 1990s, has been its key word, but success for the majority only; it will not barter or share it with anyone else; it will even pretend no one else exists; if they do, it will see to it that they cease to. I presume it is not a coincidence that the extreme measures of ethnic cleansing in Gujarat should be undertaken by those who have been the most effective proponents of the new Hinduism's mantra of material well-being. Many of the sources that fund our new kitsch Hinduism are also those that fund, or quietly encourage, a government that has a chief minister who defends and protects murderers, and a prime minister who defends and protects that minister. Then there is the largesse that flows in from overseas, from businessmen in London, from expatriates in England and America. Does it only take an *arati* to keep our gods happy?

Hinduism was never, in the past (unlike Christianity), at the heart of a revolutionary political movement, precisely because it was never an evangelical religion; it had no Word, or truth, to spread. The killings done in its name today are not part of a jihad, and nor are they the residue of a misguided evangelism; they are a brutal and calculated exercise of power in a moral vacuum: Hinduism as the punitive instrument of the powerful. Christianity has often had a quarrel with modernity, and the materialism it denotes in its eyes; Islam has a related quarrel with the West, modernity's synecdoche. That is why Islamic militancy, even at its worst, has the dimensions of an ideology, albeit a distorted one. *Hindutva*, on the other hand, has no problem with modernity, or with the West; and it rushes to embrace the latter's material benefits. This happy concordance, in *Hindutva*, of cultural extremism and materialism makes it less like a 'fundamentalist' religious movement than like fascism.

'Hinduism' and the 'mainstream'; how frequently are these words juxtaposed, and made synonymous, with each other by the ruling political party! 'Mainstream': the word that would mean, in a democratic nation, the law-abiding democratic polity, is cunningly conflated, in the newspeak of our present government[1], with the religious majority; and those who don't belong to that majority become, by subconscious association and suggestion, anti-democratic, and breakers of the law.

Ironically, saffron is the colour of our mainstream. Saffron, or '*gerua*' in the Indian languages; its resonances are wholly to do with that powerful undercurrent in Hinduism, '*vairagya*', the melancholy and romantic possibility of renunciation. At what point, and how, did the colour of renunciation, and withdrawal from the world, become the symbol of a militant, and materialistic, majoritarianism? '*Gerua*' represents not what is brahminical and conservative, but what is most radical about the Hindu religion; it is the colour not of belonging, or fitting in, but of exile, of the marginal man. *Hindutva*, while rewriting our secular histories, has also rewritten the language of Hinduism, and purged it of these meanings; and those of us who mourn the passing of secularism must also believe we are witnessing the passing, and demise, of the Hindu religion as we have known it.

We perhaps owe the politicization of the colour saffron, its recent use, in India, as a sign of national pride, to the Hindu revivalist Swami Vivekananda (1863–1902), though, as Tapan Raychaudhuri has shown, no clear line can be drawn from one to the other. We largely owe to him, too (more than we do to any other single person), the notion of 'Hinduness'. Vivekananda is a curious figure, and an exemplary one; his story is inflected with the conflicts of interest, the contradictions, of the emergence of Hinduism into modernity. Vivekananda's real name was Narendranath Datta; he was a graduate of Calcutta University, and had studied European religions carefully. Like many other middle-class, educated men of his generation, in India and elsewhere, he was a seeker after metaphysical and religious truth; but his search was related to the self-awareness of a colonial subject. After rejecting the major religions and philosophies he was surrounded by, Datta finally found his master in a rustic visionary and saint, Ramakrishna Paramhansa, who was a priest in a town north of Calcutta, who spoke in parables and homilies and claimed to have 'seen' Ma Kali. Ironically, and characteristically of the time, he first heard of Ramakrishna from an Englishman, Professor W.W. Hastie. And it was Ramakrishna who reportedly identified Datta's spiritual potential, and named him Vivekananda – 'the one who exults in a clear conscience and in discernment'.

Ramakrishna was an extraordinary man himself; he had experimented, literally, in varieties of religious experience. He could practice, for periods of time, faiths such as Islam and Christianity; his immersion, during these trance-like periods, in these alternative modes of worship was so complete that he would begin to internalize the habits and customs of other religions, to spend, for instance, long spells inside a mosque, and eat beef; he'd even experience a sort of revulsion towards his beloved deity, Kali. His experiments led him to conclude, influentially, that all paths led to God (*'jata mat tata path'* – 'there are as many paths as there are faiths'). This, then, was part of Vivekananda's liberal inheritance; but it was an inheritance quite different from that of the liberal humanism that had come to exist in Bengal by this time, and which Vivekananda, as Narendranath Datta, would probably have subscribed to had he not met Ramakrishna. It was a middle-class humanism that decreed tolerance towards all faiths, regardless of whether or not you adhered to one yourself.

Ramakrishna, on the other hand, located these various religions not in the society or nation he lived in, but in himself; it was here they coexisted and competed with each other, often annihilating each other temporarily; history animated him from within. The liberal humanism of the Bengal Renaissance formed one of the bases of the secular Indian state; the experiments of Ramakrishna, in which different ways of seeing existed in a sort of tension within oneself, formed one of the bases of the creativity of the modern Indian. It is no accident that every significant Indian writer or artist has negotiated seemingly antithetical world-views or languages in his or her work. But the relationship that the BJP and the new BJP-governed middle class have with Hinduism is prescriptive, not creative; for years now, the BJP's satellites of the far right have imposed a violent, if illegal, ban on imagined offences to the Hindu religion, and abused and harassed artists and writers for their supposed transgressions. This is not only a failure of secularism; it speaks to us of the imminent death of Ramakrishna's inheritance: leaving us unable to negotiate, any more, the different ways of seeing in a way that might create rather than destroy.

In 1893, a penurious Vivekananda travelled to Chicago to attend the Parliament of World Religions. By this time, he had abandoned the white apparel of the *brahmachari*, the celibate-devotee, for the saffron of the *sannyasi*, the wandering holy mendicant. As a follower of Ramakrishna, he had graduated from *brahmacharya* to *sannyas*, from celibacy to renunciation; and yet it was now that he and his religion would embrace the world, not only in a metaphorical and metaphysical, but in a new, global, sense. His address in Chicago, in which he announced a resurgent Hinduism to the West, made him famous; and made, by association and almost by chance, the colour he was wearing the sign of that resurgence rather than of liminality.

We might think we see some of the lineaments of today's *Hindutva* in Vivekananda's revived faith; and, while it is hard to deny the lineage, it's important to distinguish between the two. Certainly, Vivekananda wanted Hinduism to stand on its own two feet, to become less inward-looking, and exhorted it to become a more 'manly' religion. Like other figures of the Bengal Renaissance, he welcomed Western rationalism, science, and materialism, and wanted Hinduism to enter into a transaction with these things. *Hindutva* continues that journey Westward; but the West itself has become a different entity from what it was in the late nineteenth century. Vivekanada would not have foreseen a West that is synonymous, principally, with the benefits of the free market, which the twice-born *Hindutva* now rushes towards. Moreover, Ramakrishna, the rustic seer, was important to Vivekananda as the vernacular root of Hinduism; he couldn't have known that the religion he helped revive would venture so far into the world that it would become, in essence, a globalized urban faith, in Delhi and Bombay, London and New York, divorced from the vernacular experience that Ramakrishna represented. The followers of the postmodern *Hindutva* still ritually, and piously, celebrate Vivekanada, but, a hundred years after his death, no longer exult in conscience or discernment.

On the Nature of Indian Gothic
The Imagination of Ashis Nandy

The first time I met him, Ashis Nandy said to me that Mushirul Hasan had once described him as a 'de-professionalized intellectual'. We were having a conversation over lunch during which I was reflecting on my host's status as a maverick and an outsider. It is not a status one acquires by ambition; it comes, rather, from the compulsions of background and temperament, and, as Nandy pointed out to me helpfully, from not only the nature of one's work but also of one's employment. The Centre for Studies in Developing Societies in Delhi has, over several decades, with the benevolence of a patron rather than an institution, fostered and enlarged his position as maverick employee. Outsiders have generally faded from public life in India, and one of the reasons is institutional intolerance of them in this country. The place we had met for lunch, the dining room of the Indian International Centre Annexe, was itself a room bursting and crowded with rank and caste, a small area where the entrenched émigrés that comprise Delhi's political and intellectual life congregate to nourish themselves physically and, more importantly, socially. The reason for Nandy's survival in this world is his personal charm and that he seems to have made his peace with it outwardly; the fact that he seems to be on handshaking terms with many members of the establishment conceals, at least temporarily, and in everyday life, the astringency and deep oddity of his own position. (This charm is reflected in the range and generosity of the footnotes in the present book, *Time Warps*, where he acknowledges a range of sources and stimuli, some of which emerge from ideological stances subtly, and crucially, different from his own.)

What is the nature of Nandy's project? I think this book crystallizes what, for me, is one of its most powerful thrusts: to fashion a commentary on what I can only call the Indian Gothic. It is a discourse whose antecedents we must locate in nineteenth-century England. The Gothic is a category whose critical impulse was almost single-handedly defined in the middle of the nineteenth century, by the English art critic beloved of Gandhi, John Ruskin. The term's polemical meaning had been circulated by William Hazlitt, but it was Ruskin who put it to fullest and most audacious use. Although Ruskin's ostensible subject was a style of architecture, he was also, in his essay, 'The Nature of Gothic', critiquing the Enlightenment values of an England that would, in a few years, officially assume the mantle of Empire.

Ruskin completed this essay in 1853. Britain was on the verge of becoming a global imperial power, and Ruskin's essay on architecture is not untouched by the politics of Empire; it is, in fact, an early and radical critique of that politics. Mainstream European architecture is, according to Ruskin, streamlined and perfect. In bringing this to fruition, the Renaissance church or the Greek one suppresses, says Ruskin, the 'rude', the wayward, the 'imperfect'. The Gothic, on the other hand, allows these elements expression in its architectural space; and among the characteristics Ruskin notes as unmistakably Gothic are 'Savageness, or Rudeness', and 'Grotesqueness'. The Gothic is the self-expression of the 'rude' and 'barbaric' Northern temperament whose time, Ruskin believes, has come. It's worth noting that the 'barbaric' and the 'civilized' are not, for Ruskin, and as they certainly were in the time of Empire, terms used to dichotomize 'backward' states and 'enlightened' nations, or colonizer and colonized; they are a means of problematizing 'Englishness' itself as a stable category. The 'barbaric' elements Ruskin enumerates in the context of the Gothic are *within* Englishness, not outside it. The Gothic becomes an occasion on which Ruskin rewrites 'Englishness' in the terms of 'difference'.

'Rude', 'barbaric', 'savage': the political and imperial resonance of these terms becomes clear if we read Ruskin's contemporary, John Stuart Mill. The latter's *Considerations on Representative Government* was published in 1861, roughly ten years after Ruskin composed his essay, although the individual pieces that comprise it, and the rhetoric they reflect, had already been in circulation. The contradiction in Mill's work is well known: his enthusiasm for democratic governance, and the conviction he held at the same instant that democracy was unsuited to certain 'inferior' peoples. Mill's concept of the nation-state argues for the suppression of the 'rude' in the way Ruskin diagnosed its suppression in mainstream European architecture. Thus, Mill: 'A rude people, though in some degree alive to the benefits of civilized society, may be unable to practice the forbearance it demands …' For 'any people who have emerged from savage life', only a 'limited and qualified freedom' is appropriate. 'Civilized government,' Mill continues, 'to be really advantageous to them, will require to be in a considerable degree despotic …'

Placed in juxtaposition with Mill's essay, we begin to see that Ruskin's 'Gothic' is an extraordinarily prescient critique of Mill's conception of the colonial nation-state. Ruskin's account of mainstream European architecture makes it a trope for Mill's nation-state; the master-workman, the necessary 'despot', suppresses the 'rude' impulses of the 'inferior' workman; for the latter – who, according to Ruskin, becomes a 'slave' in the Greek tradition – only a version of Mill's 'limited and qualified freedom' is possible. Gothic architecture, on the other hand, doesn't suppress the 'rude' or 'savage'; it incorporates these qualities as constituents of its style by 'allowing independent operation to the inferior workman'. The freedom of the 'inferior' workman, in this equation, is inflected with the colonized's right to self-determination; the Gothic affirmation of 'rudeness' – 'betraying ... imperfection in every touch' – resonates with the political liberty of the marginalized in the imperial world.

When India gained Independence, it inherited an Enlightenment concept – the modern democratic nation-state – but, at once, embarked upon an unprecedented experiment. By opting for universal adult suffrage from the moment of Independence, at a time when the electorate was *not* largely middle-class – in fact, quite the opposite – the Indian nation-state included in the political process, besides its bourgeois citizenry, a peasant class, and, as a result, 'the agency of gods, spirits, and other supernatural beings': I am quoting Dipesh Chakrabarty on Ranajit Guha's critique of Eric Hobsbawm. The Indian state has had, thus, to negotiate two languages, two (I am borrowing from Ruskin) architectures, from its inception. The first is an Enlightenment conception of the democratic nation-state which most of us, in the middle class, inhabit mentally, and none literally or physically: an ideal of perfection, an ideal democracy. The achievement of this ideal is contingent upon the suppression, or amelioration, of the wayward. Much of our polemical energy is expended upon measuring the distance between the political 'ideal' and the 'real', and one mustn't dismiss this polemic: it is a crucial part of our democratic life.

The other language or architecture of the Indian state might be called a Gothic experiment, a space in which the 'rude' or 'savage' are indispensable to the life of the structure; where unequal groups, like Ruskin's 'inferior' workmen, allow their imaginative capacities and loyalties to mark (or, from another point of view, mar) the design of the building or nation. There are commentators who have been trying to fashion a critical and cognitive language with which to speak of the Gothic political experiment; among the foremost, and most idiosyncratic, of these is Nandy; among those whose interpretation is more exclusively political are the subaltern historians. As to the latter's philosophical analyses: Guha's critique of

Hobsbawm's 'premodern', Chakrabarty's meditation on Walter Benjamin's 'homogeneous, empty time of history', Partha Chatterjee's formulation, in response to Benedict Anderson, of the 'heterogeneous time of modernity' – all these are attempts to arrive at a discourse that doesn't divide the historical 'present' in India into pre-modern and modern components, but to create something like a Gothic paradigm, in which unequal elements alike combine to produce a single architecture, and, by implication, political and historical process.

Both Nandy and the subaltern historians are critics of the Enlightenment. The difference between them seems to me to be this: the Enlightenment, for the subaltern historians, is situated in Europe; their discourse is addressed at least substantially to the Western academy; this gives to their project its particular urgency. Nandy, on the other hand, seems to be directly confronting the Indian middle class in its incarnations as polity and intelligentsia; even closer to home, he is confronting the self. Although he speaks of the 'European' Enlightenment, the Enlightenment and the self, for him, are deeply implicated and linked; it is his 'higher' self, in a sense, he is addressing and scolding. This gives his project *its* particular urgency.

Anteriority, or posteriority, is a characteristic of the Gothic, in that it gives expression to what Enlightenment culture pushes to the back. Mikhail Bakhtin's attendance to Rabelais's portraits of the human posterior is related, for him, to being a historian of the grotesque and the carnivalesque – the latter being his metaphor for the self-expression of marginalized cultures, in the way the Gothic was for Ruskin. The Gothic relationship with anteriority in Indian modernity was an aesthetic project even before it became a political one: think of Tagore's relationship with the Santhal and Baul; moving on, of U.R. Anantha Murthy, teacher of English, drawing upon the traditions of the 'back yard' for his Kannada fiction; of A.K. Ramanujan, whose 'outer' forms, he claimed, came from English, his 'inner' from Tamil and Kannada.

But Nandy is not only our poet and theorist of the vernacular energies; he is our poet of the Indian grotesque. Just as the Indian use of the word 'secular' is both related to, and subtly different from, the Western 'secular', so the Indian word 'backside' is both akin to, and somewhat differs from, the same word in proper English parlance (although to speak of 'backside' and 'proper English parlance' in the same breath is itself a paradox). 'Backside', in English, means, as we know, the human posterior; 'backside', in Indian English, or any Indian language, refers to the rear entrance of a building, or the back of an object. That the word has a political dimension in our country was revealed to me once when I was entering Delhi in a taxi, and the driver informed me: 'Sir, that is the backside of the

Lok Sabha!' True: much of our trade in modern India is conducted in this 'backside', in unofficial quarters; most of our politics is negotiated in this 'backside.' The word, in India, has both the hint of the grotesque and the political resonance that Bakhtin once identified in it; and Nandy has been exploring those hints and resonances.

Unlike the subaltern theorists, he is not so much interested in 'resistance from below' as in the excremental echoes of 'below', in the grotesque as a counterpoint to the Enlightenment idea of the state. Thus: 'Of this Indian state ... the romantic realists have no clue ... It is ... fair to argue that more [sic] realistic analysts of the Indian state today are the criminalized elements in the polity.' The enlightenment concept Nandy calls the 'shadow state' or, echoing Anderson but inverting his meaning, an 'imagined state'; the Indian state as Gothic experiment he calls the 'present Indian state', punning on the other meaning of 'state' – as in 'state of affairs.'

Architectural tropes that conflate the Gothic and the nation-state recur in the book; and, as in Ruskin's Gothic cathedral, religion and the marginalized's self-determination are brought together: 'Religion *has* entered public life, but through the back door.' Nandy has little time for the Hindu chauvinism of the upper-caste bourgeoisie, which he calls 'an odd form of reactive Westernisation' in 'the garb of cultural nationalism'. But he is interested in the different belief-systems that constitute our Gothic national experiment, and configures this in architectural terms; here he is on deities outside the mainstream: 'They are not permitted into the main hall, but they are there, just outside the door, constantly threatening to enter the main hall uninvited ...' This is from the enthralling 'A Report on the Present State of Health of the Gods and Goddesses in South Asia'. It is about the beliefs that engender tolerance in our country; but the sentence I've quoted is also about a political process. The paradigm is the Gothic; and the essay, in its way, is as important in its metaphorical eloquence on our Indianness as Ruskin's was in relation to Englishness. The person who, generationally and figuratively, links these commentators together is, for me, Gandhi; Gandhi, who absorbed Ruskin, and who is an exemplar to Nandy. Like the Indian nation, Gandhi can be seen to be at once modern and pre-modern, political and non-political; or we could see him, and our nation-state, as a frustrating but mesmerizing Gothic paradigm, definitively political, definitively modern.

'Hollywood *aur* Bollywood'[1]

In June this year, I went to Bombay with my wife and daughter for a visit; it was two and half years since I'd been there last. This is the city in which I'd grown up; and yet there was no excuse for me to return. The city was no longer the one I'd known, despite the fact that many of the old landmarks and buildings remain exactly the same. Its name had changed, for one thing, as well as its character: exacerbated by people and cars and money and violence and politics and religion. And what's called 'Bollywood' had moved centre-stage artistically, in the space that was once occupied, in a low-key way, by music, poetry, and theatre, and become the city's main cultural output. That's why, in spite of scheming and praying for more than two years for an invitation (to read, to lecture) to a city I'd despised in my adolescence but couldn't forget, I now had to contrive to stop over there on my way to England (where I would read and lecture). Indeed, I went to Delhi, an arid metropolis by comparison, far more often, because literary 'conferences' and all-expenses-paid junkets for writers happen there with astonishing regularity; personally, I blamed Bollywood, and its stranglehold on cultural activity in Bombay, for keeping me, and the likes of me, from the city.

My wife and I decided we'd do 'nothing' for the duration of our stay; that is, meet a few friends, and amble around shops and restaurants and cafes. Neither of us remembered having taken a comparable break for more than a year; and it was in this mood that, on the fourth and penultimate day of our stay, we decided to walk across from the Yacht Club, where we were putting up, to the Regal Cinema, to watch the latest and most publicized Bollywood release, *Fanaa*. The amusement and mild pulse of excitement we felt at the prospect was itself indicative of the recklessness of our state of mind at the time; because watching a Bollywood film was, to people of our generation and background (even now, when Hindi cinema is in an unprecedentedly mainstream and ubiquitous phase), a slightly questionable adventure.

Part of the reason that I wanted to watch the film was, of course, to revisit the Regal Cinema, where I'd seen movies like *The Guns of Navarone* as a child. Built along ebullient art deco lines, something between a temple to popular culture and an immense cake, this seemingly playful, edible building has survived both multiplexes and a long two decades in which cinema appeared to have been vanquished by videos, VCDs, DVDs, and the internet. Its interior was a tiny bit shabby, but nevertheless genteel; or perhaps it had always been slightly shabby, and I hadn't noticed earlier, since shabbiness used to be an inalienable part of gentility. The fact, though, that it was showing a Hindi film (and had been showing Hindi films for about ten years) reminded you of the sort of compromises it had had to make towards survival, as well as of the place Bollywood occupies today.

The film had opened to mixed reviews. In spite of the fact that it was Kajol's comeback movie – Kajol, the most radiant of contemporary heroines, who'd married another actor, become a mother, and was now returning to acting herself, her family still intact – in spite of this, the hall was half full. The leading man was Aamir Khan, a pretty-faced hero who's evolved into one of Hindi cinema's more fastidious and articulate performers, and, with the Oscar-nominated *Lagaan*, into a canny producer. Aamir, in the film, is a tourist guide in Delhi, who runs into the blind Kajol, visiting the city from Kashmir, with, improbably, a troupe of dancers. They explore the city, fall in love; Aamir arranges for an operation that will restore Kajol's sight. And then, coinciding with the operation, there are explosions in Delhi, killing several people, including, it seems, the tourist guide. Kajol, in the hospital room, can now see; but, as the world reveals itself to her, it brings with it news of her lover's death. Kajol is with child; by the time we approach intermission, the twist in the centre of the story's clear to us – we see Aamir, alive, dressed in an expensively tailored suit, with a different haircut, in an airport, probably in Kuala Lumpur. Aamir is a 'terrorist'.

The second half is a development of this conceit. Aamir has infiltrated the Indian Army; he's an officer; he's on his most important mission, to do with a nuclear trigger that will bring unimaginable devastation to the major Indian cities. But something goes wrong, and he is pursued, in snowbound Kashmir, by Indian officers on snowmobiles in a scene out of a James Bond/Pierce Brosnan offering; he escapes, wounded, and staggers to the isolated, idyllic cottage in which Kajol lives with her parents and little son. Kajol now sees her lover for the first time; but, of course, can't recognize him. A new intimacy grows in the family; but the film, from here onward, is inexorable and doom-laden – a man who's about to destroy India can't, after all, be allowed to live. As the background music grew increasingly portentous, my seven-year-old daughter grew more and more restless; and so it was that I didn't see the last half-hour of the movie, and spent it gloomily observing, once more, the genteel shabbiness, the mirrors and the popcorn machine. But I'd seen enough to realize that, despite its token borrowings from Hollywood, this film involved a somewhat laboured, and yet intriguing, reworking of Hindi cinema's old preoccupations: to do with forgetting and remembering one's place in the world, and, connected to this, to do with the theme of doubles, of being joined, whether one knows it or not, to a different, often contradictory, version of one's self and life.

Two days later, I flew to England.

It was when I was a student in England in the 1980s that I'd properly encountered 'Bollywood' as an idea, removed, more or less, from its immediate material context: something that was at once strange, over the top, and immemorially 'Indian'. For instance, I remember a rather inane conversation from about fifteen years ago on late-night British television, between, of all combinations, Ruby Wax and Salman Rushdie. Ruby Wax, all silliness herself, began to say something about the silliness of Bollywood. Rushdie didn't take her on. Pursuing the point, she said that Bollywood films weren't 'grown-up' enough. To my surprise, Rushdie didn't argue; he wavered weakly. I don't recall having seen Ruby Wax stand up for the virtues of grown-up seriousness before or since; it was a facet of her persona I became newly aware of that night.

Of course, part of the reason Bollywood had any currency at all in conversation in Britain, and one of my main reasons for this, at best, unremarkable exchange surviving in my memory, had to do with Rushdie himself, and his novel *Midnight's Children* – Rushdie, who, in the years prefiguring globalization, had with an unfailing instinct identified what the most likely features of the 'global' (before the term possessed its present significance or usage) incarnation of India would be. 'India', so reincarnated, would involve an aggressive overturning of the older humanist ideas of seriousness; all that was most unserious about India – its loudness, its apparent lack of introspection and irony, its peculiar version of English grammar, as well as a particular notion of cinema – would be changed by becoming a powerful metaphor for the effervescence of the globalized world.

When I finally read *Midnight's Children* (I was slow to get round to it), I understood why its author had prevaricated that night with Ruby Wax. Rushdie, with this novel, had become a fantasist in public and by profession, but, like many Indians of his generation, was a rationalist in private.

The rationalist, humanist Rushdie – even the conservative Rushdie – began to emerge more and more after the *fatwa*, when he began to speak (with every justification) against the voices of unreason and Khomeini in the outraged tone, almost, of a near-defunct European Enlightenment. With 9/11, the conservative Rushdie has become more fully formed, though the fantastic tomes keep arriving, the incorrigible proselytizer for the notion that 'nothing is impossible' in a novel coming together strangely with the canny fundamentalist of free speech and democracy, George Bush. In *Midnight's Children*, though, Rushdie occupies a delicate hairline border – between the humanist liberalism which the novel embraces both in its politics and its basic vision of a world of upbeat multiculturalism, and its new, aggressive, postmodern celebration (this is where Bollywood comes in) of a popular culture whose values the older humanism always carefully differentiated itself from. But there's also a subtle differentiation within the novel itself; in it, Bollywood is over the top, energetic, but, in the end, as absurd as it would be to any middle-class Indian gentleman who'd grown up in the first two or three decades after Independence. On one thing – when it comes to Bollywood – the humanist and the postmodernist, the old-style dilettante and the modish 'cultural studies' academic, are more or less in agreement: the unlikelihood of Bollywood actually possessing *artistic value*. Today, of course, the whole question of artistic value is set aside or made irrelevant, or practised only in private like a superseded religion. Rushdie, himself, celebrates Bollywood, but we're never sure what he owes to it as an artist; indeed, his deepest artistic debts seem to be to European art-house cinema even more than to literature, his 'magic realism' less an offshoot of Marquez than of the surrealism of directors like Buñuel and Godard. No wonder he was tongue-tied at Ruby Wax's tart dismissal.

My own memories of the genre, if genre it is, go back to a time when it wasn't called 'Bollywood' at all, but 'Hindi film'. Any melodramatic out-burst in a play, or in a book, would draw from my mother the amused but contemptuous whisper: 'Hindi film'. Implausible idiocy in a Hollywood picture (there was no shortage of idiocy in Hollywood movies) would have my parents look at each other, eyebrows raised in tolerant disbelief, and murmur: 'Hindi film'. It was as if some embarrassing religious miracle had occurred in the everyday bourgeois world, some expansive gesture made, purporting that the world was more than it possibly could be. The tired expression, the whispered words – 'Hindi film' – contained a judgement at once aesthetic and moral. My parents had been formed by a Bengali humanism whose seeds were sown at the end of the eighteenth century, and which was full-blown by the end of the nineteenth; for them, the real was synonymous not only with knowledge, but with illumination. 'Reality', which their nineteenth-century forefathers bestowed upon them, along with rationality, science, and literature, represented the liberation of being who they were; it lay at the root of the political freedom that had created the India they lived in during the 1960s.

Those were the Yahoo years. I don't mean to invoke Swift here; but the term was, in the language of Hindi cinema gossip, a pejorative, and has a passing, if purely coincidental, resemblance to Swift's derision of the unreconstructed male. It derived from the sound the actor Shammi Kapoor made, some time in the late 1960s, before launching into the hit song and defiant manifesto: 'Chahe koi mujhe junglee kahe', or 'Let them say I'm from the jungle if they want to'. The song was set to a rock and roll tune, and Shammi Kapoor films had plenty of picnics, bicycles, hampers, drainpipe trousers, Himalayan hairdos culminating above the sari, and impromptu renderings of the twist. My parents hardly saw Hindi films; they had both been born into small-town East Bengal families in the 1920s (affluent families, and, in my mother's case, a very educated one, which slipped into difficult circumstances after her father's early death); and Bengali humanism, via the Tagore family and others, had, even more than colonial education, made them take a dim view of the sort of excess, in its departure from the norms of both verisimilitude and polite bourgeois society, that Hindi cinema represented. They had a taste (consolidated by the years they spent in England in the 1950s) for Hollywood 'love stories', especially historical romances – or romances based on history – like *Anne of a Thousand Days*. These are what partly provided the spark in their long honeymoon years in corporate Bombay, a honeymoon which, in retrospect, I seem to know relatively little about; now and then, they'd disappear without much explanation in the afternoon or evening, as the sisters did in the tale about the dancing shoes, and return from a different world, with stories of the Tudors, or of more mundane but nevertheless magical settings in 1950s America. Once, though, I remember they came back from a Shammi Kapoor movie, having intended, perhaps, to check out what sort of animal (idiomatically speaking) he was; this, then, was a moment in which the narrative of Hindi cinema's struggle, even greed, for respectability among the educated Indian middle classes (a respectability that would come properly two decades later, in the 1990s), and my parents' recreational adventures coincided. My mother's terse and, really, deeply moral report to me on her return was: 'Rubbish.'

My earliest memories of cinema have to do with a Hindi film my parents for some reason took me to when I was maybe four: an image survives, of a man in a suit singing to a woman by a fountain. It's evident from that flickering picture that the trappings of Hindi cinema were solemnly, sincerely bourgeois; that it was through an idea of the Indian middle class that it meant to work its scandalous magic. Soon after, in that early child-hood, I was introduced to parables of the Western bourgeoisie that also tapped into a hidden chaos: Laurel and Hardy, who, with their constant slaps, collisions, and knocks on the head, made me cry when I first saw them, while the audience around me incomprehensibly broke into laugh-ter; and Harold Lloyd, jumping onto runaway streetcars, congenitally surrounded by collapsing houses. The breakdown of order in these films filled me with fear.

Hindi film still hadn't become 'Bollywood' then; the word, I think, was coined by one of the three or four magazines in Bombay devoted to film gossip, *Cine Blitz*, some time in the early 1970s. These publications had a curious relationship with their subject: they fed off it, and yet were largely supercilious about popular Hindi cinema as a form. The magazines embodied the fun, the risk, as well as the unease of writing about an os-tensibly 'uneducated' form for an educated, if avid, readership. (English was, always, uncomplicatedly the language synonymous with education in Bombay, unlike Calcutta, where Bengali too carried with it that particu-lar prestige.) 'Bollywood', then, was a put-down, a dig at the hubris, the pretensions, of Hindi cinema by those who, officially, still gave priority and respect to faraway Hollywood, but found sustenance, without entirely admitting to it, in the common or garden, easily available contraband, Hindi film.

People who actually work in the Hindi film industry (and it is now, at last, a recognized 'industry') have long detested the term. Rakeysh Mehra, director of the recent hit *Rang De Basanti*, which is now set for worldwide release, remonstrated moodily the other day: 'I know Hollywood. It has a hill in it. Where is Bollywood? It doesn't exist. It is a notion.' And this is quite true; Bollywood is not an actual place – you can't visit it. It's an idea, even a form, perhaps a sensibility. It started life as a snide put-down from the Indian middle class when the latter was much smaller than it is now, and not the profligate, globalized entity it's become. The 'notion', then, resurfaced in the West in the early 1980s, at around the time that, coinci-dentally, the West was losing its taste for what Matthew Arnold had long ago called 'high seriousness', and finding in kitsch, pastiche, and parody modes of self-expression that were more amenable to it than patrician concepts like 'art' and 'culture'. 'Bollywood', that is, began to become an important idea in the West as the West became postmodern.

If it isn't a place, what is it? The words with which Susan Sontag (who probably would have had only a tenuous notion of it by the end of her life) opens her famous 'Notes on "Camp"' are almost as apposite to Bollywood as they are to the subject of her piece: 'Many things in the world have not been named; and many things, even if they have been named, have never been described.' Her enumeration of the qualities of Camp in the essay will persuade those who know Bollywood, since the 1980s, as a cluster of over-the-top gestures that it's a variant of the phenomenon she once provided a genealogy for. Among her 'random' taxonomy of items that constitute Camp – among others, *Zuleika Dobson*, Tiffany lamps, Aubrey Beardsley drawings, *Swan Lake*, the Cuban singer La Lupe – Bollywood finds no mention, but would have, you feel, if it had had a place in her consciousness at that time (1964). Many of her observations on the Camp artefact – that it possesses 'style at the expense of content'; that it is 'often decorative'; that it exhibits a taste for the 'strongly exaggerated'; that it is, 'from a "serious" point of view … either bad art or kitsch' – many of these observations are pertinent to the way we think of Bollywood today. So is Sontag's crucial point about androgyny; for the Bollywood hero, however macho and muscle-toned he might be, can never banish his 'softness', which derives partly from the fact that, in the film, he's always a 'son'.

Of course, all the instances Sontag cites in her marvellous essay are European, or at least white-complexioned. And yet, what she's talking about, really, without ever bringing it fully to the light, is a quality of foreignness, of 'otherness'; something that the European bourgeois sensibility cringes at, is embarrassed by, and cannot ever wholly or happily acknowledge as its own. Sontag notes this division in herself, as lots of people, including middle-class Indians, do in relation to Bollywood: 'I am strongly drawn to [it], and almost as strongly offended by it.' Two things, though, have happened to Camp since globalization: the first is that the sort of self-reflexivity Camp represents is no longer a cult or marginal taste, but a central one. It has also become a political gesture, such as Sontag couldn't have suspected at the time she wrote her notes: for her, Camp was 'a certain mode of aestheticisation … depoliticised – or at least apolitical.' The second has to do with the rise of non-Western cultures in the postmodern world; these, and the way in which they're celebrated and interpreted, have become the principal example of Camp in the last twenty five years. The queasy quality of 'foreignness' that is Sontag's real theme in her essay has burst irrepressibly to the surface; and Bollywood is part of that 'coming out'. 'Camp sees everything in quotation marks. It's not a lamp, but a "lamp"; not a woman, but a "woman".' Similarly, Bollywood is not Hollywood, but Hollywood in quotes. The writer for *Cine Blitz* sensed this years ago, had a good laugh, but couldn't have foreseen the prestige and excitement that globalization would confer on unintentional parody.

The Indian novel in the last quarter-century is another good instance of Camp separateness: its representative is never just a novel, but an 'Indian novel', akin to the novel but extravagantly different from it.

All those who wish to think and feel seriously about Hindi cinema (however impossible that may sound) will have to move, in the end, beyond the idea of 'Bollywood' and its hidden affinities with Camp; once spotted, those indisputable affinities need to be acknowledged – yet it's necessary to admit that the ironical seriousness they've given to the genre can't be the only way of discussing it. For 'Bollywood' is a droll but misleading shorthand for what's really an exceptional heterogeneity of periods and styles. Take, for instance, the songs in Hindi cinema; the presence of which to a large extent determines, after all, our perception that popular Hindi film is a non-realistic and stubbornly, awkwardly 'different' genre. But a comparison with the Hollywood musical tells us that the way songs were presented in the Hindi movies of the 1950s and early 1960s constitutes a genuine *cinematic* innovation. The Hollywood musical never emerges (and doesn't try to) from the shadow of its parent, Broadway. While Debbie Reynolds and Frank Sinatra jump about tunefully, or Gene Kelly gets soaked while he sings in the rain, we, the audience, are not made aware anew of the possibilities of cinema, but of sets and interiors; what we're watching is filmed theatre, Broadway magnified and brought within inches of the optic nerve. This is true even of Hollywood musicals made today, like *Moulin Rouge* – of which it's been said, interestingly, that it bears the marks of Bollywood's influence.

But the Hindi film in the 1950s took the song outside, into the open; even when it was filmed in a room, it was the irradiation of space around the singer – casual, irrelevant, but part of the frame – that was emphasized. Movement and actors were kept to a minimum; usually, the camera concentrated only on the couple, and on close-ups, which revealed subtle movements of the eye, and of, say, windblown hair. Aleatory natural movement was recorded, usually of the wind, but also of the moon, and of water. Many of the most famous songs of that era are about a breeze, or the moon; about the tactile or the visual. Nothing much happens during these songs: their main drama has to do with the play in them of the principal medium of cinema – light. Conceiving and arranging a song visually was called, in Hindi film parlance, 'picturization', and a great deal of art and cinematic mastery have gone into the best 'picturizations'. In the narrative-driven, intermittently melodramatic genre emerging in the 1950s, the songs are moments of stillness and contained emotion, a poetic arrest of the 'here and now' at certain points in the story. They are related more deeply to the modernist image than either to Hollywood or any traditional Indian art form; their provenance lies in neo-realist cinema and the early films of Renoir and Carne.

I myself began to discover these films in the England of the 1980s when I was there as a student, often through British television, at a time when BBC2 and Channel 4 still hadn't been tamed by the brunt of Thatcherism. Other Indian students were discovering them too; those songs were not only a currency of expatriation, but a collective memory, their melodic yearning speaking to what was most personal in us as products of Indian modernity, and very different from the extroverted Bhangra rap that the 'Asians' loved. The Hindi cinema of the 1980s I ignored completely; it represented the mutation of the genre into 'Bollywood' style in its least imaginative version. When I returned to India at the very end of the last century, I realized, as I channel-hopped through my television's new satellite-supplied repertoire, that something interesting had happened to Hindi cinema in the 1990s. For one thing, the 'song picturization' had changed: it was still largely being shot outdoors, but in 'foreign locations' – Canada, Switzerland, English manor houses. Of course, songs had involved excursions in the 1960s as well (the Shammi Kapoor character was, for instance, well-travelled and could leap, singing, into the frame anywhere) – to other parts of the country, especially the presently beleaguered Kashmir, and, occasionally, the world. Those outings and songs belong to a time when the middle-class daydream, the notion of travel, and the tourism industry converged with a trustfulness that now seems astonishing; they are the contemporaries of tea board and tourism board posters, of solicitous airhostesses who were also role models; they embody the belief that escape, even when it's packaged, is both innocent and possible.

In the globalized world, there is no 'outside', no escape from the global; every landscape or place is a showroom of a world transformed absolutely by capitalism; this is the reality that the new songs, in which actors prance about in the unlikeliest of locations as if it were their drawing room, remind us of. In fact, Hindi cinema's response to globalization has been far more intelligent and transformative than Hollywood's. For one thing, it has often let in, through the back door of its slightly improbable and apparently derived stories, the paraphernalia of the globalized world – cell-phones, one-day cricket matches on satellite television, international phone calls – far more readily and engagingly than, for instance, more 'serious' genres like the Indian novel in English have. Globalization has made Hindi cinema slicker but also more surreal and open-ended, more random in its elements; in the exuberance and awkwardness peculiar to the genre, and in the way it seeks out the pulse of the Indian 'diaspora' as well as the municipal school dropout, it mirrors, strangely but compellingly, the world of conspicuous excess and extreme poverty we now live in. Hollywood's response to globalization has been to take full advantage of the marketplace, but to close ranks artistically, to become determinedly simpler, more suburban, more white. Even cartoons, whether they're about an imagined ice age or the underworld of the ocean, remain resolutely situated in the heart of American suburbia; it's as if we're already in the age of *The Matrix*, dreamers transfixed by a fictional incarnation of the world we live in. The miscegenation that globalization richly represents for the West is hardly captured by mainstream American cinema.

What, then, is the difference between Hollywood and Hindi film, if one were to risk a generalization? It's not a question of songs and dances on the one hand, and plausible human behaviour on the other. It's a question of what a grown-up view of life might be. And grown-upness has less to do with rationality than we might think. Hollywood gives us a strangely cocooned universe; it leaves intact the beliefs that were fostered in us by our parents and our school – that the world can be understood; that if you act intelligently, you will prosper; that you can control your fate. It often does this metaphorically; by making reality persuasive but simple, by making the protagonist free of family and bodily functions. In truth, the passage of time makes things less, not more, familiar to us; it wears us down and shakes our resolve. The world in the Hollywood film is linear and realistic, but it is not marked by the passage of time, or at least the same sort of time we live in; that's why we emerge from watching it, whatever violence or devastation we might have witnessed in it, with our childhood convictions essentially unthreatened – however many bullets might have whizzed past the leading man, and buildings and even countries been blown up, we know the world is the place we were taught it was. What Hollywood gives compellingly to us (there are, of course, notable exceptions to the norm) is a particular experience that's summed up by a compound word: 'feelgood'. What *is* this experience, which leaves us feeling fulfilled in a slightly dubious sort of way? It seems to me that 'feelgood' is a displaced form of nationalism; Hollywood's most persistent subject, whether the movie's about a bank heist, or falling in love, or going to Mars, or discovering treasure, is 'winning'. It's a theme deeply implicated, especially in America, in the audience's vicarious participation in the life of the nation-state.

The Hindi film, like Hollywood, largely believes in happy endings, and has its fair share of jingoism too; but it's slightly less interested in 'feelgood' than in allowing its protagonist to rediscover his place in the world. Unlike Hollywood, it's a genre, I think, that is marked deeply by the passage of time, and the separations time visits on us; it is not an innocent genre – it knows that the notion that we control our destiny is a myth. This isn't just the wisdom of the ancients; it's a very contemporary, but tender-hearted, realism, a realism quite different from anything in Hollywood. This doesn't mean Hindi cinema is fatalistic or metaphysical; its exuberance is indispensable to its conviction that life is an unrecognizable, rather than categorizable, thing. Time reveals this to us gradually as individuals; and the way Bollywood reveals it to its audience is through a series of devices: for example, coincidences; doubles; brothers separated at birth. These devices make the Hindi film embarrassing, but also, at its best, very moving; sometimes they make it embarrassing and moving at once.

One of the devices film-makers have been using recently in India has to do with placing contiguous characters within proximity of one another without their knowing it. This is an extension and refinement of the way doubles have, for decades, populated the genre. In the film *Hum Tum* (*The Two of Us*), which I saw by chance on television the other day, a mother (discernibly a member of the new affluent and geographically mobile class) is gently bewailing to a friend the fact that her beautiful daughter has gone very quiet ever since her fiancé died. 'Sometimes I don't know that she's in the same room,' she says; there is a quick, brief flashback – she is sitting on a sofa, her daughter standing silently at a window behind her; and, turning, the mother becomes aware with a start of her daughter's presence. The Hindi film is subtly punctuated today with such starts and intakes of breath. The double occurs also as something between a cheesy out-of-body experience and a spiritual circling about and indecisiveness; in *Veer Zara*, a story of a couple separated by Partition, the actor sings in solemn despair on a verandah while his image rises from him and hovers beyond. In *Kal Ho Na Ho* (*Whether or not There's a Tomorrow*), a film I saw in Germany ('Bollywood' has become a cult there, and Germans are trying to analyse gravely why it affects them so deeply), the protagonist, a terminally ill heart patient (a condition almost no one else knows about), is often shown sitting next to his friends, listening to their conversations, though they neither see him, nor are aware of his proximity. This proximity is oddly superfluous, quite distinct from the way in which he organizes and influences his friends' lives in the film; and the unexplained superfluity is oddly moving. The protagonist's appearance at these moments has no supernatural explanation; the clever tricks with which he helps his best friend advance in love are reminiscent of Hollywood, even American sitcoms; but the recurrent, superfluous sightings to which only we have access undermine the certainty that those whom we know most intimately can be, even *should* be, knowable.

The actor playing the protagonist in both *Veer Zara* and *Kal Ho Na Ho* is Shahrukh Khan, the biggest star now in Hindi film, master of the exaggerated, emotional twitch and gesture, as well as of occupying the fringes of the frame as his own double, the Shahrukh Khan the millions do not know. Sometimes he seems to enter a film in a brief 'guest appearance', not as a leading man, but solely to be a double of himself, a shadowy but talismanic character. Towards the end of the film *Saathiya* (*Companions*), a woman who's been gravely injured in an accident with a car is admitted to a hospital; on several occasions, the estranged husband, who's looking for the wife who hasn't returned home, and Shahrukh Khan, the wealthy husband of the person who was driving the car that ran over the woman, and who's now waiting in the hospital, pass by one another without knowing it in the waiting area. Such parallel moments might be used in a Hollywood thriller to build up suspense; but seldom, I think, to convey the seemingly pointless but poignant drift of human lives, the hit-and-miss quality, as well as the life-giving interdependence, of human contact as they are in this film. Not only does the language of Hindi cinema tell us that the theme of doubles is crucial to our experience of the world we live in, a world of immense disparity and miraculous conjunctions; it shows us there's a deeply human way of approaching this theme. Perhaps we can remove Hollywood and Bollywood, twins severed by geography and circumstance, one, for a long time, unknown to the other, from talk of parody and pastiche and quotation marks, and bring to that relationship the same humanity and unexpectedness?

The View from Malabar Hill

Like Suketu Mehta, I was born in Calcutta, a city 'in extremis', in Mehta's words, and, like him, grew up in Bombay. His father, who worked in the diamond trade, and mine, then a rising executive in the corporate world, probably moved to Bombay from Calcutta for the same reasons; to do with the migration, indeed, the flight, in the 1960s, of capital and industry from the former colonial capital in the East to the forward-looking metropolis in the West, in the face of growing labour unrest and radical politics in leftist Bengal – the troubled context that 'in extremis' presumably refers to.

By the early 1970s, Calcutta had ceased to be a major centre of commerce and industry; Howrah, just outside Calcutta, where the factories were once located, became, now that the major players were absent, a purgatory for small enterprise, with businesses – among them my uncle's – waiting, sometimes for years and years, to die. The lights went out in Calcutta, literally; 'load-shedding', or power rationing, became frequent, until, in the early 1980s, the city had to occasionally make do without sixteen hours of electricity in a day. Jyoti Basu, the astringent, unsmiling Communist Chief Minister of West Bengal, a barrister from London and a *bhadralok* (that is, a member of the liberal but patrician middle class), whose first name means 'light', began to be called, in weary jest, '*Andhakaar*', or 'Darkness', Basu. Bombay, on the other hand, began, slowly, to dazzle; I have no memory of it ever not dazzling. From the twelfth-floor apartment in the slightly, but not altogether, extravagantly named Il Palazzo, where I grew up, in Bombay's most exclusive locality, Malabar Hill, I could see the row of lights called the Queen's Necklace, fluorescent and aquamarine at the time (they're now a pale golden sodium), and, further on, the great signs in lights, saying ORWO and BOAC and other things. It was an existence remarkably open to breeze, birds, and rainfall, to the arrival of daylight and evening, and it was also strangely, unselfconsciously, enclosed. It was not Suketu Mehta's Bombay.

For all this, I knew, growing up in the 1960s and 1970s, that Calcutta was India's one great modern city. Its pioneering 150-year-old tradition in literature and the arts, and the way its own history was deeply implicated in the traumas and awakenings of colonial and nationalist India, was embodied in its heat and noise and architecture; it possessed the contradictions, the shabby grandeur, of modernity, and the volatile energy that the great cities of the world possessed before globalization, and I could sense this during my visits as a child. The Bombay I knew was safe, orderly, and a bit crass in comparison.

By the 1980s, the rise of the BJP in India, and its alliance, in Maharashtra (the state of which Bombay, now, officially, 'Mumbai', is the capital), with a once-minor fascist party of Marathi, and, then, Hindu identity, the Shiv Sena, changed Bombay, seemingly for good. It was at this time that Suketu Mehta's 'maximum city' – burgeoning, and in the process pulling down the barriers that had kept the middle-class employee and the entrepreneur on the make, governance and criminality, politics and religion, in distinct physical and mental spaces – it was at this time that *this* version of the city, which Mehta records so thoroughly, even lovingly, began to become visible to those who'd ignored it earlier.

I left, then, for England; and my parents, next year, moved to the Christian suburb, Bandra (one of the 'local train' stops at which a bomb went off on 11 July), an area on the brink of transformation in 1984, but still possessed by, and offering, a sort of enchantment. My parents lived here for five years before selling their flat and moving to Calcutta in 1989; and the discovery of Bandra, with its churches, its low houses built on Portuguese lines, its lanes named after Christian saints, meant a great deal to me then, especially in connection with the transitions I was making, between the anonymous itinerant at University College London and the writer-aspirant with secret ambitions. But it was in Bandra, too, that I discovered, as did my parents, the desire to return to the city proper in which I'd grown up and from which I'd always wanted to escape, and in which my father had spent most of his working life; to embark on that hour-long journey by car to Churchgate or Dhobi Talao, a journey that would be almost impossible to make regularly, given the traffic, twenty-two years later. An obscure set of motives and compulsions drives people toward the hub of Bombay, or toward some place from which that hub is reachable; one of the compulsions, and a pretty basic one, is to breathe its air. I was told this by an upper-class woman who grew up in Bombay and now lives in Calcutta; she'd just returned, invigorated, from a trip to Bombay, and said: 'When I first land there, I inhale deeply.' The air, though, isn't necessarily pleasant or clean; in some places, it's bracing with the odour of dried fish, and, in others, it's odourless with chemical pollutants. What we're speaking of, then, is an addiction, such as the twentieth century was to Amis's John Self; something corrosive but indispensable to the addict. The need for that particular air I first felt, without being at all aware of it, in Bandra (the addict never knows, except in hindsight, that what he or she thinks is interest or curiosity is really an obsession); it's what makes me restless and resentful when I find myself invited to other cities, but with no excuse to go to Bombay; it's presumably what drove Suketu Mehta, who moved to New York when he was fourteen, back; it's what made the poet Arun Kolatkar, author of the classic *Jejuri*, travel every Thursday from his small apartment in Prabhadevi and make the forty-five-minute trip to Kala Ghoda, Bombay's arts and commercial district, and sit there writing, drinking tea, meeting up with friends from the advertising world he was once part of. When, to everyone's dismay, the Wayside Inn was replaced by an upmarket Chinese restaurant, he moved his Thursday afternoon location to the Military Café, which isn't far away from Kala Ghoda, although by now he was terminally ill with stomach cancer. The multiplicity of cafés, food stalls, and restaurants in the city, and the continual acts of eating and drinking, seem to be an appetite for the city itself: the hunger for it, and the persistent, difficult-to-appease desire to ingest it and consume it. I don't know if it's this sense of hunger that's called, especially after every trauma, including the last one, the 'spirit of Mumbai'; certainly, there are enough deterrents, besides the fear of explosions, to prevent people from piling into train compartments or getting into their cars to make the journeys they do, to and within Bombay. Often, the energy and tenacity – and the noisy excitement of stockbrokers on Dalal Street, and the diamond merchants in Zaveri Bazaar (where bombs went off about a year ago[1]) – seem to be the result of a chemical reaction upon the brain, like a 'high' – with its necessary, complementary 'lows'. Sometimes the 'highs' and 'lows' seem married to one another, eerily inextricable and indistinguishable; as in the case of the touching but strange 'laughter clubs' in Bombay, which have people congregating in open spaces for periods of time, breaking into rehearsed laughter as a therapy for tension.

Travelling from Bandra to the centre of the city in a car was expensive, even in 1984. That's when I began to take the 'local train', as it's called in Bombay, from Bandra to Churchgate, emerging, with a stream of commuters, into the areas in which I went to school and grew up. The first-class compartments of seven such trains were ripped apart by explosions; but the trains, even during normal 'rush hour', represent a frenetic and excessive mode of travel. Mehta writes well about them and their passengers and their daily exacerbations; the Darwinian conflict among people scrambling to get a seat, and the contradictory, incongruous human impulse to give a fellow commuter a hand. For him, these people milling about Churchgate and Victoria Terminus and other stations are the 'crowd', a synecdoche for the city; the book, like other significant works about Bombay – *Midnight's Children* and *Love and Longing in Bombay* – ends with a Whitmanesque, necessarily sentimental vision of the crowd: 'All these ill-assorted people walking towards the giant clock on Churchgate: They are me; they are my body and flesh. The crowd *is* the self, 14 million avatars of it, 14 million celebrations. I will not merge into them; I have elaborated myself into them.' The observation, 'I will not merge into them,' introduces a Naipaulean, anti-democratic glitch before flowing again into the Whitmanesque wonder at free movement and free mingling. It reminds us that Naipaul's response to the same crowd in the 1960s was one of anxiety, an anxiety about his own sense of self being swamped and smothered: 'And for the first time in my life I was one of the crowd. There was nothing in my appearance or dress to distinguish me from the crowd eternally hurrying into Churchgate Station.' Neither epiphany comes too often, one suspects, to those who use these trains daily; but those who examine the experience through memory, crystallising something that's amorphous and resistant to crystallization, will admit to having felt something of both the anxiety and the wonder. I, myself, recall the press of that 'rush hour', and was once advised by a kindly companion whom I never saw again to remain seated when the train got into Churchgate, so as to avoid being injured by the importunate crowd on the platform waiting to get on; he said I should get off only when the frenzy of boarding had died down. Generally, though, I avoided 'rush hour', and my journeys became an extension of my *flâneur*-like activities in the city on my visits from London and, later, Oxford. I travelled both second and first class. A second-class ticket cost the absurd sum of two rupees; first class a more respectable, but cheap, seventeen rupees. In second class, you usually had people in part-time employment for companions; in first class, whose interior was on the whole identical to second class, upwardly mobile traders, small businessmen, and accountants. I was reminded of Mehta's book again when the curious piece of news came in that a group of diamond traders, who commuted habitually with their pockets stuffed with diamonds, had been killed in the explosions.

It was in the mid-1990s in Oxford that I gradually came round to believing that Calcutta, where my parents had moved to in 1989, had ceased to be India's most interesting metropolis; that it was Bombay that had begun to display the contraries, the unexpectedness, and the capacity for self-renewal that characterize the great cities of the world. Globalization had acted upon it like alchemy. I, who'd grown up scorning it, and had viewed my parents' move to Calcutta with indifference and even satisfaction, believing that it wasn't possible for me to have any emotional attachment to Bombay (certain that, in time, I'd forget it), remember stopping one day at a window at Blackwell's bookshop, where Raghubir Singh's book of photographs, *Bombay: Gateway to India*, was opened and displayed, and staring, for about a minute, at the two pages which a large rectangular photo occupied. It was a picture obviously taken from a balcony or a window of an apartment on Malabar Hill, such as the one I lived in. One of the attractions of these apartments is their view of the sea and South Bombay, and here, too, the curve of the Marine Drive, the astonishingly thick clusters of skyscrapers and low buildings, looking a bit charred in the daylight, the Arabian Sea on the right, and then visible again on the left behind the densely inhabited land mass, the smudges of the islands of Elephanta and Trombay that I once could see morning and afternoon from the balcony, and, closer, the back of an apartment, with potted plants on the terrace – all this was contained in the picture, qualified only by the wobbly lines of skeletal bamboo scaffolding: the building from which Singh had taken the photograph was being painted. Each time I passed through Broad Street, I stopped at that window: the window of Blackwell's and the one in the photograph. I was moved by the clarity of the poor but sturdy bamboo, by the way it both impeded and framed the view. Later, I found the book in the India Institute library in the New Bodleian, and studied it carefully, photograph by photograph, as Naipaul, in the odd but excellent conversation that comprises the introduction, says you must. For me, this is still the most expressive work on Bombay I've encountered; deeply moving in the shift in sensibility it registers in the work of an already established and gifted photographer, a shift made not too many years before he suddenly died, and one that represents a conundrum, a moment, faced by all artists who'd been formed by modernity and modernism, and now found themselves faced, in their backyards, by the globalized world. Singh's major work on a metropolis before this one had been the book on Calcutta, where his pictures show the influence and the quirky humanity of Cartier-Bresson, Satyajit Ray, and, indeed, the sort of aesthetic that Calcutta itself had represented for a century and a half: of uncovering, through a modernist paradox, the intimate and the natural in urban disrepair and industrial decay, of recuperating the secretly familiar and quickening in the shabby and inhospitable. In the new book, though, as Naipaul observes shrewdly, the recurring metaphor and motif is glass, the glass of a shop window, or of a door to a plush department store or hotel: glass, which introduces an element of surface and polish, which skews the photographer's image by producing its own, which at once separates and gives access. It's not quite possible to feel 'at home' in the city of these pictures; glass not only invents the city it encloses, reveals, and reflects, but also the photographer taking the picture – Singh says to Naipaul that he's quite content to become inadvertently part of the frame, his outline and flash contained in the glass. In many ways this book explained to me why, imaginatively, Bombay's time had come, and Calcutta's had passed. It was not just to do with the failure of one city, and the success of the other; for 'failure' itself had been an integral part of modernist creativity. It was to do with the onus of creativity passing, in the globalized world, from the individual to a variety of scattered sources, to a terrain that marginalized the artist and reproduced its own images. In India, Bombay had become that terrain; and Singh's book is way of acknowledging what that subtle but decisive change means to the photographer, to the witness and by-stander.

'The writer just sees a few details, and he has to look hard at these,' says Naipaul to Singh, 'while the photographer has to see it all'; to which Singh responds, 'No. The writer does too,' and points out to Naipaul a scene from his own *India: A Million Mutinies Now*. Mehta's book has the silent intrusiveness, the busyness and ubiquity, the voraciousness of a book of pictures, as well as the largesse that prose gives. But Mehta doesn't stand at the crossroads in which Singh found himself when confronted with Bombay; the shift has already occurred, and we are in a new world with *Maximum City* – the book is a giant embrace, not only of a city, but of hope, and its more complex, earthly incarnation, desire, in the age of the free market. It performs this embrace brilliantly and passionately. It is not, really, a nostalgic book, in spite of all it says about loss, displacement, and the act of returning; its most strained notes are the elegiac ones. The book possesses the hard-headed exuberance of the nineteenth-century novels, their fascination with the spirit of compromise and with survival skills, their complete understanding of the importance of the mercantile and the pecuniary. All this it engages with not by examining the lives of the major industrialists in the city, which it also might have, but by looking at its low life – the dancing girls in bars, the whores and transsexuals, the hit men in gangs, the lowly cadres in political parties that do the dirty work during the riots. Like the elephant-headed Ganesh, who transcribed the *Mahab-harata* as the sage composed it aloud, Mehta sits uncomfortably close to garrulous hit-men, typing their memories and impressions of murder into his laptop. But he's also very good at capturing the speech-rhythms, inflections, and mannerisms of leaders of dubious organizations, political and criminal, at teasing out from them their sinister discourse made up of edict, threat, autobiography, emotional turbulence, and *Reader's Digest* homilies. This is from his conversation with Bal Thackray, the leader and father-figure of the Shiv Sena:

> I start. 'I am writing a book about Bombay – '
> 'Mumbai,' he corrects me.
> 'Mumbai,' I agree.
> He speaks to me in fractured English. He is a thin, bony man of average height, with a suspiciously jet-black crop of hair, wearing very large square spectacles.

'"Mumbai," I agree', says Mehta, though we know, from the title of his book and what's in it, that Mehta does not agree with the enforced renaming, by the Shiv Sena, of his city; the title, then, is a small act of revenge; and the little scene, deftly plotted, dramatizes the importance of deferred rebellions and immediate compromises in Bombay. Towards the end of the meandering interview, Mehta asks this dangerous man 'what accounts for his charisma'. Thackray turns lyrical: 'If you have a flower in your hand and it has a typical fragrance, how can you say that where is the fragrance, where does it come from? A fragrance cannot be seen; a charisma cannot be explained.' From Chhota Shakeel, gangster on the run and expatriate 'don' of Bombay's underworld, Mehta extracts, among other things, a quote from John F. Kennedy: '"My intention is, What can I do for my country. Not, What has the country has done for me?" Then he adds, "Think about that."' I don't think Mehta is just laughing at these people, whose actions are partly responsible for the incendiary, ever-returning disruptions that Bombay suffers today; I think he's carefully recording the defensively opaque speech of people for whom violence and self-love can substitute for, and are interchangeable with, patriotism. As with the nineteenth-century novelists, respectability and the desire for it is, to a considerable extent, Mehta's slightly dated but unexpectedly pertinent subject; for even Chhota Shakeel wants to be respectable. So does the city I grew up in; like a heroine of dubious origin and inexhaustible energy in a novel by the other Thackeray, it keeps inventing and reinventing itself, bruising itself as it looks for acceptance – and it's to this drive, this desire, that Mehta's book is so exceptionally attuned.

Stories of Domicile

Although I was born in Calcutta, I naturally have no memory of the flat my parents moved to shortly after my birth, situated in the suburban idyll of New Alipore. One random moment seems to survive, however, from the flood of moments of which one's first self-awareness must be composed, of sitting on the verandah, interestedly studying a 'poached' egg flecked with pepper, and my mother pointing out a passing cow on the road and saying 'Hamba!' History was being unmade around me; such images, in their flattering calm – the verandah, the main road, the nuclear family, company space – conceal and suggest equally that unmaking. In a year and a half, we – my parents and I – were gone from Calcutta, and then my father returned to it briefly with a new job in Britannia Biscuits. But in 1965, both we and Britannia Biscuits left for Bombay, apparently for good, joining the famous exodus of capital from the city. That movement, and the question it raises – 'What if?' – has haunted me and my writing ever since, in ways I still don't understand. What if we'd never left, and I'd grown up in Calcutta? What if that turn in history and politics that made those migrations inevitable and necessary had never occurred? These aren't actual questions I ask myself; they're subterranean stirrings. In asking them now, I'm not only preoccupied with a personal itinerary, but with the larger question of exchanging, in my life, one idea of metropolitan existence for another. That's why my childhood memories of Calcutta are not only full of a deep nostalgia for the past, but are imbued with an idiosyncratic sense of value that's perhaps impelled and misled me equally.

As industry moved out, my trips back to Calcutta from the late 1960s onwards possessed the ancient, stealthy happiness of homecomings as well as the thrill of living, for a month or a little more, another life, a different existence, an unthought-out but concentrated response to that 'What if?'; I became, during those holidays, the Bengali child that I never really was, and part of the sort of family that I didn't come from. From the moment we entered the city, I had a sense of its multifariousness, from the giant neon teapot pouring tea into a cup in Chowringhee (one of my earliest memories of the startlement of recovering the city), to the advertisement for cigarettes on slats on one end of Park Street, which changed direction every few minutes and, in the duration of a traffic jam, transformed into a different advertisement. Then the long vista of Pratapaditya Road, where my uncle lived, where Congress and Naxalite cadres fought each other in the evening, while my cousins and I peered out from the green Venetian shutters. Part of the exacerbated magic of this world were also the mysterious covers of the Puja annuals that belonged to my cousins, as well as the array of semi-inhabited terraces that swam away from us in every direction, as we ourselves looked out in triumph, our chins resting on the stone of my uncle's terrace.

In 1999, I made a calculatedly 'permanent' homecoming to Calcutta, deciding, after sixteen years in England, to return to India and actually live in my birthplace. I realized quite soon, in a way I hadn't before, that I didn't really 'belong' to this city, that, not having grown up or been educated here, I possessed neither the credentials nor the friends to pass for an authentic member of the community – and Calcutta, as is borne out by its theories of congregation under the rubric of '*adda*', and the different phases of its literary history, notwithstanding the solitary, prickly figure of Tagore, is a city that lives and often writes through its friendships. I'm thinking here of two subsequent generations who mythologize themselves and their artistic and political milieu in prose and verse: the *Kallol* generation of Buddhadeva Bose, and especially the perpetually adolescent and extraordinarily wise and gifted *Krittibas* generation (both named after the influential magazines that became synonymous with their temper) of, among others, Sunil Ganguly, Shakti Chattopdhyaya, Sandipan Chatterjee, and the intriguing, slightly marginal and angular figure of Utpal Basu. It's now too late, anyway, to convincingly insinuate myself into the fabric of Calcutta. I'm told by many who live here that this is a good thing, almost a blessing; and that tells us a different, more ambiguous, story than I would have expected about this metropolis of friendships, camaraderie, comradeship, and, as I used to see it, relations.

When I moved here, Calcutta was barely stirring from its twenty or thirty years of being caught at the fag-end of one sort of history, to do with a culturally definitive but politically marginalized middle class, and emerging into another one – whose possibilities seem, at once, thrilling, banal, and shocking – of a newly empowered diasporic population, and a suddenly disenfranchised agricultural constituency. Job Charnock was being demoted from shadowy founding father to unverifiable imponderable around the time of my return. Then there was the breach of taste that the renaming of the city represented; to name things on nationalist and religious lines is, I suppose, unavoidable sometimes, but to *rename* something for the same reasons is a deeply disconcerting gesture. If the new official name, Kolkata, was meant to recuperate the mythic metropolis of modernity, or the village on the riverbank from which it reportedly grew, it only reminded us, as such things do, the distance the city had travelled from that history: reminded us that there was no going back.

Now, as I write this, as we know too well, the state of West Bengal is groomed for economic revival by the Communist government; the groundwork is being laid, with a mixture of trepidation and short-sightedness on all sides, for land that was once 'redistributed' by this government to be acquired, seized, and handed over to large companies like the ones that had fled the state when I was a child; once more, Bengal is in conflict with itself, as it was before and during Partition, and in the Naxal period in the late 1960s. As it often has been with modern Indian history, some place either forgotten by or unknown to the urban middle class – Chauri Chaura, Naxalbari, Ayodhya, Kargil, Godhra, and, in this instance, Nandigram and Singur – bursts into the consciousness, becomes the focal point of a conflagration at once real and symbolic, and part of a larger, national anxiety. As far as the Bengali is concerned, the terrifying promise of a changed, unrecognizable Bengal and a changed Calcutta has always been held in a melancholy equipoise by the horrifying prospect of perpetual changelessness and paralysis. Tagore lulled the reader with a melodious version of this trauma in this poem he once wrote for children: 'O what a dream of dreams I had one night!/ I could hear Binu crying out in fright,/ "Come quickly and you'll see a startling sight:/ Our city's rushing in a headlong flight!"/ ... Tottering and lurching/ Calcutta goes marching/ Beams and joists battling/ Doors and windows rattling ...' (Sukhendu Ray's translation).

The comfort offered by the final couplet – 'Then at some sound, my dream came to a pause/ To find Calcutta where it always was' – has ceased to be reassuring for more than two decades now; the dreams are changed today, and represent a deep, unresolvable conflict of interest.

In what way does the outsider, the person with strong but often inexplicable ties to the place, relate to Calcutta? We forget, sometimes, that it's a city of visitors, refugees, migrants, some of them crucial to the city's self-conception, some important to others' conception of it. To the first category belongs, for instance, the novelist, poet, and critic Buddhadeva Bose, who moved here from Dhaka as a student in the mid-1920s, and who, along with his contemporaries, inserts the displaced, occasionally

East Bengali, migrant's Calcutta, of the mess, boarding-houses, makeshift employment, improvised means of study and of exchanging 'culture' (for the last, think of his essay on *adda*), into the modernist metropolis's poetry of exile. It is with the exile, the migrant, and, by extension, the vagrant and loiterer, that the city shares its secrets in both Bose's time and Sunil Ganguly's and Shakti Chattopadhyaya's.

For Tagore, many of whose formative moments (barring the epiphanies at the house on Jorasanko and on Sudder Street) seem to have taken place on trips with his sage-like father to the mountains, or on his riverine journeys – for Tagore, the city was a conundrum as he attempted to create a modernist language of perception out of his experience of the natural world. Space, light, and nature *were* what he understood as radical, disruptive freedom. Desperate – as, at once, a subject of colonialism, a human being, and an internationalist – to locate himself in an Indian 'enlightenment' which had its source in Hinduism's vision of nature, he saw, I think, the modern city as an agglomeration of institutions, an emblem of the institutional oppressiveness he associated, as a child, with the classroom, as a young man with imperialism, and as the older, public man with nationalism, and which he so feared. The city, then, never became for him a place of anarchic, disruptive play, as it did for his successors; 'play', or '*khela*' and '*chhuti*', and the city, or '*mahanagar*' and '*shahar*', largely occupied, for Tagore, antinomial positions; for the generations to follow, the two would come together, sometimes in noticeably unsettling ways.

In age, clearly troubled by accusations, coming principally from Bose, of not being modern enough (the accusations stemmed from a particular Eliot-indebted idea of what it meant to be 'modern' as an artist), Tagore wrote a poem about the city, 'Banshi', or 'The Flute', in which he ventriloquizes Bose and the younger generation's voice and incorporates their subject matter – in effect, the East Bengali migrant's Calcutta – transformed, symbolically, into the modernist city of exile. The poem is a revealing failure, and reminds us of the parameters that informed, between Tagore and a subsequent generation, the struggle to create an aesthetic of the city. The poem's protagonist is modernism's small man, a nameless, rent-paying, tenement-occupying, but nevertheless cultured clerk, the type that, in 'real life', would contribute deeply to a peculiar brand of Bengali cosmopolitanism, which involved a sense of inner exile, an intellectual eclecticism, and an oddly depreciated sense of property and inheritance. And yet (this will be borne out, I think, if one looks at the writings of Bose and Jibanananda Das) the city and its spaces possessed, at once, an odd, resistant frisson as well as an intimacy for this type, and it's this tension – of making a home out of nowhere – that gave rise to a certain literature of

Calcutta; even a certain cinema (think of Ray's delineation of Apu's frayed, hospitable rooftop room in *Apur Sansar*).

But, as the clerk in Tagore's poem moves through his neighbourhood into his tenement room, there is neither that resistance nor that intimacy (both of which I'd sense, as a child, while entering the city); nothing but an obstinate hollowness. Only when an invisible neighbour plays a raga upon a cornet does the clerk experience an utter sense of release and re-valuation; only then does he transcend his immediate environment and discover that all human beings are equally regal, that he and the Emperor Akbar are, after all, one; and, again, a much-recalled scene from the past, concerning a woman he was to marry in a village by the banks of the river Dhaleshwari (which flows from Assam into East Bengal), returns to him in its absolute perfection. So, what started out, in all earnestness, but deceptively, as a modernist poem, turns, relieved, into what it always wanted to be (at a time when Tagore was cultivating all kinds of disjunctive forms in his verse and his paintings): a romantic lyric, culminating in a variation of the Wordsworthian 'spot of time'. Just as in 'I wandered lonely as a cloud' (which is quite probably a London poem rather than a Lake District one), a sensory signal – daffodils – leads the poet to negate his immediate environment and be transported into memory (the image of the dancing daffodils) and towards the 'inward eye', so the cornet in 'Banshi' urges the clerk's retreat into his own inward eye, and a negation of what's at hand. The modernist epiphany entails a paradoxical, momentary embrace of the urban and the decrepit, the 'here and now'; but Tagore's poem isn't interested in moving towards it, but in rehearsing, as the early Yeats did, the private Romantic moment on the 'pavement grey'; to enable the recovery of Innisfree, or, here, the Dhaleswari, in the 'deep heart's core'. Yet Tagore is perspicacious enough to sense the current of East Bengali migration that underlies, to a significant extent, Calcutta's new urban modernism, and he gives it room in its poem; but won't, probably can't, enter its imaginative possibilities, its way of remaking the city on its own terms.

In the second category I mentioned earlier – of visitors who've been important not so much to Calcutta's self-conception as to others' conception of it – the foremost literary figure would be, I suppose, Günter Grass. There is Mother Teresa, whose continued presence in newsprint had, for a while, superseded all others'; but I'll leave her aside for now, because it's an aesthetic of the city, of *this* city, that I'm concerned with tracing. And, like Bose and Tagore, it's an aesthetic position, or a position about the aesthetic, that Grass is concerned with formulating in relation to Calcutta, and he brings to it the moral ferocity with which writers approach problems of the imagination and of formal expression. Not just 'How does one write about Calcutta?' but 'Should, in Calcutta, one write at all?' is what exercises Grass. It's a brutal query, and, in its way, a self-indulgent one (P. Lal's pained and effective riposte provides a provisional answer); but one can't doubt its integrity, and one needs to place it in context – not that of Calcutta, but within the growing Western unease with 'literature' in the second half of the twentieth century.

Grass came to Calcutta as a novelist, but swiftly turned here into a haunted German post-war intellectual; by, in effect, denying Calcutta its language and literature, he was invoking post-war guilt and Adorno's affirmation that poetry is no longer possible after Auschwitz. And so, Calcutta became an epiphany, a readymade holocaust, in Grass's story of expiation as a post-war artist who, despite Adorno's declaration, had dealt copiously with words; no literature of Calcutta, then, was tenable except a literature of bitter penitence and bearing witness.

Was a different response possible from a German writer, one less absolute, and more alive to history and process? For an answer to this, you might look at Grass's contemporary, the playwright Heiner Müller, one among a group of artists and intellectuals that, after the Second World War and the reallocation of Europe, decided to stay on in and practise their art in the East – mainly in East Berlin and the GDR – rather than in the 'free world'. For Müller, an exceptionally subversive and intelligent artist, the decision was, I suspect, a means of bypassing Adorno's holy stricture; to create forms out of silence and oppositionality rather than certainty. 'The Eastern bloc has a very large "third world" within it,' he said in a late interview, 'and we in the East are in a state of constant osmosis with it.' And, referring to the Turkish population in West Berlin, he remarks, 'The future of European cities lies in their ability to be in osmosis with the "third world" within them.' Müller isn't speaking of 'multiculturalism' here; he's talking about an ongoing, often difficult, transaction that undermines the utopian dichotomy, which transfixes Adorno and Grass, of holocaust/perfect society. To write about Calcutta is also, in many ways, to be part of that osmosis rather than to bear witness, to stand somewhere in between that idealised dichotomy. An osmosis between disrepair and civility, breakdown and order, the colonial and the local, has directed the relationship of the writer – who, by definition, is an outsider, a settler, a person who made a choice to stay on – to this city.

Notes on the Novel after Globalization

Some time in May in 2005, I was sitting in a flat in Cambridge, England, and watching television – the expected plug for the Hay on Wye Festival. A programme on books, with three novelists, Kazuo Ishiguro, Julian Barnes, Jonathan Coe, in conversation: so rare are these today that I was willing to forget – perhaps was hardly aware of – the fact that almost every discussion on culture on contemporary television (interviews with authors, readings from books) is connected to a publishing or media moment and is, in essence, a plug. Critics and authors have succumbed to this arrangement and its conveniences, and negated, almost unknowingly, the irrelevant, expansive, and almost purposeless space for literature in the media. The waywardness and surprise of literary discussion have largely disappeared with that space; because the plug is a deeply ritualistic activity, a totemic observance, in which you know in advance what you're supposed to do and say.

In retrospect, this might be why the discussion in which Barnes, Coe, and Ishiguro (three admirable writers) took part was respectful, low-key, and slightly peculiar. At one point, the interviewer promised that he'd ask them, after a commercial break, about what the free market was doing to the novel; once the break was over, though, the discussion veered toward a predictable direction – the life and health of the novel. 'Is the novel dead?' asked the interviewer. 'V.S. Naipaul said it is.' 'And then he wrote another one,' said someone wryly. No, the rumours of its death were hugely exaggerated; the novel was alive and well, all agreed.

This wasn't the first time I was witness to this ritual – and what can one call it but a ritual of obeisance, and, like all rites, an occasion of empty, terrified praise as well as prevarication? Why, after all, should a genre that's flooded shelves in bookshops, that has flourished almost monstrously while other genres – poetry, the short story, the essay – have been buried or prepared for burial – why should the novel, of all things, require a periodic certificate of health, a circumlocutory announcement, every

few months, that it is ailing and, then, that it was always well? Surely this
is behaviour characteristic of closed, tyrannical kingdoms, in which the
despot is pronounced ill and well at regular intervals, leading to a constant
cycle of mourning and celebration; while other deaths and annihilations
go unnoticed?

The novel's been around for a long time, but only in the last thirty years has
it achieved a curious sort of pre-eminence, in that it's the one literary genre
in which certain convergences possible only after globalization – between
'serious' and 'popular' culture, between theoretical or intellectual validation and free-market or material investment – take place. The reception of
the novel reminds us that there are no real oppositions and dichotomies
in the globalized world, and that the celebration of narrative is also a confirmation of the intolerance of oppositionality.

 The dismantling of binaries was one of the primary moral functions of
the post-structuralist, postmodernist moment, because of the hierarchies
of power that, historically, they at once concealed and expressed. The rise
of narrativity has been intriguingly continuous, or concomitant, with the
decline of the binary. As I've already said, in the cultural politics of the free
market, the *reception* of narrative – or the novel – is also involved in the
overturning of the binary that separates 'serious' writing from 'popular',
commercially successful from critically acclaimed writing. For the larger
narrative of the globalized free market in which the smaller one, the novel,
is located, that dichotomy is a nuisance and an inconvenience. Faced with
the engulfing, all-embracing, narrative-like movement and proclivities of
globalization, is it time to recuperate the binary, and give it back a measure
of polemical strength and moral dignity?

Let me go back, briefly, to another memory, one that precedes, by a couple
of years, my sighting of these writers on television. I was in New York,
teaching; it was the autumn of 2002. I made several trips outside the city,
some, to Pennsylvania and Boston, on Greyhound buses. The mythology
of the Greyhound bus, memorialized in so many popular songs, faded
quickly; as did the mythology of travel, the American romance of the highway. It was on one of these trips that I realized how difficult it was, in the
globalized world, to escape, to convincingly take refuge in namelessness
and anonymity. I was going through all the motions of travel; as the bus
took the highway in the evening, I sought to be cocooned by movement
and invisibility. But there was a false note. I could never bring myself to
believe I was completely alone (this had nothing to do with the strangers
on the other seats, who, typically, contribute to the traveller's aloneness

rather than take away from it). I gradually understood that the problem was the sense of my own identity being constantly linked to and inescapably meshed with numberless gestures of disclosure I was half-aware of and constantly involved in: if I were to use my credit card, for instance, to buy a packet of crisps and a newspaper at a 'gas station', or if I were to call a friend on a hypothetical mobile phone which I didn't actually possess. The highway, and darkness, provided no assurance of melting away; and none of the lanes in the small towns we rushed past really dissolved into the unknown; the magic of concealment was no longer a tenable one. It was only two years after the bombing of Afghanistan, and recent coverage told us that even the most obscure settlements in the least known parts of the world could be recorded, studied, and, if it proved necessary, destroyed. There is no 'outside' in the globalized world.

Globalization, then, is a text, in the special but influential meaning that the word 'text' has taken on in the last thirty years: a fabric of lateral connections and intersections that abhors, and negates, verticality. The lens of the satellite studying us from above is not really an instance of verticality, or of the Foucauldian god-like panopticon, because it's as much *in* the text as we are. Space, too, is part of the text; 'pure' emptiness isn't possible in free-market globalization, and neither, as a result, is a sense of dissolution. There's no escape for us from an infinitely lateral and discursive grid of connectedness; nor is there any escape from it for the satellite.

The philosophical underpinnings of globalization as a form of lateralness can be found in theories, or vulgarized versions of those theories, that have predominated thought in the last three or four decades, some of them originating in radical developments in philosophy, or in the social sciences, or in cultural history, often finding a new life when transposed to literary departments. These theories, of course, play a significant, even definitive, role in the way we think of the novel today, in our privileging the narrative and discursive over the poetic, the fragmentary, and the unfinished; but they also, I think, prepare in some measure the intellectual ground on which our larger acceptance of the lateral and of narrativity, and of the moral rightness of narrative, is based; and they explain our suspicion – a suspicion the free market implicitly shares and nurtures – of the poetic, of verticality, of a breach in the narrative.

Among the first theorists to give a moral and political value to – and speak up in the cause of, as it were – narrative was the Russian formalist and philosopher, Mikhail Bakhtin. The 'novel' was not a genre for Bakhtin (Forster's humorously anodyne and pointed description of the novel as a work of fiction exceeding 50,000 words would hardly have sufficed for him); instead, he fashioned it, unprecedentedly, as a polemical term. It's clear that, when he referred to the novel, it was a particular *kind* of novel he was interested in reinventing, a text that was marked by lateral and side-ways movements, 'a system of intersecting planes', to which end he created a vocabulary suggesting simultaneity and socialized space – heteroglossia, polyphony, dialogue, carnival – all conjuring a radius within which more than one voice was speaking, more than one person moving. The 'dialogic' novel, whose paradigmatic proponent was Dostoevsky, was then part of an attack on the 'high' cultural, enclosed, monological nature of the 'poetic': represented, in Bakhtin, not so much by a poet as, oddly, by the novels of Tolstoy. This is perhaps the first time the 'poetic' falls into disrepute not because of the layman's usual impatience with obscurity or irrelevance, or the Platonic disdain of daydreaming and the untrustworthiness of the poet, but because of a new anti-metaphysical politics to which privileging a certain notion of narrative is crucial. Later, important modulations on Bakhtin, such as Julia Kristeva's 'intertextuality', also involve a refutation of the essentially metaphysical notion of anteriority; Kristeva warns us that 'intertextuality' is not a 'banal study of sources' or influences, but an attempt to engage with the way sign-systems interpenetrate one another, in effect, laterally. Bakhtin was, one might recall, largely unknown outside his own country for much of his life, but his work was made available in France after his death in 1975, and gradually canonized in the American academy in 1980s; that is, his critique of the 'poetic' remained, when he was actually formulating it, unknown to the practitioners and theorists of 'high' modernism and existentialism in Europe (just as their work seems largely ignored by this student of, among other things, the seventeenth, eighteenth, and nineteenth centuries). It's only in the 1980s that his par-ticularly weighted celebration of narrative began to circulate in academia, and became one of the coordinates in preparing the groundwork for how we see narrative today; how we find it unnecessary to critique it, partly because we still think of it, in the light of the Bakhtinian legacy, of itself being a subterranean and indispensable critical tool: of the old enemy, 'high' culture.

What are some of the other coordinates responsible for preparing what I've called the 'intellectual groundwork' for narrativity? Among the most con-siderable and stimulating is, surely, Benedict Anderson's subtle and probing *Imagined Communities*. In taking pains (though 'taking pains' is probably not the most apt way of speaking of a book with such a light, alchemical touch) to differentiate the old kingdoms from the modern nation-states,

Anderson makes an essentially Bakhtinian distinction, between centrip-
etal societies converging towards a vertical, monarchical point, divinely
sanctioned, and centrifugal ones, held together by the observance of secular time – the clock and the calendar – and what he calls 'print capitalism'.
Because Anderson is interested in rewriting (the punning figurative usage
is, I suppose, inescapable) the nation as a form of narrative, the activities
of reading and of producing novels become not only important examples
of evidence shoring up his argument, but metaphors for discursivity. That
is, reading novels isn't just something that people who live in nations happen to be doing; for Anderson (and for Bakhtin), the novel isn't only *about*
society, or a mirror of it, but the most typical instance, and a tissue, of the
conditions of narrativity in which it, the novel, is located. It's important
to see that the novel, despite the physical characteristics of its being –
pages bound within a hardback jacket – is not an enclosed, bounded entity
within another enclosed, bounded entity, a book sealed by its cover within
a nation defined by its borders, but (like the nation itself) something in
constant transaction with the narrativity it's produced by, and to which
it constantly contributes. (I say this in spite of Anderson's contrast of the
physically circumscribed condition of the book with the loose nature of
a pound of sugar; for his study is not a humanist exploration of how the
novel might reflect the conditions of a nation, or how the latter might
come together to produce a certain kind of novel. These dividing lines are
really untenable for Anderson, and untenable because the way he views
both nation and novel are in some fundamental way informed by the idea
of the 'text'.) In this sense, Anderson's 'nation', too, in spite of its bounded
nature, is, like his 'novel', a precursor of globalization, an infinitely lateral
web of intersections, and print-capitalism a brilliant metaphor for – and,
once again, a precursor of – the sort of technology that not only produces
narrative, but is imbricated in it.

Anderson's book was published in 1983, and it's clearly marked,
despite bearing all the animating characteristics of the European cosmopolitan imagination, by the new postmodern affirmation of the lateral and
discursive. The point at which this shows up most interestingly is in his influential gloss of Walter Benjamin's notion of 'homogeneous, empty time'.
Anderson's interpretation is really proto-postmodernist, invoking narrative through an imagery of lateralness and 'simultaneity', a 'simultaneity
[which] is, as it were, transverse, cross-time, marked not by prefiguring
and fulfilment, but by temporal coincidence, and measured by clock and
calendar'. Add to the last two, as Anderson does in the next paragraph,
the novel and the newspaper, and the reinterpretation of 'homogeneous,
empty time' as a continuum that makes narrativity or textuality possible

is complete. Anderson's choice of word – 'imagining' – in relation to the two printed material objects mentioned is curious, given the 'imagination' is private, vertical, non-material, and often, in its self-absorption, at odds with narrative; the implications of this slight, but fundamental, incongruity of phrasing are never fully investigated in the book. Certainly, Benjamin's own concept of 'homogeneous, empty time' is a modernist one – a utopian linear flow (where clock and calendar not only stand for simultaneity, but for an unfolding) which makes possible the idea of development and the 'concept of the historical progress of mankind'. Benjamin's attack on 'homogeneous, empty time' also takes on its revolutionary Marxist purpose (inveighing against historicism) through a characteristically modernist aesthetic – the aesthetic of the present moment, the Messianic 'Jeztzeit', in which present and future come together, and create a rupture in linearity. In Anderson's 'homogeneous time' of nationhood, narrative, and discursivity, the 'imagination' in his title could have plausibly fulfilled that Messianic/romantic role, but will not, or perhaps cannot.

The parameters for narrativity were already put in place, of course, by the time Anderson was writing, by Foucault and Derrida. This was done, as we know, in different ways by the two philosophers, but, in both cases, by eroding the border separating language from what was putatively 'outside' it; by using linguistic terms – 'discourse' and '*écriture*' – in a particular way, so as to suggest that 'reality' (largely ontological and phenomenological in Derrida; political and institutional in Foucault) was inextricable from the language that purported to convey or represent it. All this gradually brings into motion, or creates the moral context for, the banishing of the 'outside' that is so much an unquestioned part of existence in the globalized world. 'There is nothing outside of the text,' said Derrida in *De la grammatologie*; or at least he did in Gayatri Chakravorty Spivak's translation. In his essay, 'Ideas of the Book and Histories of Literature: After Theory?', Peter D. McDonald, looking again at the original, '*Il n'y a pas de hors-texte*', calls Spivak's version 'clumsy', a clumsiness that 'Derek Attridge's 1992 version ("*There is no outside-the-text*") improved only slightly … Both missed the punning force of the original, which set *hors-texte*, a technical bookmaking term roughly translated as "plate" (as in "This book contains five colour plates") alongside *hors texte*, which Attridge's translation comes closest to capturing. This play on words (or on a hyphen), which reflects Derrida's lively bibliographical imagination … does not, of course, provide a key to the talismanic sentence's meaning. What it does indicate is that "*Il n'y a pas de hors-texte*" announced neither a triumphant nor a culpable break with history.' The word 'text', though, in the way Derrida uses it, involves a radical demolition of an 'outside' to narrativity. A 'text' is not a 'book'; a book, like language itself in the old days of humanist criticism, is delineated physically and symbolically from the world around it; the book is *about* the world. After Derrida's 'text', narrative no longer refers to, reports on, describes, or captures the world; it becomes the system of lateral transactions by which we understand what we used to call 'the world'.

I'll end this section with a brief consideration of the way Foucault's *Discipline and Punish* represents a noticeable and significant development in this story of narrativity, and also of how, in its restatement of the role of suffering and punishment in Western culture, it moves subtly but firmly away from the 'doubleness', or the double resonance, of suffering in the West from antiquity to modernity. Foucault chooses Mettray, a French prison founded in 1840 for juvenile delinquents, as his example and his metaphor – really, as an entry into the realm of narrativity in the new (and, since he published his study in 1975, pioneering) postmodern manner. Incarceration is a 'continuum' for Foucault; and one of the ways in which it displays narrative features, especially in the instance of Mettray, is the abolishing of the separation of 'high' and 'low' – such as would later characterize New Historicism and cultural studies – articulated, here, in terms of the interchangeability of major and minor punishment, as well as major and minor offence. Foucault quotes E. Ducpétiaux from his contemporary account: 'The least act of disobedience is punished and the best way of avoiding serious offences is to punish the most minor offences very severely.' Then, moving on from Mettray towards the more general principles of punishment and imprisonment in the latter half of the nineteenth century, Foucault reiterates his postmodern idea of the 'carceral' as a narrative (or 'continuum') in which certain boundaries between major and minor, the institutional and the non-institutional, are, in contrast to earlier times, dissolved. So:

> The frontiers between confinement, judicial punishment and institutions of discipline, which were already blurred in the classical age, tended to disappear and constitute a great carceral continuum that diffused penitentiary techniques into the most innocent disciplines, transmitting disciplinary norms into the very heart of the penal system and placing over the slightest illegality, the smallest irregularity, deviation or anomaly, the threat of delinquency. (Alan Sheridan's translation)

The dissolution of the border between the disciplinarian space and the 'normal' one, the 'penitentiary' regimes and 'the most innocent disciplines', the heinous offence and 'the smallest irregularity', makes both the institution and the crime (and, by extension, the individual) in effect superfluous; Foucault's sentences observe, even while differentiating between transgressions, this inescapable circularity: 'You will end up in the convict-ship the slightest indiscipline seems to say; and the harshest of prisons says to the prisoners condemned to life: I shall note the slightest irregularity in your conduct.' Foucault, here, is moving beyond history-writing towards establishing an idea of narrative to replace the old continuities and contrasts between free and penal spaces, institutions and individuals, major and minor: 'As a result, a certain significant generality moved between the least irregularity and the greatest crime; it was no longer the offence, the attack on the common interest, it was the departure from the norm, the anomaly; it was this that haunted the school, the court, the asylum, or the prison.'

That Foucault's account is not only a reassessment but a repositioning of great consequence becomes clear when he makes a fleeting reference to Solzhenitsyn in his phrase 'carceral archipelago'. The reference, as we know, is to *The Gulag Archipelago*, Solzhenitsyn's fictional representation of Soviet incarceration; but Foucault seems to have forgotten, for the moment, the distance separating the Russian writer's metaphysical symbolism of suffering from his own conception of the narrative characteristics of the nineteenth-century 'carceral continuum', which is, really, an attack on metaphysical notions of verticality. As the title of another one of Solzhenitsyn's novels on a similar subject, *The First Circle*, reminds us, imaginative accounts of suffering and punishment in the post-Renaissance West have most often been located in the Christian inferno: in modernity, in particular, in the Dantesque one. This encompasses an immense amount of the Western imagination's engagement with punishment and dereliction: to name a few examples at random, Milton's Satan, Marlowe's Mephistopheles, Goya's sketches of infernal dismemberment, Conrad's controversial descriptions of African labourers in *Heart of Darkness*, not to mention the explicit references in T.S. Eliot. Yet the metaphysics of this space of imprisonment and punishment, preceding the postmodern narrative moment announced by Foucault, is a curious and compelling one; its compulsion and curiosity consist of its doubleness, which explains its attraction to the artistic imagination in those periods. The damned are clearly delineated from the blessed, as the inside (or, in this context, the imprisoned interior) is from the outside (or freedom); and yet these categories, in the imagination, are always being mixed up, reallocated, and inverted. The damned, in spite of their condition, have a specifity and particularity that the paradisial, which is abstract and general, lacks; they, both despite and because of their abjection, possess a tragic refulgence. It's this investment in the particular, as well as an energy that belongs to that domain, that makes Milton, as we well know, construct his long poem written 'to justify the ways of God to man' in a peculiarly double way, or makes delight such an undeniable ingredient of Goya's horrifying drawings. Foucault's profound modulation on the Western conception of suffering and wrongdoing involves taking away, famously, the 'outside'; as well as dismantling, by means of the postmodern narrative, the illusory border between the penal institution and the ordinary world. After his study, we realize discipline is the norm; and we realize, too, that punishment is not a differentiated, possibly a vertical, space, but a 'continuum'. This move is essential to Foucault's rebuttal of the metaphysics of suffering; to his rejection of the imagination's assignation of a refulgence to those negative spaces.

I've spent some time looking at these formative, often ubiquitous, works because of the role they played in transforming narrative into a critique that decisively overturned the old hegemonies and pedagogies: metaphysical, European, masculine. (There is, as we know, a powerful version of Derrida that can be enlisted in the cause of the 'poetic'; however, the populist version involves the Derrida of lateral interconnections, the never-ending chain of signifiers.) It must be at least partly because of this that narrative, today, brings up not so much the associations of rationality, logic, and factuality that prose did earlier, but those of liberation, delight, celebration, and radical freedom. And so, even the early chapters of Anderson's study (whose intentions are hardly as pointedly anti-metaphysical as those of the philosophers who must be responsible, to a significant extent, for giving his book its particular timbre) are infected by an excitement about the march of narrative; the celebration of print-capitalism turns narrative from a mode of telling into heroic actor. Anderson's excitement comes, surely, not only from his discovery of how nations were formed by narrative, or from the inexorable and elegant development of his argument, but has something to do with being part of larger critical campaign in which narrative plays an exemplary role, and, therefore, with the *timeliness* of his project.

With the consolidation, in the 1990s, of extraordinary changes in the realms of politics, culture, and economics, the truth is that the pernicious bygone elitisms have been rendered largely obsolete – turned into shibboleths. In the meanwhile, the postmodern conception of narrative, an infinitely lateral web, with its abolition of the 'outside', has become a form of (often seemingly benign) control enforced through a series of disclosures and constant transactionability in the domains of 'information' and the 'market'. The air of celebration that surrounded, in intellectual debate, the anti-Enlightenment thrust of narrativity in the last four decades has merged, subtly but indelibly, with the orchestrated, upbeat tone of globalization.

After post-structuralism, 'nostalgia' became a dirty word; it pointed to a longing for hieratic, repressive totalities, a malaise that could affect, at once, the fascist, the humanist, and the member of the old left. Globalization has appropriated the inadmissibility of nostalgia in its own robust way; globalization is about 'being at home in the world' in a wholly unprecedented manner – not in the 'poetic', Heideggerean sense, nor in the mode familiar to mystics, conflating the earthly and the paradisial, but in a way peculiarly sanctioned and authored by the market. For the first time, with globalization, we have not so much the West's familiar investment in the idea of the future, and of development, but an apotheosis of the present – again, an unprecedented apotheosis, quite unlike the modernists' quasi-religious recuperation of the 'present moment' or the epiphanic in their work. No, the 'now' of globaliation has little to do with – indeed, is inimical to – the epiphanic, with its potentially disruptive, metaphysical resonances.

Another coordinate that should be mentioned in this mapping of narrativity as a crucial critical and political conceit is the idea of 'storytelling'. It's a notion that didn't really exist in any persuasive way on the intellectual landscape thirty years ago. Its rise is related to the fashioning of the discourse of post-coloniality; 'storytelling', with its kitschy magic and its associations of post-colonial empowerment, is seen to emanate from the immemorial funds of orality in the non-Western world, and might be interpreted as a critique of the inscribed word, and its embeddedness in Western forms of knowledge. 'Storytelling', then, is also an alternative to disciplines like history in the Western humanities; if it is now an ingredient in history-writing, it is so precisely to mark a break with the Eurocentric, the literate, the elite. No wonder that the notion is invoked almost always with an air of glamour and celebration. Both the concordances and the distinctions between this invocation and Walter Benjamin's recovery of the figure of 'the storyteller' are instructive; for Benjamin was by no means an unequivocal advocate of narrativity. Thus, in the first paragraph of 'The Task of the Translator': 'No poem is intended for the reader, no picture for the beholder, no symphony for the listener.' Benjamin is expressing the profound modernist desire for disjunction, a breach in the lateral weave of the fabric; it's an image strikingly different from the one of simultaneous readership that comprises Anderson's nationhood. Today, in the early twenty-first century, we've entered yet another cultural and political phase, after the shifts and reappraisals represented, in their time, by modernity and postmodernity. This shift asks us to look at narrative once again; and it asks the novelist to be careful about the point at which 'storytelling' begins to collude with the narrativity of globalization.

In the breach, in the notion of the 'outside', in the poetic, probably lies the much-maligned question of value. Like the poetic, like verticality, like 'high' culture, value is one of those elitist, metaphysical bastions that have been exposed by, and replaced with, the discursive engines of postmodernity. The position of critical theory in relation to value – that it was a crucial tool for the bourgeois elite in exercising control and exclusion; that the contrast between a transcendental value in the sphere of culture and a contingent material value in the marketplace was a sham, and that both forms of value were complicit with one another, often operating and being disseminated in strategically dichotomous but essentially similar ways – the position of theory on this, at the moment its critique began to be formed, was both accurate and timely. Pierre Bourdieu, with his legacy of conceiving of culture as a 'field' (comprising publishers, literary prizes, book reviews, and literary networks) provides another significant coordinate in the mapping of lateralness and narrative; and Bourdieu played, in introducing the term 'symbolic capital', an important role in the demystification of literary value. Despite the unworldly, 'high' cultural pretensions of literary and artistic value, it is, for Bourdieu, a symbolic form of material advantage (itself engendered by all kinds of materialist networks that deal in the currency of this symbolism) with which the beneficiary can make their way up and through society.

This was, for the latter half of the twentieth century, an apposite intervention. It is now, in 2007, a dated one, just as the idea of a critical, demystifying narrativity is. 'Value', 'high' culture, and 'verticality' are no longer centres of, or metaphors, for power; narrative is. We're living in a world 'after theory', not because theory has died out and we could, if we chose, return to a measure of humanist sanity, but because the problem of globalization has less to do with theory's familiar villains than with the process of reification that globalization entails.

There is, for instance, the reification of value; and it's what makes the 'symbolic' in Bourdieu's 'symbolic capital' anachronistic. Even fifteen years ago, it was possible to say, 'Stocks in Elizabeth Bishop were relatively low in her lifetime, but shot up remarkably in the 1980s,' and refer, in speaking of an underrated poet by means of a financial metaphor, almost entirely, and figuratively, to the domain of 'high' culture. The specific use of the words 'stocks' reminds us that the structure of signification within which literary value operated in bourgeois modernity was always related to the structure of signification wherein market value was decided. And yet there's a powerful, subversive irony in the sentence, in the way 'stocks' is used to describe a poet who was, and is, a writer's writer, and a genre that never had a huge public. Value in the domain of culture may have been complicit with market value, but it contained a residue of the ironic sensibility that pervades, for example, much of religion, and which devotional poets have frequently tapped into. So the Indian saint-poet Khaalas could say, 'Why did you abandon chanting the Name?/ You didn't abandon anger, you didn't abandon desire,/ Why did you abandon the real treasure?' The 'real treasure' here – '*asli ratan*' in the original – is ironical usage, the word 'treasure', or '*ratan*', in straddling two worlds, that of the marketplace and eternity, carrying with it a polemical doubleness, and the word 'real' ('*asli*') emphasizing the irony.

George Herbert structures his sonnet 'Redemption' around the doubleness of the notion of value, and the two possible registers of the word:

> Having been tenant long to a rich lord,
>> Not thriving, I resolved to be bold,
>> And make a suit unto him, to afford
> A new small-rented lease, and cancel the old.
> In heaven at his manor I him sought:
>> They told me there that he was lately gone
>> About some land, which he had dearly bought
> Long since on earth, to take possession.
> I straight returned, and knowing his great birth,
>> Sought him accordingly in great resorts:
>> In cities, theatres, gardens, parks, and courts.
> At length I heard a ragged noise and mirth
>> Of thieves and murderers: there I him espied,
>> Who straight, *Your suit is granted*, said, and died.

It's impossible to express, or put to argumentative use, this scouring sense of how related but antithetical registers of value operate in different spheres of the world unless the domain of culture reserves a degree of verticality to itself, unless it is situated both within the narrativity of the world, 'in great resorts:/ In cities, theatres, gardens, parks, and courts', and outside it. There is, however, no 'outside' in globalization; and, as a consequence, both culture and value have largely lost their doubleness. When I, at this moment, say, as a published writer, 'My stock is high,' or 'It's low at present', I may seem to echo the comment on Bishop, but I'm speaking, really, much more closely according to the logic and metier of the market. Today's writers *are* stocks and shares; the ironical register of the term 'value' is, on the whole, no longer available to us.

Let me recapitulate briefly and look at where we stand in relationship to narrative at present. The dominant tone of modernism was, I think, poetic; that is, it was haunted by totalities – to do with culture, mythology, religion, and nature – that seemed to have been available organically to pre-modern man, although it couldn't, itself, approach those totalities except in a state of ambivalence, and through the fragment and allusion. Modernity is the last phase of humanism, and is caught between its two resonances: between progress and the perfectibility of the human on the one hand, and nostalgia and loss on the other. Modernism aestheticizes this in a new and influential way: the *avant-garde*, for instance, is enmeshed in the vocabulary of development, in the idea of the 'breakthrough', of being at the forefront, at the vanguard – and, at the same time, it ironicizes development, for its experiments rehabilitate broken, unfinished forms, at odds with the social completeness that the world around the artistic fraternity strives for.

Postmodernity is the age of narrative, in a quite different sense from Arnold's characterization of Dryden's time as the 'age of prose'. Narrative levels out the binary of prose and poetry, as well as the latter's, and culture's, doubleness, its situatedness in humanist ideals of development and meaning as well as its special abnegation of them. The transcendental and 'disinterested' – Arnold's word – are always imbricated with the material, and narrative is the principal constituent of a critique that, once and for all, draws our attention to this fact, while also being the primary instance, the tissue, of this imbrication. In fashioning this critique, postmodern theory still relies, I think, on a crucial degree of irony; as Derrida points out, there is, in fact, no new anti-metaphysical language to replace the old metaphysical language with; you must turn the old language 'upon itself'. And yet the insight, or strategy, suggests that the formulation of this critique takes place in a domain somehow separate from, or outside of, the spheres in which language is ordinarily at work; it's that space, that significant gap, that makes the critique manoeuvrable.

Globalization represents a new phase – that of the rapid, incremental reification of the special postmodern notion of narrative. The postmodern philosophers, obsessed with the hubris of modernity, couldn't have foreseen how the on-and-on lateral movement of narrative, perpetually eschewing closure and delaying the finality of a fixed 'meaning', would turn from ironical critical strategy into, increasingly, the literal context for lives in free-market globalization. Neither could they have predicted what free-market reification would do to the 'old' humanist language; rather than simply turn it upon itself, the 'old' language has been transmuted by the market into an ideological discourse to whose tonalities contemporary criticism is only beginning to alert itself. The ideological language of globalization is made up of terms from older discourses, terms such as (to name a few) 'freedom', 'democracy', 'popular', 'people'. These words, once located in antithetical world-views and rival interpretations – in liberal as well as socialist ones – still carry, confusingly, echoes of their old, conflicted meanings while never really referring to them; they lack anteriority, depth, verticality, and, in effect, disruptiveness; they're catchwords in the new-found reification of the discursive. Let me touch upon, very briefly, perhaps cursorily, what's happened to the language of culture and literary criticism in this context of discursiveness.

Just as ellipsis and disjunction were the signatures of modernism – and, to a considerable extent, of modernity – in characteristic 'poetic' tension and timbre, a rhetoric of excess, plenty, and a relentless engulfing inclusiveness is the hallmark of globalization, with its powerful narrative and prolix impulses. Globalization is the tragicomic rhetoric of putative plenty overwhelming the awareness of palpable want. In India, for instance – as is the case, I'm sure, in Europe and America – want is all around us; and yet we don't really need to do business with it, as we did in modernity, because it can no longer occupy a definitive, oppositional space 'outside' us; it has been incorporated into and domesticated in the narrative abundance. This is not an 'ideology' in the old sense, in that it is not a propagation of a point of view; it's a self-referential form, for narrativity is the instrument of globalization, as well as its sole repository of value. And we're now at a moment when the theories of narrative abundance in the last forty years – the infinite play of *écriture*, the notions of 'carnival' and 'dialogue', the tide of print-capitalism and the communal imagination, the inexhaustible fund of post-colonial 'storytelling' – begin to collude with globalization's text and script of ever-increasing plenty. It's here, in the reified plenitude of narrativity, that we must situate the statements and announcements of exponential abundance: not only about the spread of democracy and 'freedom', but claims such as, 'More and more people are reading the novel.' Narrativity, as postmodern critical theory has demonstrated, is self-generating; it can produce abundance without the bogeys of privation, struggle, or development. This does something odd to linear time where the market's version of 'culture' is concerned; it either compresses it extraordinarily, or *anticipates* it. Thus, 'masterpieces' are announced before they're published, and it's also because of this lateral generation of plenty, this disposal of linear development, that we have such an unprecedented number of first-time novelists publishing 'masterworks'. At no point in history when value and accomplishment were related to linear development could such an efflorescence of immediate, readymade talent – an efflorescence of the 'now' of globalization – be possible.

A quick glance at the itinerary, superannuation, and rewriting of the word 'world' in the new language. It's a word, again, that possesses a certain post-Enlightenment doubleness, in that it refers to a horizontal, physical entity, the sum total of the geographical mass we inhabit, and, in embodying profound universalist aspirations, has a verticality and interiority premised on ideals common to the human subject everywhere. We sometimes use 'global' and 'world' as if they were interchangeable, without taking into account that the two are not only at odds with one another, but related hierarchically. Globalization abhors verticality and the universal, except when it reconfigures the latter on its own terms; and it negates the old-style internationalisms and cosmopolitanisms that worked like barely visible networks between the 'high' cultures of different nations. The principal tool and figure for globalization is the English language; if we're insufficiently aware of this, it's because one is never fully conscious of the material contexts and drives of universals when one is living in the midst of them. But it is, for instance, always a task to enter a mainstream music and DVD store and search for the corner that displays 'world' cinema. It reminds us that the 'world' – which, in the case of cinema, still represents, across languages, the persistence of a 'high' modernist internationalism that once occupied centre-stage in 'culture' – that the 'world' is now a poor suburb of the global, or even an unacknowledged squatter who's annexed a section of globalization's large and ever-increasing mansion. Similarly, 'world' music, which is largely a post-globalization construct comprising a mish-mash of classical, folk, and popular traditions from non-Anglophone countries. In this case, the 'global' anthropologizes the 'world'; makes it remote, ornamental, tribal.

Here are two comic analyses of the writer in the midst of plenty – the narrative of abundance, which is not unrelated, as I've attempted to show, to the abundance of narrative. The first instance comes from the maladroit, disturbing, faintly unsavoury French novelist Michel Houellebecq, from his first novel, *Extension du domaine de la lutte*; what drew my attention to it, really, was Theo Tait's acute article on Houellebecq in the *London Review of Books*. According to Tait, 'All Houellebecq's books have some theoretical underpinning: a modest extension of the argument of the *Communist Manifesto*, proposing that what we call sexual freedom is in fact the last stage in the free market's resolution of personal wealth into exchange value.' And he quotes a droll section of the novel, which, he says, 'explains its ironically grandiose title':

> Just like unrestrained economic liberalisation, and for similar reasons, sexual liberalism produces phenomena of *absolute pauperization*. Some men make love every day; others five or six times in their life, or never. Some make love with dozens of women; others with none. It's what is known as 'the law of the market'. In an economic system where unfair dismissal is prohibited, every person more or less manages to find their place. In a sexual system where adultery is prohibited, every person more or less manages to find their bed mate. In a totally liberal economic system, certain people accumulate considerable fortunes; others stagnate in unemployment in misery. In a totally liberal sexual system, certain people have a varied and exciting erotic life; others are reduced to masturbation and solitude.

This is, in effect, Houellebecq's attempt to place not only the sexual human being but also the writer in what I've called globalization's 'tragicomic rhetoric of putative plenty overcoming the awareness of palpable want'. Compare this with the Croatian novelist Dubravka Ugresic's essay, 'How I Could Have Been Ivana Trump and Where I Went Wrong'. Many of Ugresic's essays are to do with the strange transformation of the East European writer after the disappearance of the Soviet bloc, and are related to the sense of dislocation she experiences on stepping out into the 'free world' and being confronted with another, less expected disappearance – that of the domain of the literary, and of culture. This leads to a comedy of misreadings and thwarted desires. 'Who is Ivana Trump?' Ugresic asks us, and answers her own question: a fellow East European, a champion skier and a model who emigrated to Canada in 1973, and, 'three years later ... traded up her brief career as a model and [the skier George Syrovatka's] wife for the career of being Donald Trump's'. After her divorce from Trump, Ivana inherited the Plaza Hotel on Fifth Avenue, New York, and 'lavish severance pay, and became a successful businesswoman, writer, and active participant in the international jet set'.

None of this would have much to do with Ugresic had she not read a 'lengthy review of Ivana Trump's novel' in the *New York Times Book Review*, in the same issue that published 'an unjustly malicious review' of Joseph Brodsky's *Watermark*. 'One reviewer vilified Brodsky for his language "jammed with metaphors", and the other praised Ivana for her analytical intelligence.' Ever since, Ugresic has been following Ivana's trajectory with bemused interest; her return to Croatia, her purchase of 'hotels, casinos, department stores ...'; her purchase of the 'Split daily newspaper *Free Dalmatia*. She would not get involved in editorial policy, she said, she would

just take a column that she would write herself.' These days, when students
in Ugresic's creative writing class ask her 'how one becomes a writer', she,
by her own account, replies with 'complete authority': 'Take up a sport
and train like hell. Anything else could lead you in the wrong direction.'
For, 'having become a writer of world renown, it would have been difficult for Joseph Brodsky to become a brilliant skier, while it was easy for
Ivana Trump to go from being a skier to a writer, even a brilliant analyst
of political conditions in her former communist homeland ...' Moreover,
'Having myself become a writer, I have little prospect of ever becoming
a soccer player, but every soccer player can easily occupy my territory:
literature. Thus the well-known soccer player, Davos Suber, announced
after 1998 World Cup, when the Croatian team won third place: *No offence
to Croatian writers, but we have probably just written the greatest fairy tale in
the history of Croatian literature.*'

   These sardonic-surreal observations are located, as a gesture of defiance, within the narrative of abundance, and within, as well, the illusory
abundance of narrativity. They also alert us to the fact that the market for
the novelist, the purveyor of representation, and his or her relation to
the erstwhile 'reader' have changed with the reification of narrative. If, as
Walter Benjamin claimed in 'On Some Motifs in Baudelaire', the 'crowd',
in the democratizing nineteenth century, wanted to see and read about
itself in the novel ('It became a customer; it wished find itself portrayed in
the contemporary novel, as the patrons did in the paintings of the Middle
Ages'), the situation today is somewhat different, as not only Ivana Trump,
but the various versions of Pop Idol, as well as the high levels of tolerance
for tuneless singing on the two-decade-old Indian television show Close
Up Antyakshari remind us. The 'crowd' no longer wants to consume its
representation; the spectator wants, now, to 'be' the artist. In the plenty
of globalization, this transposition is not just possible; it's logical. Meanwhile, the 'real' writer, whoever he or she might be – someone who can do
nothing else, who cannot, by an act of the will, escape their writerliness,
who has nothing to show for themselves but their craft and their work,
whose identity as a writer, in other words, has an anachronistic ontological weight – may well be subjected, in Houellebecq's term, to 'pauperiza-
tion'; be reduced to 'masturbation and solitude'; in other words, to being,
in English slang, a 'wanker'.

It's impossible, one will have noticed, to speak up these days for art.
Academic criticism and paid-up scholars are silent, for reasons I've already
discussed and enumerated, about the question of art and its value; while
the *language* of 'disinterested' valuation has been relocated in the market-

place with an entirely new intentionality and purpose. 'High' art has been made to take responsibility for twentieth-century history; specifically, for the excesses of Western man. In the process, held hostage, as it were, it's been made indefensible. The shifting of 'blame' from the human being to the 'work of art' began as an ostensibly tragic, but conveniently exculpatory, gesture within late modernity itself; this is what informs, for instance, George Steiner's fraught and slightly grandiose and self-congratulatory reply to Christopher Bigsby's question 'about the question and value of art itself', a reply that, unwittingly, gives the entire onus of valuing, and then the urgency of dismantling the value, of art to history, specifically Western history:

> Why did the great culture of Europe not resist more effectively when the inhuman came? Why did the nation of Beethoven and Bach, of Kant and of Goethe, become the nation of Auschwitz?
> ... I kept asking the question and was forced to the conclusion that people trained to love art supremely, people like you and I for whom a great play, novel or poem was of true significance, must acknowledge that the cry in fiction blots out the cry in the street ... that imagination trained to imagine, to fictionalize, is lamed in the face of actual, concrete inhumanity.

At first, the ritual genuflection toward, and defence of, the novel (which I described at the beginning of this piece) might seem curious in the present climate. It needs, straightaway, to be distinguished from a defence of the artistic; the defence of the novel by Ishiguro, Barnes, and Coe is *not* a defence of art. Its tone of moral seriousness and piety is different from the piety of the custodians of culture and aesthetics in modernity; it's a piety that (despite Coe's interest in bygone cultural spaces that made possible the work of experimental novelists like B.S. Johnson) arises not from the patrician certainties of 'high' culture, but from the contemporary aggressiveness, and righteousness, of narrativity. Here, Naipaul's curmudgeonly, possibly mischievous, pronouncement about the death of the novel serves as a provocation; it contains, perhaps, a concealed nostalgia (barely admissible to Naipaul himself) for the superannuated realm of 'culture'. The mere utterance causes disruption; it reminds us of the low tolerance for, and the marginalization of, the disruptive, the poetic, and the anti-narrative in globalization.

What I've been struggling to articulate is my strong and returning sense of globalization's reinvention and appropriation of narrative. And I'm also trying, I suppose, to dwell and pause with my own puzzlement, a puzzlement arising from my suspicion that there is no critique of this reinvention, but only a dogged and dated critique of hierarchy. Like all people on the cusp of something, or at a crossroads, the lack of urgency and focus in the language we use, as well as an intimation of its subtle and far-reaching transformation, trouble me; for that particular critique of hierarchy has largely lost its immediacy because of the way hierarchies have relocated and radically reframed themselves. This is the thing, one gradually learns, about hierarchies and absolutes: that they are not only static – they are at once static and fluid, and their absoluteness is not incompatible with their constantly taking on new guises; becoming, even, their own opposite as they do so.

This is not, by any means, an essay against popular culture. We do need to continue to take popular culture seriously; we also need to reframe a language to understand what 'popular' culture means in the context of the present – for the word, like 'freedom', has been re-formed and almost made theological in the unipolar world. How do we develop a critique of the global without at the same time pretending that globalization hasn't happened? It is impossible – untenable – to formulate a critique which says, 'All this is terrible, globalization is bad, let's go back.' I have no intention of subscribing to the violence of 'going back'; at the same time, how do we make our knowledge of globalization, of discourse, of power, negotiate, in a way different from ever before, the close reading, the specificity, that gave us pleasure?

Anti-Fusion

In 1999, after returning to India after sixteen years in England, I began once more to listen to my old record collection. It comprised, in large part, a once-beloved array of American singer-songwriters, British rock musicians, and a fastidious selection of the blues and jazz, all of which I'd ostentatiously turned away from in the early 1980s as I grew more and more involved in North Indian classical music, and as my subterranean writerly aspirations began to become increasingly powerful, especially after my arrival in England. But, in 1999, listening, again, after almost two decades to, say, Hendrix, I noticed what I had in the late 1970s, when I played the guitar and had begun to learn the *raga*, and two or more musical systems had briefly overlapped in my life: that the pentatonic blues scale is identical with certain pentatonic *ragas*. This led, in turn, to a sort of double hearing as I listened, now, to Hendrix; where the conscious mind was registering one sort of performance or form, and the subconscious was stirred to recall another. Further, this then created experiences of what I call 'mishearings': for instance, one morning, when I was practising the *raga* Todi, as I usually do at that time of day, I heard the riff to Clapton's 'Layla' in a handful of notes I was singing. I began to wonder, surreptitiously, whether some sort of hybrid musical vocabulary – distinct from the bringing-together we ordinarily associate with Indo-Western 'fusion' – might result from these 'mishearings'. It was this speculation that, in short, led to the experiment in music I've been involved for the last three years, called 'This Is Not Fusion'.

But a person who's titled a project in music 'This Is Not Fusion' had better have some thoughts on what fusion *is*. And this is the question I'd like the listener who's heard the music, confronted the title, and been either amused or offended, to ask; not just, 'Why is it not fusion?' but 'What *is* fusion, after all?' For it's a word we use, especially when talking about music, and in the context of Indo-Western contemporary music in particular, as if it referred to a particular sort of activity that needed no further explanation. West, East; sitar, drums, tabla, marimba, bass guitar – these are just some of the components of 'fusion' as we understand it today, especially in India. Permeating these combinations are unexamined beliefs about identity and where we come from; beliefs which should be challenged in the course of a 'fusion' performance, but which are routinely reconfirmed during it because they're never brought out into the open.

A common assumption – call it prejudice or conviction, depending on which side of the divide you are – is that 'fusion' comprises a departure, scandalous or liberating, from the canonical musical traditions. Yet we all know that these traditions (I'm speaking of the Indian musical landscape within which I work, but I suspect the examples could be changed and the point still be made) – say, Indian classical music, or jazz, or film music, or rock, or Tagore-songs – came into existence as hybrid forms; that their richest periods will be the ones of assimilation, the fallowest in which their proponents subscribe to an inherited version of that music. Canonical traditions at once protect themselves from the arbitrariness of fusion and thrive on it in practice; they both domesticate and accommodate fused elements.

Domesticate, in that when we listen to, say, a song composed by the great music director from 1950s Hindi cinema, O.P. Nayyar, we aren't actually listening to it as if it were a form in which unrelated musical sounds and cultural registers had come together, but as a variety of a genre we recognize as 'Hindi film music'. Accommodate, because we're nevertheless led to wonder at the magical juxtaposition of the double bass and the *sarangi*, a stringed instrument used for accompanying classical vocalists, in a single song. Similarly, when we listen to the Pakistani classical virtuosos Nazakat and Salamat Ali singing, we're aware of listening to a *khayal* (the principal classical genre for vocal music) and not to an unexpected bringing together of *dhrupadi* (an earlier classical form) and sufi-inflected *qawwal* elements; but if we attend carefully, we'll notice those disparate registers inflecting their rendition. It's the inner tension between domestication and accommodation in canonical traditions that produces anxiety, pleasure, development, and the genuinely new treatments and compositions.

Why does it often seem to me that it's difficult to find this inner tension in 'fusion' music; that, while there might be a long-standing quarrel between fusion and the canonical traditions, there is no quarrel *within* fusion, and therefore no development; that the fusion we hear in India today is fundamentally little different from the sounds Shakti produced thirty years ago? One of the reasons for this, surely, is that Eastern and Western elements in fusion have a designated static quality that they don't in their own contexts, where they're embroiled in histories and debates. In East-West fusion as we know it here, for instance, the Indian representative is commonly a classical performer, and the bearer of an ancient tradition; the Western representative often a jazz musician, a well-known type of modern, the exhausted Romantic who's had enough of modernity, and must renovate himself (it's usually 'himself') through contact with immemorial cultures. If we listen to Hindi film songs or advertisement jingles, however, we realize that 'Indian' music isn't just immemorial: it comprises the classical lineages (themselves fairly modern inventions), regional and folk forms, swing, blues, techno and, with a self-reflexivity that only the creators of the thirty-second fillers on MTV seem to tap into, those film songs and jingles themselves.

The random list I've produced reminds us how bewilderingly music is located, in class, history, physical environment. One of the more problematic features of fusion is its wide-eyed transcendence not only of nationality but of locality, with the old ideal of the 'universal human being' reworked into the cunning, grasping innocence of our globalized world. And so, while jazz emerged from urban neighbourhoods, and Indian classical music from families and regions, fusion seems to inhabit a continuum without physicality, one that has no smoke, traffic, interiority, weather, or furniture. It's this unmappable continuum that habitually engenders, unsurprisingly, compositions with names like 'Rebirth', 'Destiny', and 'Journey'; and it's this quasi-mystical space that allows compositions to have no clear delineation, and to sound like each other; it's why, after all these years, we have trouble identifying a classic of the genre. Genres, compositions, even the troubled notion of the 'classic', are informed by history and its dissonances; 'fusion', though, belongs to some universalist – now globalized – plane where two unlikes constantly, ardently, embrace, and where conflict is not openly admissible.

If fusion still has potentiality, it's because it constitutes a search; not just for interracial contact, but for an idiom adequate to the spaces we've inhabited. Most importantly, unlike the canonical forms, it has the capacity to abjure domestication; to always remind us, with a degree of mischief, knowledge, and musical conviction, that there is both such a thing, and that there's no such thing, as 'Eastern' and 'Western' music. For me, problems and opportunities present themselves through the fact that there are no clear demarcations of Western and Indian music in my memory, although I do feel these categories exist in tension with one another. At the root of my indecision and ambivalence is, I suspect, my metropolitan upbringing in 1960s and 1970s India, which indefatigably and startlingly reallocated the 'Indian' and the 'Western', in ways we still haven't quite come to terms with. It's a sound that might be true to that hybrid metropolitan milieu, something that might have been born from, and be played in, one of its neighbourhoods, rather than some pointed and repeated gesture of musical commingling, that I've been looking for.

Part Two

Alternative Traditions, Alternative Readings

Arun Kolatkar and the Tradition of Loitering

When *Jejuri* was published in 1976, I was fourteen years old. I heard about it only the following year, when the *Times of India* announced it had won the Commonwealth Poetry Prize, and carried a piece on Arun Kolatkar. Later, if I remember correctly, the *Times* featured, on a Sunday, an article on the poet, the book, and the actual town of Jejuri, a site of pilgrimage in the state of Maharashtra; it was probably when Kolatkar's droopy moustache and longish hair became familiar to me from a photograph. It seems extraordinary that this newspaper, which, for a decade now, has pretended there's no such thing as literature, should have devoted so much newsprint to a poet; but the ethos in Bombay was still friendly, in an almost unthinking, unformulated way, toward Indian poetry in English, in a spirit of friendliness towards what it saw to be various recreational pastimes.

I first met Kolatkar in early 2000, when I was in Bombay to launch a novel. I'd extended my stay in order to seek him out; I hoped to ask him to give *Jejuri* to the international publishing house who published me at the time (for whom I'd just begun to edit a series that would give modern Indian classics, both translated and in English, a fresh lease of life), and so make *Jejuri* available to the worldwide audience I felt it deserved. At the time, the book was not only not published internationally; it was only available – though it had acquired a reputation as a key work of contemporary Indian literature in the years since it had first appeared – in limited print runs at a couple of bookshops in Bombay and, I was told, Pune from Pras Prakashan. This small press was run by Kolatkar's friend Ashok Shahane, a man who was, as Kolatkar said in an interview to the poet Eunice de Souza, 'very active in the Marathi little magazine movement.' *Jejuri*'s author was, by all accounts, content, even determined, that this was how things should continue to be.

I was told by Adil Jussawalla, one of the most respected and defining figures of Bombay's poetry scene in English, that Kolatkar could be
found at the Wayside Inn on Thursday, after half past three. The Wayside
Inn was in a neighbourhood called Kala Ghoda, which means 'black
horse': so named because of the statue in black stone of King Edward VII
on his horse that once stood at its centre, in the space that's long since
been converted into a car park. Shaped by the colonial past, reshaped by
republican and nationalist zeal, Kala Ghoda had become a cosmopolitan
'here and now', located at the confluence of downtown and the arts and
commercial districts. Wayside Inn itself overlooked the Jehangir Art Gallery and Max Mueller Bhavan, the centre for German culture; Elphinstone
College, the David Sassoon Library, the Regal Cinema, and the Prince of
Wales Museum were a short distance away; Rhythm House, for a long
time Bombay's largest music store, was next door. The banks and offices of
Flora Fountain, one of the city's more venerable business districts, weren't
far away either. In the midst of office-goers, students, and people heading
towards matinee shows and art exhibitions, were the small families of the
homeless who had settled down on the pavements around the Jehangir
Art Gallery and Rhythm House, the prostitutes who appeared at night and
sometimes loitered about in the afternoon, and the pushers in front of the
Prince of Wales Museum, who, by the late 1970s, had come to stay. The
friends Kolatkar met up with at the Wayside Inn were from the intermittently overlapping spheres of art and commerce, poets and friends from
the advertising world in which, for many years, he'd made his living; but it
was the low-life, the obscure daily-wage-earners, and the itinerant families
of Kala Ghoda he looked upon from the open window, and whom he'd
been writing about for twenty years. The sequence, *Kala Ghoda Poems*,
was published shortly before his death by Ashok Shahane.

I was familiar with the area; I'd spent a year at Elphinstone College
in 1978. It was then that I'd bought *Jejuri* from Thacker's Bookshop in the
same area; both it and the Wayside Inn no longer exist; the latter's been replaced by an upmarket Chinese restaurant. But in 2000, I found Kolatkar
there on the Thursday afternoon; three or four meetings, another trip to
Bombay, and long-distance telephone calls to a neighbour's phone (he
didn't possess one himself) followed in my attempt to make him sign the
contract. I found him a mixture of unassumingness, reticence, mischief,
and recalcitrance. His well-known prickliness about contracts came not
so much, I think, from a feeling of neglect, or a bogus, but not uncom-
mon, claim to nationalist pride among *arriviste* Indian writers, as a sense
of allegiance to a subculture that had, by now, largely disappeared; the
subculture that had given him his wariness as well as his writer's cunning

and resources. At one point, I was interviewed at the Inn by a group of friends, including Shahane – a sort of grilling by the 'firm' – while Kolatkar occasionally played, in a deadpan way, my advocate. His questions and prevarications regarding the contract betrayed a fiendish ingeniousness: 'It says the book won't be published in Australia. But I said nothing about Australia.' Only my reassurance, 'I've looked at the contract and I'd sign it without any doubts in your place,' made him tranquil. Finally, he did sign; something more extraordinary to me, and of which I'm more proud, than if I'd been an agent who'd secured a multi-million-dollar deal. Why the series fell through, and why I left that publisher, is a matter I won't go into here. But, in the long term, the bitter disappointment turned out to be a blessing. It's the reason why the edition you now hold in your hands exists; and I should add that Kolatkar, who died in September 2004, was pleased, without reservations for once, at the prospect of its existence.

Kolatkar was born in Kolhapur in Maharashtra (the Western Indian state of which Bombay, now Mumbai, is the capital) in 1932. Kolhapur is famous for its kolhapuris – chappals, or slippers, that are designed for outside wear and can be found for sale on the streets, but also as an exorbitantly finished and priced object in shops for the rich. In its casualness, its air of classless elegance, and its itinerary through bewilderingly diverse locations , the kolhapuri is not unlike the bohemian, artistic set in the 1950s, 1960s, and 1970s, who indeed made of it a mark of its identity. Members of this set had an abhorrence of fixity; they could be found on the street, walking past hawkers, prostitutes, and traffic lights, as well as in art galleries, seminar rooms, and drawing rooms and cafes with their rituals of food and drink. This was a peculiarly Bombay mixture of proximity and transcendence; Nissim Ezekiel – who was the oldest, and also the chief spokesman, of the poets writing in English who began to emerge in the Fifties – sought to compress it in these lines from 'In India':

> Always, in the sun's eye,
> Here, among the beggars,
> Hawkers, pavement sleepers,
> Hutment dwellers, slums
> … I ride my elephant of thought,
> A Cézanne slung around my neck.

The journey negotiated in Ezekiel's lines – physical and cultural – between the teeming road in Bombay and Cézanne, between recalcitrant, perspiring everydayness and the work of art – or, more specifically, the art-world – was a real journey to many of the Bombay poets. Ezekiel himself;

Arvind Krishna Mehrotra, his MA student at Bombay University; Gieve Patel; Adil Jussawalla – all these poet-critics poached and encroached upon the territory of painters (Patel became a considerable painter himself), especially the J.J. School of Art, which, at the time, was producing, in F.N. Souza, M.F. Husain, and others, a premier post-Independence generation (remarkably heterogeneous in class, religious, and regional backgrounds) of Indian painters. The poets seemed to have realized, instinctively, the importance of the moment and of this proximity; for instance, Ezekiel's and Jussawalla's essays on the Baroda painter Bhupen Khakhar (who'd later be taken up by Rushdie), written in the early 1970s, are extraordinarily shrewd readings of the then unremarked-upon elements of kitsch and homoeroticism in Khakhar's work. That this liaison between a dormant, semi-visible literary culture and a semi-visible tradition of modern art has a parallel in the now publicized liaison between similar worlds in 1950s and 1960s New York is indisputable; so is the fact of the richness of the interaction. It's unlikely, though, that the Indian poets, despite their admiration for twentieth-century American poetry, their enviable and intriguing up-to-dateness, would have known then of Frank O'Hara or John Ashbery. Two comparable but not directly relatable metropolitan flirtations between artistic subcultures seem to have taken place in two continents within a few years of, and at some points overlapping with, each other. The literary history that might describe, in serious terms, the significance of what happened in that context in Bombay is still to be written, perhaps because the writer in English was, in India, till Rushdie came along accompanied by Booker-inspired fanfare, a sort of elite pariah, a 'missing person', in Jussawalla's words, a figure marginal to the larger, and solemn, task of nation-building.

It was into this hybrid society that Kolatkar inserted himself; in 1949, he enrolled at the JJ School of Art, after which it seems a mysterious phase of drifting and formal as well as spiritual education followed, which few people appear to be clear about. At any rate, he took his diploma as late as 1957; but by this time he was already a graphic artist for the vibrant and upwardly mobile advertising world in Bombay. He was, in advertising jargon, a 'visualizer'; and was to become one of Bombay's most successful art directors. All this seems very far away from Jejuri, both the place and the book. The place itself would have been fairly well known to a certain kind of pilgrim-devotee and follower of the local Maharashtrian deity Khandoba (who began his career as a folk-god, a protector of cattle and sheep, and graduated slowly to Brahminical acceptance as an incarnation of Shiva); but it would probably have been obscure to Kolatkar and his friends. An interdisciplinary, but not disciplined, reader – 'I read across disciplines, and don't necessarily read a book from beginning to end,' he said to the poet Eunice de Souza – he claimed, in the same conversation, that he discovered Jejuri in 'a book on temples and legends of Maharashtra … there was a chapter on Jejuri in it. It seemed an interesting place.' He went there first in 1963, with his brother Makarand, and his friend, the Marathi novelist Manohar Oak, both of whom, indeed, make appearances in the poem, in laid-back, deadpan incarnations that are variations of the narrator.

The 1960s, for him, was a time of reappraisal and ferment. After the break-up of his first marriage, he married his second wife, Soonoo (who survives him). The discovery of, and journey towards, places like Jejuri in a time of inner transition, and all that such journeys represent, from the redemptive to the terrifying, is described in Marathi poems like 'The Turnaround':

> Bombay made me a beggar.
> Kalyan gave me a lump of jaggery to suck.
> In a small village that had a waterfall
> but no name
> my blanket found a buyer
> and I feasted on plain ordinary water.
>
> I arrived in Nasik with
> peepul leaves between my teeth.
> There I sold my Tukaram
> to buy some bread and mince.

> (Kolatkar's translation)

He was writing extraordinary Marathi poems, about the extremities of urban and psychological experience, which seem to be the product of a social outcast who's been dabbling in mind-altering drugs while reading up on Surrealism, William Burroughs, Dashiell Hammett, Indian mythology, and Marathi devotional poets like Tukaram. The last of these was a real enthusiasm, and Kolatkar was translating, into English, the medieval poet's rather prickly, belligerent hymns to God. These were as much translation as occasionally tough-guy reworkings of some of the songs; an unsettling form of ventriloquizing. Machismo seemed to have interested him; not only its aura of power, but its disorienting humour. The proximity between the disreputable, the culpable, and the religious – a living strand in Indian devotional culture, and an everyday reality in places like Banaras and Jejuri – becomes, in the act of translation, an aesthetic:

It was a case
Of God rob God.
No cleaner job
Was ever done.

God left God
Without a bean.
God left no trace
No nail no track.

The thief was lying
Low in His flat.
When he moved
He moved fast.

 Tuka says:
Nobody was
Nowhere. None
Was plundered
And lost nothing.

And so some of his own 'Marathi' poems of the 1950s and 1960s are written in the Bombay argot of the migrant working classes and the underworld, part Hindi, part Marathi, which the Hindi film industry would make proper use of only decades later. These poems he then often translated into an Americanese which, at the time, would have made respectable Americans blush, '*maderchod*' rendered, for instance, as 'motherfucker'. Bombay, in the 1960s, gave him these languages and also the passages of transition between these worlds, the movement from street to library to cinema hall.

There was also, at this time, a musical transformation, a musical moment. Kolatkar had learnt Western musical notation. He'd also taken lessons in playing the *pakhawaj*, the venerable Indian drum that predates the *tabla*; in the early 1970s, he began to compose his peculiar and compelling versions of rock music. He recorded a demo of four songs with a group of local musicians in a studio in 1973; he was forty one years old. Though nothing came of that experiment, it sounds now, more than ever, like groundbreaking, astonishing stuff. The first song, 'I am a poor man from a poor land', has an *ananda-lahari* – one of the instruments played by Baul singers, mendicant devotees of Krishna, in Bengal – in the background. The first line is something Kolatkar read on a piece of paper of the sort that the semi-educated beggar in India used to hand out to people, often stating his profession and including a message in English, perhaps to keep some of his dignity intact. In the foreground is Kolatkar's scolding but very musical vocalizing; a spin-off on the beggar's plea that becomes a demand to the consumer, the singer asking his listener to pay up for his 'damn' good song'. The genre, here and in the other songs, is metropolitan and immediate and hybrid; inescapably but complicatedly 'Indian', without any of the sentimental assumptions of 'world music'. It's a style that hasn't occurred before or since. As in *Jejuri*, the devotional is inserted forcefully into the economic, where it always resided anyway in India, into the bread-and-butter transaction, the duty and slightly disreputable compulsion to earn a living.

Some time after the demo, Kolatkar, in December 1973, began to write *Jejuri*. The impetus was provided by the twenty-six-year-old Arvind Krishna Mehrotra, who'd just returned to India from the University of Iowa's International Writing Program, and had been asked by its director, Paul Engle, if he'd compile an anthology of Indian poetry for the program's anthology series. Mehrotra asked Kolatkar if he had a suitable poem for the compilation. It was now that Kolatkar got down to writing the poem-sequence. Amazingly, he'd written a version before, from which a single poem, 'A Low Temple', had been published in a little magazine of the mid-1960s in Bombay, *Dionysius*. The editor lost the manuscript; there was no copy. Kolatkar finished *this* sequence, with all its immediacy, a few months later after he began it, in early 1974, and sent it to Mehrotra; though the compilation was never completed, the entire poem was published that year in the *Opinion Literary Quarterly*.

This wasn't the first time Kolatkar had published a poem-sequence in English (few poets have cultivated the sequence as Kolatkar did); in 1968, 'the boatride' had appeared in Mehrotra's little magazine, *damn you/ a magazine of the arts*. With this poem – an arresting record of a steamer ride taken from the Gateway of India – Kolatkar had announced what his métier would largely be as an English poet: the urban everyday, or a view of the material universe informed deeply by it. The banishment of capital letters, the treasuring of the concrete: these features of 'the boatride', as well as of the magazine it was published in, alert us, again, to the presence of the Americans – e. e. cummings, William Carlos Williams, Marianne Moore, the 'Beat' poets. A generation of Indian poets in English (A.K. Ramanujan, Mehrotra, Kolatkar) had turned to the idiosyncratic language, and the capacity for eye-level attentiveness, of American poetry to create yet another mongrel Indian diction – to reorder familiar experience, and to fashion a demotic that escaped the echoes of both Queen's English and the sonorous effusions of Sri Aurobindo's *Savitri* and the poorly translated but ubiquitous *Gitanjali* of Tagore; to bypass, as it were, the expectations that terms like 'English literature' and 'Indian culture' raised.

Jejuri is, on its most obvious level (and a very rich level that is, in terms of realism, observation, irony), an account of a man who arrives at the pilgrimage town on a 'state transport bus', in the company of people whose intent is clearly more devotional than his is, and has less to do with a seemingly unfathomable curiosity. They seem to, thus, reproach him by their opacity, their inaccessibility, their very presence: 'Your own divided face in a pair of glasses/ on an old man's nose/ is all the countryside you get to see.' The rest of the poem is about the narrator's idiosyncratic reading of the place; Jejuri, which seems to him a mixture of temples in disrepair, unreliable priests, and legends and religious practices of dubious provenance, nevertheless excites him oddly, though not to worship, but to a state akin to it but also quite unlike it. He leaves later on a train from the railway station, still, evidently, in a state of confusion over what's secular and what miraculous: 'a wooden saint/ in need of plaster/ … the indicator/ has turned inward/ ten times over'. The typographical flourish in the penultimate poem, in, and through, which the narrator records the experience of witnessing cocks and hens dancing in a field on the way to the station, is the closest the poem comes to imitating a religious ecstasy and abandon, on the brink where both irony and the verbal are obliterated.

Jejuri was received with unusual enthusiasm by the standards of poetry publishing in Anglophone India; the book was reprinted twice at short intervals, and then twice again at longer ones. The critical response, by any standards, was unremarkable and intermittent. One of the reasons was that the poem, like its author, was resistant to being pigeonholed into quasi-religious categories; in response to an interviewer asking him, in 1978, if he believed in God, Kolatkar had said: 'I leave the question alone. I don't think I have to take a position about God one way or the other.' This discomfort with the either/or lies at the heart of the poem. Most of the Marathi critics opted, conveniently, for simplification and chauvinism. The novelist and critic Balachandra Nemade's response, in a 1985 essay, is characteristic: 'Kolatkar comes and goes like a weekend tourist from Bombay.' There was, of course, the occasionally sensitive retrospective reappraisal, of which Bruce King's chapter on Kolatkar in *Modern Poetry in English* is an example; but the poem was to receive, decisively, a fresh lease of life, and the oxygen of good criticism, from Mehrotra in his anthology, *The Oxford India Anthology of Twelve Modern Poets*. Sixteen years after the poem had first appeared, Mehrotra seemed to be in no doubt about its place in the canon of Indian poetry in English: 'among the finest single poems written in India in the last forty years'. The religious question he settled robustly and acutely, if, perhaps, temporarily: 'The presiding deity of *Jejuri* is not Khandoba, but the human eye.'

I've said that, in the larger, unfolding story of the independent nation, writing poetry in English was a minor, marginal, and occasionally controversial activity. This remained so in spite of Nissim Ezekiel's attempts to invest the enterprise with seriousness, to stir Anglophone readers as well as writers in the vernaculars, both of whom were busy with more important projects, to see it as something more than, at best, a genteel and harmless preoccupation; at worst, as a waste of time, even a betrayal. Ezekiel defied this combination of indifference and moral and nationalistic chauvinism with a critical puritanism, and had a small measure of success. But marginal endeavours have their own excitements, disappointments, and dangers. Among the excitements was the creation, in 1976, of Clearing House, brought into being by Jussawalla, Mehrotra, Kolatkar and Gieve Patel to publish, in the first instance, their own poetry. Like the writing of the poetry itself, the publishing venture was undertaken as things are in subcultures: with love, as a semi-private affair, partly for the eyes of other poets and fellow travellers. Books were supplied to a handful of bookshops, and also on the basis of 'subscriptions'; that is, orders from friends and supporters. The four titles published that year were Patel's *How Do You Withstand, Body*; Jussawalla's *Missing Person*; Mehrotra's *Nine Enclosures*; and *Jejuri*. Kolatkar had designed the covers, and chosen the typeface, turning the books – again, this is something we associate with subcultures rather than mass markets – into *objets d'art*.

But, along with their passion and enterprise, subcultures are also characterized by disabling forms of self-doubt that often express themselves as doubts about the larger world. In the case of the poets I've just mentioned, this took the form of a wariness about committing words to paper, or the written word to print, or the printed word to wider circulation. This is not writer's block, but a strategic and partial withdrawal from the world; at its best, writing for a handful of readers, some of them friends, entailed a greater sense of responsibility, of judiciousness, about the task of writing. In Kolatkar's case, it meant that he wrote steadily after *Jejuri* (as he had before its publication), in both English and Marathi, but published only very sporadically in journals. Two collections of his Marathi poetry appeared in 2003; but the English works, the *Kala Ghoda Poems* and the political/mythological fable in verse *Sarpa Satra*, would see the light of day only after he knew he was dying. The book launches of his final works were, bizarrely, events surrounding a dying man who, on the evidence of his poetry, was still possessed by the youthfulness of the Sixties: both celebration, then, and premature memorial.

When I first met Kolatkar in 2000, Bombay had already become Mumbai, and the Hindu chauvinist parties, the Shiv Sena and the BJP, were at their most active and aggressive in the city – perhaps in prescient nervousness at an election defeat later that year. Bombay was trying to rebuild its old cosmopolitanism and sense of personal and physical freedom, its delight in the wayward and the aleatory, after more than a decade of religious and economic divisiveness, and after having become the commercial capital of a globalized India. My trip coincided with Valentine's Day, and it re-emphasized the different, exacerbated, poles of 'Mumbai'. On the one hand, the Valentine's Day industry had reached a new zenith, and well-to-do teenagers were wandering about in an ingenuous swoon of love; on the other, Shiv Sena cadres were vandalizing shops selling the day's parapher-nalia, and, in a ritual meant to attract the media, burning Valentine's Day cards. The distance between this moral policing and the xenophobia that animated Shiv Sena slogans like 'Mumbai for Mumbaikars', where 'Mum-baikar' really meant Maharashtrian Hindus, was frighteningly small.

The Shiv Sena, which started as a Marathi chauvinist organization under the leadership of Bal Thackray, a cartoonist and admirer of Hitler, reinvented itself as a Hindu chauvinist one and came to power in Mahar-ashtra in 1995 in an alliance with the BJP, and soon changed the name of its capital city to Mumbai. Both parties had taken advantage of a moral vacu-um in secular politics at the time, as well as a new state of polarization that had been building up between Hindus and Muslims. This polarization was confirmed with the destruction of the Babri mosque in Ayodhya by BJP extremists in December 1992. Bombay bore the imprint of these events: in the riots and violence in early 1993, and then the series of explosions in March that year. It also bore the most visible imprint anywhere in India of the economic 'liberalization' that took place in 1991; the troubled city was booming, and growing beyond recognition. What was once outskirt or hinterland was now integrated into the city's teeming, self-generating expansion.

When I reread *Jejuri* now I realize how important the modern me-tropolis – the city as it was before globalization – with its secret open-ings and avenues, its pockets of daydreaming, idling, and loitering, its loucheness, is fundamental to Kolatkar as a way of seeing, as a means of renovating experience. For no other Indian poet in English, and for few other writers, is Walter Benjamin's *flâneur* an analogue for receptivity and creativity as he is for Kolatkar, in a way, and in contexts and situations, that perhaps Benjamin wouldn't have been able to imagine. What the German writer (whom Kolatkar wouldn't have read) discovered in Paris, and imagined his *flâneur* came upon in the nineteenth-century Parisian boulevards and arcades, Kolatkar did in Kala Ghoda – not only a range of details and particulars, but a restructuring of the way we experience them. Hannah Arendt, in her revealing commentary on Benjamin, notes how the line that divides interior from exterior, domestic from public space, even the 'natural' from the urban and manufactured, is dimmed and blurred constantly for the *flâneur*; he loiters about on the street, inspecting its everyday marvels (or what to *him* is marvellous), as if it were an extension of his drawing room. Even the sky in Paris, says Arendt, took on, for the *flâneur*, the artificial appearance of a great ceiling.

When I think of Kolatkar by his window in the Wayside Inn, looking out, for decades, on families of pavement dwellers and itinerant workers bathing themselves, eating, and raising their children before the Jehangir Art Gallery, I'm reminded of that indeterminate space, where the street turns into an interior, and which complicates the urban boundary separating room from pavement, that's so crucial to the *flâneur's* experience of reality. For Kolatkar, in his personal life, what was dwelling and what place of transit was at times almost interchangeable. During some of his most successful years, Kolatkar and his wife were 'paying guests' – that is, lodgers – in one of Bombay's most expensive areas; they then moved to a single-room, book-lined apartment in Prabhadevi, a fairly middle-class location that's not anywhere near the centre of the city. Notwithstanding a very happy domestic life, and the fact that he wrote productively in his tiny flat, he did spend a great deal of time, sometimes breakfast onward, at the Inn, at the confluence of public and street life and private reverie.

I am reminded of these things as I reread *Jejuri*; that, although it's about a journey to a remote (for many) pilgrimage town in Maharashtra, it's less about the transformations of the journey than about a man who never left the city, or downtown, or a cosmopolitan, modernist idea of the metropolis; that his journey, and his sense of travelling and of wonder, brought him back to where he was – and where he was is metropolitan, shabby, and dislocating. And so, in the third poem itself, the four-line 'The Doorstep', the newcomer to the pilgrimage town speaks in the voice of the *flâneur*, for whom the line dividing public from private space is never final; the title names an object, a threshold, while the first two lines retract that meaning: 'That's no doorstep./ That's a pillar on its side.' The *flâneur* stops, starts, pauses again, ponders, constantly struck by the unremarkable object that the city's passers-by don't notice. Things, thresholds, buildings that have either fallen out of use or look like they have, that disturb and ironicize the logic and flow of capital (and, in independent India, Bombay has been as much the centre of expanding capitalism as Paris was in France in the nineteenth century) – this is what he's besotted with. So, in *Jejuri*,

part network of shrines, part downtown, he's transfixed by the journey of
a 'conduit pipe' around a wall; by a broken door that's leaning against an
'old doorway to sober up/ like the local drunk'; by the invitation to what
seems to be 'another temple' – 'The door was open' – but turns out to be
'just a cowshed'.

Benjamin discovered, on his first visit to Paris in 1913, that the houses
that formed the Parisian boulevards 'do not seem to be made to be lived in,
but are like stone sets for people to walk between'; in other words, architecture and buildings – the locations of life and livelihood – become a sort
of theatre, but a theatre that's only available to the loiterer. Similarly, the
temple that becomes a cowshed; the slightly off-kilter construction and
vision of the concluding lines of 'Heart of Ruin', 'No more a place of worship this place/ is nothing less than the house of god'; the theatrical gap
between assertion and reality that was enacted in 'A Doorstep' and recurs
in 'A Low Temple': 'Who was that, you ask./ The eight-arm goddess, the
priest replies./ ... But she has eighteen, you protest.' This is the moment
of theatre that neither the pilgrim at the holy shrine nor the ordinary city
dweller can see. Both invest their surroundings with certain unalterable
meanings; and it's these unalterable meanings that make the *flâneur's*
drama and his irony, as well his odd sense of wonder, possible. The difference between the pilgrim – or, for that matter, the office-goer – and the
flâneur is the latter's passionate disengagement; he doesn't rush toward a
site hallowed by authority or tradition, he gravitates towards, hovers, steps
back, idles, stands outside, dawdles. So, in 'A Low Temple', after his experience with the 'eight-arm goddess', the narrator 'come[s] out into the sun
and light[s] a charminar': the *'charminar'* being a cheap filtreless cigarette
once popular with the artistic fraternity. In another poem, 'Makarand', the
narrator, invited to offer prayers inside a temple, replies, 'No thanks.' He
has both a *flâneur's* democratic generosity and his curious at-homeness in
thresholds and spaces that have no clear function, rather than in interiors
that have designated uses: 'you go right ahead/ if that's what you want
to do,' he reassures his companion, while confessing, 'I will be out in the
courtyard/ where no one will mind/ if I smoke.'

The junk of the urban everyday – a stained doorknob, a disused
threshold, a tile – fills the *flâneur* with momentary excitement and adoration; these random items seem to possess a mystery that derives from
being part of a larger narrative, an unspoken theology or mythology. The
objects the *flâneur* lights upon in streets, by-lanes, alleys, have, for him, an
aura, an air of sacredness, that's almost religious. Kolatkar's metaphor for
urban junk transformed by a small abrasion into something significant,
or poetic, is, in *Jejuri*, the simple stone or rock – like junk, entirely useless

– which is changed by a mark into a holy object. So, in 'The Horseshoe Shrine', the 'nick in the rock/ is really a kick in the side of the hill', where the hoof of Khandoba's horse struck it 'like a thunderbolt' as he rode with his wife 'across the valley', like a spark 'fleeing from flint'. The astonishing translation of urban junk into the realm of the modern imagination is what informs these famous lines from 'A Scratch': 'scratch a rock/ and a legend springs'; it is this process of translation and refashioning, and not devotion, that makes Yeshwant Rao – 'a second class god' whose place 'is just outside the main temple', a 'mass of basalt,/ bright as any post box,/ the shape of protoplasm/ or a king size lava pie' – an object of the poet's wry wonder. The religious is implicit in the transitory objects that Benjamin's *flâneur* discovers, hoards, and cherishes in the city; Kolatkar reworks and inverts this casually, but profoundly, in *Jejuri* – in his poem, a religious landscape is pregnant with the implications, the wonders, of the urban.

In 'Heart of Ruin' (which describes how a temple to the god Maruti is now inhabited by a 'mongrel bitch' and her puppies), there are lines – 'The bitch looks at you guardedly/ past a doorway cluttered with broken tiles'; 'The black eared puppy has gone a little too far./ A tile clicks under its foot.' – which lead us directly to a moment and to the exposition of a certain sensibility in Benjamin's 'The Return of the *Flâneur*'. This essay, written in 1929, became available too late in the day to the Anglophone world for Kolatkar to have read it in the early 1970s, but the concordances in imagery and in sentiment are startling. Benjamin asks us why the *flâneur* is 'the creation of Paris', and not Rome, despite the latter's various landmarks and monuments. He quickly concludes Rome is 'too full of temples, enclosed squares, and national shrines to be able to enter undivided into the dreams of the passer-by'.

> The great reminiscences, the historical *frissons* – these are all so much junk to the *flâneur*, who is happy to leave them to the tourist. And he would be happy to trade all his knowledge of artists' quarters, birthplaces, and princely palaces for the scent of a single weathered threshold or the touch of a single tile – that which any old dog carries away.

The inversion in Benjamin, where history and its imperial monuments (for which 'Rome' is a metaphor) become 'so much junk', and junk, like the tile that 'any old dog' might carry away, is aggrandized and magnified – this inversion is especially true of the Kolatkar of *Jejuri* (where the puppies and the loose tile in the temple supersede the importance of the temple, the monument, itself) and the *Kala Ghoda Poems*. The latter, indeed, abounds in images of junk; of the spokes and wheels that the children of pavement-dwellers recycle for their own recreation. Benjamin's notion of *flânerie* is crucial to our understanding of Kolatkar's poetics, and also of his position in the narrative of Indian writing in English.

In 1981, five years after *Jejuri* had been published, *Midnight's Children* inaugurated a monumental view of Indian history in literature – in fact, a monumental view of literature itself in India. It brought into being, in effect, a lineage of writing about the 'great reminiscences, the historical *frissons*', everything that was 'so much junk to the *flâneur*', as Kolatkar's art had so passionately and contrarily proved. I'm not setting up a crude opposition between the two writers here; Kolatkar admired Rushdie's novel, as Rushdie does Kolatkar's work. But I am suggesting that there is another lineage and avenue in Indian writing in English than the one *Midnight's Children* opened up, along with an obsession with the monumental; and its source lies in *Jejuri*. Younger writers haven't looked at the possibilities of this lineage, with its idiosyncratic delight in the freedom to withhold, assign, and create meaning, its consignment of history to the scrap-yard, and its bringing of the scrap-yard into history, closely enough. If it does exist in some form, critics haven't done enough to uncover and identify it. Had they done so, our view of Indian writing in English would be a different, a more heterogeneous and unexpected, one than it has been in the last twenty-five years. For now, the place of Kolatkar's legacy – no less far-reaching, potentially, than that of *Midnight's Children* – hovers on the edges; which is where, as we see in *Jejuri*, he liked to be.

Learning to Write
V. S. Naipaul, Vernacular Artist

No writer has written more tellingly about the vocation of writing than V.S. Naipaul. His career began almost five decades ago; and this new novel[1] shows us that Naipaul's absorption in how he came to be a writer is still fresh. The protagonist of the novel is Willie Chandran, a writer, named by his father after William Somerset Maugham. In one of his many essays on the subject, Naipaul comments on how the urge to 'be a writer' mysteriously preceded, in him, having anything to actually to write about. This, then, was the first fiction that Naipaul created, long before he'd written a word worth publishing, the fiction of 'being a writer'. It began with an air of fraudulence, with Naipaul hesitating to put the word 'writer' on official forms before he'd produced at least six books, and is approaching an irascible, even oracular, aftermath, where older writers and reputations are brought down – but all is permeated by the pressure and trajectory of his vocation.

In *Finding the Centre*, Naipaul's very fine record of his beginnings as a writer, he tells us how important his place, and tools, of composition were to him: 'a BBC room in London', 'an old BBC typewriter', and 'smooth, "non-rustle" BBC script paper'. There is a description, a few pages later, that invokes the physical process that writing is:

> … I should say that my own typing posture in those days was unusual. My shoulders were thrown back as far as they could go; my spine was arched. My knees were drawn right up; my shoes rested on the topmost struts of the chair, left side and right side. So, with my legs wide apart, I sat at the typewriter with something like a monkey crouch.

On the one hand, this passage is an enactment of the cliché, 'breaking through'; obstacles – the English language, the disadvantage of coming from a small colony – have to be physically pushed aside before the unprecedented work can be created. There's also a reference, in the phrase 'monkey crouch', to Caliban, and it reminds us that Naipaul was not always 'Sir Vidia'. Unlike most Indian writers in English today, who belong to the upper class of a large post-colonial democracy, Naipaul, the grandson of a Brahmin indentured labourer, emerged from nowhere, and had to strain bodily, as in the passage above, against silence. Most movingly, Naipaul's passage echoes the scene in *Great Expectations* in which the recently literate Joe Gargery tries his hand at writing. Dickens, with great compassion, delineates the physical dimensions of the task; the account is narrated by Pip:

> Evidently, Biddy had taught Joe to write. As I lay in bed looking at him, it made me … cry again with pleasure to see the pride with which he set about his letter … At my own writing-table, pushed into a corner and cumbered with little bottles, Joe now sat down to his great work, first choosing a pen from the pen-tray as if it were a chest of large tools, and tucking up his sleeves as if he were going to wield a crowbar or sledgehammer. It was necessary for Joe to hold on heavily to the table with his left elbow, and to get his right leg well out behind him, before he could begin …

As in Naipaul's portrait of his own posture – something between 'monkey crouch' and battle readiness, 'shoulders thrown back' – there is a hint of comic belligerence in Dickens's comparison of the pen to 'a crowbar or sledgehammer', and a poignancy in the way he relates writing, through these words, as much to the dignity of physical labour as to mental activity. The presence of Dickens's passage in Naipaul's alerts us to the way the latter, in attending to this difficult physicality, is taking us back to his grandfather's indentured labourer past even as he draws a picture of a young man about to embark on a life of writing. The phrase, 'his great work', with which Dickens describes a neo-literate's letter, suffuses the passage by Naipaul, who intended to write 'great works' of his own, with its deflating irony; and the echo of Joe Gargery introduces the trope of illiteracy, helplessness and innocence into this self-portrait by one who, according to Irving Howe, is 'a master of the language'.

The theme of illiteracy, and the conflation of writing and labour, is also part of Seamus Heaney's early work; Heaney, too, like Naipaul, came from a background of agriculture and labour – 'My grandfather cut more turf in a day/ Than any other man on Toner's bog,' as he says in his poem, 'Digging'. By the end of that poem, the pen has usurped the spade, and yet remains an instrument of labour: 'Between my finger and my thumb/ The squat pen rests./ I'll dig with it.' Writing, for Heaney, becomes both an annihilation, and continuance, of his father's occupation. In Naipaul's great novel, *A House For Mr Biswas*, it is through Anand's father, the eponymous

Mohun Biswas (in many ways, based on Naipaul's father, Seepersad), that
the author celebrates the physicality of writing, and the English language
as a vernacular. Biswas begins his working life as a sign-writer, learning the
trade from a friend, Alec; together, they are assigned the job of painting
the message, 'IDLERS KEEP OUT BY ORDER'. Here, Naipaul, in one of
the most beautiful prose passages in English, praises, through his father,
the idea of English as a vernacular, and, again invoking Joe Gargery, suggests both the difficulty and joy of, literally, 'learning how to write':

> ... his hand became surer, his strokes bolder, his feeling for letters finer.
> He thought R and S the most beautiful of Roman letters; no letter could
> express so many moods as R, without losing its beauty; and what could
> compare with the swing and rhythm of S? With a brush, large letters were
> easier than small ...

The father, in modern Western culture, represents, famously, social
aspiration, the law, and bourgeois hierarchy. There is an entire tradition
of literature, from Kafka's 'Metamorphosis' to the emasculated patriarch
in J.M. Coetzee's *Disgrace*, that reflects this. But there is another tradition, seminal to the emergence of the modern novel, that is situated in
working-class or colonial experience, and in which the Freudian model is
overturned; here, the figure of the father is synonymous with the socially
censured, the creatively liberating, and the vernacular. *Great Expectations*
itself is an example of this; Pip wishes to be a proper gentleman in London,
but the principal father-figure in the novel, the escaped convict Magwitch,
is not so much an upholder of the law as a transgressor of it. Again, in
Lawrence's *Sons and Lovers*, it is the mother who represents bourgeois
aspiration, the life of the mind, while the father, the miner Walter Morel,
always animated or intoxicated, whistling as he works, is identified with
the physical. In Joyce's *Ulysses*, the father-figure is the petit-bourgeois
copywriter, Leopold Bloom. As a copywriter, he is allied to the modern,
urban version of the vernacular, the language of advertising, the very opposite pole of the world of literature and Shakespeare that Stephen Daeda-
lus inhabits, but not too far from the world of Mohun Biswas, sign-writer
and, later, journalist. Biswas, himself, married to a woman from a powerful
business family, is a daydreamer, with ambitions to 'be a writer', and, as
a journalist, to see his stories in print. Isolated by his wife's family, he is
an inspiration to his son Anand; *A House For Mr Biswas* must be counted
among those great but idiosyncratic modern novels that are impelled by
a transgressive father-figure, symbolizing creativity rather than authority,
at their centre.

Both Naipaul's father and, one feels, the writer R.K. Narayan preside over the early work, culminating in *Biswas*. Tragicomic dreamers like Seepersad Naipaul populate Narayan's Malgudi; and Naipaul's slyly accurate description of Narayan's characters – 'small men, small schemes, big talk, limited means' – could be a reference to his father's world. Indeed, Narayan served as a conduit between father and son when they discussed writing. In 1952, Seepersad wrote to his son in Oxford, 'You were right about R.K. Narayan. I like his short stories ... he seems gifted and has made a go of his talent, which in my case I hadn't even spotted.' The transaction between father and son, with Narayan as intermediary, is as palpable inside Naipaul's novels as it is outside them; it is Narayan, one suspects, who helps Naipaul realize that the minor, daydreaming figure of his father is central to his work, and to ironize the comically ambivalent position of the writer in colonial societies. But as Naipaul enters his middle period with his novels about post-colonial Africa, *In A Free State* and *A Bend in the River*, he exchanges Narayan's influence for Conrad's; the father-figure disappears, and what we have then is the metaphor of travel, the lone figure moving through what is, on one level, a metaphysical landscape.

The idea of Africa as metaphysical terrain is something Naipaul inherited from Conrad. For Conrad, Africa, especially in *The Heart of Darkness* (to which Naipaul's response was profound), is an infernal or purgatorial landscape. Conrad didn't advertise his debt to Dante as some of the other modernists did, but, certainly, Dante's *Inferno* helped him construct Africa as 'a place of darkness', a nether region of the imagination. Dante gave Conrad also the disengaged observer who moves, himself untouched, through the dark landscape, as Dante does in his own poem through Hell. Although Marlow belongs to a secular world, he speaks of Africa in religious terms, as 'the centre of the earth', and 'the gloomy circle of some Inferno'. Conrad's Marlow, in turn, gave Naipaul the trope of travel and *his* disengaged observer, traversing, in Dantesque manner, the disintegrating 'half-formed societies' around him.

In ascribing to Africa the fixity of a religious symbol, Conrad opened himself to the charge of racism from readers like Chinua Achebe; and, in apparently doing much the same as Conrad, Naipaul is (and has been) vulnerable to the same charge. But it is interesting how many of his effects Naipaul achieves by overturning Conrad. For, while both Conrad and Marlow come to the Congo from Europe, Naipaul was himself born, in his own words, in 'one of the Conradian dark places of the earth'. Marlow is an outsider moving through a foreign landscape, but Naipaul's Dantesque travellers, like the 'half and half' people in the African section of the new novel (expatriates, settlers) are inner émigrés, who both belong to the in-

fernal landscape and don't belong to it, with all the resonances that being
in that position brings.

Although *A Bend in the River* is said to be Naipaul's most Conradian
work, it is *The Enigma of Arrival* that is his most audacious overturning of
The Heart of Darkness. Marlow comes to the Congo by sea; in exactly the
reverse journey in the later novel, a Trinidadian of Indian origin arrives in
England, and the de Chirico painting (of a harbour in an unnamed city
where passengers have disembarked – never to return, feels the narrator)
which gives Naipaul's book its name introduces the motif of the ship and
the sea, of arriving but never returning. Naipaul's narrator, then, is both
Marlow and Kurtz, in that he is both traveller, and settler, doomed never
to go back to the country he travelled from. Marlow, describing to his
English audience the experience of entering Africa, compares it to 'prehistoric earth', and to what England might have been like when the Romans
got there – 'I was thinking of very old times, when the Romans first came
here, nineteen hundred years ago …' Naipaul's narrator, inverting this,
lives in Wiltshire, on the Salisbury Plains, not far from Stonehenge, from
the beginnings of 'prehistoric' England. When he sets out upon one of his
walks in the countryside, he too recalls the Romans as he reflects on his
neighbour's geese:

> I heard on the radio one morning that in the days of the Roman Empire
> geese could be walked to market all the way from the province of Gaul
> to Rome. After this, the high-headed, dung-dropping geese that strutted
> across the muddy, rutted way at the bottom of the valley … – Jack's geese –
> developed a kind of historical life for me …

An unknown post-colonial's discovery of England in an age when
the Empire has ceased to exist becomes a parody of Marlow's discovery of
Africa in the heyday of colonialism.

In his next novel, *A Way in the World*, Naipaul showed his impatience
with the closed structure of the conventional novel; the assortment of different narratives in it was reminiscent of the way a much earlier novel, *In
A Free State*, had been put together, and Naipaul has attempted something
similar, on a smaller scale, in the construction of *Half A Life*. The 'half' in
the novel's title refers to, among other things, the 'half and half' people in
the book, the emigrants who belong nowhere; but it is also a comment on
its own deliberate incompleteness. Yet, for all its incompleteness, most of
Naipaul's earlier preoccupations inform the three 'unfinished' narratives
in the book.

The first section is set in India; it is, on the surface, the least 'real' part
of the book, and has the symmetry of a fable. It is about the protagonist's

father, a college teacher and Gandhian, who marries, to spite his own father, a lower-caste woman as an act of sacrifice, and becomes a social out-
caste. As he sits in a temple in a strategic show of defiance and silence, he is
noticed by a visiting writer, Somerset Maugham, who becomes fascinated
with his story, and bases a character in *The Razor's Edge* on him. This man
names his son William Somerset as a homage to the writer, but the son
grows up despising his father; although it is in reaction against him that
he begins to write stories. The historical background to this section might
have well emerged from the interviews Naipaul conducted for *India: A Million Mutinies Now*. But we have encountered transgressive fathers before in
Naipaul's fiction, in Biswas and *The Mimic Men*, and, outside his fictions,
in Seepersad Naipaul. As with Willie Chandran and his father, Seepersad's
relationship with his own father was unhappy, and yet not unconnected
to writerly self-discovery; in *Finding the Centre*, Naipaul says, 'My father
never forgave his father. He forgave him only in a story he wrote …' Again,
like Willie Chandran's father, Seepersad too, in Trinidad, had once offered
a sacrifice of a goat to 'mollify' Kali, in order to ward off the danger of
death, and this event, curiously, had been reported by the *New York Herald
Tribune*, probably as a piece of exotica, in 1933 – transplanted to the West,
in effect, as Chandran's father's story is by Maugham. Naipaul himself only
came to know of the event after he had published *Biswas*.

The second section has Chandran move to London; it is set in London, and conveys jubilantly, and humorously, the sense of discovering a
world and a vocation. Chandran enters London's immigrant bohemian,
and journalist, life; he makes progress with his stories, is published and
reviewed. These pages glow, and bear comparison with anything that Naipaul has done. The material is fresh; Naipaul had mentioned the London
bohemian life in passing in *Finding the Centre*, but never before written
about it. The peripatetic mapping of London, how its dingy bars and sites
of illicit love-making seem a world away from the offices of editors and
publishers, while they are actually within walking distance of each other,
is almost casually, but beautifully, achieved, and recalls Naipaul's own
response to Jean Rhys's marginal life on the Left Bank, and her mapping
of Paris. Publication brings, not fame, but an admirer, a woman from a
Portuguese colony in Africa; in the final section, Chandran marries her
and they leave for her estate in the colony.

He spends eighteen years there, like the man in the de Chirico painting who has arrived but can't return. They become part of a post-colonial
society of 'half and half' people, 'second-rank Portuguese'. He finds a
lover; the colony becomes, even as it disintegrates, the site of Chandran's
sexual awakening. The adulterous courtship begins at a reception in the

'little governor's house … the oldest building in the town … a mixture of museum and historical monument', even as the last rites of the colony are to be performed. Chandran, in a Conradian moment, reflects on what the house might have been like 'two hundred and fifty years ago' when the colony was still new, unexplored, and, as in the de Chirico painting, 'the sea always blue and transparent … the strange small ships appearing … the town hardly a settlement'.

This reflection about the governor's house 'was like being given a new glimpse of our history', just as Jack's geese 'developed a historical life' for the narrator of *The Enigma of Arrival* when he thought about the Romans. This small novel, then, captures in miniature the exceptional trajectory of Naipaul's oeuvre; the figure of the father, the life of the writer, and, finally, an inquiry into the origins of the colonial landscape itself, into how one came to exist in 'one of the Conradian dark places of the earth'. This novel is not one of Naipaul's major undertakings, but I don't think it was meant to be. It is intended to give us yet another perspective on his oeuvre, where one detail illuminates another. There is no point in placing this book in the current climate of publishing, or in the context of rivalries and reputations, or suspending our critical faculties by comparing it to the other books on the Booker longlist. To understand the progression it represents, it must be related to Naipaul's own works, and situated in that particular imaginative universe.

A Bottle of Ink, a Pen and a Blotter
On R.K. Narayan

In the obituaries of R.K. Narayan (1906–2001), written by the 'talkative men' of modern India who once knew the writer slightly or quite well, there were one or two remarks about his habit of walking around without any apparent purpose. Here, for instance, is Khushwant Singh on a visit to Mysore forty years ago: 'Being with Narayan on his afternoon stroll was an experience. He did not go to a park but preferred walking up the bazaars … He would stop briefly at shops to exchange namaskaras with the owners, introduce me and exchange gossip with them in Kannada or Tamil.'

Singh speaks as though he had expected Narayan to behave like one of his characters – and Narayan evidently didn't disappoint him. He emulated his characters in other ways, too: when questioned about his writing, he had the evasiveness of some of his creations, and hardly ever said anything revealing. The protagonist of 'The Storyteller', for example, would from time to time break his long spells of silence to 'enchant' his village audience with his tales, and then return, puzzlingly, to silence.

Like Chandran, the young hero of *The Bachelor of Arts*, Narayan made it a policy to withhold rather than confess: 'Chandran was just climbing the steps of the College Union when Natesan, the secretary, sprang on him and said: "You are just the person I was looking for. You remember your old promise?" "No," said Chandran promptly, to be on the safe side.' The movement of these sentences finds its mirror-image in Narayan's memoir, *My Days*, where he describes his beginnings as a writer. 'Do I hear aright when people say that you plan to be a writer?' his uncle would ask him. 'I could not say "Yes" or "No." There was danger in either.'

In spite of this authorial reticence, or strategic ingenuousness, the seemingly easy-going, affable nature of Narayan's fictional universe has encouraged critics to think they have it figured out. Some readers have found it all too simple-minded and straightforward; reading an early draft of Narayan's first novel, the uncle portrayed in *My Days* said the kinds of thing that would often be said as Narayan's readership grew:

> He held . . . [a typed sheet] to the light and read out: '"It was Monday morning." Oh, oh, Monday! why not Tuesday or Friday?' He glanced through the others and said: 'What the hell is this? You write that he got up, picked up tooth powder, rinsed his teeth, poured water over his head – just a catalogue. H'm . . . I could also become a novelist if this was all that was expected, but I have no time to write a detailed catalogue.'

Others besides the uncle have assumed that it's easy to write novels like Narayan's, and perhaps this is one of the reasons (besides his immense subtlety) he hasn't engendered a school of writing – no one thought it worth emulating such an unremarkable feat.

In fact it was Graham Greene who was responsible for the publication of his first novel, *Swami and Friends*. Narayan had instructed a friend to throw the manuscript into the Cherwell if he couldn't find a publisher for it, and the friend sent it to Greene, who recommended it to Hamish Hamilton. It was published in 1935. More novels followed, and as an increasing number of readers grew acquainted with what they saw as the unambivalent charm of Narayan's writing, critics in the West, especially in America, started to praise his work for presenting a microcosm of 'timeless India', transcending history, that Western-manufactured complication, while critics in India condemned it for presenting a microcosm of 'timeless India', stubbornly oblivious to the liberal, educated Indian's burden, history. Yet if there is anything that criticism of the Indian novel in English itself lacks, it is a sense of history; both in the West and at home, Indian fiction is almost always addressed as if it were produced in a void, and each individual novel is treated as if it were self-sufficient, and bore little relation to anything beyond the reality, or fantasy, that it described. When critics look into Narayan's work, it's as if they see only themselves: the 'timeless India' they discover in his fiction is a mirror, or a metaphor, for the ahistorical nature of their own response.

The subject of Narayan's fiction is, if anything, the fictionality of 'timeless India', which, it tells us, is a thoroughly modern invention, a figment of the contemporary imagination. To this end, he creates a trope for inventedness, Malgudi, a place that, like 'timeless India', exists nowhere; and then both lovingly nourishes and mocks our need for its existence, by providing maps and street-names and recounting sensuous, vivid and persuasive details to impress us with its verisimilitude.

At the same time he keeps telling us that Malgudi, and its characters, and 'timeless India' are inventions. Through a series of minor accidents,

Raju, in *The Guide*, ends up, rather reluctantly, as a godman invested, in the eyes of adoring villagers, with holy power, when in fact he is an unemployed loiterer recently released from jail, who, in a previous life, was that most unglamorous and unmystical of things, a tourist guide. Scratch a relic, or emblem, of 'timeless India' in Malgudi and you discover a reality that is suburban, modern, dreary, mercantile and petit-bourgeois. Narayan's work wipes away the sheen of the eternal and reveals the tawdriness of modern, small-town Indian life. Although it is entirely set in India, *The Guide* can also be read as a response to Narayan's contact with America and its tyrannical credulity. The Indian villagers, in their own way, are not unlike American suburbanites, rock stars and Hollywood directors, for whom the holiness of India is a fundamental necessity; and the book records, and parodies, the way holiness is invented. It is no surprise to learn, in *My Days*, that it was 'during my travels in America' that the idea of *The Guide* 'crystallised in my mind. I stopped in Berkeley for three months, took a hotel room, and wrote my novel.'

Similarly, the opening of *The Vendor of Sweets* seems to derive from the high philosophical India of Professor Radhakrishnan, the first President of India and a former Spalding Professor of Eastern Religions and Ethics at All Souls, but quickly metamorphoses into the languors and evasions of a small-town bureaucratic conversation between superior and subordinate. '"Conquer taste, and you will have conquered the self," said Jagan to his listener, who asked: "Why conquer the self?" Jagan said: "I do not know, but all our sages advise us to."' This exchange reworks the rhythm and structure of the exchange that opens *The Bachelor of Arts*, which itself finds an echo in the exchange in *My Days* in which writing is discussed by Narayan and his uncle: a question is posed; the answer is non-committal, slightly furtive. It rehearses, too, Narayan's own replies to his interviewers.

Narayan's fictions, faced with the 'eternal' questions, with the 'ouboom' of the Marabar Caves, cough with the same comic evasiveness. His characters, like Jagan the sweetmeat vendor, who has a son in America and an American daughter-in-law, start out as spokesmen for 'timeless India' and become, as in the conversation I quoted, its apologetic accomplices. The timeless and the short-term and mercantile are never very far away from each other, as in Jagan's shop: 'The air was charged with the scent of jasmine and incense and imperceptibly blended with the fragrance of sweetmeats frying in ghee, in the kitchen across the hall.'

In the 1930s when Narayan began writing, the cultural legacies of the Orientalist scholars, and of the Bengal Renaissance, with its transcendental strain, were still dominant, contributing to an idea of India as a country with an ancient philosophical and religious, mainly Brahminical, tradition; figures like Tagore (largely misinterpreted in this respect, but with his own collusion) and Radhakrishnan loomed large as examples of high-minded, unworldly 'Indianness'. (Narayan's own youthful reading included, he tells us in *My Days*, Tagore's *Gitanjali*, as well as Palgrave's *Golden Treasury*, and the World's Classics edition of Keats. His juvenilia included a poetic effusion called 'Divine Music', a title that is almost a literal translation of *Gitanjali*, which he 'composed in a state of total abstraction', convinced it was 'going to add to the world's literary treasure'.) A 'timeless India' was being set in opposition to the aggressive materialism of the West, rather than an India that was historically and politically in flux. Although Narayan is accused of having turned away from the historical and the political, Malgudi subtly situates itself in history by rejecting that timelessness. Through Malgudi, he presents a small India of material desires and ambitions, and gently mocks the transcendentalism of the Bengal Renaissance and the Orientalists' vision of India with its grand spiritual heritage. He was certainly not the first writer to do this, but he was the first to achieve it in English, and before a worldwide audience.

There are, however, some unexpected concordances between Tagore's early life and Narayan's, which have to do with their attitude to education. Tagore's aversion to school, English lessons and to higher education in general, is well known. As the youngest of fourteen children, he was educated for a period at home by private tutors, and when eventually he went to school he hated the incarceration of the classroom, experiencing what he called in *My Reminiscences* 'the degradation of being a mere pupil'. Like most young men in Indian upper-class families, he was then sent to England where in 1878 he enrolled at University College London, but soon returned to India without completing his degree. He remained an opponent of conventional education all his life, and founded a school, Shantiniketan, that advocated a freer style of learning, with a penchant for the arts. Several pages in *My Reminiscences* describe the hours that he used to spend daydreaming, imprisoned in the house, and looking out:

> Just below the window of this room was a tank with a flight of masonry steps leading down into the water; on its west bank, along the garden wall, an immense banyan tree; to the south a fringe of coconut palms. Ringed round as I was near this window, I would spend the whole day peering through the drawn Venetian shutters, gazing and gazing on this scene as on a picture-book.

The words *chhuti* ('holiday'), *khela* ('play') and *kaaj* ('work') recur in his songs, poems and stories, with the holiday and the idea of play representing creative activity, and *kaaj* carrying the resonance of bur-densome intellectual toil, reminiscent of the classroom. This, of course, made Tagore a problematic figure for those in India who required creative activity to be a form of *kaaj*, a responsible endeavour in the larger task of nation-building.

Narayan, too, as he says in *My Days*, 'instinctively rejected both edu-cation and examinations, with their unwarranted seriousness and esoteric suggestions. Since revolt was unpractical I went through it all without conviction, enthusiasm, or any sort of distinction.' Later, he would fail the university entrance examination, and spend a year drifting insouciantly. It was at this time that he began to write. 'My natural aversion to aca-demic education', he says in his memoir, 'was further strengthened when I came across an essay by Rabindranath Tagore.' The classroom, for both writers, stood in for the academy; and their creative work has a powerful anti-academic impulse. In *Swami and Friends*, the view beyond the class-room window is described in terms similar to Tagore's account of the boy looking out at the world beyond the 'Venetian shutters' in the house in Jorasanko: 'To Swaminathan existence in the classroom was possible only because he could watch the toddlers of the Infant Standards falling over one another, and through the windows on the left see the 12.30 mail glid-ing over the embankment, booming and rattling while passing over the Sarayu Bridge.' Of course, the academy took its own revenge on these writ-ers. Nirad Chaudhuri remarks how, in the early decades of the twentieth century, the Bengali paper at Calcutta University quoted passages from Tagore and instructed examinees to render them into 'chaste Bengali'. Narayan has been largely neglected in post-colonial English departments. When I was teaching the 'Commonwealth and International Literatures in English' paper for the English Tripos in Cambridge, I found he was hardly taught, or read.

In an essay on Narayan in the *New York Review of Books*, Pankaj Mishra observes that his novels begin with great energy and promise, and then fail to resolve themselves. This, he says, is because in their structure and movement, they mirror the societies in which their characters live – societies in which fulfilment is rapidly succeeded by exhaustion. The narrative arc of the novels, then, becomes the melancholy undertow to their ostensibly comic subject matter. This is well said, and sets out part of the reason Narayan's novels seldom seem complete, or self-sufficient. Another reason is that Narayan is less interested in the perfected and self-enclosed novel than he is in the recycling of familiar, used material; Malgudi, for him, is not so much the crystallization of a solitary impulse, as it is an occasion for a small-scale but continual transaction, or series

of transactions, in the currency of his material. In this, again, he resembles the protagonists – the 'vendor of sweets', 'the painter of signs', 'the
guide', 'the financial expert' – who inhabit both his fiction and the shabby
but resilient mercantile society of small-town, post-Independence India.
These characters deal not so much in single, graspable commodities as in
lending, borrowing, reselling. Similarly, Malgudi is not a commodity or a
product whose outlines are clear or recognizable – a novel or a place – so
much as a web of multiple transactions undertaken by its characters and
its author, the 'writer of novels'. Not all of them will bear fruit, but they
are engaged in with gusto even so. Margayya, the eponymous 'financial
expert', satirizes such activity in the opening pages of the novel; here he is,
conducting his not quite legal business in the environs of a co-operative
bank once managed by an English registrar:

> The ghost of the Registrar had many reasons to feel sad and frustrated.
> All the principles of co-operation for which he had sacrificed his life were
> dissolving under his eyes, if he could look beyond the portals of the bank
> itself, right across the little stretch of lawn under the banyan tree, in whose
> shade Margayya sat and transacted his business. There was always a semi-
> circle of peasants sitting round him, and by their attitude and expression
> one might easily guess they were suppliants . . . He was to them a wizard
> who enabled them to draw unlimited loans from the co-operative bank . . .
>
> His tin box, a grey, discoloured, knobby affair, which was small enough
> to be carried under his arm, contained practically his entire equipment: a
> bottle of ink, a pen and a blotter, a small register whose pages carried an
> assortment of names and figures, and above all – the most important item –
> loan application forms of the co-operative bank. These last named were his
> greatest asset in life, and half his time was occupied in acquiring them ...
> When a customer came, the very first question Margayya asked was, 'Have
> you secured the application form?'
>   'No.'
>   'Then go into the building and bring one – try to get one or two spare
> forms as well.'

Like the storyteller in Narayan's short story, who casts a spell of
'enchantment' on the villagers as they listen to him, Margayya too sits
beneath a banyan tree, a 'wizard' to the 'semi-circle of peasants sitting
round him', who wear expectant expressions, as if listening to a story.
Margayya is a liminal actor in the world of low, makeshift capitalism, who
belongs outside the 'portals of the bank'; he is one of the figures Swaminathan might have caught sight of outside the classroom window. Like the
writer, he has a 'bottle of ink, a pen and a blotter'; most important, the
paraphernalia of his business – the loan application forms – are borrowed
materials, hoarded for future use ('try to get me one or two spare forms as

well'). If Margayya represents the Narayanesque author, then Narayan is not so much the originator as the vendor of his diffuse material; and, just as Margayya saves the extra application forms for another day, so, too, the business of Malgudi never arrives at a conclusion with the end of a novel; the ending becomes a pretence, or occasion, for yet another endeavour or excursion. The only way for these transactions to cease was to remove the author, and this has now happened; and yet they continue to ramify in their desultory fashion in the actions of his characters.

'A Feather! A Very Feather upon the Face!'
On Kipling

In 1857, eight years before Kipling was born, Indian soldiers in the north of the country rebelled against the representatives of the East India Company. The uprising was known as the Sepoy Mutiny and, later, somewhat romantically, as the First War of Independence. Although its impact on the Indian and Anglo-Indian middle classes was probably not as immediate and direct as it has been made out to be in subsequent colonial and nationalist narratives, it brought to an end, as historians like C.A. Bayly have pointed out, a period of cultural exchange between different races. The late eighteenth and the first half of the nineteenth century had seen the commercial and colonial expansion of the East India Company in Bengal and other parts of India, thanks to a series of military victories and not a few dishonorable transactions, but it was also a time of commingling, especially in Calcutta, between the new, post-feudal Indian middle class and members of the British scholarly and administrative classes. William Jones, whose researches at the Fort William College in Calcutta were largely responsible for inaugurating Orientalist scholarship and the reconstruction of Indian history, wore native clothes made of muslin in the heat – the sola hat and khaki uniform that Beerbohm has Kipling wear in one of his caricatures were not yet de rigueur. There are early portraits depicting English men with their Indian wives, dressed in a mishmash of Persian and Hindu styles. In the first half of the nineteenth century, the Fort William College , and later the Hindu College, saw teacher and student, Englishmen, Indian and Eurasian, engage in a colloquy at a crucial moment of modern history – people like the educationalist David Hare, the Anglo-Portuguese poet and teacher Henry Derozio, the great Bengali poet

Michael Madhusudan Dutt. If Kipling had been born fifty years earlier, it would have been impossible for him to write the cheerfully assonantal but bleak lines: 'O East is East, and West is West/ And never the twain shall meet!' It would have been equally difficult for the narrator of the story 'Beyond the Pale' to make his seemingly unequivocal statement: 'A man should, whatever happens, keep to his own caste, race and breed.'

With the Sepoy Mutiny, attitudes hardened, and the rule of the East India Company passed to the crown. Psychological boundaries came in to existence, to reinforce the physical ones – the 'White' and 'Black' town – that were already there. The social and racial structure of the India Kipling was born in and later returned to as a journalist was determined by the Mutiny and, later, by the defeat of the Ilbert Bill (in effect, the comprehensive amendment of the bill in its original form), which would have been given Indian magistrates the right to try Englishmen. But by the time Kipling wrote *Kim* in 1900, the Mutiny was an unthreatening, dreamlike memory, and it is represented in the novel by a retired Indian soldier who had fought with – not against – the British, 'an old, withered man, who had served the Government in the days of the Mutiny as a native officer in a newly raised cavalry regiment':

> The government had given him a good holding in the village, and though the demands of his sons, now grey-bearded officers on their account, had impoverished him, he was still a person of consequence. English officials – Deputy Commissioners even – turned aside from the main road to visit him, and on these occasions he dressed himself up in the regiment of ancient days, and stood up like a ramrod.

Later, after Kim has entertained and shocked his native audience with sensational reports of an imminent 'war', he 'enjoyed a most interesting evening with the old man', who 'brought out his cavalry sabre and, balancing it on his dry knees, told tales of the Mutiny and young captains thirty years in their graves, till Kim dropped off to sleep'.

What we see here is Kipling's subtle rewriting of history. The adjectives 'old, withered' naturalize the man; he is portrayed not as an anomaly but as part of his surroundings. With his sabre and his uniform he represents the confluence of the colonial and the native; ramrod-straight, he is almost a national flag without being a nationalist. His apparent agelessness (his sons are 'grey-bearded officers') suggests the immemorial continuity of the benign order he represents. The Mutiny, the passing of British rule from the Company to the Crown, the formal inception of Empire, all are rendered musical and painless in the shining phrase 'ancient days'. History, with its intransigencies, is made seductive, a lullaby that soothes Kim to sleep. These paradoxes make Kipling a very great writer, and also a writer of fictions in every sense of the word.

Earlier in the novel, before Kim and the lama set out on their journey from Lahore, Kim arranges, for the lama's benefit, a meeting with the curator of the museum – the 'Wonder House'. The Curator is a tribute to Kipling's father, John Lockwood Kipling, who moved to Bombay as curator of the J.J. School of Art in 1865, the year of Kipling's birth. But through the figure of the curator, Kipling also indirectly acknowledges the existence of a colonial India of intellectual collaboration between cultures: unlike Kipling, who was shaped by an environment in which boundaries were more clearly and viciously drawn, and who could dismiss the *Mahabharata* as a 'monstrous midden', the curator belongs to the world before the Mutiny. Here he shows the museum's collection of Buddhist icons to the lama:

> Out shuffled the lama to the main hall, and, the Curator beside him, went through the collection with the reverence of a devotee and the appreciative instinct of a craftsman.
>
> Incident by incident in the beautiful story he identified on the blurred stone ...
>
> Here was the devout Asita, the pendant of Simeon in the Christian story, holding the Holy Child on his knee while mother and father listened; and here were incidents in the legend of the cousin Devadatta. Here was the wicked woman who accused the Master of impurity, all confounded; here was the teaching in the Deer-park; the miracle that stunned the fire-worshippers; here was the Bodhisat in royal state as a prince; the miraculous birth; the death at Kusinagara, where the weak disciple fainted; while there were almost countless repetitions of the meditation under the Bodhi tree; and the adoration of the alms-bowl was everywhere. In a few minutes the Curator saw that his guest was no mere bead-telling mendicant, but a scholar of parts. And they went at it all over again, the lama taking snuff, wiping his spectacles, and talking in railway speed in a bewildering mixture of Urdu and Tibetan ... For the first time he heard of the labours of European Scholars, who by the help of these and a hundred other documents have identified the Holy Places of Buddhism ... The old man bowed his head over the sheets in silence for a while, and the Curator lit another pipe.

This is an uncharacteristically jubilant homage to the transforming powers of narrative and translation that lay at the heart of polyglot India in the early nineteenth century. A new narrative about India was being formed through collaborations between Indian and European scholars, and the stories told in the passage above formed a part of it. The excitement communicated between curator and lama, at one moment in an argot of Urdu and Tibetan delivered at 'railway speed', at another in silence, as the curator lights a pipe, is an echo of the intellectual excitement that must have been palpable in late eighteenth- century and early nineteenth-century Calcutta, and which had been suppressed by the time Kipling was writing *Kim*, in an age of more confrontational politics. Kipling himself was a spokesman for a particularly unpleasant racial theory. Yet, when the lama and the curator part they exchange gifts, the curator gives the lama his spectacles in exchange for the lama's 'scratched' ones – 'A feather! A very feather upon the face!' the lama exclaims as he tries them on – while the lama, in turn, gives the curator a pen 'of ancient design, Chinese, of an iron that is not smelted these days'. This, too, is a trope for a cultural reciprocity that largely belonged to a time earlier than Kipling's own. The symmetry is neat: the pen, with which the European will inscribe another culture; the spectacles, through which the lama will see himself, translated, anew.

The defeat of the original draft of the Ilbert Bill in 1883 increased the distance between the Indians and their rulers. As Harry Ricketts points out in his fine biography, *The Unforgiving Minute*, Kipling was, at the time, a very young journalist on the *Civil and Military Gazette* at Lahore. The newspaper was 'strongly against the Ilbert Bill', as most Englishmen were, but was pressured by its 'larger sister-paper, the *Pioneer*', to make more supportive noises. 'One evening after work,' according to Ricketts, 'Rud walked into the Punjab Club in Lahore to find himself "hissed" by all the other members, because that day's CMG carried a leader ... voicing ... approval of the bill.' Kipling describes the scene in *Something of Myself*: rather than making him recoil, the 'hissing' leads him to 'see a great light', and come round, fully, to the point of view of the Bill's opponents. Ricketts explains this capitulation by pointing out that Kipling was, as he would be all his life, an outsider who 'desperately wanted to fit in'; and not a little of his racist posture stems from that desperation.

As the gap between 'native' and European worlds widened, crossing the boundaries had, for Kipling, an air of illegality about it, as, indeed, had the act of writing itself. Kipling's prose was erotic in its texture and effects, in its elisions and momentary absorption in small shocks of pleasure. He would always have to reconcile his devotion to the artistic, with its fluid, feminine, even 'Eastern' associations, with the more grandiose and masculine overview of Empire. In *A Passage to India* Forster points out that the furthest Ronnie Heaslop, the City Magistrate in Chandrapore, was prepared to go in the direction of Art was to sing the national anthem – and Kipling was always prepared to launch into the national anthem as a counterpoint to the subtler melody of his prose. Writing became for him a matter of subterfuge and concealment: a nocturnal activity, distinct from the preoccupations of his daytime world. It would lead to the ulcer that tormented and, eventually, killed him, as if his more vituperative side had turned on him. Like this writing, his forays into the 'native' city were also largely undertaken at night. Of one excursion into Lahore, he observed:

> It was impossible to sit still in the dark, empty, echoing house and watch the *punkah* beat the dead air. So, at ten o'clock of the night, I set my walking-stick on end in the middle of the garden, and waited to see how it would fall. It pointed directly down the moonlit road that leads to the City of Dreadful Night.

The ideas of poetic inspiration producing a physical restiveness that can be allayed only by perambulation and of the illicit transgression of a boundary are conflated here. The native world, which is not quite possessed of legitimacy under the Crown, is perceived in fragments: 'There was a sharp clink of glass bracelets; a woman's arm showed for an instant above the parapet, twined itself around the neat little neck, and the child was dragged back, protesting, to the shelter of the bedstead.' The word 'instant' links Kipling to the modernist enterprise (Ricketts points out that, in his ellipses and his exploration of the shifts of narrative voice, Kipling is a precursor of the modernists), to Joyce's 'epiphany' and Woolf's fleeting 'moment' of heightened perception and 'being'. But Kipling's instant is also situated in colonial history, for, in the latter half of the nineteenth century, the subcontinent, for the resident colonial, was unweighted by history – it had become, at least in one sense, insubstantial. Whatever complexities of dialogue had existed in the early years of the colonial encounter, as the different races delved into each other's cultures, had largely vanished: the land, to the white man, had become the backdrop for a series of random perceptions, 'sights, smells and sounds', vivid but indirect, without substance or context, but, occasionally, oddly beautiful and compelling. It is this India, mysterious not because it withholds its secrets, but because the colonial enterprise demands that it withhold them, that constitutes Kipling's sound-inflected landscape.

What, then, was the principal secret? It was, first of all, the formation of modern India itself: of a hybrid but nationalistic middle class, created by history and the colonial encounter and to which both the intelligentsia and the administrative, clerical cadre belonged. From this class would emerge writers, social reformers, professionals and, later, politicians like Nehru and Bose and Gandhi. Kipling, in fact, was born during the first efflorescence of the putative, but palpable, Bengal, or Indian, Renaissance. Michael Madhusudan Dutt, after years of attempting to become a canonical 'English' poet, published in 1861 his epic, *Meghnadbadhakabya*, a revisionist work based on an episode in the *Ramayan* and inspired by *Paradise Lost*, an inaugural text in modern Bengali and, in effect, Indian literature.

In the year that Kipling was born, Bankimchandra Chatterjee, a magistrate who had already written one of the first Indian novels in English, *Rajmohan's Wife*, wrote the first significant modern Bengali, and Indian, novel, *Durgesnandini*. These writers, and others, were, to paraphrase what Pound once said about Tagore, singing India into existence. The Renaissance, by reconfiguring the Western and the local, was providing, for Indians, a reinterpretation of what it meant to be Indian. Tagore himself was born four years before Kipling, and if Kipling made a dazzlingly precocious debut with *Plain Tales from the Hills*, Tagore's first book of poems, *Prabhat Sangit* (*Morning Songs*) published even more precociously when he was sixteen, and his second, which appeared three years later, made no less unsettling an impact. When Kipling published his stories, however, they were treated as if they were almost unique in having contemporary India as their subject; and this notion persists, quite commonly, in Britain and America. Indeed, no one reading Kipling would suspect that Tagore and Chatterjee might be living in the same world as Kim, Mehboob Khan, Shere Khan and Mowgli. So profound was the effect of British colonial policy on post-Mutiny India, so fiercely was the division between the races enforced, that it is still difficult to reconcile the neighbouring worlds of modern, 'Renaissance' India and Kipling's fiction. If there is one lacuna, in Ricketts's even-handed and sympathetic biography, it is the one created all those years ago by British colonial policy: the absence of the modern India in which Kipling was situated, which he did his best to ignore, and which nevertheless left its imprint on his writing.

The social and intellectual force of the Renaissance is represented in Kipling by cameo appearances of bowdlerized Bengali gentlemen who suffer various humiliations. Of these caricatures, the most sympathetic is Hurree Chunder Mookerjee in *Kim*, an MA from Calcutta University – as it happens, one of the most significant sites of the Renaissance. Mookerjee is singular not only because he's a Bengali who quotes Shakespeare (in this, Kipling implies, he is tediously typical), but because, surprisingly, he is working on behalf of British espionage. In this he is an unlikely precursor to a fair number of his compatriots – among them, Kshudiram Bose and Bagha Jatin who would later be labelled terrorists because of their anti-Government activities. Kipling records Mookerjee's advice to a bewildered Kim:

> There were marks to be gained by due attention to Latin and Wordsworth's Excursion (all this was Greek to Kim), French, too, was vital, and the best was to be picked up in Chandernagore, a few miles from Calcutta. Also a man might go far, as he himself had done, by strict attention to plays called Lear and Julius Caesar, both much in demand by examiners. Lear was not

so full of historical allusions as Julius Caesar; the book cost four annas, but could be bought secondhand in Bow Bazaar for two. Still more important than Wordsworth, or the eminent authors, Burke and Hare, was the art and science of mensuration. A boy who had passed his examination in these branches – for which, by the way, there were no cram-books – could, by merely marching over a country with a compass and a level and straight eye, carry away a picture of that country which might be sold for large sums in coined silver . . .

Said the Babu when he had talked for an hour and a half: I hope some day to enjoy your offeecial acquaintance. *Ad interim*, if I may be pardoned that expression, I shall give you this betel-box, which is highly valuable article and cost me two rupees only four years ago.

Mookerjee delivers his long speech to Kim in 'volleying drifts of English after having had a huge meal'; the suggestion of flatulence is not far away. Yet the description is permeated by contemporary history, even as it rewrites it; in its constant, mischievous transposition of meaning, the passage mirrors, while it mocks, the process of redefinition in late nineteenth-century India. Kipling captures perfectly the Bengali's pronunciation in the word 'offeecial', but thereby slyly renders both the word and Mookerjee's English, unofficial. He is accurate, too, in his recording of the Bengali's obsession with university degrees and English literature (Presidency College and Jadavpur University continue to have two of the most flourishing English departments in the country); and the second-hand copy of Julius Caesar in Bow Bazaar is also significant. When I had finished school in Bombay, and embarked on the unusual course of taking my A-levels there, I was assisted in my study of Macbeth and Othello by my 'Banerjee'. Each 'Banerjee' was a cheap, bound, annotated edition of a Shakespeare play, so called because the notes had been written by a Professor Banerjee, a Bengali Brahmin, the name would imply, like Kipling's Mookerjee; these books, though useful, were unrecognized by the school reading list, and were 'unoffeecial'. But the presence of Julius Caesar in Bow Bazaar (an old commercial section of North Calcutta) also reminds us that modernity, in Renaissance Bengal and India, entailed a radical relocation of what was foreign and what local. Shakespeare, and the English language, for instance, are sites of ambiguity where the indigenous and the colonial are made to reassess themselves. Shakespeare is of the colonizer's party, but, in his incarnation in Bow Bazaar, and as a crucial element in Mookerjee's self-definition, he is also of the colonized's history without his, or probably Kipling, knowing it. This thread of ambiguity runs through much of modern Indian culture: many of the great writers in Bengali, Urdu, Hindi and the South Indian languages were students, or teachers, of English literature.

The early nineteenth century saw a debate about education policy between Orientalists and Anglicists, about whether, as the Orientalists desired, what was imparted in schools and colleges should be emphatically 'Eastern' in content, or whether Indians should be given a Western education. That the Anglicists triumphed, thanks to Macaulay's Minute in 1815, is revealed by Mookerjee's reading list of Shakespeare, Burke, Wordsworth; but the mention of the classical European languages also recalls the preoccupations of the Orientalist scholars whose researches established the family of Indo-European languages with Sanskrit, Greek and Latin as the originary ones. 'All this was Greek to Kim': Kipling wonderfully revivifies the cliché by slipping yet another language of antiquity into the passage, echoing and parodying the debates that went on for most of the century to decide what was Indian and what European. That European culture, narrated by a Bengali, should be 'all Greek' to an Irish boy who happens to be Indian, tells us casually that colonial India was a comedy of inversions and untenable identities.

One of the chief instruments in the triumph of Anglicist education was a Bengali and forefather of the fictional Mookerjee and others like him: the polyglot Raja Rammohun Roy, who knew, besides his mother-tongue, Latin, Sanskrit, Greek, Persian and English, who campaigned for Western education for Indians, and who died in Bristol in 1833. Kipling mocks Roy's fictional descendant by having him, quite plausibly, despite his knowledge of Shakespeare and Latin, omit the indefinite article when he says to Kim: 'I shall give you this betel-box which is highly valuable article'. In giving Kim the 'highly valuable article', Mookerjee has lost the more precious article, 'a'; this is the key that would have let him into a club reserved for Englishmen, but Kipling denies him access, and the absent 'a' denotes the unbridgeable gaps of post-1857 India. The missing article also reminds us that Mookerjee is bilingual, thinks in both Bengali and English, and, occasionally, constructs sentences in one language according to the grammatical rules of the other. He is more like his creator than his creator seems to realize: when speaking to his parents as a child, Kipling, as he points out in Something of Myself, 'haltingly translated out of the vernacular idiom one thought and dreamt in'.

By the time Kipling was born, the exam- and crammer-loving Bengali had begun to make inroads into the realms of colonial governance by negotiating the difficult entrance examination to the 'heaven-born' Indian Civil Service. Indians, too, had discovered that a certain kind of knowledge is power, as is evident from Mookerjee's advice to Kim to master 'the science and art of mensuration', in order to possess and control the land both figuratively and literally, to 'carry away a picture of that country' which 'might be sold for large sums in coined silver'. Satyendranath Tagore, one of Tagore's elder brothers, was the first successful examinee; but such a representative of the modern, colonial India would have been anathema to Kipling. It was not that Kipling was anti-modernity: the technological wonders, the heroes, of colonial progress and expansionism – ships, radios, motor-cars – are also the heroes of his books; more than any other English writer, Kipling, in stories like 'Wireless', brought into the province of the imagination what was romantically seen as antithetical to it, as Wordsworth said the poet eventually must. It was just that the 'modern' and the 'native' in colonial India were mutually incompatible categories: the 'modern' was represented by the English and by Empire; India was 'native', outside history and mysterious. Modern Indians (the word 'Indian' has a quite different connotation from 'native', and is rarely used by Kipling) like Mookerjee are at best ridiculed, or dealt with violently, as in the story 'The Head of the District'.

Even today, informed but commonplace Western notions about Indian history involve the work done on classical India by Orientalist scholars in pre-Mutiny India, as well as certain episodes in the Nationalist movement before Independence; the intervening years, in which Indians reformulated their history, are largely a blank, as is the continuation of this process in the post-Independence years. Kipling's intimacy with an Indian vernacular tongue – the Hindustani spoken to him by his servant and ayah – came to an end in early childhood; by that time, other vernacular languages such as Bengali were replacing English as the language of the middle class. In much of Kipling's work, the vernacular is located colourfully and exuberantly in a local and timeless India; while in nineeenth- and early twentieth-century India, the vernacular had actually become an instrument of bourgeois sensibility and cosmopolitanism. Distanced from such realities, Kipling exchanged the grown-up world of history and modernity that was contemporary India for an infantile universe of animals, 'natives' and adventure. For years, in fact, he was thought of as a children's writer. Henry James, an admirer of Kipling, complained:

> In his earliest time I thought he perhaps contained the seeds of an English Balzac; but I have quite given that up in proportion as he has come steadily from the less simple in subject to the more simple – from the Anglo-Indians to the natives, from the natives to the Tommies, from the Tommies to the quadrupeds, from the quadrupeds to the fish, from the fish to the engines and screws.

This regression must have had something to do with the dwindling of Indo-British relations that accompanied Kipling's development as a writer. His infantilizing of the natives and the landscape was typical of British racial attitudes in the post-Mutiny years: natives were judged to be like women or children, and officers in the British Army were the 'mai baap' (mother and father) of Indian soldiers. Any modernity in India outside the colonial machinery was strenuously wished out of existence – to the eventual detriment of the colonizers. This infantilization must have had at least something to do with the fraught relations the colonizing sahib of late Victorian England had with his own childhood, parents, family and home, leading to a psychopathology of Empire (Ashis Nandy has an interesting discussion on this subject, and on Kipling, in *The Intimate Enemy*). The colonizer's frequently uncomfortable relations with his own 'mai baap' meant that England became an uneasy, unfamiliar terrain, and the colonized world, where relations between colonizer and colonized were less confusing, became home and family, and was often spoken of in familial terms. For this cosy sense of the family to sustain itself in the colonies, it was necessary that the 'native' be constructed as an infant, and that grown-up complexity should not intrude on the 'native' universe. Kipling's otherwise loving and supportive parents made the mistake of sending him to a private tutorial home in Devon when he was seven, where he was tortured by his landlady and her son, until he was rescued by his mother and taken back to India. This experience of abandonment is revisited to devastating effect in the story 'Baa Baa Black Sheep'. In one of his more rhapsodic but ambiguous moments, Kipling said: 'England is the most marvellous foreign country I have ever lived in.'

The powerful allure of Kipling's Indian stories, and of *Kim*, is that, in their special construction of India, they make it a metaphor for belonging, a 'dwelling' in the sense that Heidegger yearned for in the homeless twentieth century. It's not only the English who respond to the rare fullness and magic in his work about India: middle-class Indians, like those Kipling shut out (Nirad Chaudhuri, for example, who thought Kipling was the greatest writer about India in the English language), have also found a home in this fiction. Yet it would be a mistake to conclude that the child's-eye view of much of Kipling's Indian fiction means that he doesn't address the contradictions of modern India – Kipling is a great poet (in English prose) of the shifting meanings of the colonial universe. The caveat that D.H. Lawrence once issued in another context is apposite here: 'We like to think of the old fashioned American classics as children's books. Just childishness, on our part.' Apposite because the stories so often undermine what Kipling holds to be true or amenable, as Lawrence pointed out stories were in the habit of doing. The British Empire may have showered Kipling with honours, but his tales, especially those once deemed fit mainly for children's consumption, were often untrustworthy. They played, chameleon-like, as one of the characters in disguise in them might, on both sides of the Great Game. (Disguise, in Kipling, is itself a metaphor for the way the writerly imagination can enter spaces made inaccessible by taboos enforced by race or colonial policy.) As Walter Benjamin pointed out in an essay on toys, the child's imaginative world is partly a grown-up construct: toys are made for children by adults, who assign 'childish' meanings to them, which children don't always go along with. The ambiguities of the child's world, where adult and childish definitions overlap and compete, are extended in Kipling's work, which poses oppositions between colonizer and native, ancient and modern – categories themselves open to interrogation.

If, as Kipling's critics say with some justice, his stories use infantile material, animals and inanimate objects to bring to his fictional world a simplicity to rival the more brutal simplicities of the white colonial's India, it is through this same material that he introduced his readers to a universe of contested meanings, of things let loose from their origins and redefined in another context: the colonial world in flux. Even in the very early 'Story of Muhammad Din', Kipling's tendency to write about things – what James called 'engines and 'screws' – as if they were characters with a will of their own is evident:

> The polo-ball was an old one, scarred, chipped and dinted. It stood on the mantelpiece among the pipe-stems which Imam Din, *khitmatgar*, was cleaning for me.
> 'Does the Heaven-born want this ball?' said Imam Din deferentially.
> The Heaven-born set no particular store by it; but of what use was a polo-ball to a *khitmatgar*?
> 'By Your Honour's favour, I have a little son. He has seen this ball, and desires it to play with. I do not want it for myself.'
> No one would for an instant accuse portly old Imam Din of wanting to play with polo-balls. He carried out the battered thing into the verandah; and there followed a hurricane of joyful squeaks, a patter of small feet, and the *thud-thud-thud* of the ball rolling to the ground.

The conversation between the 'Heaven-born' and his servant is well-meaning but circumlocutory: they don't quite understand each other. This dialogue is echoed and modified in the dialogue between the child and the polo-ball; here, the interaction is an equal one, and takes place outside the more official relationship between master and servant, just as the India that modern Indians inhabited existed outside the line drawn by white colonial society. On this side of the wall, the conversation is polite but ornately official. On the other side, another exuberant language is heard – composed of 'joyful squeaks' – as two parties come together, not the colonizer and colonized, but the 'native' appropriating the hardware of Empire, which might be a polo-ball, or the English language, or some other instrument of 'play'. Things, as James observed, take on an independent life in Kipling's stories ('the *thud-thud-thud* of the ball') and this is so precisely because the technologies of Empire – the steam engine, printed books – took on a life of their own in the colonies, one quite unpredictable to the colonizing imagination. Things were reconstituted in another landscape, where they could no longer be wholly identified with themselves or their owners. As a cultural sign, the polo-ball is no longer complete, unambiguous: it is 'scarred, chipped and dinted', displaying the marks of conflicting significations.

When the Russian formalist Viktor Shklovsky was working out his theory of 'defamiliarization', by which, according to him, writers alter our perception of reality by using devices to estrange us from it, he used as an example a passage from a short story by Tolstoy, in which a horse's perspective on the world becomes a means of transforming reality through language. Shklovsky would have found several instances in Kipling in which the animal viewpoint not only defamiliarizes reality, but reveals the colonial world to be a constantly unexpected place, in which there's ceaseless conflict over meanings and their attribution. In the story 'Rikki-tikki-tavi', for instance, we enter, with the mongoose, the world of colonial settlement, of the 'Englishman who had just moved into the bungalow' with his wife and son. A drama ensues in which a mongoose, a cobra and its mate, a tailor-bird and its family, a colonial, his wife and their son Teddy, even the bungalow and the garden, participate to narrate the tumult of colonial history. The mongoose itself, as is appropriate to a figure that belongs to two places – outside the colonial space of the bungalow and inside it – is portrayed as a wearer of disguises; partly of 'nature', partly an invention of language and a certain multiplicity of seeing. In this it is not unlike Kim, or Hurree Chunder Mookerjee, or indeed its creator.

> He was a mongoose, rather like a little cat in his fur and his tail, but quite like a weasel in his head and his habits. His eyes and the end of his restless nose were pink … he could fluff up his tail till it looked like a bottle-brush.

The mongoose is rescued by the English family from their garden after a 'high summer flood'. Revived, almost a family pet, Rikki-tikki-tavi explores the bungalow: 'He nearly drowned himself in the bathtubs, put his nose into the ink on a writing-table, and burnt it on the end of the big man's cigar, for he climbed up in the big man's lap to see how writing was done.' At first, this sentence would seem to be an instance of 'defamiliarization': through Rikki-tikki's eyes a perfectly ordinary domestic reality is made to look larger than life. But the estrangement has a double, overlapping quality. On the one hand, one might be tempted to associate the freshness and magic of the mongoose's discovery of the bungalow with the 'native's' wonder at the British colonial universe. Yet, perhaps unwittingly, but powerfully nevertheless, Kipling also celebrates, through the mongoose, the mental landscape and hierarchies of the late nineteenth-century white colonial's India, where the interests of a small island could somehow consume the huge country the colonial lived in. So large has the unremarkable English furniture become that it has swallowed up an entire landscape, a subcontinent; oceans exist in the bathtub, and a rather ordinary English family has become a family of giants. This vivid sentence, as animated as the mongoose, is a small essay on power and its inversions.

Outside in the garden, when Rikki-tikki asks the tailor-bird superciliously, 'Who is Nag?' the cobra himself replies, 'I am Nag,' and, before issuing the warning, 'Look, and be afraid!' recounts his origins: 'The great God Brahm put his mark upon all our people when the first cobra spread his hood to keep the sun off Brahm as he slept.' But Rikki-tikki has already begun to see details in terms of the paraphernalia of the English interiors he's become familiar with: Brahm's mark looks to him like a 'spectacle-mark', 'exactly like the eye part of a hook-and-eye fastening'. This is the second time in his fiction – the first was the curator's gift to the lama of his glasses – that Kipling uses spectacles to suggest the ambiguities and richness of an cross-cultural vision. The mongoose replies with some temerity: 'Well … marks or no marks, do you think it is right of you to eat fledglings out of a nest?' This could be a satire of an early nineteenth-century conversation between a conservative Brahmin and a social reformist Hindu full of demystifying zeal; it is not unlike, in tenor, Rammohun Roy's debates, conducted through published pamphlets, with Bengali Brahmins. These debates are a preamble to the battle between Nag and Rikki-tikki, between an antique India and a 'modern' one, enacted in a colonial theatre, the bathroom. The energy and conflict in Kipling's children's stories are not unconnected to the energy and conflict in colonial Indian history.

By the time Kipling died in 1936, he was, despite his public honours, more or less ignored by the literary establishment. The banishment had begun a few decades before his death; Max Beerbohm, never an admirer, drew a cartoon of Kipling as an Oriental idol on a shelf, with the caption 'Kipling on the Shelf'. Efforts to revive the reputation of this incomparable artist and often deranged racial supremacist came from the more perceptive critics of a former colony: Randall Jarrell and Edmund Wilson, the title of whose essay, 'The Kipling Nobody Reads', tells its own story. Perhaps his ghost has done penance enough; time seems to have pardoned him for writing well and to have forgiven him his views. Ricketts's biography, and Andrew Lycett's more recent one, both published to acclaim, are themselves evidence of renewed attention. The range of his living admirers is noteworthy – Craig Raine, Tom Paulin, Edward Said (who, not long ago confessed in these pages to the sort of bilingualism that was nascent in Kipling: 'Every time I speak an English sentence, I find myself echoing it in Arabic; and vice versa') – but the range of their political sympathies reminds us how endlessly problematic the relationship is between a great writer's politics and his art, and the reader's engagement with both.

Returning to Earth
The Poetry of Jibanananda Das

'Jibanananda' is a Tagorean name; its meaning, 'the joy of life', recalls, for me, the lines from a famous song in the *Gitanjali*, in which Tagore's defiant Nietzschean mood is contained, as it almost always is, by decorum and serenity: '*Jagate ananda jagne/ Amaar nimantrana*' – 'I have been invited/ to the world's festival of joy.' Of course, Tagore had to earn those lines' triumphal affirmation, and also their irony; by the time he wrote them, his wife was dead, as were two children, a son and his favourite daughter, Rani.

Das found himself invited to the 'festival of joy' in 1899; from the evidence of his poems and fiction, it doesn't appear that he thought life – '*jiban*' – an unqualified benediction. There is, not infrequently, a note of bewilderment in the way Das's poems speak of earthly existence, the bewilderment of a person who wakes to find himself in a place of transit from which he must soon move on. The nameless speaker in the poem 'Banalata Sen' begins wearily:

> For thousands of years I roamed the paths of this earth,
> From waters round Ceylon in dead of night to Malayan seas.
> Much have I wandered. I was there in the gray world of Asoka
> And Bimbisara, pressed on through darkness to the city of
> Vidharbha.
> I am a weary heart surrounded by life's frothy ocean.
> To me she gave me a moment's peace – Banalata Sen from Natore.

The translation is Clinton B. Seely's, of the Department of South Asian Languages at Chicago, from his superb literary biography of Das, *A Poet Apart*. From the beginning, Das, an elusive, deeply private writer, reluctant to make himself better known, reluctant, in some crucial instances, to publish his own work, has had his champions, who've attempted to bring his work to the attention of the Bengali, and now the Anglophone, reader. The most important of these was the poet and critic Buddhadeva Bose, Das's contemporary, probably the most influential Bengali writer of that bristly, fascinating post-Tagorean generation, whose generosity in supporting a fellow poet was, and still is, as unusual in the republic of Indian letters as was his critical farsightedness and acumen. The poems are now part of the Bengali consciousness, on both sides of the border dividing India from what was Pakistan and is now Bangladesh; it's safe to claim that Das is the pre-eminent and best-loved Bengali poet after Tagore. Those who know his work first-hand are convinced that he is among the twentieth century's great writers, and so the process of recuperation continues, now in English. Like some of those writers – one thinks of Pessoa and Kafka – Das felt, for some reason, compelled either to suppress some of his most important writings, or to locate them in a secret life. Seely's excellent work, as translator and biographer, represents a sustained effort that's been ongoing for a few decades now, a project, however, dogged by the sort of inexplicable delays and impediments (his translations have still to find a publisher), the sort of nebulous cloud, that occasionally seemed to keep Das's contemporaries (despite the enthusiasm of Bose and some younger writers, and Tagore's qualified but genuine admiration) from seeing the true value of his work. Now the English poet Joe Winter's translations, collected in two slim but not insubstantial volumes, *Naked Lonely Hand*, a selection of some of the best-known poems, and *Bengal the Beautiful*, which contains the sonnets that were published posthumously and made him a household name in Bengal, give the process of dissemination, and the cause of Das, a fresh impetus – a small but significant contribution which will not be, hopefully, scuppered by Saturn.

Both translators, Seely and Winter, have either taken the trouble to master Bengali (Seely's doctoral thesis was on Bengali literature) or to make themselves intimate with it – Winter, until recently, lived in Calcutta, and returned to England after several years; it was in Calcutta, I believe, that he discovered Das's poetry. Seely has been revising and revising the translations, including the one of Das's single most famous poem, from which I've quoted, above, the opening stanza. Winter's version announces a translator who's happier with looser forms, whose diction has a not-unattractive roughness and simplicity that is probably more characteristic of Winter's own writing as well as of some post-war British poetry than it is of Das. Unlike Seely, Winter is also intent on preserving Das's glancing, sometimes unnoticeable, rhymes – a constraint which, paradoxically, produces some of that looseness of structure, as well as occasional awkwardnesses of phrasing. Here is the same opening stanza in Winter's version:

> For thousands of years Earth's path has been my path. I have passed
> at dark of night the sea of Ceylon and the ocean of Malay;
> the ashen worlds of Bimbisara and Asoka I've encompassed,
> and Vidarbha town's dark distance, in life's far ocean-foam-play ...
> and a touch of peace came to me once, the tiredest of men –
> there and gone, the gift to me of Natore's Banalata Sen.

One of the reasons that Winter is trying to preserve the original
structure of the three-stanza poem and its rhymes is, surely, to adhere to
the summation, in the original, of the last line of each verse with '*Natorer
Banalata Sen*'; or 'Natore's Banalata Sen'. This is a rounding-off, a coda,
at once mysteriously resonant and mock-resounding; it enacts a characteristic and essentially modernist comedy, although comedy is not what
one usually associates with this poem or its author, 'the most solitary',
according to Bose, 'of our poets'. Yet comic is what, in the first instance,
Natore's Banalata Sen is, as is the idea of her simultaneously physical and
transcendent redemptive quality; for Natore is what in India is called
a 'mofussil', a prototype of the sort of small town that came into being
(in this case, in East Bengal) in the time of colonialism, usually with an
administrative centre, a post office, a school, a hospital, a railway station.
Banalata is the kind of name a young middle-class woman of Das's generation might have had; 'Sen' a surname that ordinarily denotes the *vaidya*
caste, the caste Das's own family belonged to before it became Brahmo
(the protestant reform sect among Bengali Hindus founded by Rammohun Roy). The fact that she's called 'Banalata Sen' rather than 'Banalata
Devi', 'devi' a respectful honorific once used to address women in lieu of
the surname or maiden name, tells us that she belongs to the new educated
bourgeoisie, and probably appears to our exhausted traveller, after his
sojourn through mythic and historical time, in a drawing room. In other
words, Natore and Banalata Sen are at once glamorous and banal, these
two unrelated qualities converging in them as they did in several aspects
of not just modernity, but what the Indian social scientist Partha Chatterjee calls 'colonial modernity' (it's natural, in this context, to think of
Joyce). That the ordinariness, the replicatedness, of the colonial modern
should somehow be both embedded in the monuments of the past and
of the world (the *Odyssey*, the kingdoms of Asoka and Bimbisara), and
yet be involved in a huge inversion of value, where *it* (here Banalata Sen)
possesses, in its banality, a magic greater than that of myth, is a crucial part
of the comedy, and its revelatory intent. As critics have shown earlier, the
poem is not only haunted by the passing of civilizations, but freighted with
allusion. There are references to Poe's 'To Helen'; and, as an excellent essay by the Bangladeshi poet and critic Kaiser Haq demonstrates, to Pater's

eulogy of the Mona Lisa. But it's the ordinariness and the singularity of the colonial modern, of Banalata Sen, that gives it its special shape, and sets it apart from the piece by Pater and the poem by Poe.

Das himself was born to educated, even accomplished, Brahmo parents (his mother a poet, his father a schoolteacher) in an important mofussil, Barisal, in what was then East Bengal. The mofussil had some of the characteristics we ordinarily associate with small towns – of being a backwater, of being a place to escape and get out of. But it does seem to me, from the evidence and the quality of my parents' memories, both of whom also grew up in a mofussil in East Bengal, that it was, to a significant extent, a place of discovery, subversion, possibility (these are registers I find in the phrase 'Natorer Banalata Sen'), and, noticeably, ambition. At least until Independence, it represents a crucial stage of self-fashioning, between the pathshala (the traditional school, such as my father went to when he was very small) in the village and the university (such as also my father went to) in Calcutta. That is, the mofussil was not all provincialism and dullness, as is, so often, the case with the American small town, at least in its literary incarnation; nor was it a Naipaulean 'half-made' entity. It was a place of both constrictedness and hope, and, keeping figures like Das, Nirad C. Chaudhuri, and even my parents (my mother a singer of some repute, my father a successful corporate man) in mind, one of professional and artistic experimentation, and a real seedbed for cosmopolitanism. I have mentioned ambition as a quality of the mofussil (sometimes formerly landowning) bourgeoisie; it's something that Das appeared to lack, or to interrogate terribly and turn inside out. Das went to Calcutta first as a student of English literature at Presidency College, gaining a second class in both his undergraduate and his MA degrees, and then took up various forms of employment, including that of part-time lecturer (the second-class degree foreclosing academic advancement). Whether it was ambition that took him there or whether it was something else isn't clear. Whether it was ambition that made him publish some of his poems, and never publish many of them, and kept him from publishing his short stories or the novel *Malyaban*, or whether it was something else is also open to question. Whether it was intention or unmindfulness that made him step in front of a tram in Calcutta (a pretty difficult thing to do accidentally) in 1954, leading, of course, to his death, has never been fully explained. Indeed, intentionality, and its robust mofussil cousin, ambition, are never transparent or clearly stated in Das's life, or in the lives of the drifting protagonists in the poems ('For thousands of years Earth's path has been my path. I have passed/ at dark of night the sea of Ceylon and the ocean of Malay;/ the ashen worlds of Bimbisara and Asoka I've encompassed') and the fictions.

What Das did take from the mofussil is what one might, for want of a better descriptive term, call its palpable dream-life, a mixture of daytime fantasy and the images that populate our sleep, and inform, at any given point in history, the very decisions we make. It's this dream-life that gives to my parents' memories their still-contemporary mixture of colour and cosmopolitanism – a peculiar mixture of emotion, desire, and the secular word that seems to have occurred at that time – for which words like 'cosmopolitan' actually sound tentative and inadequate, and 'dream', in the end, seems almost more apposite. Das's poems make this dream-life explicit in their susceptibility to astonishment, and in their particularly eccentric take on historical time. Here are the opening stanzas of 'Windy Night', in Winter's translation:

> The wind was fierce last night – a night of innumerable stars.
> Nightlong an immense wind toyed with my mosquito-net;
> at times the net billowed out like the monsoon ocean's maw,
> at times it tore free of the bed
> on a whim to fly to the stars,
> there were times I felt – half-asleep maybe – there's no net over my
> head,
> it's flying like a white heron in a blue ocean of air to graze the side of
> Swati's star!
> Last night was such a splendid night.
> Then all the dead stars were awake – not the hint of a gap in the sky
> –
> there too in the stars I saw the faces of the ashen, all the dear dead of
> the world;
> all the stars shone in the dark like the dew-glistening eye of a
> courting
> male kite at the top of an *aswattha*-tree;
> the vast sky glittered like a shawl of shining cheetah's-skin over the
> shoulders of the Queen of Babylon on a night of moonlight!
> Last night was such an amazing night.

This is an account of an inner tumult, as well as of the positioning of one's relationship to one's art and to certain transformative moments; the process that produced it is part of the same one, you suspect, that produced Raymond Roussel's and Henri Rousseau's visions, as well as their ambivalent, double-faced relationship to the public persona of the artist. These imaginations – Das's, Roussel's, Rousseau's – are often cartographical and historical; they don't balk at making impossible, even ludicrous, journeys through time, spaces, horizons; and yet often their mode, in the lives of their authors, is secrecy, a jealously guarded privacy, that undermines the two poles – the exoticist and the cosmopolitan – in which the eclectic, internationalist sensibility most often falls in the twentieth century. They emanate from a nameless dream-life that constituted the submerged universe of the more visible and recognisable forms of cosmopolitanism, a universe that was to be found in the mofussil, in the suburbs of Calcutta, as well as in the *Jardin des Plantes* which Rousseau visited frequently, and the affluent Parisian street on which Roussel lived. It's this submerged universe, linking Bengali mofussil to Paris, that I became aware of, in a circuitous way in my own consciousness, when I first heard of Roussel's *Impressions of Africa*, a title that came to me with the curious bit of information that Roussel had never actually journeyed to equatorial Africa. This, then, immediately reminded me of Bibhutibhushan Banerjee's *Chaander Pahaad* or *The Moon-Mountain*. Banerjee is the author of the classic novel, *Pather Panchali*, and *The Moon-Mountain* is set in Africa, to which Banerjee had never been. I also recalled, at once, that this last fact had been conveyed to me, when I was a boy, by my uncle, who'd grown up in one mofussil, Sylhet, then moved to another, Shillong, just before Partition, where he'd read *Chaander Pahaad*. 'One day,' he said to me, 'I received a letter from my older brother, who was then a colonel with the King's Engineers (it was the time of the War), and I immediately knew from the postage stamp that it had come from Africa. Do you know why? Because I had read *Chaader Pahaad*. But it was not an Africa of elephants and lions. The picture on the stamp was of a railway platform and railway tracks. *That* was the Africa Bibhutibhushan had written about.' In other words, the Africa my uncle recognized was at once mofussil, enmeshed in Partha Chatterjee's semi-comical and specificity-cherishing 'colonial modernity', as well as imaginary continent; a place simultaneously alive and immediate as well as being one that was experienced absolutely second- or third-hand. This is the submerged, rather than the visible, world of cosmopolitanism from which many of Das's trances and visions seem to emerge, with rents in the mosquito net and cheetah-skin all intact.

Here is the unnamed protagonist again, in the poem 'Naked Lonely Hand' (from which the collection takes its title), reminiscing, bringing back to the present a more composed but nevertheless slightly unfathomable setting:

> Again in the *Phalgun* sky the darkness lowers:
> as if a mysterious sister of light, this darkness.

> Like that lady who has always loved me
> and yet whose face I have never looked upon,
> that very lady,
> the darkness deepens in the *Phalgun* sky.

I seem to hear a tale of a lost city,
the beauty of an ash-gray palace wakes in my heart.

On the Indian Ocean shore
or else beyond the Mediterranean coast
or out beyond the Sea of Tyre
not now, but once, a certain city stood,
a certain palace,
a palace of the richest furnishings:
Persian carpets, cashmere shawls, round-sheer pearls and coral of the
    Bering wave,
my lost heart, my dead eyes, my extinct dreams and desires,
and you lady –
all was once in that world.

The 'lady' is one of Das's many compulsive variations on the Banalata figure, here lifted out of the colonial modern and made metonymic, presented in the world of the poem only as a 'naked lonely hand'. The only suggestion, here, of the modern – not the colonial modern, but the post-1860s Bengali refashioning of the 'modern' – is, curiously, in the recurring reference to the Bengali month which coincides with spring, *Phalgun*. Both the Indian seasons and the Bengali calendar are pointedly observed and run as a counterpoint and as a parallel time-cycle to the Gregorian calendar in Bengal's nineteenth and twentieth centuries; and this counterpoint in time is an essential characteristic of Bengali modernity. In the poem, *Phalgun* is the present moment, the settled, familiar, homely moment of Bengali bourgeois modernity, from which the other time-frame, the Gregorian calendar of history, is seen in a perspective that narrows and converges till it becomes invisible, or visible in another way:

Phalgun's darkness is here with a story from over the sea,
a pain-filled outline of exquisite domes and arches,
the smell of pears, now gone,
ash-pale parchments in profusion of lion-hide and deer-skin,
glass panes rainbow-coloured,
and at curtains coloured like peacocks' fanned-out tails
a momentary glimpse
of rooms, inner rooms, more rooms, further rooms –
a timeless stillness and wonder.

Curtains, carpets spread with the blood-red sweat of the sun!
Blood-crimson glasses of watermelon wine!
Your naked lonely hand …

your naked lonely hand.

But who is the narrator, and what is he doing in these unexpected locations? About intention and ambition, Das was always unclear, and unsettlingly challenging. Living in Calcutta and producing poetry in the 1930s and 1940s, at a time when Bose and his contemporaries were trying desperately to delineate a space for their practice that was distinct from the ageing Tagore's ('it was impossible not to imitate Rabindranath, and it was impossible to imitate Rabindranath': thus, Bose), Das seemed aloof from the quarrel about what constituted the 'modern': 'an uncomfortable word, a cause of confusion and brewer of battles' – Bose again. It remains an 'uncomfortable word' in India, for all sorts of reasons. Among the causes Bose is thinking of are its anti-Tagorean, un-Indian (this second reason still exercises many, Indian and European, to this day) connotations. Das appeared, however, elusive, and aloof from the debate, and from what would be called the Kallol age after the magazine Bose edited (kallol means 'wave'): according to Bose, 'shy, sombre and a little frightened of what is popularly known as life …' Indeed, says his friend, 'Jibanananda is so obstinately himself that he seems to have abandoned the homeland of tradition in favour of a gnomeland all his own. His world is one of tangled shadows and crooked waters, of the mouse, the owl and the bat, of deer playing in the moonlit forests, of dawn and darkness …' This was written in 1948, soon after Independence and Partition had consigned Das's birthplace to the other side of the border, and when he had already made his name with four mature volumes of verse; he was in a loveless marriage and had been moving from job to job. Not frightened of life, perhaps, but of intentionality, that impetus that makes us return to life, to adhere to it, to persist with it. In this – Das's savage examination of intentionality – he overturns the polite, socially acceptable idea of 'ambition' on which much of the professionalized, educated Bengali middle class was created. I've asked whether it was ambition or something else that directed Das's creative and personal life, as well as the lives of his narrators and protagonists: for he had a persistent sense of the inexplicable 'something else', and in one of his poems he has a name for it: 'bodh'. The word gives this poem its title; in Bengali, it means many things, principally 'understanding', 'awareness', or 'realization'. It derives from the etymological root that produced 'buddhi', or 'intelligence', or 'buddha', 'person who has received spiritual illumination'. Das, though, dismantles the word, and makes it into an occasion of inquiry into desire, and what he clearly believes, in poem after poem, the most bewildering desire of all, the desire for existence. Winter translates the word as 'sensation'; and in doing so, he's right to imply, I think, that Das wishes to take it out of the realm of the intellect, free choice, and the will; to take it out of the realm of conscious control, as it were. Here are the opening lines of 'Sensation':

I journey through light and dark. In my head
is no dream, but a certain sensation instead
is at work. No dream – no love – no rest –
a certain sensation inside my breast
is born.

These lines are a critique of Tagore's notion that the often frustrated fumblings of creativity, even creation, are necessitated by love, or *prem*; they also represent a dissonant rewriting of the Hindu concept of *leela*, which also fascinated Tagore, which posits the idea that the universe, with its seemingly arbitrary allocations of wonders and disappointments, is the consequence of divine, childlike play, essentially innocent, essentially self-absorbed and opaque. There's long been an indulgent, forbearing bafflement regarding the divine purpose in Hindu thought, and an interesting tragic decorum about not trying to explain it too much; the shift in Das involves changing the object of bafflement from divinity, or the creator, to intentionality:

Those who were born here on this Earth
as if its children – who gave birth
over and over to children, and so their time spent;
or those for whom birth-giving's imminent;
or those who have come to the seed-fields of the Earth
for this, that they too will give birth –
have I a different head from theirs?
Have I a different heart from theirs?
Different feeling? Different seeing?
What brings this difference to being?
– But I am this different being.

But in another sort of mood, Das can be affectionate about the convergence of play, pointlessness, and life, as in 'Cat':

All day long on my way out and back I keep meeting a cat:
in tree-shadow, in sun, on a rabble of brown leaves;
a satisfying few scraps of fish-bone somewhere, and then
in the pale ground's skeleton
I see it preoccupied all with its own heart, like a bee …

In 'Suchetana', the poet states as plainly as he ever has why (because 'why' is the powerful, unanswered query) this time-traveller, who keeps turning up on earth at various points in history, keeps chancing upon things, looking at them afresh – why this traveller bothers to revisit these locations at all:

> Drawn to the Earth's ground, to the house of human birth
> I have come, and I feel, better not to have been born –
> yet having come all this I see as a deeper gain
> when I touch a body of dew in an incandescent dawn.

The 'body of dew', in Das, means several things: nature, that which is outside of human existence, Bengal itself, and very often, implicitly, death. Nature, art, and death are almost coeval in Das; and the closest he comes to revealing this is in the great short poem 'Tangerine' ('*kamlalebu*'), which, for some reason, is absent from Winter's selection; here is Seely's version, from the biography, and I quote it in its entirety:

> When once I leave this body
> Shall I come back to the world?
> If only I might return
> On a winter's evening
> Taking on the compassionate flesh of a cold tangerine
> At the bedside of some dying acquaintance.

Das's peculiar and relentless longing to escape the body – in effect, his longing for death – and then, characteristically, to revisit, almost help-lessly ('If only I might return'), existence – even a transitory and perishable existence in the form of the 'cold tangerine' and the 'dying acquaintance' – is also an almost fatalistic enactment of the creative act. The art-work often seems to Das not so much the result of intention as of that inex-plicable '*bodh*', the unfathomable will that leads deathward, and then, as unfathomably, back towards birth. And that it is art that's being referred to in 'Tangerine' is something we become aware of through its echo of Yeats (whose work, with Hardy's and Poe's, Das clearly loved), and its rewriting and reversal of these lines from 'Sailing to Byzantium':

> Once out of nature I shall never take
> My bodily form from any natural thing,
> But such a form as Grecian goldsmiths make
> Of hammered gold and gold enamelling
> To keep a drowsy emperor awake …

Yeats wishes to be taken 'out of nature' into art and history; Das, con-stantly, out of human identity into history (the worlds of Bimbisara and Asoka; the coast of the Mediterranean and the Sea of Tyre), into nature ('to be born as grass in grass, from some deep grass-mother's/ womb', as he says in another poem), and into a state and place of return he calls *Bangla*, or 'Bengal'. Das's echo of Yeats alerts us to the death-wish that's latent in the latter's Byzantium poems; and it reminds us of the intimate contiguity between art, death, and making in his own work. It's in this intersection that we must situate the *Bangla* in the extraordinary sonnets that comprise the posthumous collection named *Rupasi Bangla* (*Bengal the Beautiful* in Winter's translation). *Bangla* invokes various registers: it's a fierce expression of the death-wish, or the extinction of the personality into nature; it's a justification, against all wisdom and judgement, to return, having accepted, dubiously, the invitation described in Tagore's lines, 'I have been invited/ to the world's festival of joy'; and a very delicate drawing out of the tension contained within *bodh*, which is a compulsive desire for both death and for existence. I quote the first sonnet, in Winter's translation, in its entirety:

> You all go where you like – I shall stay here beside
> this Bengal bank – I'll see jackfruit-tree leaves losing hold
> at dawn, and at dusk a *shalik*'s brown wings turning cold –
> yellow-legged beneath some fair fluff it performs its bird-stride
> in dark in the grass – once – twice – all at once a *hijal* has cried
> from the forest for it to fly to its heart's stronghold;
> the tender arms of a woman I'll see ... like a conch-note that's rolled
> on grey air her white bangles cry out – she stands there, at the
>> pond's side
>
> at dusk – as if to take a duck, *khoi*-coloured, to some fabled place –
> about her soft body the aura of old tales seems to fall –
> in the nest of this pond she was born, from its *kalmi*-weed shawl –
> in quiet she washes her feet – to leave in mist's pall
> for a land unknown – yet I know I will not lose trace
> of her in Earth's crowd ... she is on the bank of this my Bengal.

As Winter says in his introduction to *Bengal the Beautiful*, '*Rupasi Bangla* ... was discovered after the poet's death in an exercise-book dated 1934, twenty years earlier. The manuscript was left not quite complete, with an alternative wording here and there and one poem half a line short.' Like the poem above, each one of the sonnets comprises a single, unfolding sentence, its quick transitions held together by punctuation marks, its shape closely allied to breath. (One thinks, briefly, of Dickinson, a quite different sensibility. Perhaps to work towards that utopian object, the absolutely private poem, inevitably involves transposing the rhythms of breathing into the signs of language and one's handwriting.) Although preserving the rhymes, almost inaudible in the hypnotic low-voiced originals, is always a risk, Winter does well to give us the sense of the Das sonnet as at once a difficult formal exercise and a spontaneous declamation, a habitation for multifarious ways of noticing and a single observation.

Each sonnet is a fresh beginning, a fresh attempt to say the same thing (as in the second sonnet: 'I have looked on the face of Bengal: nowhere else shall I go to see/ the loveliness of the Earth ...'); a draft, in effect, of one poem. It stands somewhere intriguingly between the Worsdworthian sonnet, with its aspiration to be an individual lyric poem of fourteen lines, and the Renaissance sonnet, which, whatever its subject, is an improvisation that's situated in a workshop, a work-in-progress meant to be shared with a coterie of friends. Here, there are no friends, there is no audience, at hand (which is probably why – because they were meant for no one – the poems have such currency in the Bengali imagination today); and the romanticism of each individual sonnet is constantly turned into an echo, a declaration made at one remove, through repetition. The *Rupasi Bangla* sonnet seems to come to us, thus, without ground or origin. On the one hand, through, and even despite, its subject, *Bangla*, or Bengal, it fashions an argument for existence (so crucial, as I've pointed out, for Das) that's deeper than nationalism. At the same time, reiteration, by giving primacy to the word over the 'real', pushes 'Bengal', the place, the country, into a sort of ambivalence.

It's difficult to say this with certainty, of course, but it is not improbable that the sonnets were always *meant* to be discovered and read posthumously. I offer this because of the returning and continual presence of a poem by Thomas Hardy in Das's work. Das was much taken with Hardy: an unhappy mofussil character in one of his unpublished stories takes out an old copy of *Wessex Poems* from his trunk, wipes the dust off it, and takes it with him before starting out on a journey. The correspondences between Hardy's and Das's practice too are palpable and illuminating. *Wessex Poems*, like Das's stories, novel, and sonnets, represents Hardy's secret life; it contains the poetry he wrote for the thirty or forty years he was a professional novelist, and which he published only after his disenchantment with the novel. Both Hardy and Das used silence and cunning by investing in literary forms they weren't identified with; and Hardy the novelist uses his poems to elegize a sexually cold marriage, just as Das explored, more darkly, his failed marriage in his stories. Certain autobiographical material can be approached by certain writers only, it seems, when they exchange their principal literary practice for an alternative one.

But it appears, too, that Das drew, during his life as a mature poet, upon a single late poem by Hardy, 'Afterwards', a poem that he revises in several ways, and whose Keatsian subject, a 'posthumous existence', is at the core of Das's concerns and of the polemics central to his oeuvre: the desire for annihilation poised against the necessity of return. Indeed, much of *Rupasi Bangla*, and some of the earlier poems – which, together, record, in meticulous acts of *noticing*, the earthly joys of the Bengali landscape – have their source in Hardy's poem and the question it poses:

> When the Present has latched its postern behind my tremulous stay,
>   And the May month flaps its glad green leaves like wings,
> Delicate-filmed as new-spun silk, will the neighbours say,
>   'He was a man who used to notice such things?'

The voice of the observer, who is both rooted in place and itinerant in time, who expects to vanish tomorrow and yet continue to regard, through the eyes of others, his landscape, the poem's conjunction of the physical, the concrete, with the ghostly and the posthumous: these are the elements that inform, in any number of permutations, Das's poems, especially the sonnets. Hardy's Wessex, Das's *Bangla*: one is a 'real' place whose reality is contingent upon its fictional incarnation, the other an imagined paradise – concomitant, as paradise always is, with death – that becomes incarnate in poetry. The first two lines of Hardy's second stanza, for instance ('If it be in the dusk when, like an eyelid's soundless blink,/ The dewfall-hawk comes crossing the shades'), recur in Das, signifying the sudden awareness of the passing of a great expanse of time, in compressed, glancing allusions. It's echoed at the close of 'Banalata Sen' ('At day's end when evening is here at last/ in syllables of the dew; and a kite cleans its wings of sun's smell'), and at the end of 'After Twenty Years' ('Like an eyelid silent-descending where do the kite's wings stop – /... golden golden kite, the dew hunted it, took it from here ... / after twenty years in that mist suddenly to be with you clear!'). In the sonnets, Das asks the question in Hardy's first stanza in a variety of ways:

> The day that I part from you all – to make my way out
> into a far mist – where death in darkness shall beg my body away –
> on this shore of Bengal, this blue shore of Bengal, on that day –
> ah, what will be in my mind?
> (Sonnet 9)

And

> When I lie in the sleep of death – in dark by the jackfruit-tree
> under the stars, where the Dhaleswari or Chilai flows on its way,
> as it may be – no face is near the burning-ground all day –
> yet the shade of Bengal's jackfruit and *jaam* is falling over me ...

Yet, in the end, Hardy's poem was always meant to be read in his lifetime; the voice, with its speculation about 'the neighbours', is an austere but sociable one. We don't know who the 'you' or 'you all' (*tumi* and *tomra*) of Das's sonnets are; they are not us; we are now eavesdropping, as we were always meant to be. Not ambition or intention, but maybe *bodh* – something that entirely preoccupied the poet, but about whose workings even he could not have been wholly conscious – prepared the notebook for posthumousness; death gives to the sonnets and to Das's 'Bengal' their now recognized shape; and in the midst of this strange, compelling domain Winter has provided us with an effective and loving renewal.

Women in Love as Post-Human Essay

I was in my final year at University College London in 1985, when my tutor, the South African novelist Dan Jacobson, told me that I'd read a great deal of poetry but not enough prose. He asked me to read four novels, the earliest of which was *Moll Flanders*, the most recent *Sons and Lovers*. I remember reading the Lawrence in my studio apartment on Warren Street, my days lit by the glow of the fires in the pit, my unremarkable room overlooking the street changed by the smell of Mrs Morel's ironing. Afterwards, I felt I'd made a discovery; not so much as a student, but as a reader and a writer-aspirant groping for his true subject.

At twenty-three, I was in awe of the modernists, especially Eliot. A very different sort of poet preoccupied me as well: Philip Larkin. What must have drawn me to them, as a young man ill-at-ease in England, in the Bombay he'd left behind, and even in the early 1980s, was, I think, their nostalgia for and sense of loss in relation to certain utopian sites of culture – Europe, antiquity, middle England. Their political conservatism (which I innocently thought of in purely aesthetic terms), where the urge to preserve and cherish, as well as to exclude, informed even the experiments in language and tone they undertook, must have also appealed to me; as did their transcendental longing for an elsewhere, a hereafter, a longing which, I think, permeates Larkin's work despite his rejection, in 'Aubade', of the notion of an afterlife, and of religion as a 'vast, moth-eaten brocade'.

What I found in the writer who had composed *Sons and Lovers* was an extraordinary refutation of this anguished longing, an anguish I'd thought I must at least vicariously make my own. On several levels, it opened my eyes to my own temperament as a writer, and even (though I use the term with the utmost wariness) as an 'Indian'. It wasn't the Oedipal paradigm in the novel which interested me; it was its profound rejection of tragedy (which my own creativity, too, was turning away from in order to discover itself), a rejection which I sensed was (though I dared not say it of this most 'English' of novels) fundamentally non-Western. Already, in this great, early work, Lawrence is delineating, in the most immediate imaginative terms possible, a refutation and, at once, a celebration whose nature he'd describe not long before his death in *Apocalypse*, and which was to mark him out from his modernist contemporaries: 'Whatever the unborn and the dead may know, they cannot know the beauty, the marvel of being alive in the flesh. The dead may look after the afterwards. But the magnificent here and now of the flesh is ours, and ours alone, and ours only for a time.'[1] This isn't just a Dylan Thomas-like statement about the heroic poignancy of carnality; 'life', for Lawrence, is a complex and loaded word, denoting neither a continuity, nor a spontaneous occurrence, but a historical crisis, a break between the old and new, and between cultures. It is part of his polemic against European humanism and its metaphysics, as the 'here and now' too is; but to see how Lawrence's ideology, his anti-metaphysic, is also an aesthetic, we must turn to his poetic manifesto, 'Poetry of the Present', where the religiose 'unborn and the dead' of *Apocalypse* is translated into literary terms – 'the perfected, crystalline poetry of the past and the future' – from which the 'poetry of the moment', the 'here and now' (the poetry Lawrence believes he's written), constitutes a radical departure. In *Sons and Lovers*, that break has begun to be effected; the 'magnificent here and now' is vividly present in the novel, but it already has an unprecedented revolutionary sharpness (in this, the least strident of his works) quite different from the 'here and now' invoked by his famous modernist contemporaries.

This becomes clear when we read the essay on poetry which became Lawrence's introduction to his *New Poems* (1918), written, it seems, around the time he was completing *Women in Love*. And what Lawrence is working towards in the novel, in terms of formal and spiritual ambition, informs his discussion of poetry; 'poetry', which becomes a metaphor for Western literature in general, and for the 'classics' of English literary tradition:

> The poetry of the beginning and the poetry of the end must have that exquisite finality, perfection which belongs to all that is far off. It is in the realm of all that is perfect. It is of the nature of all that is complete and consummate. This completeness, this consummateness, the finality and the perfection are conveyed in exquisite form ... Perfected bygone moments, perfected moments in the glimmering futurity, these are the treasured gemlike lyrics of Shelley and Keats.[2]

Against this, Lawrence posits an aesthetic which relinquishes 'perfection' and 'exquisite form' – relinquishes, in a sense, both *Sons and Lovers*, which possessed these qualities, as well as the canonical definition of what comprises a 'work of art'.

But there is another kind of poetry: the poetry of that which is at hand: the immediate present. In the immediate present there is no perfection, no consummation, nothing finished. The strands are all flying, quivering, intermingling into the web, the waters are shaking the moon. There is no round, consummate moon on the face of the running water, nor on the face of the unfinished tide ... There is no plasmic finality, nothing crystal, permanent. If we try to fix the living tissue, as the biologists fix it with formalin, we have only a hardened bit of the past, the bygone life under our observation.[3]

At first glance, this might seem like a somewhat febrile, overwritten version of the Joycean 'epiphany', or any of those modernist preoccupations that trace their history to the Romantic 'privileged moment', the Wordsworthian 'spot of time', in which an extraordinary, transformative experience is made available to the artist. Another look at Lawrence's essay tells us, however, that he's speaking of something that lacks the repose and self-containedness of Wordsworth's 'emotion recollected in tranquillity' or Pound's 'emotional and intellectual complex in a moment of time', or the elevated status (Joyce is careful to introduce an element of the sacred with his choice of term: 'epiphany') that the Romantic or modernist moment has. The latter renovates the banality of the present by opening it, almost randomly, and yet fortuitously, onto the past; thus Proust's narrator, tasting the 'petites madeleines', ceases to feel 'mediocre, contingent, mortal', and is transported to a realm where he has 'infinitely transcended those savours' of 'the tea and the cake',[4] although he's still unsure of what that realm might be. Lawrence's moment deliberately claims its 'difference' from this poetic rehabilitation of the world through an instant in time: he rejects Proust when he rejects the 'hardened bit of the past, the bygone life under our observation', and when, in the same essay, he says: 'Don't give me the infinite or the eternal: nothing of infinity, nothing of eternity. Give me the still, white seething ... the moment, the quick of all change and haste and opposition: the moment, the immediate present, the Now.'[5] Lawrence is struggling to take the Romantic/ modernist moment out of its canonical, humanist lineage; and the overwriting in these passages is at once a sign of that struggle, as well as a gesture towards the radical incompatibility of that Lawrentian 'here and now' within the English canon. (This incompatibility is something I'll continue to return to, later, in this introduction.) Much of the imagery in the extracts I've quoted above is, as it happens, common to the language he's fashioning in *Women in Love* at that time to deal with his preoccupations; the face of the 'quivering' moon upon the water also appears in the strange, coded dreamscape in the famous 'Moony' chapter in the novel.

After the relative tentativeness of his first two novels, Lawrence discovered a remarkable visual style in *Sons and Lovers*, only to muddy it (I use the word advisedly, for 'mud' is an integral Lawrentian trope in the assault upon transparency and clarity that became so important to him) in the next two novels, *The Rainbow* and *Women in Love*. 'I shan't write in the same manner as *Sons and Lovers* again,'[6] he said in the famous letter to Edward Garnett. And in another letter to Garnett defending his new style:

> I have no longer the joy in creating vivid scenes, that I had in *Sons and Lovers*. I don't care much more about accumulating objects in the powerful light of emotion, and making a scene of them. I have to write differently.[7]

One shouldn't underestimate, in spite of this, the break that *Sons and Lovers* itself represents, nor ignore the continuities the novels he wrote after it, and the rhetoric he'd develop about 'art' and 'life' in his later writings, have with that early work. What's fascinating, though, is Lawrence's sense that the novel is an artistic moment he must leave behind, and what this departure, this apparent severance of ties, this dissolution might comprise. Certainly, one might say that, with *Sons and Lovers*, Lawrence had grown into some of the key aspects of modernism – to do with language and its mediation and renovation of reality – in a style quite unlike his precursors or even contemporaries like Arnold Bennett, but in many ways consonant, in the novel's response to sensory perception, and its use, especially, of the image, with the modernist project. One of the characteristics of modernism is that it doesn't simply take 'reality' as a fact or a given to be reported upon, as naturalism does, but as a potential transmitter of value to the self, or the subconscious. This value is not obvious or visible, but, in many ways, has to be recovered or 'created' by the artist. It's a transaction that has its origins in Romanticism, of course, but which modernism relocates from the natural world to the bourgeois city. The value in question is residually, but indisputably, religious, although, since the 'spot of time' is secular, its religious provenance must remain at once hidden and palpable. This contradiction marks the oxymoron with which Wordsworth describes the quality of the 'spot of time' in *The Prelude*: 'visionary dreariness'. Proust makes apparent the simultaneous suppression and indispensability of religious wonder in modernist sense-perception in his metaphorical construction of a scene in which the narrator stops at a hawthorn hedge:

> I found the whole path throbbing with the fragrance of hawthorn blossom. The hedge resembled a series of chapels, whose walls were no longer visible under the mountain of flowers that were heaped upon their altars; while beneath them the sun cast a checkered light upon the ground, as though it had just passed through a stained-glass window; and their scent swept over

me … as though I had been standing before the Lady-altar, and the flowers … held out each its bunch of glittering stamens… in the flamboyant style like those which, in the church, framed the stairway to the rood-loft … How simple and rustic by comparison would seem the dog-roses which in a few weeks' time would be climbing the same path in the heat of the sun, dressed in the smooth silk of their blushing pink bodices that dissolve in the first breath of wind.[8]

As a midpoint and phase of transition between English naturalism and modernist suggestion, *Sons and Lovers* is an extraordinary example. Take the passage below, which struck me even the first time I read it, and which is startlingly reminiscent, in its deliberate evasions and in the way in which it insinuates a sense of wonder, of the one I've quoted from Proust; here, the pregnant Mrs Morel has been locked out of her house at night by her drunken husband; wandering about, she's exhausted and angry but constantly distracted by the world around her:

Languidly she looked about her; the clumps of white phlox seemed like bushes spread with linen; a moth ricochetted over them, and right across the garden. Following it with her eye roused her. A few whiffs of the raw, strong scent of phlox invigorated her. She passed along the path, hesitating at the white rose-bush. It smelled sweet and simple. She touched the white ruffles of the roses. Their fresh scent and cool, soft leaves reminded her of the morning-time and sunshine.[9]

Here are the wholly unexpected, but, once made, supremely apposite associations between physical outline and memory, combined with the strategic, irrelevant detail – 'the clumps of white phlox … like bushes spread with linen; a moth ricochetted over them' – that are characteristic of modernism's off-kilter transaction between language, reality, and the subconscious (the metaphor of clothing and domesticity – 'linen', 'ruffles' – taking us back to Proust's 'silk' and 'blushing pink bodices'). The association is sometimes stated, as in the 'cool, soft leaves' reminding Mrs Morel of the 'morning-time and sunshine', but not explained, as it would be in a metaphor or simile. But sometimes it is suppressed, as in the observation about the rose-bush (which again recalls, but also extends further, Proust's 'simple and rustic' dog-roses): 'It smelled sweet and simple.' These adjectives struck me when I was an undergraduate: 'sweet', yes, but in what way 'simple'? How could a smell be 'simple'? Proust, the pioneer of the olfactory in modern literature,was referring, after all, to a thing and not a smell when he used the word. Something had been suppressed, and 'simple' was anything but simple; it was an ambiguity. Lawrence, then, had learnt the same lessons the modernists had, and learnt them exceptionally well: of control over the conflicting registers of language and memory, over expression and concealment. With *The Rainbow*, and especially *Women in Love*, he loosened, for some reason, that control, and muddied (a very different project from making ambiguous) his language. Why he should have done so, and with conscious, intellectual and spiritual intent, remains intriguing and significant, and distinguishes him further from the other major practitioners of the time.

Like certain other writers, Lawrence believed he was living during a time of crisis and unprecedented historical change, a change that has a peculiar charge in Lawrence's work because it's made available to us not only in spite of, but in, the element of the banal in the lives of, say, Birkin, Ursula, Gudrun, Gerald, and Hermione in *Women In Love*; in the flirtations, arguments, conversations, confessions of love, teas, parties, and visits to country houses. What emerges from our reading of this novel is a sense of two seemingly conflicting impulses explored simultaneously: on the one hand, an absolute commitment on the author's part to his characters, and, therefore, an unspoken taking for granted of the humanist basis from which the idea of 'characterization' emanates; on the other, the impulse to make the crisis of the human a condition for the conception and the inner life of the work. There was, of course, the personal crisis: *The Rainbow* had been banned because of obscenity, and for four years Lawrence worked on his next novel without being assured of a publisher or an audience. Then there was the war, which Lawrence, with his relentlessly inverted diagnostic analyses, his constant, almost compulsive, redefinitions of what was the disease and what the cure, would probably have seen as one of the symptoms of a crisis rather than a crisis itself. As he says in a foreword he wrote later for *Women in Love*:

> It is a novel which took its final shape in the midst of the period of war, though it does not concern the war itself. I should wish the time to remain unfixed, so that the bitterness of the war may be taken for granted in the characters.

That 'crisis', nevertheless, was on his mind in regard to the novel Lawrence makes clear in the penultimate paragraph; though here, too, he allows its historical provenance and features to remain 'unfixed':

> We are now in a period of crisis. Every man who is acutely alive is acutely wrestling with his own soul. The people that can bring forth the new passion, the new idea, this people will endure. Those others, that fix themselves in the old idea, will perish with the new life strangled unborn within them.

That last sentence is, of course, among other things, a reference to the musical orchestration of unnatural deaths in the novel, from the prophetic death of the drowned child who strangles, underwater, the doctor who tries to rescue her, which sets off two other deaths: the deceptively 'natural' death of the elder Mr Crich, the owner of the mines who dies mourning the child, and of his son Gerald, who, despite his new ideas about the business, is even more 'fixed' in the 'old idea' of control than his father is; his death, then, appropriately, has a frozen immobility.

These powerful symbolic, even allegorical, impulses in Lawrence are made at once complicated and material to us, in *Women in Love*, by being translated into the realm of style; style is where the concerns of the abstract symbolic order of the novel are turned into actual process. Lawrence is deliberate about his intentions, and it is the reason why he could not 'write in the same manner as *Sons and Lovers* again'; both before and after the paragraph in which he declares, 'We are now in a period of crisis', and speaks of the struggle with the 'soul', he's busy commenting on the business of translating that struggle into the processes of language, thereby making material, in the act of writing, the conflicts explored in the novel's mental symbolic order. It's no accident that, in the preceding paragraph, Lawrence points out that the 'struggle for verbal consciousness should not be left out in art'; and, in the final paragraph, the theme of 'crisis' is, once and for all, related to his preoccupation with style:

> In point of style, fault is often found with the continual, slightly modified repetition. The only answer is that it is natural to the author: and that every natural crisis in emotion or passion or understanding comes from pulsing, frictional to-and-fro, which works up to culmination.

Most modernists felt, of course, they were in a time of historical and spiritual crisis: David Jones and T.S. Eliot to do with the war, and with the disappearance of cultural resources, both pan-European and, in Jones's case, local and Welsh. For Ezra Pound, the crisis had to do with the contemporary scene in literary culture, a scene at once radical and dispiriting, as explored in *Hugh Selwyn Mauberley*; but also with the spread of the free market, resulting in the anti-Semitism that informed his championing of culture. (Art and culture, for Pound, as for others, were prey to the market and to business: 'Usura rusteth the chisel,' he said in the famous 'Usura' canto, 'It rusteth the craft and the craftsman/ It gnaweth the thread in the loom ...'[10] And the stereotypical Jew, as the title of the canto itself hints at, is, for Pound, a figure for the threat of the market. For Virginia Woolf, the crisis had to do with reality itself, and its representation in literature, a taking stock that directed both her experiments in fiction and her critique, in her essay, 'Mr Bennett and Mrs Brown', of the sort of 'realism' practised by Arnold Bennett. These are significant, sometimes disturbing, points of departure, and responses to the changed world; and, above all, they are significant because they're of their time and are characteristic of how we think of that time. Lawrence's crisis is significant, on the other hand, because it is odd and out of place and seems to occur some fifty or sixty years prior to its recognized moment; it has to do with a loss of faith in the Enlightenment, with the fact that the 'human', in its European construction, is finished, and that new epoch is defined by transactions of both power and fecund exchange between the self and the 'other', which, for Lawrence already, and increasingly, is the non-West. He is almost the first modern writer anywhere, let alone the first English one, to respond to the fact of what we now understand as 'alterity' and 'difference', and in a way that's at once more demanding, exhausting, moving, and less pat than the manner in which post-colonial writers (for whom 'difference' might be seen to be, at least in the eyes of the current orthodoxy, a legitimate concern) have often responded to the same things.

What's extraordinary about Lawrence's reaction to the crisis he perceived, to the inroads of the 'other' and to what he saw as the end of humanism, is that it's undertaken not only as prophecy and insight, but, especially since *Women in Love*, made deliberately material on the level of style. In particular, his constant testing, after *Sons and Lovers*, of the notion of 'good' or 'fine' writing, perplexing earlier admirers, is itself an attempt to breach paradigms like the 'literary', which make features, and even departures and experiments, in language recognizable within humanist conventions of reading. Indeed, to many of the earlier admirers, Lawrence appears to be marring, or, as I said before, 'muddying' his own work. And so, the struggle for, and spiritual negotiation of, power that Hugh Stevens,[11] for instance, sees as characteristics of both this novel and the story 'The Prussian Officer' (composed before it), can be seen to be played out not only in narrative, in the characters' lives, but in the act of composition itself; the author's relationship to language is not symbolically disjunctive or alienated, as it was with Eliot or Kafka, but agonistic.

For the modernists, language – and by implication, the act of creation – is often a metaphysical, Sisyphean burden, as well as compulsion. Kafka's work, thus, is full of images of fruitless and mysteriously obsessive labour; Beckett's narrator, at the end of *The Unnamable*, confesses, '… in the silence you don't know, you must go on, I can't go on, I'll go on';[12] and Eliot, in beautifully controlled language, speaks of the betrayals of language:

> ... Words strain,
> Crack and sometimes break, under the burden,
> Under the tension, slip, slide, perish,
> Decay with imprecision ...[13]

But Lawrence isn't interested in the metaphysical tension between language and silence, saying and not saying; what absorbs him is the relationship of power between author and material: 'Never trust the artist, trust the tale.' The implications of this are what preoccupy Lawrence when writing his review of Thomas Mann's *Death in Venice*, and in his view of Flaubert. The review was published in 1913, after he'd made his 'break' with *Sons and Lovers*, and begun to fashion the new language he'd explore first in *The Rainbow* and then, more comprehensively, in *Women in Love*. Mann's novella, for Lawrence, is an example of the 'will of the writer' striving 'to be greater than and undisputed lord and master over the stuff he writes which is figured to the world in Gustave Flaubert.' And further:

> Thomas Mann seems to me the last sick sufferer from the complaint of Flaubert. The latter stood away from life as from a leprosy. And Thomas Mann, like Flaubert, feels vaguely that he has in him something finer than ever physical life revealed. Physical life is a disordered corruption against which he can fight with only one weapon, his fine aestheticism, his feeling for beauty, for perfection, for a certain fitness which soothes him, and gives him an inner pleasure, however corrupt the stuff of life might be.[14]

Once more, 'physical life' or 'life' is, for Lawrence, a complex oppositional weapon in his attack upon the old language of humanism; it represents an opening out in that language, and not just a grand disavowal of the aesthetic, as is, say, Wilfred Owen's declaration in his manifesto for his war poems, 'Above all, I am not interested in poetry'. Lawrence himself, in *Women in Love*, is interested in opening himself to the 'other', not only in terms of subject matter, but on the experiential and material level of style. He wishes to open style out, unprecedentedly in the strategic deliberateness of this ambition, on to its 'other', 'bad' style (one thinks of Eliot's innocently supercilious, 'To me, also, he seems often to write very badly: but to be a writer who had to write often badly in order to write sometimes well'), on to overwriting, to the 'continual, slightly modified repetition'. It's not a question, any more, after *Women in Love*, of writing 'badly' or writing 'well' – 'I shan't write in the same manner as *Sons and Lovers* again,' he'd said – but of involving both author and material in an agonistic relationship that would exist on various levels: between writer and craft ('Never trust the artist, trust the tale'), the self and the 'other', the West and the non-West, style and 'bad writing'. 'The latter stood away from life as from a leprosy,' he said of Flaubert; Lawrence not only wanted, it seems, his work to be *about* life, but, strange as it may sound, as style, to *become* it. One should add immediately that he didn't want to anthropomorphize style ('How stupid anthropomorphism is!' reflects Ursula; Lawrence detested anthropomorphism, as another attempt to impose a human paradigm upon the non-human, and, by metaphorical extension, the non-Western), nor to organicize it, to 'breathe life' into it; by turning style into 'life', he wished to effect a radical break between it and its humanist conception.

The shrewd Mann, whom Lawrence underestimated, would have been one of the very few novelists at that time who'd have seen, in a more accurate way than Eliot, what it was that so profoundly exercised Lawrence – not perhaps to pursue the latter's example himself, but to allow that vantage-point to transform his own thoughts, especially in *Dr Faustus*. At one point in that late work, Mann implicitly critiques his own work in the terms that Lawrence had earlier; critiquing it, that is, not from the emergent position of the modernism of the time, where style and form are caught between the poles of the conventional and the experimental, but where they are situated on the dividing line between culture and its 'other'. And so, when the academic Serenus Zeitblom points out to the composer Leverkühn that 'the alternative to culture is barbarism', Leverkühn replies that 'barbarism is the antithesis of culture only within a structure of thought that provides us the concept. Outside of that structure the antithesis may be something quite different or not even an antithesis at all.'[15] For Lawrence, the oppositional friction between man and woman in *Women in Love* is only one part of its constant argumentation on what's culture and its 'other'; as is, crucially, style. Here, in this brief, animated discussion in the 'Moony' chapter between the two sisters, the schoolteacher Ursula (who's in love with Birkin, the Lawrence-figure in the novel) and the artistic Gudrun, we are reminded of the 'impossibility' of Lawrence's quest ('impossible' both in the literal sense, and in the social one, meaning 'wearing' or 'frustrating') – to move toward the 'antithesis' that is 'something quite different or not even an antithesis at all':

> 'Yes', cried Ursula, 'too much of a preacher. He is really a priest.'
> 'Exactly!' He can't hear what anybody else has to say – he simply cannot hear. His own voice is so loud.'
> 'Yes. He cries you down.'
> 'He cries you down,' repeated Gudrun. 'And by mere force of violence. And of course it is hopeless. Nobody is convinced by violence. It makes talking to him impossible – and living with him I should think would be more than impossible.'

'You don't think one could live with him?' asked Ursula.

'I think it would too wearing, too exhausting. One would be shouted down every time ... He cannot allow that there is any other mind than his own. And then the real clumsiness of his mind is its lack of self-criticism – . No, I think it would be perfectly intolerable.'

Lawrence is ironicizing himself, of course, as he does brilliantly in the chapter 'Gudrun in the Pompadour', in which a group of Birkin's bohemian acquaintances read out and mock one of his high serious, exhortatory letters in a café. But self-mockery, comedy, characterization, are as indispensable to the economy of the novel as is its utter investment in the notions and experiences of 'clumsiness' and the 'intolerable', notions which these staged scenes expertly introduce. Certainly, the openness to the 'other' brings, from this novel onwards, an element of 'clumsiness' and the 'intolerable' to Lawrence's writing; in his response to the 'other', to the non-West, even to 'primitive' art, and in the way he responds to them, Lawrence both belongs to, and departs radically from, the modernist temper. *Women in Love* is scattered with references to, and encounters with, African art; but the 'primitive' is not brought into the domain of 'high' culture, as it is with modernism – it remains a wonder, but also a breach, an 'obscenity' (and it was obscenity, as defined then in England, that had got Lawrence's previous novel into trouble); 'obscenity' not only as vulgarity, but as the incongruous, the 'intolerable'.

> It was an ordinary London sitting-room in a flat, evidently taken furnished, rather common and ugly. But there were several negro statues, wood-carvings from West Africa, strange and disturbing, the carved negroes looked almost like the foetus of a human being. One was of a woman sitting naked in a strange posture, and looking tortured, her abdomen stuck out ... The strange, transfixed, rudimentary face of the woman again reminded Gerald of a foetus, it was also rather wonderful, conveying the suggestion of the extreme of physical sensation, beyond the limits of physical consciousness.
>
> 'Aren't they rather obscene?' he asked, disapproving.
>
> 'I don't know,' murmured the other rapidly. 'I have never defined the obscene. I think they are very good.'

Gerald's interlocutor is the Russian who, with the members of the bohemian set described in this chapter in the 'rather common and ugly' London flat, will arraign and ridicule Birkin's letter in the Pompadour Café; will arrive, through the letter, at a definition of the 'obscene'. In the 'Pompadour Café' chapter, Lawrence implicitly, but palpably I think, connects the question of 'otherness', the 'rather wonderful' but 'rather obscene' statues in the London flat, to the question of style and language, in this case in Birkin's letter, which Halliday, the one reading it out, calls, sneeringly, 'absurdly wonderful'. The 'other' or the non-Western does not figure in the economy of *Women in Love* as the African mask does in Picasso, or the Japanese prints in Van Gogh, as a fresh and untapped vernacular resource; or as the directives from the *Upanishads* at the end of *The Waste Land* do, transformed into a cosmopolitan, high cultural utterance. In each of these cases, the non-Western enters, and then is domesticated, in a humanist/ modernist economy of representation; in *Women in Love*, the 'other' figures as a relinquishing of Flaubertian 'control', a feature of language that's 'impossible', 'clumsy', 'obscene', 'absurdly wonderful', 'intolerable'.

Here, in *Women in Love*, Lawrence begins to create a critical language of binaries that he'd develop thenceforth till the end of his life; but these binaries are made problematic and aesthetically challenging – they aren't 'fixed', to use a common Lawrentian pejorative, but are in a state of bewildering but intriguing realignment, and for a number of reasons. One of them is the curious but astonishing way in which Lawrence manages to insert his overarching quest, the quest to go outside of Western humanism, into the English novel of the great tradition, so making that novel 'different' from itself. He doesn't 'move on' from the great tradition, or break it up formally, or introduce, paradoxically, the epic into everyday bourgeois space, all of which the modernists do; instead of abandoning the language of the great tradition, he turns it, in *Women in Love*, upon itself. Never have the English realist novel and post-humanist essay come together in this way before or since. The binaries are caught and embedded, always, in this transition, and meshed in the language's turning upon itself; they are never quite available outside it. Often his very imaginative powers as a novelist give to whatever seems negative or 'fixed', on the level of the narrative's relentless theorizing, an incomparable elegiac force. Gerald is such a character, cast in the Flaubertian mould of being 'greater than and undisputed lord and master over the stuff' of 'life' and its 'disordered corruption', emblematizing, then, part of the architecture the novel wants to shake off – yet in the contradictory pull we, and Birkin, and, indeed, Lawrence, feel toward him, he's essential to that act of 'shaking off' remaining 'unfixed' and in a Lawrentian way 'impossible'. Lawrence's polemic never lets up, but neither does the performance of its compositional dynamics and writerly emotion; and this is what makes reading *Women in Love* such an unsettling and unique experience, where we're constantly traversing the distance between resistance and awakening. The resistance is caused by the odd, heavy proximity between the writing and the ideas; between the insistence of the style, the argument, and the very world that's being described. It is not a 'novel of ideas', though it's nothing without them, and nor is it the opposite of such a novel, the novel of style and sensation and psychology, such as Eliot ascribed to James, when he said that the latter had a mind so fine that it was never marred by a single idea; our awakening as readers comes in the midst of our grudging realization that *Women in Love* is 'difficult' in a Lawrentian, rather than modernist, way, that it is perverse and will not accept the common ground on which such distinctions are erected.

Lawrence's binaries, to do with 'light', 'the sun', the 'crystalline', the transparent, and the 'fixed' on the one hand, and with the 'melting', the 'muddy', 'flux', 'corruption', and especially 'darkness' on the other, are complicated by the fact that at least some of them derive from a common pool that has been made use of before, and would continue to be used by the modernists and the symbolists. 'Light' and 'dark', the binary that derives its immemorial authority from religion, is powerfully coopted, as we know, into the secular metaphysics of symbolism and, later, absurdist literature; but Lawrence's use of the binary, which might seem to locate him in the common pool I mentioned, is actually quite different, and is part of an anti-metaphysic. Claiming to abandon the visual mode after *Sons and Lovers* – 'I have no longer the joy in creating vivid scenes … I don't care much more about accumulating objects in the powerful light of emotion, and making a scene of them' – Lawrence speaks in a curious and striking rhetorical language that leads us to Derrida's insight about 'light' and 'seeing' being foundational tropes for Western metaphysics. Something like a premonition of the Derridean critique about the controlling dimension of the visual is already at play in the uneasy statement about 'accumulating objects in the powerful light of emotion'. Derrida, of course, notes the tropes of light in the language of what he calls 'Western metaphysics' – for instance, when we speak of the 'clarity' of an idea, or of 'seeing' the way in which an argument makes sense, or an idea as an 'illumination', or of understanding something in the 'light' of an idea. A source of metaphorical light in language makes it possible for us to think of the mental and actual worlds we inhabit in terms of clarity, perspective, distance, transparency, as well as of their absence; as M.H. Abrams, a critic of Derrida, but one of his most lucid commentators, remarks, the 'sun … serves Derrida himself as a prime trope of the founding presence, or logos.'[16] The visual as a medium of power, and a metaphor for absolute knowledge: this is what Lawrence means when he speaks about 'accumulating objects' in a 'powerful light' – 'powerful' in a theological and authoritative sense. Again and again, the image of water at night-time, 'unfixed' and refractive, preoccupies the novel, as in the 'Water-Party' chapter, in which people in boats move about with lanterns on the lake:

The dark woods on the opposite shore melted into universal shadow. And amid this universal undershadow, there was a scattered intrusion of lights. Far down the lake there were fantastic pale strings of colour, like beads of wan fire, green and red and yellow. The music came out in a little puff, as the launch, all illuminated, veered into the great shadow, stirring her outlines of half-living lights, puffing out her music in little drifts.

Here is a chapter that begins as an eerie celebration of community and ends as a doom-laden record of the individual consciousness, with the drowning of a child and a young man. If light is humanist consciousness, the chapter becomes an essay in which argument is translated into experience, event, and form – never rejecting the visual, but grappling with it – while uncannily foreseeing Lawrence's own words in *Apocalypse*: 'There is nothing of me that is alone and absolute except my mind, and we shall find that the mind has no existence by itself. It is only the glitter of the sun on the surface of the water.'[17]

Indeed, sun and daylight and consciousness are brought together in the story of the Criches, the powerful mining family, as it's gradually transformed from a moving realist tale about the vicissitudes of English economic power into an apocalyptic narrative about humanism. The elder Crich, Thomas, dies more than midway into the novel, 'slowly, terribly slowly … only half-conscious – a thin strand of consciousness linking the darkness of death with the light of day'. That consciousness is to be inherited and sustained by the son, Gerald; and Lawrence's uncharacteristic pun on 'son', as Gerald stands at the dying man's bedside, restates his insistent polemic against light: 'Every morning, the son stood there, erect and taut with life, gleaming in his blondness.' Birkin, on the other hand, is 'wavering, indistinct, lambent'.

Again, these dualities between the principal characters culminate in the chapters at the end, beginning with 'Snow': familiar modernist symbolic terrain rewritten in the terms of Lawrence's anti-metaphysic as Birkin, Ursula, Gudrun, and Gerald come to Innsbruck for what will be a tragic vacation for the latter: 'Birkin was on the whole dim and indifferent, drifting along in a dim, easy flow, unnoticing and patient, since he came abroad, whilst Gerald, on the other hand, was intense and gripped into white light, agonistes.' (Indeed, the words from *Apocalypse* are echoed again, in regard to Gerald, after the friends' arrival at their hotel: 'When they had bathed and changed, Gerald came in. He looked shining like the sun on frost.')

After *Sons and Lovers*, Lawrence would recurrently explore the relinquishing of the visual (in spite, or perhaps because, of being such an astonishingly visual, even visionary, writer), and what that implied in terms of 'contact' – both literal 'contact', or touch, as well as the metaphorical but profound confrontation with 'otherness'. In the story, 'The Blind Man', the eponymous protagonist, thus, 'seemed to know the presence of objects before he touched them':

> It was a pleasure to him to rock thus through a world of things, carried on the flood in a sort of blood-prescience ... So long as he kept this sheer immediacy of blood-contact with the substantial world he was happy, he wanted no intervention of visual consciousness. In this state there was a certain rich positivity, bordering sometimes on rapture. Life seemed to move in him like a tide lapping, lapping, and advancing, enveloping all things darkly.[18]

In the story, touch leads to an inadmissible form of 'contact' – between the blind protagonist and another man, a visitor to the house. The abnegation of the visual, tellingly, leads to a fluid and liquid state, a 'flood ... of blood-prescience', 'a tide lapping, lapping ... enveloping all things darkly'. We begin to understand now what Lawrence is attempting with his images of darkness, water, and the moon (contrasted always with images of fixity, frozenness, and solidity) in *Women in Love*: not so much to abandon the visual, as to turn the visual against itself.

All the while, in this novel, but especially in the last chapters set in snow country, Lawrence is developing the poetics of an anti-humanist style. To this end, he reiterates and orchestrates here a series of what will become increasingly familiar contrasts. On the one hand, we are told of the crystalline ('For Gudrun herself, she seemed to pass altogether in the whiteness of snow, she became a pure, thoughtless crystal'), and the deathly, as well as of the culture of the 'late eighteenth century, the period of Goethe and of Shelley, and of Mozart', which Gudrun and Loerke take a 'sentimental, childish delight in' praising as 'by-gone things ... the achieved perfections of the past'; and, on the other, we are shown Ursula's longing to escape the 'terrible static, ice-built mountain-tops' into 'earthy fecundity' and 'dark earth'. Here, Lawrence is citing fixity, conflict, and process not only as the novel's preoccupations, but its very language and form. Soon after he completed *Women in Love*, he would, in attempting to arrive at a radical definition of poetic form in 'Poetry of the Present' (written 1918–19), seem to refer to the snowed-up landscape and its tragic denouement, its vision of crystalline fixity in ice and Gerald's frozen corpse, again:

> The ideal – what is the ideal? A figment. An abstraction. A static abstraction, abstracted from life. It is a fragment of the before or after. It is a crystallised aspiration, or a crystallised remembrance: crystallised, set, finished. It is a thing set apart, in the great storehouse of eternity, the storehouse of finished things.19

As I've said, it's difficult, in this great novel, to discuss his binaries as if they were categories that preceded or stood outside the language they were formulated in. Lawrence's crucial oppositions in its final chapters, between the 'static, ice-built mountain-tops' and 'earthy fecundity', are, 'Poetry of the Present' reminds us, to be found in language, while at once being *of* language:

> There is poetry of this immediate present, instant poetry, as well as poetry of the infinite past and the infinite future. The seething poetry of the incarnate Now is supreme ... In its quivering momentaneity it surpasses the crystalline, pearl-hard jewels, the poems of the eternities.[20]

The 'poems of the eternities' are, the essay tells us, the 'treasured, gem-like lyrics of Shelley and Keats', the products of the 'late eighteenth century, the period of Goethe and of Shelley, and of Mozart' that Gudrun and Loerke spend hours discussing in the snowed-up hotel. With this novel, Lawrence departs, as Birkin and Ursula do briefly toward the end, before returning to the scene of tragedy, the 'great storehouse of eternity, the storehouse of finished things'; and the binaries that govern the narrative become problematized by becoming entangled in his exploration of, and struggle with, style.

Champion of Hide and Seek
Raj Kamal Jha's Surrealism

This book begins to narrate its story, or stories, with the picture on the jacket; the story has begun, then, even before we've reached the first page. After a dedication to the author's parents, we encounter a quotation from Paul Auster's *Mr Vertigo*, which expresses, deadpan, the following view on flying, or weightlessness, or 'hovering in the air': 'Deep down, I don't believe it takes any special talent for a person to lift himself off the ground and hover in the air. We all have it in us – every man, woman, and child.' Then we arrive at page one, whose opening sentences calmly exhort us: 'Look at the picture on the cover, there's a child, a girl in a red dress; there's a bird, a crow in a blue white sky. And then there are a few things you cannot see.' We look, and there is indeed a picture of a girl in a red dress, an anklet around her left ankle, hair coming down below her shoulders, standing very straight and looking out from a balcony, while a bird flies to her right.

In *If You Are Afraid of Heights*, his second novel, Raj Kamal Jha seems to be trying to make the book, in its material incarnation, a part of the narrative experience; to bring to it life and motion, not in a magical or anthropomorphic sense, but in a way that's nonetheless unexpected and strains at the limits of possibility. This impulse to involve the inanimate or the non-human in the story, to give it agency, is evident again in the description of a building on the first page. Having told us to 'Look at the picture on the cover,' the narrator goes on to discuss 'a few things you cannot see' in it; for instance, the building on whose balcony the girl in the red dress is standing:

> a building that, from the street outside, looks like a crying face. Its windows are the eyes, half-closed by curtains, smudged and wrinkled. Rain, wind and sun of countless years have marked the wall, streaking it in several lines, two of which look like lines of tears, one falling below each window. The

mouth is the balcony, curved down under the weight of iron railings, rusted and misshapen. Like the stained teeth of someone very sad. And someone very old.

Jha isn't interested here in personification or allegory, or in exhuming the discredited pathetic fallacy. As you read the novel, you discover that, though the three stories that comprise it have human characters and a mystery or quest at their centre, it's the casual but persistent non-human or disembodied elements in each tale – a child's cry, trams, an antique shop, a crow – that both withhold meaning from, and confer it on, the characters, and the readers. The characters themselves – with the exception of some in the second story – are deliberately emptied of psychological inwardness, and have the odd plangency of figures in a primer (indeed, in the last story, the connection between the novel's characters and those in a child's English primer is made more explicit). The world of insensate things – of machines, rooms and objects – and of animals has an eerie unpredictability, a suggestion of menace and a capacity to astonish. What you get in this novel is not a cute anthropomorphism – although a man flying above the city on a crow is central to it – or a magic realist addiction to the miraculous and to allegories of national history. I was reminded more of Dalí: 'After Freud it is the outer world, the world of physics, which will have to be eroticized and quantified.' It is with the eroticization of 'the outer world', beginning with the cover of the book and the exhortation to study it, that Jha's novel is concerned, and it's a project that few other novels in the English language – although there are notable lineages in European art and cinema – have undertaken with comparable seriousness and imagination.

The first story begins with a paragraph that briefly summarizes what it's about:

> Once upon a time in the city, there lived a woman called Rima and a man called Amir and late one night, they met in an accident, face to face, she picked out the shards of broken glass from his face, they fell in love and just when it seemed they were settling down to live happily ever after, a strange little thing happened one night: Rima woke up hearing a child cry.

The rest of the story fills out what happened until the night 'Rima woke up hearing a child cry'. Amir works in a post office in 'this dying city', which the narrator never names, but which, to judge by the landmarks, descriptions, and some of the street names, is Calcutta. He is an 'Extra Departmental Agent' – someone who has 'a government job' which 'isn't a permanent one'. He lives in the building that, 'from the street outside, looks like a crying face'. Inside his flat, things aren't much better: his 'toilet bowl is white, cracked in several places where his shit gets stuck so that even though he pours in half a bottle of acid every other morning, the stains don't go away'. Amir is of 'medium height, medium age, medium weight . . . everything medium. Even in colour, he's medium brown.'

In a way, Amir is reminiscent of Auden's 'unknown citizen' who 'was found by the Bureau of Statistics to be/ One against whom there was no official complaint' and 'worked in a factory and never got fired/ But satisfied his employers, Fudge Motors Inc.' However: 'Was he free? Was he happy? The question is absurd:/ Had anything been wrong, we should certainly have heard.' There are differences between the ironic martyrdom Auden confers on his 'unknown citizen', and Jha's sense of the social injustice faced by Amir, which – although the narrator tells us there are 16 million others like him in the city – is compounded by a sense of mystery and even desire. Auden calls his unknown person a 'saint', 'in the modern sense of an old-fashioned word'; Jha places his protagonist in a deliberately implausible and abortive relationship with Rima. The novel's eroticism is emphasized by its silences: the narrator doesn't point out that Amir is a Muslim name, Rima a Hindu one; the names' mirror images, their concordances and dislocations, nudge our subconscious, as the word 'ambulance' does when its letters are seen the wrong way round – distress and terror are momentarily subsumed by confusion, mystery and comedy.

One afternoon, after finishing work at the post office, Amir takes a desultory walk down Park Street, peering into, and being rebuffed at, one of its antique shops, and later strolls down Free School Street to pay his customary visit to a prostitute. Later still, presumably close to midnight, he takes a tram to Esplanade, and is knocked unconscious in a freak collision with another tram: the first collision of its kind, the papers report the next day, to have taken place in the city. Amir wakes up to find himself in an impossibly luxurious apartment at a great height, being looked after by Rima, who apparently picked him up at the site of the accident. It gradually dawns on him that he's in Paradise Park, an extraordinary new building of mythical height and stature which he's heard of but never been inside. As he recovers, he rediscovers the city from one of the windows in his room, toy-like and transformed, its furthest, most hidden corners now suddenly visible. He begins a relationship with Rima; they start to go out for secret walks. On one of these excursions, they go to Amir's old flat, the flat in the house with 'a crying face', with its cracked and stained toilet bowl and its badly lit rooms. Here, tending to an injured bird they pick up off the street, they begin to lead a proxy life, the man still not going to work, the woman absent from her home; they lead this life, that is, till the woman repeatedly hears a child's cry – the moment at which the narrative began. Going out one night to find where the cry was coming from, she vanishes; Amir can't find her.

Jha was born and grew up in Calcutta, and as this novel and his first, more tentative work, *The Blue Bedspread*, show, it's crucial to his imagination; it's equally clear that Jha doesn't want to write a novel of place – that, in some senses, he's mysteriously fascinated with unravelling such a novel. In this book, there is a feeling that a story and locale have been composed, arrived on the brink of recognizability, and then have gently been taken apart. This gives the reader the mixture of freedom, participation and abnegation from volition that people have when they're dreaming – the sense, at once, of helplessness and agency. Real streets and roads in Calcutta are combined with sites and structures that are both fantastic and imaginary, like Paradise Park. (It's true, however, that more and more walled cities for the rich are being built in Calcutta, and often have similarly mawkish names: Sherwood, Highland Park etc.) Everyday details or the flotsam of the contemporary world – a sign at a beauty parlour, a poster for *Indecent Proposal* – coexist with a man on a crow, flying above the city and looking into people's lives.

These disjunctions aren't undertaken with magic realist euphoria, however, but have a compelling ordinariness. The phrase that J.G. Ballard uses to distinguish Dalí's work from that of other Surrealist painters – 'hallucinatory naturalism' – is also apposite to Jha's writing in this book. 'For the most part,' Ballard says, 'the landscapes of Ernst, Tanguy and Magritte describe impossible or symbolic worlds – the events within them have "occurred", but in a metaphorical sense. The events in Dalí's paintings are not far from our ordinary reality.' While the 'symbolic world' of Ballard's Surrealists allegorizes the subconscious, the magic realists allegorize history. Here, too, Jha is singular in the way he relinquishes any straightforward relationship to national history, while situating his fantasy imperceptibly but firmly in the tumult of a globalizing India. This sentence from Ballard's essay on Dalí's art describes Jha's work, at first glance, even better than it does Dalí's: 'Elements from the margins of one's mind – the gestures of minor domestic traffic, movements through doors, a glance across a balcony – become transformed into the materials of a bizarre and overlit drama.' I'd only replace 'overlit', which is apposite to Dalí, with 'underlit': there's a strong sense in the preponderantly nocturnal landscape of Jha's novel of poorly lit rooms and streets.

The subject of the second narrative is hinted at in the first one, in a newspaper headline Amir notices casually as he's having sex with the prostitute: 'He moves inside her, his faces inches above hers, she moves, her hair brushes against his eyes, he brushes it away, he can see yesterday's newspaper stuck to the window frame, *Girl Found Dead in Small Town*, he reads.' The eleven-year-old found raped and possibly murdered next to a canal in a small town outside the city may or not be the girl in the newspaper in the prostitute's room; according to the post-mortem report, she was wearing a red frock at the time of her death, like the girl on the cover. What do these connections add up to? As if to uncover their significance, a reporter from the city, a woman called Mala, arrives at the small town on a day of rains and waterlogging, and interviews the 'Post-Mortem Man', who works in a 'small building, red in colour with an asbestos roof that gleams in the half-light of this half-afternoon'; she also interviews the girl's mother, one of the many part-time workers who live in the town, who responds in detail to Mala's questions about the girl's red frock, an object of desire in a shop window that had been bought recently; she interviews, too, after a journey through the waterlogged streets, a police officer. She finds out nothing. The only help she gets, which doesn't amount to very much, is from a mysterious intruder in her room, a man called Alam. Again, Alam's name is a mirror-image of Mala's; that the first is a Muslim name and the second a Hindu one is, once more, not remarked on.

The last, and shortest, section is narrated by a girl who lives with her parents in the house with 'a crying face'. There's been an epidemic of suicides in the city lately, and the girl is seized by a terror that her parents might be the next to die. One night she finds a 'friend' underneath her bed, a man who calls himself the 'Champion of Hide and Seek', a man you can't ordinarily see, who reassures the girl that her parents will be all right. He has been keeping an eye on the mother and father – simultaneously – and taking photographs of the father's day. He shows her the photographs: they are hypnotically unremarkable – what comes to mind is again Ballard's phrase, 'hallucinatory naturalism'. Father at a bus stop; Father in his office; Father looking at a poster in a shop window; Father – and this picture was apparently the most difficult to take – by a window inside a tram. Now the man's task is over; as he leaves, he does something extraordinary: he gets onto the back of a crow and, as the girl watches from the balcony, flies away. We are being asked not only to partake of the truth of a childish fantasy, but to return to the picture on the cover and study it, to participate in Dalí's 'eroticization of the outer world'.

One reason *If You Are Afraid of Heights* is *sui generis* is that its provenance is not literary at all, but lies in film, in what's misleadingly called 'world cinema' (as if Hollywood weren't part of the world, or the world were an obscure suburb of Hollywood). Tarkovsky, with his obsessions with time, space and the supernatural; Buñuel and Almodóvar, with their peculiar, tragicomic transitions – these films are destined to remain foreign, even to those who speak the language they're made in, because foreignness is their impulse and topos: in spite of their Russian or Spanish temperament, they speak another language. One might say the same of Jha's remarkable novel.

Midnight at Marble Arch
On *The Reluctant Fundamentalist*
by Mohsin Hamid

In 1989, I was invited to a party in London. I was a graduate student in Oxford, supposedly writing a dissertation on D.H. Lawrence, but actually doing nothing of the sort. Instead, I'd completed a short novel; an extract from it had appeared in this paper, as had a poem and a review. It was on the basis of these that I must have been invited that night to the party, which was a celebration of the *London Review of Book*'s tenth anniversary.

Generally uncomfortable at literary gatherings, as all of us probably are, I was cushioned against the brunt of celebrity and erudite chatter by Dan Jacobson, my former tutor at University College London, and my fellow interloper for the evening. Various covers of past issues were on display, I seem to recall; one of them had a photograph of Salman Rushdie, which both Dan and I looked at disbelievingly, as you might at someone you'd known as a child, who'd become famous for some unforeseeable feat, like holding their breath for ten minutes underwater, or journeying to Jupiter; for the *fatwa* had been recently announced. In the midst of the laughter and condiments of the evening, we were suddenly reminded of what a serious business literature, and life, really were.

I was introduced to several people I admired, and mistaken for another Indian contributor, the late Raj Chandarvarkar, by Ian Jack. I ate canapés, searched for something to say to Frank Kermode, and had a glass of red wine. I generally feel neither one way or another about drinking, but my listlessness about consuming alcohol only offends Indian acquaintances, not Western ones. However, in Oxford, imbibing the occasional Port or wine was proving unavoidable, and not unpleasant.

It was mildly wet that evening, but it had stopped drizzling by the time I'd reached the stop at Marble Arch for the Citylink coach back to Oxford. It wasn't very late, and it must have been a weekday, because there was hardly anyone else at the stop. The other figure beside me, I realized with a sort of relief (certain emotions are as unpredictable as intakes of breath), was a South Asian – or, as I'd have probably thought in those days, 'someone from the sub-continent' – a man of my height and age. He warmed to me as well; just the nature of our glances was enough to establish that we weren't unhappy to see each other. Soon we began to talk; he was from Pakistan. This, after the small delay between hearing this and understanding it, pleased me; it gave a new dimension to the encounter; of the seemingly familiar becoming imperceptibly unfamiliar – and, as a result, promising.

He was not, I realized in a few minutes after we'd begun to talk, from the same class background as myself. His clothes were of a different weave; his English was different. And this, along with the fact that he was from Pakistan, not to speak of an openness and charm he had, was one of the reasons for my being attracted to his company. There are many upper-middle-class people in South Asia (as there probably are anywhere else) who feel at once less than themselves in, and superior to, their own class, and are drawn to people outside it. This might be a form of naivety as well as a sign of youthfulness; it's to invent someone else, and also to never quite delve properly into why one can't be with them for more than an hour-long journey, or the duration of a momentary encounter, to gloss over the reasons for meeting and separation, and the cause of the division. There's no real and enduring equality between the classes in India; yet the idea of class itself presupposes a notional human equality in a way in which caste, for instance (which plays a subliminal role amongst all religions in South Asia), doesn't. And yet, for all that, class, in this part of the world, carries with it an old, autochthonic magic, and, as a consequence, an offering – and often, by the upper classes, a presumption – of certain kinds of comfort. In a realm of putative equality, such as the Marble Arch coach stop, the lower-middle-class person might appear to possess a simplicity that is childlike to the upper-middle-class one, as well as a patience and clear-sightedness that reminds the latter of his parents, of the wisdom of age. It's possible that, for the lower-middle-class man, the other seems to be at once more privileged and educated, and less worldly-wise and intelligent; that he'd view him, then, with a mixture of envy and forbearance. Neither is absolutely sure, in their exchange with each other, of who's the child and who the adult, and at which particular point of time. This gives the encounter its promise as well as its misunderstandings and its share of unhappy surprises.

When the largely empty coach arrived, our casual but solicitous bonhomie, our comfortableness in one another's presence, meant that we sat next to each other without giving it too much thought. The conversation continued; until – I can't remember what took it in that direction – the subject of religion and belief came up. I didn't mind this. It's another thing I'd noticed in encounters of this sort as a student: that, talking across a semi-familiar, barely acknowledged divide of difference and even inequality, it's possible to broach the big subjects. The discussion might almost inevitably, at some point, tackle God, or destiny, or death. This might be an implicit, sly reference to the fact that fate – something that was seemingly entirely arbitrary – brought us together, and gave us our different futures. I was always deeply moved and illuminated by what I heard, because of the straightforwardly human, rather than oracular, quality of what was said. These were subjects and instincts you had to suppress among people of your own background; 'matters of life and death', for them, was incontrovertibly a euphemism – for deadlines and social commitments. In Oxford, for graduate students in the English department, it was even forbidden, I'd noticed, to speak about literature. This had little to do with an ideological position derived from critical theory, which belonged relatively to the background in 1989; it was simply a taboo that was commonly observed. Among Indian students, talk about human emotion in particular – falling in love, homesickness – was considered imbecilic; you had to talk about Junior Research Fellowships, Indian politics, American universities, or the joys of visiting Venice. In the end, I think it must have been homesickness that drew me to this man.

'But there is something I do not understand about Hinduism,' he said at one point, polite but forthright – yet maybe not absolutely forthright, because he was troubled by something beyond the question. It looked like a moment of reckoning, much-delayed, had come.

'What is it?' I asked; my smile was meant to be accommodating, but also to remind him, I hoped, that I wasn't a representative of the Hindu faith.

'The idea of reincarnation – I have a problem with it,' he said.

'Well, it's difficult to take literally,' I conceded.

'No, it is not a logical idea,' he persisted, frowning as the coach approached the darkness of the motorway without urgency. He was following a train of thought, and now he turned and confronted me, still, however, courteous. 'Suppose you were to die, but, some time before you died, you were to have relations with your wife.' There was no one at this time I knew that I wanted to marry, and I remember envisioning a faceless, elusive, vaguely Indian, woman. 'Suppose just after you died after having relations your wife became pregnant.' He looked at me and I nodded at the complexity of this strange, already posthumous future. 'Then,' here was the clincher, 'your soul, or whatever you call it, can enter the foetus in your wife's womb?' He stared at me in expectation; I was silent, and he took it to mean that I wasn't convinced. 'Can it not?' he asked, and I nodded distantly: 'I suppose it can.' 'That is,' he concluded vigorously, 'according to this idea, you can be born as your own son.'

He probably hadn't meant to challenge me; he'd probably sensed that I wasn't religious, and took this as an opportunity to clear up a metaphysical glitch with someone who at least nominally belonged to the faith.

'Religions are not rational,' I responded weakly; and then, because I could get childish in an argument, added, 'The Koran isn't completely logical, is it?'

'It is completely logical,' he corrected me. I have a memory of the eerie Hoover building passing by.

'Really?' I said. 'Everything in it makes sense?'

He turned to me, unruffled, as if to someone who was ignorant about the basic facts of existence. 'The Koran is completely logical because it is the only book in the world that is the word of God.' This was spoken with almost a publisher's zeal, a sales pitch to end all sales pitches.

My childish stubbornness was growing. 'How do you know?' I asked. He stared at me, again, as at an ignoramus, and I said, 'How do you know it is the word of God?'

'Because it says so in the Koran,' he replied. Instantly, his expression changed, as if he'd decided he wanted to shrug off this business; it didn't interest him any more. 'Excuse me, if I am not mistaken, you have been drinking?'

I stared at him, astonished that the anniversary wine, this residue of literary hobnobbing, should still be issuing from my breath (no wonder they call alcohol 'spirits'). Indignant, but not insulted, I said, 'I wasn't "drinking". I just had a glass of wine.'

After this, we reached a sort of impasse. We must have pretended to doze; I remember the lights coming on, and him getting off somewhere on the outskirts of Oxford. The episode has receded; but I've never forgotten it. It would be simple enough to dismiss the man's remarks as stereotypical; and yet I couldn't wish away his warmth, accessibility, the sense of comfort he gave forth. It was a comfort I couldn't have expected from someone of my own background (we might have never entered into a conversation); this was part of an older equation, thrown out of its own context, involving an old sense of dependence, and possibly, on my part, a subtle taking-advantage-of. Whether or not that equation was unfair and weighted on one side, which it was, it was useless to deny that its emotions were complex and real, especially in new and improvised situations. Our equality – at once both false and true – inside the coach had led him to open up with me, with such awkward results. Like Richard Dawkins and Christopher Hitchens, I believe that there are certain statements and positions you just can't agree with. Unlike them, though, I have a pathological inability to take extreme opinions or actions, including religious ones, at face value. I don't only mean that political parties – the BJP in India is a good example – blatantly manoeuvre religion for political gain (the issue of immigration for British political parties is a subtle, undeniable modulation upon this); I mean that there are certain views and acts – voiced on evangelical radio stations, executed by suicide bombers – that make you speculate about them beyond their stated motives and objectives. The realm of 'equality', too ill-defined and opaque a parameter, leads to some of these actions and opinions coming out into the open, and is ill-equipped to make sense of them once they do. Then, confusingly, there's the curious human affinity that draws us – not through conscious effort, or as a result of an education in multiculturalism – to those who are, culturally and in other ways, unlike us, until, sometimes, we realize with a shock that we don't know them. The unsaid is at work in motives and actions on both sides; in the group of people we call 'us', and in those we begin to name, at certain points of time, 'them'. The unsaid undercuts the dichotomy that Hitchens imposes on the debate, between the 'literalists' – the archbishops, priests, and mullahs, the unemployed bus driver or corporate professional turned 'fundamentalist' – and the 'ironists', or novelists like Salman Rushdie. Acceptably, irony is a manner of not saying something, or saying something and meaning the opposite; but the unsaid that governs the terrorist's attenuated destiny, the mullah's rant, and Hitchens's polemic, isn't irony, but something else.

As reviews of Mohsin Hamid's second novel began to appear earlier this year, I was reminded, for some reason, of that encounter from almost twenty years ago. Not that my story and Hamid's are exactly similar; but there are several points of contact. Sometimes, while reading reviews of a book, you find (especially if there's something about it that's begun to intrigue you) that you've begun to invent it, that you're already becoming familiar, in a silently persuaded way, with a work you really don't know; and, at some point, my story became part of what I imagined Hamid's novel to be. What had brought these two stories together – one a memory, the other an outline of a novel I hadn't read – in my mind was the crucial piece of information that Hamid's book was a monologue, or a possible dialogue in which you never heard the other voice, which emerges from a chance, even bizarre, encounter: between a Pakistani man and someone who at first appears to be an American tourist, on the streets of Lahore. The novel is structured around this encounter, but it isn't directly about it – what it's *about* (in the form of the long confession addressed to the hapless and increasingly 'reluctant' interlocutor) is the speaker's previous life in America, leading up to his present one in Lahore. But the idea of the encounter, and, along with it, of the present moment, the here and now, is an all-important one to the novel, despite the fact that – or maybe precisely because – it's a structural device, and primarily a part of what used to be called 'form', and only secondarily, and by implication, informing 'content'. These elements must have led to that feeling of growing recognition and to that interweaving in my mind; the notion of the unforeseen encounter, and its consequences, or its ultimate lack of consequence, and, more pressingly, that of the urgency of the present moment, its magic and deceptions, its spaciousness and promise, its political immediacy, and the constant, unfulfillable sense of illumination it offers.

Having become almost too well acquainted with my construct of the novel, I risked being disappointed when I read it. That wasn't to be so. The former was quite different from the latter, but the journey from one to the other was nevertheless seamless, and, from the start, I was gripped. The differences were obvious. Hamid's narrator, Changez, is neither entirely like me nor my companion on the coach. He is one of South Asia's proliferating, and, by now, customary success stories, the sort magazines probably leap to associate with India, but is equally true of Pakistan: a Princeton graduate, like his creator, Changez – again, not unlike Hamid – has worked in what might loosely be called the corporate-financial world of New York, a driven and exceptionally energetic domain. In contrast to, I strongly suspect, the man I met in Marble Arch, Changez used to be a believer in Western corporate meritocracy. Indeed, he'd been a star performer for an acquisitions firm called Underwood Samson; the fruits of belief have been tangible, and the costs – which Changez becomes more aware of after September 11 – intangible and alienating, as they often are. Changez had a girlfriend, Erica (most reviewers have pointed out Hamid's penchant for allegorical naming), a delicate, privileged, quite probably WASP woman with literary talent and ambitions with whom he had a curious, largely asexual relationship, something long on the verge of being resolved. The relationship, like Erica's sanity, begins to come undone by the second half of this short novel; she, under some mysterious psychological duress, possibly to do with Chris, a lover who died (several works are glancingly but effectively invoked by Hamid, including 'The Dead'), becomes increasingly inaccessible and remote. At the same time, Changez's treasured American self, especially after it experiences a contradictory and scandalous moment of happiness upon witnessing the destruction of the Twin Towers on television in a hotel room in Manila, begins to crumble, as does his sense of his corporate mission:

The following evening was supposed to be our last in Manila. I was in my room, packing my things. I turned on the television and saw what at first I took to be a film. But as I continued to watch, I realized that it was not fiction but news. I stared as one – and then the other – of the twin towers of New York's World Trade Center collapsed. And then I *smiled*. Yes, despicable as it may sound, my initial reaction was to be remarkably pleased.

Your disgust is evident; indeed, your large hand has, perhaps without your noticing, clenched into a fist.

'Not fiction but news': Hamid is unobtrusively, but constantly, hinting at us how to read his novel; how not to be manipulated and led in the way that, in a sense, Changez's companion is, but to become attuned to its hidden, recurrent inversions. There's an almost delightful allegorical symmetry to the flow of events, as well as a sensuousness and finish that might belong to some other form or art: music, perhaps. Despite its minute probing into the narrator's thoughts, this is not a conventional psychological novel; much of its magic – the enchantment and innocence of the relationship, the absolute familiarity and foreignness of America, the fragrant boisterousness and menace of Lahore – hinges on the unsaid. Hamid manages marvellously well in creating a novel that's rendered entirely in terms of the spoken word, and governed constantly by the shape of what's evaded or not uttered. Two registers of the word 'formal' come to mind as one reads. One has to do with politeness, etiquette, and even over-elaboration and circumlocution. In the book, it has to do with the way in which something spontaneous and immediate, like speech, is constantly qualified by adornment ('irresistibly refined or oddly anachronistic', as Changez says while speculating about the qualities in him she might have been drawn to), and comes to seem disorienting and at one remove. The other has to do with Hamid's own craft and practice; his working within the genre of the novella, James's 'blessed *nouvelle*', with its unique tensions, restrictions, and essential playfulness. The pressures and deflections of the form allow Hamid to visit the various genres that are common to South Asian Anglophone writing, which are often connected with the revelation of identity – autobiography; travelogue; the novel of diaspora or exile – and to commit himself to none of these. For both author and narrator are involved in certain kinds of disclosure, and yet are always making the temptations of disclosure and topicality (to do with Pakistani, immigrant, or Muslim identity; to do with 9/11) surrender to formal – in both senses of the word – considerations. The result is a cool equipoise such as is not possible in 'real life', where our desires for both the earthly and the immutable generally end up being so messy; but no less moving or true for having achieved a sort of perfection.

Beyond 'Confidence'
Rushdie and the Creation Myth of Indian English Writing

Just as there are two creation-myths in the Old Testament – the first to do with the making of the universe ('And God said let there be light'), the second with the creation of the human race – (Adam, Eve, the apple, the serpent) – there are two parables about the foundations of Indian writing in English. They move in a direction opposite to the one in Genesis. First, there's the story of temptation, deflowering, exile, retold in the metaphors of colonialism; the creation of Macaulay's bastard children is the equivalent of Adam's exit from Eden. The triumphal moment, the counterpart to the seven days of creation, comes more than a century later and can be dated: to AD 1981, when *Midnight's Children* was published and, more importantly, won the endorsement of the Booker Prize. Both award and awardee were thrown into the firmament like angels we've been contemplating, agog, ever since. Then, inevitably, the other planets, stars, and constellations began to appear.

This is how the parable of Indian writing in English runs for most Anglophone Indians, from the academic teaching English in San Jose to the journalist in Delhi. No argument, no appeal to history or fact, toward fashioning an alternative account, or accounts, of the brief history of this literature is going to penetrate the minds of those who feel they've been transformed by the revelatory force of the parable; cults have a particular immunity to history. What passes for discussion is really the sort of semi-paranoiac gossip that breeds inside cults; signs of loyalty and telltale marks by which to identify who belongs and who doesn't preoccupy the discussants. Does the author live in Europe or in America? Do they include a glossary in their work?

The analogy with the cult can only be stretched so far; for cults are fatally drawn to self-destructiveness. The *arriviste* middle-class Indian, however, who's largely taken over the discourse of English writing in India, is deeply enamoured of longevity, success, and, importantly, power. The literature, then, is described, by both critic and reporter, in terms ordinarily remote from criticism but perfectly sensible to the parvenu: 'Indian writing has arrived.' *Midnight's Children* is indispensable to this narrative. Ever since its appearance, 'confidence' has been a buzz-word in literary chatter: 'The new writers have a confidence the old ones didn't.' In what way is 'confidence' a characteristic of creativity? Self-doubt shapes and even makes necessary the act of creative exploration, an act accompanied, conversely, by self-belief, a very different thing from confidence. I can think of confidence as a descriptive term for artistic endeavour only when it comes to certain kinds of experimentation and risk-taking; John Coltrane's rendition of 'My Favourite Things' shows not only confidence, but audaciousness. The word might also be used of Muriel Spark's slender, peculiar, relentless novels; in India, in recent times, it's the Tamil writer Ambai who possesses that quality, in her ability to do very strange things, with a modicum of means, with the short story. It's lightness of touch, not grandeur of ambition, that requires confidence in writing; because it risks being misunderstood, or, what's more common, going unnoticed.

This isn't the sense in which those who speak of 'confidence' in Indian writing understand that term. What they mean is visibility, success, proximity to power. This confidence is a general, seamless metaphor for India in the age of globalization. Indeed, Indian writing in English, since Rushdie, has participated in a subtle but significant shift in register in the way India views itself and others: from a once-colonized nation 'finding its voice', to quote from V.S. Pritchett's review of *Midnight's Children*, to a player on the world stage with a 'say' in the world. A thin line divides post-colonial pride from imperialist ambition, separates the India trying to consolidate its democratic traditions from the India with Security Council aspirations; the story of Indian writing in English traverses, in the last twenty years, this journey, and is located where the dividing line's at its most blurred.

And so the Indian writer in English must be coopted into this narrative of success and record growth; anything else, during this watershed, is looked upon with anxiety. The writer mustn't cause anxiety; in our family romance, he's the son-in-law – someone we can be proud of, can depend on, who is, above all, a safe investment. He is solvent; preferably settled abroad. He's capable of addressing questions consonant with our emerging prestige. He is not a failure, a daydreamer, a misfit. The Anglophone intellectual tradition in India, unlike other intellectual lineages in modernity, has developed no space for daydreaming, irresponsibility, failure, or for the outsider; it has little understanding of the role these play in shaping the imaginative life. It is baffled, if not offended, by an indifference to lofty themes and causes; in the end, it's baffled by an indifference to power.

The triumphal narrative of Indian writing in English bores me; personally speaking, as a reader and writer, I feel almost no connection with it. I find no echo in its values and excitements of the sense of value and excitement that once brought me to writing. I think this sense of alienation (and at least some of us will have felt it, and, feeling it, wondered if it's an illness peculiar to ourselves) is more than vague disgruntlement; it's an important point of departure, a chance to abandon optimistic but invented paradigms in the interests of exploring fresh perspectives. Rushdie himself becomes a more complex and intriguing symbol once we start to look for him outside that story of empowerment – to locate him among his enthusiasms, his memory, his contradictions. For Rushdie's a great and often moving enthusiast; and what he enthuses over – painting, for instance, for which he has an eye; the astonishing Gujarati artist Bhupen Khakhar – makes him seem sometimes like a Bombay writer: not just a writer *about* Bombay, but, intellectually and emotionally, of it, possessing the gift of curiosity that the Bombay poets Nissim Ezekiel and Adil Jussawalla had, and which, in turn, drew *them* to the art-world and Khakhar in the 1970s. This sort of writer is at once interloper and observer; he has the air of a student, a learner. We find this writer in the Rushdie who admires a heterogeneity of stimuli besides the fabulist forebears he's associated with; the Rushdie who's quickened by Kipling, JG Ballard, Arun Kolatkar, and who's occasionally drawn irresistibly to an artist with an aesthetic radically different from his own, such as Satyajit Ray. It's difficult to fit this Rushdie into a bureaucratic paradigm. This Rushdie is louche, perpetually open to enthusiasm, incomplete, in the process of being made; we don't know him completely, but he has an odd intimacy, a neighbourliness, that the Rushdie of the other narrative doesn't.

We might say the same thing of modern Indian writing: that its most complex, persuasive, and delighting incarnation lies outside the story of empowerment and, by extension, of power. Both the Sanskrit aestheticians of antiquity and, much later, Philip Sydney, writing in the country that would one day colonize India, conceived of poetry and literature as a realm of radical freedom and autonomy. This, too, is how the site of literature and culture was delineated in modern India, around the middle of the nineteenth century: a realm of freedom that presaged and predated political freedom by almost a hundred years. But artistic and imaginative autonomy differed from the political autonomy that was to be fought for, and which would eventually come, in one fundamental respect: that while the latter necessarily entailed a hardening of identity, of Indian-ness, and a conflictual relationship with the colonizer, the former – the realm of imaginative autonomy – reserved the right to constantly redefine Indianness, to have no single, exclusive notion of it, and to be related to European culture not only oppositionally, but by creative curiosity. That's why Indian writing, in the last one hundred and fifty years, represents not so much a one-dimensional struggle for, or embodiment of, power, as a many-sided cosmopolitanism. It isn't enough, today, to celebrate Indian writing's 'success', after having identified what its marks of success are (as if a whole tradition must only, and constantly, be thought of as an *arriviste* would be); one needs to engage with its long, subterranean history (as hard-earned as political freedom itself) of curiosity and openness.

Notes

Introduction: On Clearing a Space

1. Chatterjee has thought in his own interesting way about this problem. See his essay, 'The Fruits of Macaulay's Poison Tree', in *The Truth Unites: Essays in Tribute to Samar Sen*, ed. Ashok Mitra (Calcutta, 1985).
2. Dutt (1824–73), author of, among other works, the poem *Meghnadbadhakabya* (1861), his refashioning of an episode from the *Ramayana*.
3. Naidu, 1879–1949, popular poet, first Indian woman to become President of the Indian National Congress, and first woman to be governor of an Indian state.

Poles of Recovery

First published in a different version in *Interventions: A Journal of Postcolonial Studies*, 2002

1. That conviction has been belied by my taking up the guitar once more as a compositional tool for the kinds of musical experimentation I'm now interested in.

In the Waiting-Room of History: On 'Provincializing Europe'

First published in the *London Review of Books*, 2004

The Flute of Modernity: Tagore and the Middle Class

First published in the *New Republic*, 1999

1. *Rabindranath Tagore: The Myriad-Minded Man,* by Krishna Dutta and Andrew Robinson, St Martin's Press.
2. Since this piece appeared, the monograph has been reissued, thankfully, by Papyrus; but it is still difficult to locate in bookshops.
3. *Rabindranath Tagore: An Anthology,* edited by Krishna Dutta and Andrew Robinson, St Martin's Press

The East as a Career: On 'Strangeness' in Indian Writing

First published in the *New Left Review*, 2006

1. I mean to imply, by this term, a mixture of an openness to markets and a fidelity to the conventions of Western art that's quite different from the partly ironical and belligerently playful intentions of 'magic realism' in postmodernity.

Argufying: On Amartya Sen and the Deferral of an Indian Modernity

First published in the *Times Literary Supplement*, 2005

'Huge Baggy Monster': Mimetic Theories of the Indian Novel after Rushdie
First published in the *Times Literary Supplement*, 1999

1.   R.K. Narayan wittily introduces the theme of 'copying' and its relationship, in the context of post-coloniality, to creativity, in *The English Teacher*, where the protagonist passes off 'She was a phantom of delight' as his own poem to his wife

Two Giant Brothers: Tagore's Revisionist 'Orient'
First published in the *London Review of Books*, 2006

Travels in the Subculture of Modernity
First published in two parts in the *Times Literary Supplement*, 2003

1.   2002.

2.   In this context, see, while making the necessary distinctions and qualifications, Hannah Arendt's summary, in her introduction to *Illuminations*, of Walter Benjamin's 'ideal of producing a work consisting entirely of quotations', where, oddly, the excerpts 'constituted the main work, with the writing as something secondary'. In an anthology, of course, the excerpts are the 'main work' – an agglomeration of other people's work. But if the anthology is conceived of as an essay, that is, not only a selection from a literature, but as a commentary on, and critique of, a literature and its means of representation, then the predominance of the quotation or excerpt must serve to challenge or ironicize the idea of the 'main work'. For, in the conventional essay, the quotation is always distinct from, and 'secondary' to, the commentary.

3.   In this context, one might recall, for the sake of comparison, Kafka's repression of his own body, of which he was ashamed because of its thinness. In *The Lessons of Modernism*, Gabriel Josipovici has spoken of the fact that one of the many things that Kafka envied, admired, and resented in his father was his 'mere physical presence'. Josipovici also relates how Kafka decided not to accompany his fiancée Felice and her friend Greta Bloch to the Baltic because, as he confessed later in writing to a friend, 'I was ashamed of my thinness and my usual pusillanimity.' In a letter, Kafka speaks of how he used to once row up the river Moldau in a bathing-suit; at one point, he says, he would 'let the current take me down' as he stretched out on his back while the boat passed under the bridges. 'An employee of the office,' he says, 'who had once seen me from one of the bridges ... summed it up in these words: it reminded one a little of the Last Judgement at the precise moment when the lids of the coffins are lifted and the dead still lie there, motionless.' Elias Canetti comments: 'The figure of the thin man and the dead man are seen as one and the same ...' Post-Renaissance, the body, in Western art, is almost always idealized; the thin or ungainly body is repressed, unrepresented, or, as Canetti notes, made synonymous with death. Perhaps something like this neurosis is both concealed and mutated in the metamorphosis in Kafka's story of the same name. With Gandhi, however, we see the state of undress, the thin or ungainly human body, performing a radically different function. His 'half-nakedness' (Churchill's term) brings

into the public domain, and into the political process, the absurdity of a colonized race partaking of, and revising, the Enlightenment notions of self-consciousness, self-expression, and self-governance; Gandhi's 'corporeality', provoking tenderness, suspicion, and embarrassment in equal measure, signifies, in effect, a shift in register in the language.

I must reiterate, here, that I use the words 'absurd' and 'unthinkable' not in the metaphysical sense familiar to us from Western modernism, nor to denote the self-aware meanings of these terms in postmodernity, but to signify a change in register introduced into an economy of expression to which it doesn't ostensibly belong. The example of Basheer reminds us that the political and cultural processes of the sort of plurality I'm describing were in place long before Independence, and foresee the Indian nation-state as we might presently theorize it: as an Enlightenment concept in which apparently inadmissible changes of register occur. This could be, as well, a working definition of the fictions and stories I've been discussing. To say that the 'change of tone' is a result of the pressure exerted by 'local' or 'unofficial' or 'pre-modern' traditions on the writer is both germane and too easy, and brings with it problems of critical language. The recovery of the 'local' or 'unofficial' has, of course, been constitutive of Indian modernity right from the inception of its 'high culture': Tagore's borrowings from Baul and Santhal culture are an early instance. But the question remains – why do some of these borrowings become domesticated in the 'high cultural' economy of certain texts, and certain writers, while becoming disruptions or embarrassing changes of register in others? A more specific example and contrast: why does the recuperation of the local in Satyajit Ray's *Pather Panchali* not disturb the 'high cultural' integrity of that work, although the same process both threatens and enriches, in a series of changes in tonality, Ritwick Ghatak's *Ajantrik* and *Teetash Ekti Nadir Naam*? It's as if there were two notions of plurality at work here in the conception of a 'modern' work of art in India; one of them transcendental, in which the various elements have been harmonized, and the inadmissible naturalized, and the other makeshift and experimental, in which the process becomes open to view.

4.   To speak of the pressure of a 'local' or 'pre-modern' tradition on the modern Indian writer or artist brings with it, too, another set of problems. They have to do with the assumption that there is, within the space we call Indian 'modernity', another space that is somehow 'pre-modern', and, thus, both anterior to, and outside of, modernity. The stories in the anthology, or those discussed here, however, indicate something else: that no such 'outside' exists; that the existence of such an 'outside' would have made this modernity self-enclosed and recognizable; that the modernity in these stories, on the other hand, has no clear boundary or closure; it is surprising rather than recognizable, disruptive rather than canonical.

5.   May I say, in a brief aside, that there was an aspect of the American literary sensibility that brought the 'unthinkable' and 'intolerable', to use Panikkar's terms, into the realm of American democratic life, as a hidden value that was compensated for by an exaggerated eloquence. This register was first

heard in Whitman, and later in Ginsberg; it sounds a note, as in Basheer's exclamation marks, of the 'excessively melodramatic' and the 'painfully true'. Interestingly, exclamation marks are 'rife', to use Mia Alvar's adjective, in the works of these poets. Their poems have invoked, in different ways, both embarrassment and admiration in the reader. The hidden value here is homosexuality, in the days before it was domesticated; it stretched the limits of American pluralism as a means of tolerating 'a variety of opinions', and introduced it to the 'unthinkable', the 'absurd', and the 'intolerable'. It was this hidden pluralism in American society that gave these poets, I believe, their simultaneous air of self-parody and deep seriousness.

Thoughts in a Temple: Hinduism in the Free Market
First published in the *Times Literary Supplement*, 2002
1. At the time this was written, the government was made up of the BJP and its allies.

On the Nature of Indian Gothic: The Imagination of Ashis Nandy
First published in the *Hindu*, 2003

'Hollywood aur Bollywood'
First published in a slightly different version in the *Observer Magazine*, 2006
1. A reference to the Hindi films made in the 1970s about twins with rhyming names separated at birth, like *Seeta aur Geeta* and *Ram aur Shyam*; '*aur*' meaning 'and'.

The View from Malabar Hill
First published in the *London Review of Books*, 2006
1. 2005.

Stories of Domicile
From the introduction to the forthcoming *Penguin anthology of Calcutta*

Notes on the Novel after Globalization
First published in *Meanjin*, 2007

Anti-Fusion
Published in the *New Statesman*, 2007

Arun Kolatkar and the Tradition of Loitering
First published as the introduction to the *New York Review of Books Classics* reissue of *Jejuri*, 2006

Learning to Write: V. S. Naipaul, Vernacular Artist
First published in the *Times Literary Supplement*, 2001
1. *Half a Life*, Picador, 2001.

A Bottle of Ink, a Pen and a Blotter: On R.K. Narayan
    First published in the *London Review of Books*, 2001

'A Feather! A Very Feather upon the Face!': On Kipling
    First published in the *London Review of Books*, 2000

Returning to Earth: The Poetry of Jibanananda Das
    To be published in the *London Review of Books*

'Women in Love' as Post-Human Essay
    First published as the introduction to the Penguin Classics edition, 2006

1. D.H. Lawrence, *Apocalypse* (London, 1981), p. 110.
2. Vivian De Sola Pinto and F. Warren Roberts (eds.), *The Complete Poems of D.H. Lawrence* (Harmondsorth, 1977), p. 182.
3. Ibid., p.182.
4. Marcel Proust, *Remembrance of Things Past*, trans. C.K. Scott Moncrieff and Terence Kilmartin (Harmondsworth, 1983), p. 48.
5. *The Complete Poems of D.H. Lawrence*, pp. 182–3.
6. George J. Zytaruk and James Boulton (eds.), *The Letters of D.H. Lawrence*, vol. II (Cambridge, 1981), p. 132.
7. Ibid., p.142.
8. *Remembrance of Things Past*, p. 150.
9. *Sons and Lovers*, p. 60.
10. Ezra Pound, *Selected Poems* (London, 1975), p. 148.
11. Hugh Stevens, 'Sex and the nation: "The Prussian Officer" and *Women in Love*', in Anne Fernihough (ed.), *The Cambridge Companion to D.H. Lawrence* (Cambridge, 2001), pp. 49–65.
12. Samuel Beckett, *The Unnamable* (London, 1975), p. 132.
13. T.S. Eliot, *Collected Poems 1909–1962* (London, 1974), p. 194.
14. D.H. Lawrence, *Phoenix* (London, 1968), p. 312.
15. Thomas Mann, *Doctor Faustus*, tr. John E. Woods (New York, 1997), p. 66.
16. M.H. Abrams, *Doing Things with Texts: Essays in Criticism and Critical Theory* (New York, 1989), p. 327.
17. *Apocalypse*, p. 110.
18. D.H. Lawrence, *Collected Stories* (London, Everyman's Library, 1994), p. 431.
19. *The Complete Poems*, p. 185.
20. Ibid., p. 183.

Champion of Hide and Seek: Raj Kamal Jha's Surrealism
    First published by the *London Review of Books*, 2004

Midnight at Marble Arch: On 'The Reluctant Fundamentalist' by Mohsin Hamid
    First published in the *London Review of Books*, 2007.

Beyond 'Confidence': Rushdie and the Creation Myth of Indian English Writing
    Published in the *New Statesman*, 2006

Index

Abrams, M.H.   291
Achebe, Chinua   63, 238
adda   66-7, 190, 192
Adorno, Theodor   194
Ahmed, Aijaz   122
Almodóvar, Pedro   300
Alvar, Mia   153
Ambai   46, 309
Anderson, Benedict   66, 90, 168,
   198-200, 203, 204
Anderson, Perry   109, 111
Andrews, C.F.   106
Annals and Antiquities of Rajasthan
   (Tod)   73
Anquetil-Duperron, Abraham-
   Hyacinthe   123, 123-4, 125, 127, 128
Aparajito (Ray)   18
Apocalypse (Lawrence)   280, 292
Apur Sansar (Ray)   19, 193
Arendt, Hannah   67, 231
Argumentative Indian, The (Sen)   100,
   107, 130
Arnold, Edwin   126
Arnold, Matthew   42, 48, 110, 111, 126,
   175, 207
   and culture   112
Ashbery, John   224
art and its value   211-12
asymmetric ignorance   91
Attridge, Derek   200
Auden, W. H.   157, 158, 297

Aurobindo, Sri   227
Austen, Jane   157
Auster, Paul   295
Autobiography of an Unknown Indian,
   The (Chaudhuri)   47, 48, 49-50

Babri mosque, Ayodhya, destruction
   of   230
Bachelor of Arts, The (Narawan)   243,
   245
Bakhtin, Mikhail   119, 168, 169, 198-9
Balaka (Tagore)   133
Ballard, J.G.   298, 299, 310
Bandyopadhyay, Manik   86
Banerjea, Surenranath   20
Banerjee, Bibhutibhushan   86, 114,
   270
Banerjee, Tarashankar   105, 114
Bangla (Das)   274
Barnes, Julian   195, 212
Basheer, Vaikom Muhammad   151-3
Basu, Jyoti   182
Basu, Utpal   190
Baudelaire, Charles   58, 59, 133, 211
Bayly, C.A.   102, 251
Beckett, Samuel   151, 286
Beerbohm, Max   251, 263
Bend in the River, A (Naipaul)   63,
   238, 239
Bengal the Beautiful (Das/
   Winter)   266

Bengal   22, 24, 26, 64, 69, 109, 110, 118,
    133, 182, 191, 192, 226, 251, 263, 266,
    267, 271, 274, 276, 277
    culture   41, 44, 66, 67, 111, 129, 132
    humanism   13, 14, 18, 163, 173, 174
    middle classes   41, 48, 49, 55, 60,
        65, 69-84, 118, 126, 182, 183, 190,
        191, 259, 272
    Naxal period   197
    nationalism   24, 40
    and Orientalists   65
    and Partition   197
    significance of education   257
    and Tagore   18, 67, 69-84, 94, 127,
        129-30, 131, 132, 137, 247
    under British rule   112, 113, 120
    see also Dutt, Renaissance, East and
        West Bengal, Tagore
Bengali (language)   12, 22-3, 29, 41,
    42, 54, 67-8, 73, 76, 77, 118, 175, 259
    literature   19, 20, 21, 42-3, 44, 48,
        50, 69, 71, 74, 78-9, 80, 114, 128-9,
        142, 145, 158, 255, 256, 259, 266,
        272
    critics   86, 132-3
    poetry and nursery rhymes   20,
        22, 23, 50, 74, 84, 124, 251-2, 272
'Bengaliness', concept of   49, 51, 54,
    69
Benjamin, Walter   32, 33, 57ff, 60, 66,
    199, 200, 204, 231
    and flâneur   32, 58-9, 67-8, 230,
        232-3
    philosophy and ideas of   58-9, 63,
        168, 211, 261
Bennett, Arnold   282, 286
Bergman, Ingmar   46, 53
Berlin, Germany   58, 194
bhadralok   24, 49, 55, 81, 83, 126, 182
Bhagavad Gita   106
Bhangra rap   178
Bhanusingha (Tagore)   78-9
Bhanusingher Padabali (Tagore)   79
bhasha (writers in Indian
    languages)   13, 89, 155, 156, 159
Bhusan, Bibhuti   114

Bidyapati   79
Bigsby, Christopher   212
Birla temple   160-1
BJP   92, 100, 161, 163, 183, 230, 305
Blue Bedspread, The (Jha)   298
Bollywood   92, 170-81
    origin of term   175
    compared to Hollywood   176-7
    influence of   177
    Hindi film   151-2, 170-1, 173, 174,
        175, 177-8, 179-80, 181, 215, 216,
        226
Bombay (Mumbai)   28, 55, 56, 164,
    170, 174, 175, 182-8, 222ff, 253, 279,
    310
    renaming of   183, 188, 223, 230
    'spirit of Mumbai'   184
Bombay: Gateway to India
    (Singh)   186-7
Borges, Jorge Luis   103, 105, 107,
    116-17
Bose, Buddhadeva   75, 80, 86, 95, 102,
    114, 118, 132-3, 190, 191-2, 193, 261,
    266, 267, 272
Bose, Kshudiram   255, 256
Bose, Sarat   49
Bose, Sugata   102
Bourdieu, Pierre   205
Bradbury, Malcolm   46
Brahmo Samaj   19, 20, 23, 40, 75-6,
    78, 109, 128, 139, 267
British Empire   49, 129, 166, 239,
    260-1, 262
    debate over policy in India   258
    colonial modern   267, 268, 270,
        271
    colonial policy   261ff
    in India   64, 69, 81, 83, 105, 124,
        257ff
    psychopathology of Empire   260
Brodsky, Joseph   210, 211
Brook, Peter   116
Buñuel, Luis   173, 300
Bush, George   173
Byron, Lord   126, 157

Calcutta   13, 48, 49, 51, 54, 59, 60, 64,
    67, 93, 102, 160, 162, 163,175, 182-88,
    189, 190, 192, 193, 194, 251, 254, 266,
    268, 270, 272, 298
    and Bengal Renaissance   64
    and Bengali   175
    historical development   64,
        69-70, 71, 75, 103, 106, 251, 254
    and Dutt   19, 40, 43, 44, 112
    and East India Company   69, 251
    and globalization   186-7
    renaming of   191
    and Tagore   19, 69, 71, 75, 125, 126,
        129, 130, 133
Camp, concept of   176-7
Captive Ladie, The (Dutt)   40
Carne, Marcel   178
Cartier-Bresson, Henri   186
Centre for Studies in Developing
    Societies, Delhi, India   165
Chaander Pahaad (*The Moon
    Mountain Banerjee*)   115, 270
Chakrabarty, Dipesh   59-67, 91, 106,
    124, 132, 133, 134, 167, 168
    and postcolonialism   59-60
Chandidas   79, 124, 137
Charnock, Job   190
Charulata (Ray)   19
Chatterjee, Bankimchandra   65, 74,
    105, 128, 256
Chatterjee, Partha   14-15, 16, 98-9,
    105, 168, 267, 270
Chatterjee, Sandipan   190
Chattopadhyay, Sunitikumar   66-7
Chattopadhyaya, Shakti   190, 192, 215
Chaudhuri, Amit:
    childhood and poetry   118, 174-5
    cultural heritage of   13
    education of   57-8, 216
    family   52, 55, 173, 174, 179, 183,
        185-6, 189, 268, 269
    and American newspapers   145-6
    and Ashis Nandy   165
    and Bombay   13, 19, 39, 55-6, 57,
        170, 182ff, 189, 195, 222, 257

    in Calcutta   13, 160, 182ff, 189ff,
        190, 191, 195-6
    and cinema   170-2, 173, 174-5
    in Delhi   168-9, 170
    as editor   44, 140, 221-2
    in England   178, 183, 185, 195, 214,
        279, 301ff
    and English literature   279ff
    and Jejuri   221
    and Kolatkar   221-3, 230
    in Lille   16
    in London   39, 141, 183, 185, 279,
        301
    and music   55-6, 214-7
    in New York   145ff, 159, 196-7
    in Paris   146
    and Sahitya Akademi award   155
    teaching at Columbia
        University   140ff
    university education   141-2, 279,
        301
    writings of   39-40, 155, 206
    visit to Birla temple   160ff
Chaudhuri, Nirad C.   47-52, 53, 67,
    86, 114, 247, 260, 268
    as writer   47-8, 49-50, 51-2, 96, 117
Chauduri, Sukanta   22, 25, 131
Chokher Bali (Tagore)   128
Christianity   161, 162, 163
Cine Blitz (magazine)   175, 176
Civil and Military Gazette,
    Lahore   254
Clare, John   134
Coe, Jonathan   195, 212
Coetzee, J.M.   237
colonialism   17, 34, 40, 48, 54, 62, 65,
    103, 104, 105, 124, 127, 138, 174, 183,
    192, 222, 238, 239, 241, 308
    colonial attitudes and rhetoric   23,
        44, 115, 260, 251ff
    colonial modern   267, 268, 270,
        271
    colonial period   30, 64, 69, 71, 82,
        83, 90, 92, 96, 106, 110, 114, 123,
        143, 158
    Kipling and   251ff

neo-colonialism   98
  Said and   119, 123
  Tagore and   26-7, 80, 84, 126, 137,
    192
  see also Indian nationalism, post-
    colonialism
commercialism   12
Communist Manifesto (Marx/
  Engels)   209
Conrad, Joseph   63, 203, 238
*Considerations on Representative
  Government* (Mill)   166
cosmopolitanism, Indian usage   16,
  27-8
cultural studies   14-17, 63, 207
culture: 20, 30, 31, 33, 88, 93, 100ff,
  109ff, 115, 120-1, 122ff, 175ff, 195,
  203ff, 216, 279
  categories of   13
  Bengali   41, 48, 64, 66, 78, 81, 84,
    129, 132, 135, 192
  colonial   34, 40, 44, 53, 54, 64, 67,
    111, 122, 125
  emergence of culture   35, 70,
    109-12
  high   14, 15, 16, 17, 21, 27, 32, 34, 35,
    53, 55, 63, 102, 111, 120, 145, 146,
    156, 198, 205-6, 207, 209, 289
  high art212
  in India   40, 41, 47, 64, 70, 81, 84,
    100ff, 111-12, 115, 119, 122, 168, 224,
    225, 228, 252-3, 254, 257, 210
  interactions between cultures   44,
    88, 106, 216, 253ff
  literary   10, 195, 208, 224, 285ff
  and modernity   140ff
  popular   13, 15, 17, 31, 53, 63, 92, 93,
    105, 119, 147, 171, 173, 196, 213
  and religion   109, 110
  role of culture   109
  subcultures   140ff, 158, 159, 222,
    229
  Tagore and   21, 31, 71, 79, 84, 126,
    135
  Western   64, 87, 107, 109, 110, 122,
    129, 168, 201, 212, 222, 237, 258

Dalí, Salvador   296, 298, 299
Dante   238
Das, Jibanananda   118, 192, 265-78
  works   279-81
Dawkins, Richard   305
Day, Rev. Lal Behari   22
De la grammatologie (Derrida)   200
De Souza, Eunice   221, 225
Death in Venice (Mann)   287
defamiliarization, concept of   94-5,
  98, 99, 262
democracy, multucultural   28
Derozio, Henry Louis Vivian   40, 70,
  73, 74, 103-4, 135, 251
Derrida, Jacques   61-2, 119, 120, 200-1,
  203, 20, 291
developmental paradigm   65
Devi, Mahashweta   46
Dickens, Charles   75, 158, 236, 237
Discipline and Punish (Foucault)   201
Disgrace (Coetzee)   237
Dostoevsky, Fyodor   158, 198
Dr Faustus (Mann)   288
Dublin   59
Ducpétaux, E   201
Dune, William   71
Durgesnandini (Chatterjee)   256
Dutt, Michael Madhusudan   20, 21,
  45, 46, 47, 48, 50, 51, 52, 53, 55, 56,
  112, 130, 251-2, 255
  biography   39-44
  and Bengali language   41, 42, 49,
    74
  and colonialism   41
  influence of   56
  travels of   42-3
  writings of   40-4, 45, 46, 50-1
Dutta, Krishna, and Andrew
  Robinson   74, 77, 80, 84, 127

East Bengal   51, 52, 174, 192, 193, 267,
  268
East India Company   69, 124, 126,
  251, 252
eclecticism   28, 123, 1248, 192
Eliot, George   157

Eliot, T.S.   53, 110, 126, 131-2, 133, 140, 192, 202, 279, 285, 286, 287, 288, 291
elitism   14, 16, 34, 55, 88, 102, 106, 203
Engle, Paul   227
English language   135-6, 209, 235, 237, 257
 and choice of other languages   45-6, 48, 49, 89, 94, 168, 259
 Indian poetry in English   40, 143-5, 168, 221, 222, 223, 227, 228-9, 230, 255
 post-colonial use   12, 20, 35, 50, 54, 79, 85ff, 95, 96, 116
 and post-modernism   114, 158
 Indian novel in English   11, 20, 30, 74, 85ff, 113-21, 127, 158, 178, 228, 244, 256, 296, 308-11
 Tagore and   129, 130, 131
 use of English in India   12, 13-14. 16, 17, 20-4, 35, 50-3, 71, 73-4, 77, 85ff, 91, 94, 95, 96, 118, 155, 158, 168, 172, 175, 224, 234, 236, 237, 257, 259, 260, 266, 308-9
Englishness   134, 166, 169
Enigma of Arrival, The (Naipaul)   239, 241
Enlightenment   32, 35, 101, 115, 119, 134, 136, 137, 138, 145, 148, 154, 166, 167, 168, 169, 176, 192, 204, 286, 314
ethnocentricity   57-8
Etruscan Places (Lawrence)   136
Eurocentrism   61, Eurocentric paradigm   65
European culture   30
evolution   57-8
exotic, meaning and use of term   90-3
exoticization   12, 98
Extension du domaine de la lutte (Houellebecqu)   209
Ezekiel, Nissim   223-4, 229, 310

Fanaa (film)   170-1
Finding the Centre (Naipaul)   235, 240

First Circle, The (Solzhenitsyn)   202
First War of Independence/ Sepoy Mutiny   251, 252
Fitzgerald, Edward   126
flâneur and flânerie   32, 58-9, 67-8, 230-1, 232, 233, 234
Flaubert, Gustave   128, 145, 147, 287, 288
Folk Tales of Bengal (Day)   22
Ford, John   54
Forster, E.M.   63, 197, 254
Foucault, Michel   61, 119, 129, 201, 202, 203
France, Anatole   151
free market economy   35, 87, 121, 130, 160ff 187, 195, 196, 197, 210, 285
 see also globalization
Freud, Sigmund   122, 151
Freudian model   22, 237

Gadamer   60
Gandhi, Mahatma   21, 63, 74, 84, 108, 154, 167, 169, 255
 responses to   23, 151, 153
Gandhi, Sonia   104
Ganguly, Sunil   190, 192
Garnett, Edward   282
GDR   194
Gibran, Kahil   80
Gitanjali (Tagore)   79, 130, 228, 246, 271
globalization   12, 35, 172, 176, 183-4, 186, 187, 196, 197, 200, 204, 206, 207, 209, 213, 216
 absence of 'outside' to globalization   178, 196, 197, 206
 expansion of   87, 209
 free-market globalization   35, 197, 207-8
 India and globalization   16, 32, 159, 164, 175, 178, 183-4, 190, 230, 298, 309
 narrative of   205, 212
 and the novel   195-213
 philosophical nature of globalization   197-8, 205

post-globalization   16, 209
  and postmodernism   159, 212-4
  reactions to   32, 179, 183-4, 190
Godard, Jean-Luc   173
Goethe, Johann Wolfgang von   70,
  136, 293, 294
Gogol, Nikolay   156
Golden Treasury (Palgrave)   246
Gorji, Mina   134
Gosse, Edmund   30-1
Goya, Francisco   202, 203
Gramsci, Antonio   60, 101
Grass, Günter   193, 194
Great Expectations (Dickens)   236,
  237
Great Indian Novel, The
  (Tharoor)   63
Greene, Graham   244
Guha, Ramachandra   28
Guha, Ranajit   60, 62, 167
Guide, The (Narayan)   96, 245
Gujarat   160, 161
Gulag Archipelago, The
  (Solzhenitsyn)   202
Guns of Navarone, The   171
Gupta, Iswar   22
Gupta, Sunetra   132

Half a Life (Naipaul)   239
Halhead, Nathaniel   69, 74
Hall, Stuart   14, 15
Hamid, Mohsin   301-7
Haq, Kaiser   267-8
Hardy, Thomas   274, 276, 277
Hare, David   251
Hastie, Professor W.W.   163
Heaney, Seamus   30, 103, 236
Heart of Darkness, The
  (Conrad)   202, 238, 239
hegemony   35, 102, 105, 112
Heidegger, Martin and his
  philosophy   29-30, 31, 33, 260
Henry, O   151
Herbert, George   206
Hindu College   40, 70, 73-4, 106-7,
  251

Hindu mela, creation of   20
Hinduism   40-2, 63, 75, 109, 123,
  160-4, 192, 245, 299
  and BJP   100, 161, 163
  see also Brahmo Samaj
Hindutva   92, 100, 101, 102, 107, 108,
  112, 161, 162, 164
historicism   62, 63, 64, 65, 66, 200,
  201
history, remapping   13
Hitchens, Christopher   305
Hitler, Adolf   58, 230
Hobsbawm, Eric   167, 168
Hölderlin, Friedrich   29, 30
Hollywood   170. 172, 173, 175, 177,
  179, 305
  compared to Bollywood   176, 178,
  179-80
  and nationalism   184
  see also Bollywood
Homi, Bhabha   65, 66
Houellebecq, Michel   209-10, 211
House for Mr Biswas, A
  (Naipaul)   236-7, 238, 240
Howe, Irving   236
Hugh Selwyn Mauberley
  (Pound)   285
Hughes, Ted   134
Hum Tum (*The Two of Us*, film)   180
humanism   11, 14, 123, 125, 125, 127,
  137, 173, 207, 286, 287, 292
  Bengali humanism   13, 14, 18, 64,
  163, 173, 174
  European   58, 134, 136, 137, 138,
  280, 290
  Indian   101-2, 107, 138
Hussain, M.F   112, 224
Hyde East, Edward   106
Hyder, Qurratulain   46, 111, 115, 158

iconic images, use of   98-9
identity, discussion of   12, 13
If You Are Afraid of Heights
  (Jha)   295-300
Ilbert Bill (legislation, 1883)   252, 254

Imagined Communities
  (Anderson)   66, 90, 198
Impressionism   32
Impressions of Africa (Roussel)   270
In a Free State (Naipal)   63, 238, 239
In Praise of Shadows (Tanizaki)   32
India:
  and concept of the foreign   34-5
  education in   174, 175, 258, 305
  literature in   14, 16, 20, 25, 30, 31,
    40, 42, 44, 45, 46, 85, 86, 87-90,
    113, 129, 131, 135, 138-9, 140ff, 183,
    192, 194, 221, 255, 266, 310
  development of literature   21
  children's literature   20, 24, 77
  post-colonial literature   142
  middle class in   17-18, 40, 49, 55,
    64, 67, 83, 88, 92, 101, 107, 112, 116,
    151, 163, 167, 168, 173, 174, 175, 176,
    178, 231, 251, 255, 260, 302, 309
  and multiculturalism   27, 28, 109,
    116, 173, 305
  philosophical narrative in   26-8
  poetry, significance of   156
  secularism in   27, 70, 109-10, 111,
    162, 163-4
  and the West   16, 101
  History of:
  antiquity   46, 89, 103, 124, 132, 134,
    136, 137, 263, 310
  medieval and feudal
    periods   79-80, 81, 83, 89, 103,
    104, 124,
  colonial period, and
    colonialism   62, 64, 69ff, 103,
    104, 105, 110, 111, 125, 183, 251ff,
    258
  pre-Mutiny period   40ff, 102, 106,
    259
  Mutiny   251,252
  post-Mutiny period   252, 256, 257,
    258, 260
  rise of nationalism in   20-2, 23, 26,
    49, 54, 103-4, 106, 107, 162, 183,
    259, 268
  colonial inheritance   167

Independence   154, 167, 266, 272
post independence/post colonial
  period   15, 16, 19, 50, 52, 98,
  111-12, 113-14, 142, 173, 224, 231,
  236, 248, 261, 305 309
modern period   26, 27, 32, 34, 100,
  101 103,112, 154, 161 169, 174, 183,
  191, 230, 255
see also East India Company,
  English, Hindu Cinema,
  Orientalism
India: A Million Mutinies Now
  (Naipaul)   187, 240
Indian Civil Service   77, 258
Indian Gothic   17, 165-9
Indian National Association   20
Indian National Congress   20
  Bengal nationalism   24, 40
  Indian identity, development
    of   105-6
'Indianness'   16, 40, 54
Indology   123, 136
Inferno (Dante)   238
intellectual, post-colonial   11
internationalism   12, 209
intertextuality   198
Intimate Enemy, The (Nandy)   260
Ishiguro, Kazuo   195, 212
Islam and Islamic culture   40, 75,
  109, 162, 163

Jacobson, Dan   279, 301
Jain, Jyotindra   16-17
Jalal, Ayesha   102
James, Henry   140, 259, 261, 261, 291,
  307
James, William   25, 26, 146
Jameson, Fredric   119
Japan   31-2
Jarrell, Randall   263
Jatin, Bagha   256
Jayadeva   124
*Jejuri: Commentary and Critical
  Perspectives* (Kolatkar)   94, 95, 96,
  99, 184, 221, 222, 227, 228, 229, 230,
  231, 232, 233, 234

Jha, Raj Kamal 295-300
Jiban Smriti (My Reminiscences,
 Tagore) 77, 129, 246
Johnson, B.S. 212
Jones, David 53, 285
Jones, William (Sir) 65, 69, 70, 71,
 111, 123-4, 136, 251
Joy babu Felunath (Ray) 19
Joyce, James 30, 88, 112, 147, 158, 237,
 255, 267, 281
Jussawalla, Adil 222, 224, 229, 310

Kafka, Franz 103, 104, 149, 237, 266,
 286
Kahn, Louis 32
Kajol (actress) 171
*Kal Ho Na Ho (Whether or not There's
 a Tomorrow)* 180, 181
Kala Ghoda Poems (Koltakar) 222,
 229, 239
 place 184, 222, 231
Kalidasa 31, 65, 69-70, 71, 72, 120,
 123, 124, 133, 134, 136, 137, 138
Kallol (magazine) 190, 272
Kanchenjunga (Ray) 118
Kapoor, Shammi 174, 178
Kelly, Gene 177
Kennedy, John F. 188
Kerala 45, 54, 109, 151
Kermode, Frank 301
Khaalas 206
Khakhar, Bupen 224, 251, 310
Khan, Aamir 171
Khan, Sharuk 181
*Khasakkinte Itihasam (The Legends of
 Khasak)* 45
Khayam, Omar 126
Khilnani, Sunil 28
Khusrau, Amir 104-5
Kim (Kipling) 252-4, 256-259, 260
King, Bruce 228
Kipling, John Lockwood 253
Kipling, Rudyard 80, 114, 129,
 251-64, 310
 presentation of India, and themes
 pursued 259ff

Kolatkar, Arun 94, 95, 96-9, 184,
 221-34, 310
 use of English 227
 quoted 97, 223, 225, 226
 see also Jejuri
Kolhapur, Marashtra 223
Kristeva, Julia 198
Krittibas (journal) 190
Kurosawa, Akira 19, 32, 101

Lagaan (film) 171
Lal, P. 194
Lalla Rookh (Moore) 126
language, choice of 39, 54, 73-4
 borders of 200
 use of 213-15
Larkin, Philip 94, 118, 279
Lawrence, D.H. 59, 136, 237, 260,
 279-94, 301
Lévi-Strauss, Claude 61-2
Light of Asia (Arnold) 126
literature as a category 85-6
London Review of Books 209, 301
Lonely Voice, The (O'Connor) 156
Love and Longing in Bombay
 (stories) 185

Mahabharata 81, 116, 137, 138, 161,
 187, 253
Mann, Thomas 104, 287, 288
Manto, Saadat Hasan 151, 158
marginality 12, 25
Marlowe, Christopher 201
Marquez, Gabriel Garcia 173
Marx, Karl 86, 120
Marxist viewpoint and
 interpretations 28, 64, 67, 104,
 122, 200
 Marxism and Bengal 109
Matrix, The 179
Maximum City 183, 187
maya (word) 29-30
McDonald, Peter D. 200
Meghaduta (The Cloud Messenger,
 Tagore/Kalidasa) 71-2, 137

Meghnadbadhakabya (Dutt)   41, 42, 111, 255

Mehra, Rakeysh   175

Mehrotra, Arvind Krishna   116, 118, 143-4, 224, 227, 228, 229

Mehta, Suketu   13, 183, 184, 185, 187-8

Midnight's Children (Rushdie)   55, 91, 113ff, 121, 172-3, 185, 234, 308, 309
  effects on Indian literature   113ff, 234, 308

Mill, John Stuart   62, 63, 140-1, contradiction within theories   170-1

Milton, John   53, 54, 74, 139, 208, 209

Mimic Men, The (Naipaul)   63, 65, 66

Mishima   32

Mishra, Pankaj   247

Mistry, Rohinton   114

Mitra, Nabagopal   20

Modernism: 16, 22, 24, 25, 32, 35, 64, 88, 111, 125, 126, 145, 148, 153, 186, 198, 208, 282, 283, 288, 289
  European   13, 15, 131
  Indian   32, 42, 54, 55, 106-7, 132, 133, 193
  and 'little man'   133, 156,
  modernist aesthetic   144 207
  Western   32, 106, 126
  Western and non-Western compared   53, 62-5

modernity   13, 14, 22, 24, 27, 31, 32, 33, 34, 35, 56, 58, 91, 140ff, 162, 172, 202, 205, 206, 207, 208, 212, 216
  in India   17, 18, 19, 40, 41, 44, 47, 53, 54, 60, 61, 62, 64, 65, 66, 69-85, 92. 100-8, 111, 112, 122, 132-3, 136, 157, 168, 178, 186. 191, 257, 270, 271, 310
  Kipling and   259, 260, 267
  European ideas of   58, 60, 112, 162, 201
  and colonial encounter   65

modernization paradigm   65

mofussil   267, 268-9, 270, 276

Moll Flanders (Defoe)   279

Monroe, Harriet   80

Moore, Charles   32

Moore, Thomas   126

Moraes, Dom   118

Moretti, Franco   142

Mozart, Wolfgang Amadeus   54, 293, 294

Mr Vertigo (Auster)   295

Mrs Dalloway (Woolf)   158

Mueller, Heiner   62, 194, 200

Mueller, Max   117, 126, 136, 222

mukti ('freedom')   21

Mukti ('Liberation', Tagore)   29

multiculturalism   27, 109, 116, 173, 194, 305

Murthy, U.R. Anantha   46, 53, 89, 114, 168

Music Room, The (Ray)   104

music   209, 214-17

Mussolini, Benito   84

My Days (Narayan)   243, 244, 245, 246, 247

My Reminiscences (Jiban Smriti, Tagore)   77, 129, 246

Nagy, Imre   45, 53, 54

Naidu, Sarojini   30-1

Naipaul, Seepersad   237, 238, 240

Naipaul, V.S.   52, 62, 63, 65, 117, 140, 185, 186, 187, 195, 212, 235-41, 268

Naivedya (Tagore)   29

Naked Lonely Hand (Das/ Winter)   266, 270-1

Nandy, Ashis   102, 154, 165-70, 260

Narain, Raj   41, 50-1

Narang, Gopi Chand   156

Narayan, R.K.   12, 238, 243-9

narrativity   196, 197, 198, 199-200, 201, 205, 206, 208, 211
  postmodern concept   209-10, 215
  power of narrative   259

nationalism   16, 17, 18, 23, 28, 30, 31, 33, 34, 35, 95, 96, 100, 107, 122, 131, 134, 169, 179, 251, 252
  Bengal   84
  growth of Indian   20, 22, 23, 24, 26, 27, 28, 49, 54, 70, 73, 74, 103,

104, 105, 106, 129, 183, 191, 222, 255
Hollywood and   184
narrative of nationalism   21-2, 90, 99, 115, 116, 119, 157, 199, 200
romantic   22
nation-state, concept of   26, 27-8, 31, 66, 76, 98, 129, 159, 167, 169, 179, 198-9, 224, 229, 247
JS Mill on the nation-state   166-7
nation and novel   158-9, 199
use of national images   98-9
Nayyar, O.P.   215
Nehru, Jawaharlal   76, 101, 114, 255
Nemade, Bhalchandra   95-6, 98, 99, 228
New Poems (Lawrence)   280
New Quest (journal)   95-6
New World, A (Chaudhuri)   155
Nietzsche, Friedrich   120
Notes on the Bengal Renaissance (Sarkar)   64
novel, Indian   45, 63, 65, 74, 80, 87, 91, 113-21, 155, 159, 177, 178, 187, 188, 192, 237, 305
novel and globalisation   195-213
and nationalism   158-9, 199
putative death of the novel   195
see also Midnight's Children

O'Connor, Frank   156-7, 158
O'Hara, Frank   224
Old Testament and creation myths   308
On Liberty (Mill)   62
On Representative Government (Mill)   62
'Oriental' tranditions   31
Orientalism (concept) and legacy   23, 60-1, 85-7, 90ff, 122ff, 160
and comparison of Western and Indian writers   65, 69
legacy of orientalism   85-7, 251
Orientalist history   73
Orientalist narrative   71

Orientalist philosophy   26
Orientalist scholars and scholarship   20, 53, 61, 64-5, 69, 70, 113, 127, 128ff, 139, 245, 246, 251, 258, 259
Orientalism within India   69-70
see also William Jones
Orientalism (Said)   87, 88, 90-1, 95, 121, 125
Owen, Jesse   58
Owen, Wilfred   287
Oxford India Anthology of Twelve Modern Poets, The (Mehrota)   143-4, 228
Ozu Yasujiro   31, 32

Paine, Tom   70, 105
Panikkar, Raimundo   154
Paradise Lost (Milton)   255
Paramhansa, Ramakrishna   163-4
Parashuram (Rajshekhar Basu)   29
Parliament of World Religions, Chicago, 1893   164
Parthasarathy, R.   144
Partition (of India)   180, 191, 270, 271
Passage to England, A (Chaudhuri)   48
Passage to India, A (Forster)   63, 254
Patel, Gieve   224, 229
Pather Panchali (Banerjee)   115, 270
Pather Panchali (Ray)   19, 54, 115
Paulin, Tom   134, 147, 264
Picasso, Pablo   106, 148, 290
Pioneer (newspaper)   254
Plain Tales from the Hills (Kipling)   256
Plato   120
Poet Apart, A (Seely)   265
post-colonialism   59, 64, 65, 84, 134, 136, 210, 309
post-coloniality   11, 15, 16, 19, 28, 44, 64, 98, 114, 117, 119, 149, 152, 157, 161, 204, 244ff
post-colonial culture   15, 16, 98, 103, 115, 117, 120

post-colonial and India   15, 51, 93,
  94, 108, 145
post-colonial language   12, 79, 118
post-colonial literature   114ff, 134,
  137, 139, 142, 192, 208, 286
post-colonial narrative   53, 54, 114,
  148, 208
post-colonial theory   11, 61, 107,
  149
Said and   122
see also colonialism, English
post-modernity   55, 115, 122, 142, 145,
  146, 147, 154, 156,159, 164, 173, 199,
  201, 202, 205, 213-14
  and post-coloniality   119, 154, 158
  post-modern world   122-3, 175,
    176, 196
  post-modern narrative   202, 203,
    207, 208
  post-modern literature   55, 114-5,
    119-20, 151, 161, 205
  West becoming postmodern   180
post-structuralism   61, 87, 119, 120,
  141, 196, 204
Pound, Ezra   53, 79-80, 126, 130, 145,
  256, 281, 285
Prabhat Sangeet (*Morning Songs*,
  Tagore)   79, 256
Principles of Psychology (James)   25
Pritchett, V.S.   309
Proust, Marcel   281, 282-3
Provincializing Europe
  (Chakrabarty)   59-60, 65-6, 91
Psychology (James)   25, 26
Pushkin, Aleksandr   156

Radhakrishnan, Professor   245, 246
Rai, Alok   142
Rainbow, The (Lawrence)   282, 284,
  287
Raine, Craig   264
Rajmohan's Wife (Chatterjee)   74,
  256
Ramanujan, A.K   12, 46-7, 53, 55, 89,
  114, 115, 118, 168, 227

Ramayana   21, 42, 54, 74, 81, 116, 137,
  255
Rang De Basanti (Mehra)   175
Rashomon (Kurosawa)   102
Ray, Satyajit   18-19, 20, 32, 54, 92-4,
  98, 102, 186, 191, 310
  and light   18
  films of   19, 104, 115, 118, 193
Ray, Sukumar   18-19
Raychaudhuri, Tapan   162
Raykar, Shubhangi   94, 95, 96-7, 98,
  99
realism   92, 93, 95, 114, 120, 173, 180,
  228, 283
religion   18, 19, 32, 35, 42, 109ff, 207,
  303
  Indian   26, 28, 29, 31, 41, 76, 92, 99,
    100, 107, 108, 109ff, 137, 138, 161-4,
    170, 206, 302
  and politics   109-10, 183
  Western   40, 109, 110, 111, 169, 279
  see also BJP, *Hindutva*
Reluctant Fundamentalist, The
  (Hamid)   301-07
Renaissance Orientale, La
  (Schwab)   123
Renaissance:
  Bengal   48, 64, 74, 79, 109, 163,
    164, 186, 245-6, 255, 257
  European   64, 125, 136, 166, 256,
    276
  post-Renaissance   202
  European Enlightenment   121, 151
  Indian   63, 255, 256, 262, 263
Renoir, Jean   54, 178
Republic, The (Plato)   75, 120
Reynolds, Debbie   177
Ricketts, Harry   254, 255, 256, 264
Rilke, Rainer Maria   111
Romantics:
  English   66, 72, 111, 136, 137, 141,
    193, 281, 282
  Indian   132, 133
  Western   217
  romanticism   27, 42, 59, 71, 135,
    276

romantic nationalism   16, 22
Roth, Philip   147
Rothenstein, William   79, 130
Rousseau, Henri   59, 86, 269, 270
Roussel, Raymond   269, 270
Roy, D.L.   129
Roy, Raja Rammohun   40, 102, 106,
      127, 128, 138, 258, 263, 267
      see also Brahmo Samaj
RSS   10
Rubaiyyat (Khayam)   126
Rupasi Bangla (*Bengal the Beautiful*,
      Das)   275-7
Rushdie, Salman   12, 52, 55, 91, 113-21,
      172-3, 224, 234, 301, 305
      influence on Indian literature   11,
          13, 87, 151, 240, 308-11
      and Ruby Wax   172
      see also Midnight's Children
Ruskin, John   59, 166, 167, 168, 169

Saathiya   181
saffron, significance of   162
Sahitya Akademi   142-3, 155
Said, Edward   63, 87, 96, 119, 122ff,
      132, 264
      on colonialism   121, 126-7
      and Orientalising   60-1, 90-1, 95,
          138
Sakai, Naoki   60
Sakuntala (Kalidasa)   70
Samskara (Murthy)   46, 47
Sarkar, Akshay Chandra   22
Sarkar, Susobhan   64
Savitri (Aurobindo)   227
Schelling, Friedrich   136
Schiller, Friedrich von   136
Schwab, Raymond   123, 136
Sebald, W.G.   147
secularism and the secular
      domain   26ff 34, 40, 41-2, 76, 81,
          82, 100-8, 109ff, 125, 134, 137, 163, 168,
          199, 228, 238, 269, 291
      secular culture   70, 83, 93
Seely, Clinton B.   265, 266
Sen, Dinesh Chandra   22

Sen, Amartya   100-8, 130
      intent   100-1
Sepoy Mutiny/First War of
      Independence   251, 252
Seth, Vikram   85, 114
Seventh Seal, The (Bergman)   46, 54
Shahane, Ashok   221, 222, 223
Shakeel, Chhota   188
Shakespeare, William:
      plays of   40, 42, 105, 135-6, 138, 237,
          256, 257, 258
      use of sonnet form   43-4
      Kalisda compared to   65, 69, 136
Shakuntala (Kalisda)   136
Shastri, Shibnath   63
Shetty Manu   89
Shiv Sena   183, 188, 230
Shklovsky, Viktor   94, 262
Sinatra, Frank   177
Singh, Khushwant   243
Singh, Raghubir   186
Solzhenitsyn, Aleksandr   202
Something of Myself (Kipling)   254,
      258
Sons and Lovers (Lawrence)   237,
      279, 280, 282, 283, 285, 286, 287, 291,
      292
Sontag, Susan   175-6
Southey, Robert   126
Souza, F.N.   224
space, definition of   14
      Indian perception   35
      Tagore and   20
      urban space   67
Spengler, Oswald   53
Spivak, Gayatri Chakrabarty   148,
      200
Steiner, George   212
Stevens, Hugh   286
storytelling, concept of   87-90, 204-5
stream of consciousness
      (concept)   25
subalternist history and studies   14,
      60, 64, 68, 101, 102, 149, 154, 167,
      168, 169
Suber, Davos   211

submerged population group"
(narrative device) 156
Subrahmanyam, Sanjay 103, 111
Surrealism 173, 178, 304, 211, 225,
295-300
Suryana Kudure ('A Horse for the Sun',
Murthy) 89
Swami and Friends (Narayan) 244,
247
Swift, Jonathan 174
Sydney, Philip 310

Tagore family 20, 75, 77-8, 81, 104,
126-8, 174
and Brahmo Samaj 75-6
Tagore, Abanindranath 92, 125, 130
Tagore, Debendranath 18, 54, 75, 76,
77-8, 93, 104, 126-7, 128, 138
see also Brahmo Samaj
Tagore, Dwijedranath 77
Tagore, Indira 133
Tagore, Jyotirindranath 77, 127, 128
Tagore, Kadambari 127, 128
Tagore, Nilmoni 75
Tagore, 'Prince' Dwarkanath 75, 81,
104, 126
Tagore, Rabindranath 13-14, 17-18,
69-84, 105, 106, 107, 108, 111, 168,
122-39, 190, 191, 192, 193, 246, 247
biographical details 69, 74-5,
77-8, 126ff, 246
on Bengali literature 22-3
and colonialism 23, 25, 27, 136, 137
definition of space 20
influences on 25, 76, 79, 111, 124,
128, 136-8, 168, 192
influences of 84, 93, 105, 108, 114,
125, 130-1, 133, 192, 266, 272, 273
and Kalidasa 71-3, 124, 133-4,
136-8
and middle classes 81-4
and nationalism 18, 21, 25, 26-7,
134
and Orientalism 124, 125-6, 131-2,
135, 134-5, 136

Oxford Tagore Translations 131,
138
philosophical position of 25ff, 32,
134, 136
poetry and songs of 71-3, 76-7,
78-9, 81, 82-3, 93, 111, 120, 132-3,
133, 191, 192-3, 215, 256, 275
writings by 19, 22-7, 29, 79, 80,
106, 114, 130, 134-6, 228, 246, 265
Tagore, Satyendranath 77, 259
Tait, Theo 209-10
Tanizaki, Junichiro 32-4, 35, 140
Taylor, Frederick Winslow 59
telos 54
Ten Twentieth-Century Indian Poets
(Parthasarathy) 144
Teresa, Mother 193
Thackray, Bal 188, 230
Tharoor, Shashi 63
Thomas, Edward 82
Thousand and One Nights 116
Tilottama Sambhava (Dutt) 41
Time Warps (Nandy) 165
To The Lighthouse (Woolf) 141
Tod, James 73
Tolstoy, Leo 198, 262
Trump, Donald and Ivana 210-11

Ugresic, Dubravka 210-11
Ulysses (Joyce) 30, 88, 158, 237
Unforgiving Minute, The
(Ricketts) 254
Unnamable, The (Beckett) 286
Upanishads 40, 54, 75, 103, 123, 124,
125, 127, 128, 138-9, 290
Urdu literary discourse and
postmodern theories 156, 158

vairagya 162
Vaishnav Padavali 79
Varma, Ravi 92, 93, 125
Vedas 75
Veer Zara 180, 181
Vendor of Sweets, The (Narayan) 245
Verma, Nirmal 115, 148-51
vernacular, use of 12, 20, 89

Vidyapati   124, 128, 137
Vijayan, O.V   44-6, 47, 53
Vikramaditya, King   69
Vivekananda, Swami (Narendranath
    Datta)   93, 162-3, 164

Waste Land, The (Eliot)   116, 125, 290
Watermark (Brodsky)   210
Wax, Ruby   172, 173
Way in the World, A
    (Naipaul)   239-41
Welty, Eudora   30
Wessex Poems (Hardy)   276, 277
West Bengal, state of   182, 191
West: 60
    civilization   63, 92, 107, 110, 119,
        136
    culture in   64, 80, 107, 109-11, 112,
        117, 119, 122, 129, 201, 202-3, 204,
        237
    Enlightenment   35, 115, 119, 134,
        136, 166, 168, 173, 286
    history   58, 59, 60, 62, 64, 109, 115,
        122, 212, 244
    humanism   134, 136, 290
    literature in   25, 30, 147, 156, 194,
        280
    modernism in   32, 53, 59, 106, 149,
        162, 175, 204
    and non-Western culture   16, 32,
        35, 62, 105, 106, 107, 120, 164, 175,
        179 214, 215ff

    and non-Western literature   51, 81,
        85, 86, 87, 90, 91, 98, 116 119, 244
    philosophy   61, 119, 291
    politics in   100, 154
    secular aspects   109-10, 168
    see also Orientalism
Western interpretations of
    India   100, 101, 108, 116, 119, 120,
        130, 246, 258, 259
Westernization   31-2, 169
Williams, William Carlos   116, 227
Wilson, Edmund   263
Wilson, H.H.   71
Winter, Joe   266-7, 269, 274, 275, 278
Women in Love (Lawrence)   279-94
Wood, James   144
Woolf, Virginia   141, 143, 144, 255,
    285-6
Wordsworth, William   24, 42, 136,
    259, 281, 282
World, The (journal, Calcutta)   71
    'world' as a concept   196, 197, 199,
        200
    see also globalization
Writing and Difference (Derrida)   61

Yeats, William Butler   79-80, 125, 130,
    132, 141, 193, 274-5
Young Bengal   40